PLATO AND THE ART OF
PHILOSOPHICAL WRITING

Plato's dialogues are usually understood as simple examples of philosophy in action. In this book Professor Rowe treats them rather as literary-philosophical artefacts, shaped by Plato's desire to persuade his readers to exchange their view of life and the universe for a different view which, from their present perspective, they will barely begin to comprehend. What emerges is a radically new Plato: a Socratic throughout, who even in the late dialogues is still essentially the Plato (and the Socrates) of the *Apology* and the so-called 'Socratic' dialogues. This book aims to understand Plato both as a philosopher and as a writer, on the assumption that neither of these aspects of the dialogues can be understood without the other. The argument of the book is closely based on Plato's text, but should be accessible to any serious reader of Plato, whether professional philosopher or classicist, student or general reader.

CHRISTOPHER ROWE is Professor of Greek in the Department of Classics and Ancient History at Durham University. His recent publications include *Plato: Phaedo* (1993) and (with Terry Penner) *Plato's Lysis* (2005).

PLATO AND THE ART OF PHILOSOPHICAL WRITING

CHRISTOPHER ROWE

CAMBRIDGE
UNIVERSITY PRESS

CAMBRIDGE UNIVERSITY PRESS
Cambridge, New York, Melbourne, Madrid, Cape Town, Singapore, São Paulo, Delhi

Cambridge University Press
The Edinburgh Building, Cambridge CB2 8RU, UK

Published in the United States of America by Cambridge University Press, New York

www.cambridge.org
Information on this title: www.cambridge.org/9780521859325

© Christopher Rowe 2007

First published 2007

Printed in the United Kingdom at the University Press, Cambridge

A catalogue record for this publication is available from the British Library

ISBN 978-0-521-85932-5 hardback

Contents

Preface

I offer in this book what is in some respects a new approach to Plato: one that attempts to take account of his strategies as a writer who writes, for the most part, in order to *persuade* his readers; an approach that attempts, in particular, to understand the way in which those strategies help to shape what he writes. In other words, my first concern is with understanding the nature of Platonic *rhetoric*. What he actually says, or has his main character – usually Socrates – say, is usually only a version of what he wants to say, designed to suit a particular audience on a particular occasion, as defined by the *dramatis personae* and the setting of the individual work; and he may well offer us different versions of the same thing, either in the same dialogue or, more usually, in others. It is one of the main claims of this book that trying to read off Plato's thinking from the surface of the dialogues is unlikely to be a reliable method for understanding him; especially when such a method is combined, as it often is, with a tendency to interpret different treatments of the same topic in chronological terms, that is, as evidence of 'developments' in his thinking. What will emerge, by the end of the book, is a Plato who will be, to most readers, and often for different reasons, unlike the Plato they have come to think they know.

At the same time, however, I am conscious of returning, in some respects, to an earlier tradition, which I identify particularly with Paul Shorey, among the Anglophones, and among French scholars with figures like Auguste Diès, Joseph Moreau, and more recently Monique Dixsaut, the sensitivity of all of whom to the complexity and sophistication of Plato's writing resists domination by any particular school of interpretation – whether one that sees Plato as a purveyor of doctrines, or one that treats him as a thinker who above all wants *us* to think, for ourselves. (These are caricatures, one of an ancient tradition of interpretation, the second of a more modern one.) This may be wishful thinking, and I may be on my own, as in some parts of the book I surely am; nor would I claim the protection of the figures just named for the outcomes of this book. It is, however, certainly true that the book finds itself opposed to the two tendencies I have just referred to. It is opposed, particularly, to the second type of interpretation, the non-doctrinalist one, which in one variety or another currently dominates Anglophone Platonic scholarship – usually in combination with a special 'developmental' thesis: that Plato started as a Socratic, but broke away in mid-career to become a Platonist. My own rival thesis is that Plato stayed a Socratic till the end. That is why, for the most part, he keeps Socrates on as his main speaker; 'Socrates', indeed, is his *alter ego*, his *persona*, his mask. And as it happens, this thesis also turns the normal non-'developmentalist', or 'unitarian' (also 'doctrinalist') type of interpretation on its head. The normal, contemporary 'unitarian' view starts from the 'mature' Plato and works backwards, so that Plato's Socraticism is submerged and obliterated. This view too I find mistaken and unhelpful, even if, over the centuries, it or some version of it has given the world what it understood as 'Plato'. So from at least two perspectives this will appear a radical book. Yet, as I have implied, I believe that this appearance has more to do with the directions that Platonic interpretation has taken in the last century than with the book's theses in themselves. As I read Shorey's *The Unity of Plato's Thought*, for example, from 1903, or Diès on Platonic *transposition* (1913), I have the sense that I am in large part only walking old and overgrown paths again. ·

However the book is not written primarily in order to argue *against* any particular view of Plato. Rather, its purpose is to argue *for* a view which happens to be in opposition to others. This is reflected in the fact that I make relatively little reference to existing literature on Plato, rarely engage directly with others on particular points, and frequently fail to acknowledge that others have arrived before me at what may look like the same interpretations. My explanation, and excuse, apart from the fact that the book is already long enough, is that despite the extended and detailed discussions of particular stretches of text that occupy the larger part of the book, my overriding concern at every point is less with those discussions in themselves than with the larger argument they are designed to support. It is chiefly for that larger argument, and the light that *it* brings to Plato's texts, that I claim whatever degree of originality the book may have. My broad characterizations of current trends in Platonic scholarship are a product of ten years' service as compiler of 'Booknotes on Plato and Socrates' for *Phronesis*, with up to fifty books a year to read – mainly in English, but also in French, German, and Italian, occasionally in Spanish (or Catalan); crude my characterizations may be, but I dare say they are true enough to life.

My argument is, inevitably, still a work in progress. Since it will never be complete (and I have already had to cut out at least a third of what I had originally intended to include), now is as good a moment as any to bring it to publication. If the book's title recalls Richard Rutherford's *The Art of Plato* (1995), and, more polemically, Thomas Szlezák's *Platon und die Schriftlichkeit der Philosophie* (originally 1985; volume II, 2004), that is accidental. *Plato and the Art of Philosophical Writing* (*PAPW*) has a much closer relationship to the book Terry Penner and I co-authored on Plato's *Lysis* (Cambridge University Press 2005), of which it is, in a way, a direct descendant. My part in *Plato's* Lysis was the first fruit of a five-year Personal Research Professorship awarded to me by the Leverhulme Trust; *PAPW* is the second – and indeed it was the original project for the Professorship. However, as it turned out, *Plato's* Lysis was a necessary first step, helping to shape many of the central ideas in *PAPW*. In some important respects *PAPW* even presupposes the earlier volume, while also applying aspects of its outcomes to a much larger quantity of text: perhaps, in one way or another, up to half of the genuine dialogues. At the same time *PAPW* brings together, and gives a fuller context and meaning to, a significant number of my other publications, whether commentaries, articles or book chapters; some of this published material has been absorbed into the new book, but nearly all of it has been completely re-thought and re-written to fit the new, larger context.

My thanks go, first and foremost, to the Leverhulme Trust, without whose support neither *Plato's* Lysis nor *PAPW* would probably have emerged until five or ten years from now, if at all; in second place to Terry Penner, who as usual has been ready with philosophical support whenever asked, but who is completely innocent of any philosophical crimes that I may have committed over the following pages; then to all those friends, colleagues and students with whom I have discussed various parts of the book, in various parts of the world, over the last fifteen to twenty years; to my talented and inspiring departmental colleagues in Durham; to Durham University, for awarding me a Sir Derman Christopherson Fellowship for the last, crucial stages of the writing of the book; to the Durham Institute of Advanced Studies, for a haven and good philosophical company over the last months; to the two long-suffering readers for the Press (one of whom was Thomas Johansen); to Jodie Barnes, Sarah Parker, Michael Sharp and especially Linda Woodward (best of copy-editors) at the Press; and last but hardly least, to Heather Rowe.

Durham, May 2007

Preliminaries: reading Plato

I INTRODUCTION

This is a book about Plato as a writer of philosophy: probably the most accomplished and sophisticated such writer the western world has known, but also one of the most puzzling. One of the chief puzzles about Plato's writing, and the one from which I shall begin, is its enormous *variety*. Why should he write in so many different ways? Philosophers, surely, only need to write in one way – as clearly and intelligibly as possible. Granted, virtually every item within the Platonic corpus is written in the same general format, that of imaginary conversations (reported or direct) between two or more interlocutors. However, this format is deployed in markedly varying fashions, and not only that, but often with what appear to be markedly varying outcomes. It sometimes appears almost as if different parts of the Platonic *oeuvre* might have been written by different people.[1] Most strikingly, while a significant number of dialogues, mainly short ones, take the form of an apparently open-ended exploration of particular subjects (often particular virtues – what I shall prefer to call 'excellences': *aretai*), led by a Socrates who continually advocates the importance of such – apparently open-ended – exploration and inquiry, other dialogues seem to show us a quite different Socrates, and a different Plato. Thus, most notoriously, the Socrates of the *Republic* – a work which will figure prominently in the present book – appears, at least on first reading, as an advocate of a closed society in which philosophy, instead of being the instrument of intellectual liberation that those other shorter dialogues seem to promise to make it, becomes the instrument of a political structure in which 'liberation' would

---

[1] By and large there is now consensus about which dialogues within the traditional corpus are by Plato and which are spurious; only one or two items are still debated, notably the *First Alcibiades*, *Hippias Major*, and *Clitophon*. (I myself think all three of these certainly spurious, along with all the *Letters*. *Menexenus* is by now surely off the doubtful list.)

evidently consist, for the majority of the population, in their control and manipulation by the few (philosophers).

How to explain this and other examples of the way Plato apparently changed, or wavered, in his approach to philosophy and to the writing of it: that will be one of the major tasks to be attempted in the following pages,[2] along with the task of explaining what it is, exactly, that Plato wanted to achieve, and thought he could achieve, by writing as he did. And that, for anyone who has seriously read any part of his *oeuvre* (i.e. by reading any dialogue from beginning to end, rather than just conning pre-selected passages, torn from their contexts), is the biggest question of all. As one of a fine group of undergraduates in Durham recently put it to me, Plato is 'weird', because he makes any reader work so hard to see what it is that he is up to – what he is using his characters to *say*, or in other words what he wants the reader to extract from his text.[3] Studiously (it seems) leaving himself off the list of speakers on every occasion, or at least not appearing in person, he leaves us to guess where to locate his voice. The best guess must be that it is normally the main speaker that speaks for him – and so, since Socrates is usually that main speaker, the chances are that Socrates' voice will also, normally, be Plato's (see section 4 below).[4] But then Socrates himself so often tells us that he has no answers – and when he does seem to come up with answers, they are not always the ones we might have expected, or hoped for (I refer again to the *Republic* as my central example).

At issue here is nothing less than what some might call the meaning of Plato, and of Platonism: 'Platonism', that is, in the sense of what it is that Plato stands for. At the most basic level, is he a philosopher who wishes for nothing so much as to *make his readers think for themselves*, somehow to make use of their own inner resources, without trying to weigh them down too heavily with doctrine? Or is he, on the contrary, someone who writes in order to impart *doctrines*? These are the lines along which the longest-running dispute among Plato's interpreters – beginning, strangely, even with his immediate successors, who might have been expected to know how to read him – has permanently been drawn. However, each of the two types of interpretation appears just as problematical as the other. If the

---

[2] The outcome of my argument will be to put the emphasis on that 'apparently' in 'apparently changed'. Plato changed a great deal less than appearances might suggest.

[3] 'Nothing is a matter of course; everything can be called into question. To read Plato demands a far higher degree of vigilance and activity than any other philosopher asks for. Time after time, we are forced to make our choice, to decide how we should interpret what we are reading' (Tigerstedt 1977: 99).

[4] See also Kraut 1992: 25–30.

first is right, then why is there so much by way of what look like positive doctrines in at least a significant proportion of the dialogues? And if the second, then why on earth did Plato not try to impart his teaching in a more direct way?

Defenders of the first type of interpretation will typically concentrate their fire on the talk of 'doctrines'. They will propose that Plato has few if any of *those*, pointing to that very richness (I called it variety) of Plato's writing, and explaining it either as proof of his versatility, or else as a sign of the kind of process of continual development and maturation that we should expect of any good philosopher. Talk of 'versatility' is in danger of suggesting that we can retreat into interpreting each dialogue on its own (as some scholars in the last two centuries have attempted to do), and there are too many connections between them, too many constants, to make that a viable proposition.[5] But again, if Plato was a doctrinalist, why was he not more open and direct about it? Because, say some defenders of the 'doctrinal' sort of interpretation, Plato thought his ideas incapable of being properly conveyed in writing; the dialogues are a sort of invitation to the feast, offering an initial encounter with fundamental ideas that could not be fully grasped without deepened contact through the medium of oral discussion within the walls and porticoes of the Academy. Yet what these interpreters generally propose for the main feast centres on a metaphysical system (including a set of first principles) that generally seems a good deal less interesting philosophically – whether to most ancient or to modern tastes – than what we find on or just under the surface of the dialogues themselves. Even more importantly, such interpreters fail to explain why, on their account, Plato needed to write out so many and such varied invitations: so many dialogues, small, medium-sized, large, massive, containing a wealth of action, argument, imagery, all sorts of other varieties of brilliance – why go on writing them, throughout a lifetime, if they were only the first step, and to be superseded by a higher (and not so far obviously more illuminating)[6] state of understanding?

Despite what I have just said, my own interpretation of Plato, or at any rate of Plato *as a writer*, as it unfolds, will turn out to have at least as much

---

[5] That is, if we want (as I presume most will want) to take Plato seriously as a philosopher. Of course if one decides in advance that he is (e.g.) a dramatist rather than a philosopher, then the objection might not apply. Grote 1865, a brilliant account in its own way, may be said to have tested to destruction the idea that we can appreciate Plato fully without at some point trying to relate systematically what we discover in one dialogue to what we discover in another. (Grote himself was reacting to what he – rightly – saw as the oversystematization of Plato by Neoplatonizing interpreters.)

[6] I refer here simply to the apparent philosophical aridity of the reconstructed 'unwritten doctrines' (Aristotle's phrase) of Plato on which such interpreters often pin their hopes.

in common with that of the second, 'doctrinal', group of interpreters as with that of the first, who may be very loosely termed 'sceptical'.[7] I shall certainly want to reject the understanding of Platonism put forward by the particular 'doctrinal' interpreters I had in mind in the preceding paragraph,[8] but there are certain things that they seem to me to have got right (as, for example, when they insist that Plato does not always say, at any one point, everything that he has in mind, or in hand; or, more generally, when they tell us that we frequently need to look below the surface of the text to find its real intention). It is interpreters of the 'sceptical' mould that I shall treat as my more immediate opponents, and among that rather broad group, one set of interpreters in particular: those who divide off certain parts of the Platonic corpus as 'Socratic' – the 'Socratic dialogues' being those mainly shorter, allegedly 'exploratory' dialogues that I have referred to, dating (it seems) from somewhere near the beginning of Plato's writing career – and who by so doing shift the locus of what is most authentically Platonic to the period of writing that followed. *The* key moment in Plato's development, from that perspective, was the break from the master, Socrates, the moment when the younger man started writing more ambitious and positive works (especially the *Republic*), whatever the degree of attachment he may have felt to the successive outcomes of these.[9]

Perhaps as much as anything else, it will be my aim in the present book to replace this way of dividing up Plato's work, which in my view has become the single greatest obstacle to a proper understanding of Plato and

---

[7] The term will roughly fit, insofar as the ancient and original sceptics – one variety of whom developed their views inside Plato's Academy itself, a few generations after Plato's death – were people who perpetually *looked* (the Greek verbs are *skopein*, *skopeisthai*, the noun *skepsis*), without ever finding anything solid they could rely on. Academic sceptics read Plato *as* a sceptic: some of the dialogues – especially the so-called 'Socratic' group (see below) – may superficially attract such a reading, but no modern interpreter would be likely to find it satisfactory. It is thus safe enough to borrow the term 'sceptical' for that broad church of non-'doctrinalist' readers of Plato. The members of this same broad church tend also to suppose that their non-doctrinal Plato was typically ready to review his ideas, to modify, abandon and replace them – to 'mature' and 'develop', as I put it in the preceding paragraph: in short, to use a standard term, the majority of such interpreters are 'developmentalists', by contrast with the 'unitarianism' of the their 'doctrinal' rivals, and I shall generally, if somewhat loosely and inaccurately, treat the labels 'sceptical' and 'developmentalist', on the one hand, and 'doctrinalist' and 'unitarian' on the other, as more or less interchangeable. I shall shortly be picking a quarrel with one very common kind of modern 'sceptical developmentalist': the kind that divides up the corpus into 'Socratic' ('early'), 'middle' and 'late' periods.

[8] These are the members of the so-called 'Tübingen school', including most importantly Hans-Joachim Krämer, Konrad Gaiser, and among contemporary scholars, Thomas Szlezák: see especially Szlezák 1985 and 2004.

[9] Since I am speaking here of 'sceptical' interpreters as opposed to 'doctrinal' ones (in my admittedly very crude distinction), the attachment will be less than would be implied by the use of the term 'doctrine'. Doctrines, for some philosophers, will not be suitable things for philosophers to have – as opposed to ideas or theories, which will be perfectly respectable.

Platonism.[10] For it will be one of my core claims that in fact the post-'Socratic' dialogues in all central respects depend and build on, even as they may extend, ideas and arguments contained in the 'Socratic' dialogues. (The scare quotes around 'Socratic' are to be taken seriously; there is in my view no group of dialogues which can helpfully be labelled 'Socratic' as opposed to others.) That is, these dialogues, along with others not normally labelled as 'Socratic' but nevertheless apparently predating the *Republic*, do crucial philosophical work which is not only not superseded by what comes later, but which we need to have properly grasped – and also to *keep in mind* – if we are fully to understand what we find in the *Republic* and other supposedly post-'Socratic' dialogues.[11] Importantly, I shall also claim that Plato remained faithful to the very notion of philosophy that is developed in, and in part illustrated by, the 'Socratic' dialogues. (Even the philosopher-rulers of the *Republic* will turn out to be formed after Socrates' image.[12] But this is to anticipate.)

For many if not most readers of Plato these will look unlikely claims – to say the least. As it happens, the 'doctrinal' interpreters[13] tend to be hardly less *Republic*-centred than the 'sceptical' ones, insofar as for them too it is

---

[10] The next greatest, in my view, is the idea, much favoured by 'doctrinalists' of all eras, that Plato was, more than anything else, an other-worldly metaphysician who thought that the highest kind of existence would be spent in the contemplation of pure being (*vel sim.*). See especially chapters 2, 7, 8 and 9 below. This approach, for its part, entails leaving out so much of the content of the dialogues, takes so little account of what Plato actually *wrote*, that I for one find it hard to take it at all seriously. Or, to put it another way, a book like the present one, which aims to explain why Plato wrote as he did, is not likely to be favourable to an approach that by its very nature leaves it entirely mysterious why Plato should have written so much that had so little bearing on what he supposedly intended his readers to sign up to.

[11] I shall not of course, impossibly, deny that there are also apparent, and important, discontinuities between the so-called 'Socratic' dialogues and what follows. But it will be my argument that these discontinuities are best seen against the background of an essential continuity – one that after all would be no less than one would expect, given that Plato keeps Socrates on, both in the *Republic* and in other 'non-Socratic' dialogues, as main speaker. I agree wholeheartedly with David Sedley (Sedley 2004: 14) that Plato 'emphasiz[ed] the continuity in his development [i.e. with what Sedley calls the '"semi-historical" Socrates featured in the early dialogues': 3] rather than acknowledging any radical break'. However while acknowledging Plato's own perspective on the matter, Sedley himself 'separat[es] an early Socratic phase from one or more subsequent Platonic phases' (ibid.), thus aligning himself with Vlastos 1991, and against Kahn 1996 – for whom the 'Socratic dialogues' are written to look forward to the *Republic* and other 'middle' dialogues, and so 'can be adequately understood only from the perspective of these middle works' (Kahn 1996: 60). My own view is exactly the reverse of Kahn's (though I register unease about the use of the term 'middle': on dating in general, see section 10 below).

[12] Still more surprisingly, from the perspective of any current interpretation, the same will be true of the members of the Nocturnal Council in the *Laws* (see chapter 10, n. 2 below).

[13] Or at least, modern 'doctrinalists'; for their ancient counterparts, it was the great cosmological dialogue *Timaeus* that counted as more central. But Plato himself takes care to link *Timaeus* with *Republic*, making the conversation represented (fictionally 'recorded') in the former take place on the day after the conversation, 'reported' by Socrates, that constitutes the latter.

the *Republic* – and other dialogues that the 'sceptics' call 'mature' – that take us closer to the heart of Plato: thinking of Platonism as nothing if not a *system* of thought, and more or less unchanging, they then propose *Republic*, along with *Philebus* and *Timaeus*, as the works that will give us the most information for fixing the outlines of that system. The so-called 'Socratic' dialogues (so-called, that is, mainly by the 'sceptics'), for the doctrinalists, are of relatively little interest in themselves, just as for the 'sceptics' these dialogues tend to represent the parts of Plato, i.e. those Socratic parts, that he left behind, whether this is taken to be a bad or a good thing.[14] One of the main tasks of the present book will be to show that both the 'sceptical' approach, which sees the *Republic* as marking Plato's break with Socrates, and its 'doctrinalist' counterpart, which tends to assimilate the 'Socratic' dialogues to the *Republic*, are mistaken: the Socrates of the *Republic is*, with certain important qualifications, the Socrates of the 'Socratic' dialogues; but this latter Socrates is not fashioned after the 'doctrinalists'' image. What should have emerged from my argument by the end of the book is a quite unusual, not to say revolutionary, picture of Plato and his thought. However whether or not this picture will appear plausible will depend entirely on my ability to persuade the reader of the usefulness of certain interpretative moves; or, to put it the other way round, my ability to persuade the reader to share my analysis of Plato's strategies as a philosophical writer. The title of the book may in this sense be taken as a true disjunction: I hope to understand what Plato stands for by understanding the reasons, methods and purposes of Platonic writing. (I admit, however, that many times over the detailed argument will turn out to be the other way round; what Plato wants to say and how he says it are mutually interdependent topics.)

It will be useful here to give a quite full and detailed outline of the key interpretative moves that will underpin my approach, before I turn, in the main part of the book, to particular themes and particular dialogues. The Table of Contents gives a fair indication of the selection of dialogues that will provide the main material for my discussion. Particularly prominent will be *Apology, Charmides, Euthydemus, Gorgias, Meno, Phaedo, Phaedrus,*

---

[14] It will be a bad thing for those who prefer what they see as Socrates' mode of doing philosophy in those dialogues to what they see as his appalling demeanour in the *Republic* (see above); a good thing for those many people who – quite misguidedly, in my own view – tend to think of Socratic methods and ideas as interesting but naive and limited. There has been talk in recent years, especially among North American scholars (of whom Francisco Gonzalez is among the most eloquent: see e.g. Gonzalez 1998), of a 'third way' of interpreting Plato, i.e. one that is describable neither as 'sceptical' nor as 'dogmatic'. Insofar as that could be said of my own reading, it too will belong to this 'third way'. However the main defining feature of this 'third' mode of reading seems to be just that it isn't either of the other two, both of which – as I began by saying – are plainly, by themselves, unsatisfactory.

Republic, and *Timaeus*. I shall have a fair amount, too, to say about *Theaetetus*, but rather little about the *Parmenides*, and nothing or virtually nothing about *Cratylus, Laws, Philebus, Protagoras* and two dialogues closely connected with the *Theaetetus, Sophist* and *Politicus*. I shall, however, advance a general thesis about those five big dialogues *Parmenides, Sophist, Politicus, Timaeus* and *Laws*, in which Socrates is not assigned the role of main speaker, as he is in every other genuine dialogue; clearly, given my overall thesis about the closeness of Plato to his Socrates, this is likely to appear a significant shift, suggesting – perhaps – that disciple did after all finally give up on master (for, as it happens, all five of these dialogues appear to be datable to the latest part of Plato's life: see section 10 below). I shall suggest, rather, that in demoting Socrates Plato distances *himself*, in varying degrees, from the positions he assigns to Socrates' replacements.

2 THE NATURE AND IMPORTANCE OF DIALOGUE, FOR PLATO

Plato evidently held dialogue to be fundamental to philosophy: Socrates never ceases to treat dialogue in this way, and for the most part – in Plato's works – carries on his business, which he calls philosophy, through dialogue. But why should dialogue be so important for the philosopher? The answer, it seems, has something and everything to do with Socrates', and Plato's, recognition of the need for *questioning*: only if we go on questioning our ideas can we ever hope to reach the truth, if we can reach it at all.

Some modern interpreters have understood this questioning in terms specifically of 'refutation',[15] because of the overwhelming tendency of Socrates' questioning, in the 'Socratic' dialogues, to end in the discomfiture of whoever or whatever is being questioned.[16] They have then gone on to propose that refutation could even somehow generate, discover, truth, by itself; and such interpreters have reconstructed on Socrates' behalf the assumptions that would be required to make that possible.[17] (I take it that

---

[15] See chapter 3 below.

[16] Such interpreters typically call Socrates' method 'elenctic'. In fact the Greek noun *elenchos* and the associated verbs, which Plato frequently applies to Socratic activity, as often refer to questioning and challenge as to refutation as such: see Tarrant 2002. I myself will propose that the fact that Socratic dialectic, in the 'Socratic' dialogues, nearly always ends in the refutation of the interlocutor has rather more to do with Plato's rejection of the positions Socrates' interlocutors represent than with the essential nature of Socratic method.

[17] Here is Donald Davidson, building on Vlastos 1983: 'the elenchus would make for truth simply by insuring [*sic*] coherence in a set of beliefs if one could assume that in each of us there are always unshakable true beliefs inconsistent with the false. It is not necessary that these truths be the same for each of us, nor that we be able to identify them except through the extended use of the elenchus. Thus someone who practices the elenchus can, as Socrates repeatedly did, claim that he does not

Socrates and Plato would have been repulsed by any special theories that find dialogical conclusions, in certain contexts, as all that there is to *constitute* truth;[18] whatever else they hold, they will certainly hold that the truth is the truth regardless of what anyone thinks it is, and indeed regardless of whether anyone at all has it in mind.) Reconstructions of this sort are a reaction, in itself noble enough, to the need somehow to square Socrates' repeated claim that he knows nothing with his more than occasional tendency to behave as if there are some things, at least, that he is pretty sure about, even knows. However the combination in Socrates of these two features – as a know-nothing, and (as one might put it) as a conviction philosopher – is perfectly intelligible without any such rich supplementation of Plato's text.[19] The most for which we have textual warrant is the idea that a continuous process of questioning, whether of one person by another or of oneself by oneself, along a particular line may lead to results that for all practical purposes are reliable and unlikely to need to be abandoned. This process of questioning represents the essence of the Socratic – and, as I hold, also the Platonic – notion of philosophy, and it is one that is most consistently displayed in action in the so-called 'Socratic' dialogues. Philosophy, as an activity, *is* the 'art of dialogue', whether internal or with others:[20] *dialektikē technē* in Greek, and hence 'dialectic'. (The 'art of dialogue': sc. through progressive questioning, and on the sorts of subjects expertise in which contributes to wisdom, *sophia*, *philo-sophia* being the love or pursuit of wisdom.)

---

know what is true; it is enough that he has a method that leads to truth. The only question is whether there is reason to accept the assumption.

'I think there is good reason to believe the assumption is true – true enough, anyway, to insure that when our beliefs are consistent they will in most large matters be true. The argument for this is long, and I have spelled it out as well as I can elsewhere' (Davidson 1993: 184–5, referring to Davidson 1983 [2001]).

[18] I mean no disrespect here to the late Hans-Georg Gadamer, whose subtle take on Plato is beautifully expounded by François Renaud in Renaud 1999; Gadamer himself accepts that a Plato who saw the true implications of his position would no longer be a Platonist ('Platon war kein Platoniker', cited by Renaud from Gadamer's *Gesammelte Werke* 2, 1977: 508).

[19] Briefly: there are things that Socrates will happily claim to be sure about, and even, in unguarded moments, to know, on the basis of argument; e.g., at the most general level, that knowledge and excellence matter more to everyone than anything else. But underlying his general position is a sensitivity to the limits of what mere human beings can achieve, which causes him typically to deny that *he* knows what he is talking about, even while he allows that others, perhaps, may know (or come to know) more than he does. See especially section 10, and chapters 1 and 8, below.

[20] Because of his position as a know-nothing, Socrates typically stresses his own need to be in conversation with others. But when Plato has others describe him, as in the *Symposium*, they vividly describe, among other habits of his, a tendency to spend long periods in self-absorbed thought; and he typically refers to examining *himself* in the same breath as he talks about examining others. See chapter 3 below; for thinking described explicitly as internal dialogue, see, e.g., *Theaetetus* 189D–190A.

3 THE RELATIONSHIP BETWEEN 'THE ART OF DIALOGUE' ('DIALECTIC') AND THE WRITTEN DIALOGUE FORM

It would be all too easy to slip from the simple proposal that all Platonic dialogues are 'philosophical' (at least to the degree that they were written by an author everyone agrees to have been a philosopher) to supposing that all equally display philosophy in action; and from there, given that the kinds of discussion we find in different dialogues are different, to supposing that Plato had different ways of conceiving of philosophy. Sometimes, as in the *Timaeus*, dialogue gives way to monologue: by the argument in question, Plato will on that occasion have given up on dialogue as the proper medium of philosophy. For the 'sceptical' brand of philosophers, this is likely to be a perfectly acceptable outcome, since few of them will share any great commitment to dialogue as such over monologue as a way of conducting philosophy in the first place,[21] and for them it might even be something of a relief to be able to think of Plato as giving up on it (as their Plato regularly gives up on things);[22] and for the 'doctrinalists'' Plato, too, dialogue may be equally dispensable – a means to a preliminary cleansing of minds from misapprehensions, and as a kind of intellectual gymnastics, but hardly the stuff of real philosophy.[23]

However, such responses would vastly underestimate the nature and complexity of written dialogue in its Platonic mode.[24] Above all, we need to remember the fact that a written dialogue possesses two extra dimensions, one of which will always, and the other will usually, be absent from a real dialogue, i.e. from any live conversation (or indeed one that is merely recorded in writing): (1) an author, and (2) an audience. It is hardly in doubt that Plato constructed and wrote his dialogues *for* an audience (or audiences), given the earnestness with which his main speakers address their interlocutors. He had a purpose in writing – he had things he wanted to say to his audience, ways in which he wanted to affect them. And he was presumably free to write as he pleased: he could set up the conversation as

---

[21] Especially, perhaps, if the dialogue may be internal; what harm will it do to redescribe any serious internal thought as a kind of questioning? (That, however, would be to miss Socrates' point, which is about the need to *challenge* one's own and others' thinking.)

[22] A special impatience with dialogue form is evinced by the habit some interpreters have – those brought up within the analytical tradition – of trying to reducing Socratic arguments to a series of numbered (and impersonal) propositions.

[23] 'Dialectic' itself, on this account, ultimately becomes severed from conversation and dialogue altogether, and becomes a term for whatever method will lead to philosophical truth.

[24] That is, whatever other writers of philosophical dialogues might make or might have made of the medium; let them be set to one side.

he liked, where he liked, and between whatever characters/interlocutors he liked. If, then, we are fully to understand what is going on,[25] and indeed if we are even to have any chance of grasping Plato's underlying argument, we have no option but to try to come to terms in each case with a whole series of different relationships: between author and text (and its argument – both the philosophical argument, and the 'argument' in the sense of the overall direction or directions of the text); between author and characters/speakers, especially the main speaker;[26] between author and audience; between the speakers themselves. But this already means that a written dialogue is something considerably more than a piece of philosophy. It is philosophy with its participants, and their utterances and actions, shaped, directed, set up, stage-managed by someone for someone else.

I do not mean to deny that it would be perfectly possible to write philosophical dialogues in which the dialogue and the philosophy (in the Socratic-Platonic sense, of progressive questioning: see above) were simply co-extensive. Interlocutor A, a voice perhaps with a name but no necessary identity, would state a position, which interlocutor B, another similarly unspecific voice, then questioned, leading A to restate the original position; if this imaginary dialogue were more than a few paragraphs long, then B would again raise problems with the new statement – and so on. This would be the basic, stripped-down version of Socratic dialectic.[27] But no actual Platonic dialogue is like this. For a start, A and B[28] will be identified as particular individuals, usually with names, and always with identifiable characteristics: A will more often than not be Socrates, and B will be a general,[29] a rhapsode,[30] a sophist,[31] a sophist/rhetorician,[32] a friend of Socrates',[33] a brother of Plato's[34] . . . And the nature and course of the conversation that ensues between A and B will always partly be determined by the choice of the person to play the role of B as much as by the choice of the person to play the role of A – which, if it is Socrates, will ensure that the

---

[25] I assume that we may ignore the possibility that Plato was a lazy author, who did not make the most of the opportunities available to him.

[26] Plato's dialogues always have a main speaker; this is no doubt itself something to be explained. (It will turn out to be significant that there is always, within a single dialogue, one perspective that is privileged – by the author – over the others.)

[27] The model is based on a combination of passages from the *Phaedrus* and the *Republic* with Socrates' actual practice in a range of other dialogues.

[28] I here for the moment leave out dialogues that lapse into monologue, i.e. where B ceases to play any audible part: *Menexenus* as well as *Timaeus* (where there is a C and a D as well as a B).

[29] Or generals: see *Laches*, where Socrates talks to the generals Laches and Nicias.

[30] I refer to Ion in *Ion*.   [31] Say, Hippias in *Hippias Minor*, Protagoras in *Protagoras* . . .

[32] Thrasymachus in *Republic* (especially Book I).   [33] Crito in *Crito*, Phaedo in *Phaedo*.

[34] Or brothers: Glaucon and Adimantus in *Republic* (especially Books II–X).

conversation is or becomes philosophical,[35] since that is his preoccupation, not to say his obsession. (Conversely, if A is not Socrates, that will leave the actual nature of the conversation in principle open: more on this possibility in a moment.) Socrates will have a different kind of conversation with a general from the one he will have with a rhapsode, and a different one with a general or a rhapsode from the one he will have with a friend of his, who is used to his ways. Or, to put it another way, a conversation between Socrates and Ion, rhapsode, on the nature of the rhapsode's and the poet's 'art', as in the *Ion*, will not be the same as a conversation between two anonymous philosophers on the same subject. The conversations on the subject of justice between the sophist/rhetorician Thrasymachus and Socrates, on the one hand, in *Republic* I, and between Socrates and Glaucon and Adimantus, Plato's brothers, in *Republic* II–X on the other *are* actually quite different: at any rate, one is confrontational in form, the other cooperative. (And even as he talks to Glaucon and Adimantus, Socrates repeatedly refers to another sort of conversation that he might have had, using different premises: see especially chapter 5 below.) Evidently Plato wanted these differences, since he put them there, and it must be our business to ask why he did so.

We may presumably begin by dismissing the possibility that the characterization (and the dramatic action: that too we must take into account) in the dialogues is for merely ornamental purposes, just on the grounds that it is so obtrusive. It is part of that 'weirdness' of Plato's texts that they force us to try to see whatever point it is that they are making through the fog of a conversation with *this* individual, or these individuals, now. I also propose to dismiss the possibility that Plato is interested in, say, Ion, or Laches, for Ion's or Laches' sake (if he is writing for us, his readers, or any of our predecessors, why on earth should he expect them, let alone *us*, to be interested in such figures, neither of whom left much else by way of an imprint on history?). Rather, his interest in them is because of the types of people they are (a rhapsode and a general), and also because the types they represent are, at least within the fictional context, real and familiar – or would have been to the original audience. That is, the *Ion*, the *Laches*, and other dialogues show the philosopher in conversation with some of the sorts of people we, or our ancient counterparts, might encounter; people who, more importantly, hold (or can be induced to entertain) *attitudes or views* that we might encounter, and might even share. To that extent,[36]

---

[35] That is, it will involve questioning and challenge – and will also be about subjects that matter (not just the weather, or the quality of the wine).

[36] And only to that extent: below, I shall enthusiastically reject the idea that Plato thinks the reader can enter into any meaningful *dialogue* with his texts (or any text).

the conversations between the interlocutors are also conversations between the author and the reader – if rather peculiar conversations, given that the reader's answers are already given for him, by the interlocutor. By the same token, to the degree that the conversations usually involve Socrates' trying to unsettle an interlocutor's apparent certainty about something, or introducing him to new points of view, or doing both things together, we may reasonably suppose it to be Plato's purpose similarly to unsettle the reader.[37] If so, the dialogues will also have a persuasive function, i.e. in addition to any purely philosophical one; and indeed in such a case the philosophical will be employed in the service of the persuasive.

The point may be generalized. If 'philosophy', as I propose, for Socrates and Plato is fundamentally a matter of progress through questioning towards a presumptive truth, then the persuasive function of written dialogue – even in the case of the 'Socratic' dialogues – will usually be more prominent and/or immediate than the philosophical one.[38] It is in principle possible that Plato's arguments reproduce internal dialogues of his own, a kind of talking to himself.[39] However some of the dialogues are clearly not like that – that is, the arguments they contain are not the kind of arguments Plato (Socrates)[40] would have with himself, since they start from other people's assumptions; and in general there seems just too large an element of *staging* – Socrates always seems ahead of his interlocutors, rather than moving along with them.[41] A dialogue like the *Ion* is less like a piece of dialectic than a dialectical clash between two views of poetry and expertise. In *Laches*, the element of dialectical progress is more prominent, and in *Charmides* and *Lysis* it is more prominent still, with the consequence that any sense of confrontation between speakers and views is gradually lessened, and agreement may even be in sight – before, in each of these three

---

[37] Any reader, that is, who is in a condition analogous to that of the interlocutor (or who knows someone who is).

[38] Some interpreters plausibly attribute a fundamentally 'protreptic' function to Plato's writing as a whole; i.e. they see it as designed (perhaps *inter alia*) to turn people towards philosophy. But as will soon emerge, I believe this understates the case, if 'turning to philosophy' is understood merely as questioning ourselves and the way we presently think: what Plato is after is to change our whole view of the world and ourselves, in a particular and determinate way.

[39] See e.g., Sedley 2003: 1 ('. . . these . . . question-and-answer sequences can legitimately be read as *Plato thinking aloud*'). This would take us some way back in the direction of an identification between dialogue and dialogue-*writing*; more on this in the following section.

[40] On the relationship between Plato and (his) Socrates, see the next section.

[41] I am aware that these are far from being knock-down arguments. Nor do I mean to rule out Sedley's option altogether (see n. 39 above), at least to the extent that Socrates' dialectical exchanges with his interlocutors will in general serve as models of how philosophy is done. I simply find this kind of explanation of Plato's use of the dialogue form unsatisfactory, and not least because there is so much in the dialogues that does not consist of 'question-and-answer sequences'.

dialogues, the conversation formally ends in *aporia*, 'perplexity' or '*impasse*'. So there is plenty of what will count as philosophical by Socrates'/Plato's measure, even if it is a written version of it (and to that extent inauthentic: it is Plato's recreation of progress that might have been made between Socrates and some other person, if they had had the occasion to talk together). But the immediate overall effect on the reader, for all that some interpreters have suggested otherwise, is likely to be less a sense of engagement in the argument, which he or she will usually find fairly baffling, than a sense of sympathy with one or other of the interlocutors. That, certainly, is how modern readers tend to feel, many of them taking at once against Socrates; I hazard that ancient readers felt much the same. (Bafflement, a sense of someone's being done down, but still also a sense of things being less settled than they were before?)

When we turn to other, allegedly 'non-Socratic', parts of the corpus, the proportion of dialectic – that is, of passages that to some degree approach my imaginary model, sketched above, of what pure philosophical dialogue might be – to other kinds of matter in most cases drops considerably. In *Phaedo*, there are four blocks of argument, carefully marked off from the rest; in *Symposium*, a solitary stretch of dialectic between Socrates and Agathon, Diotima and Socrates; *Republic* I is on the model of a *Charmides* or *Lysis*, but the remaining nine books contain relatively little by way of genuine exchange; *Timaeus*, as I have said, is virtually a monologue; and so on. Many, as I have already noted, see all this as a sign that Plato is moving away from the Socratic way of doing philosophy, i.e. through dialogue and conversation (despite *Theaetetus* and *Philebus*, both superlatively dialectical in character; both throwbacks, according to the interpreters in question). My own view, by contrast, is that what the situation in the 'non-Socratic' (or post-'Socratic') dialogues marks is a change of strategy, not a change of mind. If Plato writes in a different way, that is because he has decided to approach his readers – who, in my view, were always his first preoccupation – by a different route. His aim is always to change people's perceptions, by variously stimulating and provoking them (us); even while insisting that philosophy is the key, he by no means always uses dialectic, or the written counterpart of dialectic, to achieve that stimulation and provocation. In fact philosophical dialectic is merely one of his tools. On occasion, as in the *Timaeus*, he can leave it in his bag entirely (and indeed, in a later chapter,[42] I shall argue that Timaeus, the main speaker in that dialogue, is not a philosopher-dialectician at all, even if he has a more

---

[42] Chapter 10.

than intelligent grasp of Platonic metaphysics). Or else, as in the *Laws*, he can set up a conversation between a philosopher and two non-philosophers who are specifically identified as incapable of dialectical exchange (it simply goes over their heads); a strategy that has immediate consequences for the level of the conversation. The Athenian visitor to Crete in *Laws* cannot, clearly, carry on a discussion with the philosophically unformed Clinias and Megillus of the sort that Socrates, albeit a still youthful one, can conduct, in the *Parmenides*, with the great Parmenides of Elea – the one named philosopher other than Socrates for whom Plato seems to have had any serious time – and his acolyte Zeno.

In short, Platonic written dialogue is not the same as dialectic (philosophy).[43] But this ought not to come as any great surprise. Socrates in the *Phaedrus* tells us roundly that writing is no more than the bastard stepbrother of philosophy, among other things because it cannot answer back. Ask questions of any written document, and it goes on stolidly saying the same thing. Socrates obviously cannot be knowingly referring to the very (written) dialogues in which he participates, since from his point of view within the dialogue these are oral, but[44] we have no good reason to suppose that he means to exempt them from his strictures. Plato preferred to write in dialogue form, and he gives every sign of thinking dialogue the most valuable form of human activity. However his preference for writing in the form of dialogue is not *because* he thought dialogue so valuable as an activity (even if he might perhaps originally have started using dialogue form in imitation of, as a kind of recreation of, the real Socrates' favoured pursuit). For just as, self-evidently, there are different kinds of dialogue/conversation that one can have, most of them entirely unphilosophical, so there are many different kinds of written (Platonic) dialogue. That he employed dialogue form in different ways, some of them not portraying dialectic in action, does not in the least tend to indicate that he ever abandoned his view that *living* dialogue, based on questioning of oneself or others, on the most important subjects, was the only available means to intellectual progress. But that, in turn, need not have deterred him from continuing to place before us, in one extraordinary way after another, alternative visions of the

---

[43] And how could it be? Take the little *Menexenus*: in formal terms still a dialogue, because it begins with a short exchange between Socrates and Menexenus, but then a monologue – a mock-funeral speech – offered by Socrates to Menexenus. Then too the monologue itself contains hardly a trace of anything we – or Plato – might recognize as a philosophical argument (even while it refers implicitly to ideas that appear in more obviously philosophical/dialectical contexts). At the same time this little piece contains all the complexities, and raises all the questions (about the intended relationship of author to audience, and so on), that attach to its larger counterparts in the corpus.

[44] *Pace* Mackenzie 1982 (see chapter 11 below).

way we, and the world, are, and from presenting those visions in contrast to more familiar ones: that I take to be one of the commonest and most central functions of Platonic writing, from the smallest of its products to the largest.[45] Even if he thinks that we can only advance through dialectic, there is nothing incompatible between that and showing us how differently things might, or will, look, if only we could become able to see more clearly.

4 PLATO AND SOCRATES: MANY VOICES?

There is one standing issue in modern Platonic scholarship over which I may seem to have skated with nonchalance in the preceding section. In the present post-modernist (or post-post-modernist) age, literary interpreters in particular have become worried about the practice – enshrined in Platonic interpretation over two and a half millennia – of assuming that the Socrates of the dialogues speaks for Plato. In principle this worry seems entirely well motivated. The dialogues always contain more than one voice (except when they change to monologue, and sometimes perhaps even then),[46] and in principle it seems perfectly plausible to suppose that Plato *might* have wanted, sometimes (or even often), to side with Socrates' opponent(s) – or, at least, to see their positions as impeding endorsement of Socrates'. Or, again, he might sometimes just have wanted to distance himself from the old man. ('That's just going *too* far.') But it is hard to credit that Socrates' voice is not *in general* Plato's: why else would it always – or very nearly always – be his opponents, rather than Socrates, that are variously defeated, humiliated, or made to think again? Why, again, would Plato keep bringing Socrates back on stage, in dialogue after dialogue, in many cases to say what are often the same sorts of things and support the same sorts of positions, if he did not view those positions with favour? (I started in section 1 above with the *differences* between one dialogue, or group of dialogues, and another; the constants, despite those differences, should be obvious enough on any close reading.) In brief, the worry about making Plato's text univocal may have fine motives, but it is overdone and misplaced. By and large, Socrates is Plato's *portavoce*, his mouthpiece.

But here there is a complication. What about those occasions when Socrates says different things, instead of the same ones? What, for example, of those apparent inconcinnities between the *Republic* and the so-called

---

[45] This is not to say that all dialogues have this function, and certainly not that it is the exclusive function of all. There are also more specialized dialogues, e.g., *Parmenides*, or *Theaetetus*, and Plato is in any case far too sophisticated a writer and a thinker to be tied down by any simple description.

[46] See chapter 10 below.

'Socratic' dialogues from which I began in section 1? Of course, if these
bother us at all, that will probably be a sign that we have already proposed
to accept that Socrates speaks for Plato. To find him speaking as he does in
the *Republic* is bothering precisely because, having got used to one kind of
Platonic voice, we are suddenly presented with what looks like a new one.
'Plato has betrayed Socrates,' comes the cry (in the light of all those appalling
political proposals), and the betrayal will seem all the worse because Plato
keeps Socrates on, to all appearances simply substituting the new voice
for the old one, with the result that he has 'Socrates' endorse ideas that,
allegedly, would have had the real Socrates turning in his grave. Did ever a
pupil treat his teacher worse?[47]

I do not propose to enter into what is now an old controversy, about
the relationship between Plato's Socrates (or any of his Socrateses?) and the
historical, flesh-and-blood Socrates, beyond saying that I see no obstacle to
supposing Plato's overall portrait of Socrates to be faithful to his own vision
of the original one[48] – no obstacle, that is, unless it is the attribution to him
of unpalatable and apparently un-Socratic ideas like the ones in the *Republic*.
But in this case, as in some others, I believe we need to identify a further
feature of Platonic writing that interpreters in general have either missed
altogether or – more usually – seriously underplayed. Plato's Socrates speaks
for most of the time with his own voice (and Plato's), but he can also 'speak
with the vulgar'. That is, he can, on occasion, adopt the colouring and the
premisses of his interlocutors or opponents, as an argumentative strategy.
'I would prefer not to go that way,' he will say, by implication, 'but if you

---

47 I am here leaving to one side the further complications to the 'Socrates as mouthpiece' interpretation
that go along with separating off the 'Socratic' dialogues from others – an approach that I have
typically associated with the 'sceptical' brand of interpreters: on *their* view, of course, there will be
distance between Plato and Socrates as soon as he embarks on his post-'Socratic' period (cf. n. 14
above). I leave these complications to one side for the obvious reason that I reject the approach
from which they flow: *my* Socrates always, or nearly always, fully understands whatever it is that
Plato puts in his mouth – even when we might want to protest that it is something the Socrates of
the 'Socratic' dialogues, or the real Socrates, will never have thought of (of course, Socrates can't
know that he's a character in a written dialogue, but that will usually not matter too much). That
is, from Plato's perspective (I claim), any amount of extension, even of modification, of the kinds
of things Plato might once have got from Socrates he still sees as *Socratic* – because he sees Socrates,
and himself, as having bought into *a system of ideas* (representing the way things really are), which
requires exploration rather than construction. Plato does not see himself, and Socrates, as putting
together a theory, but rather as investigating the implications of a set of insights that he takes to be
true and fundamental.

48 A vision that will in fact be very complex, if one accepts the substance of the preceding note:
'Socrates' will not be co-extensive simply with what that particular historical person actually said
and did, but will include whatever can legitimately be identified as belonging to that truthful picture
of things that he – the historical person – had begun to sketch. For the implications of this approach
in relation to Platonic metaphysics ('Forms'), see section 10 below.

insist, I will; and even so I shall give you good reason for coming over to my side.' Every reader accepts that there is an element of this in Books II–X of the *Republic*, where Socrates undertakes to show that justice 'pays' even if the just man receives none of the rewards of being just and all of the penalties that accrue to someone who has been found guilty of the worst injustices. What is not so usually noticed, or at least given sufficient emphasis, is that the whole political structure of 'Callipolis', the beautiful or 'ideal' city, is designed to cure a city that is already 'fevered' and *un*ideal;[49] and that even the analysis of the four excellences or virtues (*aretai*) in Book IV, which derives from the construction of Callipolis, depends on the evidence of the behaviour of souls that are internally conflicted and thus themselves out of sorts. As I shall argue in detail in chapter 5, the net outcome is that there is a question-mark over the level of Socrates' (and Plato's) commitment to – or, perhaps better, enthusiasm for – the political and psychological analyses conducted in *Republic* IV: there is more than enough in those analyses that Socrates can accept to allow the overall argument to follow through, but the argument is itself shaped as much by the interlocutors' assumptions and starting-points as by his own. Left to himself, as I shall claim Socrates makes quite clear, he would have rather different things to say about the best kind of city, and the best state of the soul, just as he would argue differently[50] for the claim that justice 'pays'.

This is, however, already to anticipate a set of claims that need to be established in detail if they are to be introduced at all. At this early stage of my argument, my concern is still no more than to indicate the main interpretative strategies that I shall be deploying in the following chapters; and in that spirit I shall simply assert, for now, that I take it to be one of the key features of Plato's use of Socrates that he not infrequently does have him argue from premises other than his own. However – and this is a crucial corollary, without which 'Socrates' might be in danger of being reduced to one of the 'eristics'[51] that he likes to criticize – when Socrates *does* argue from others' premises, Plato is always careful to avoid having him commit himself to anything that he would not accept on his own account. Thus *if* the best city had to address itself to the curing of internal 'fever', then

---

[49] The political arrangements sketched in Books II–IV are 'good', even 'correct' (V, 449A1–2); VI, 497B–D comes close to saying that the constitution of Callipolis is 'best', but in the sequel it is the issue of its possibility, and sustainability, that comes to dominate the discussion.

[50] And in fact has, already (in *Republic* I). None of this is intended to deny that the main political diagnosis of the *Republic*, and its prescriptions, are seriously meant; the question is just about where the argument should *start from*. See further chapter 5.

[51] 'Eristics', in brief, are those who argue merely in order to win, without any regard to the truth; star examples are Euthydemus and his brother Dionysodorus in the *Euthydemus*.

it would look something like Callipolis; *if* we observe conflicted souls in action, then an account of the virtues or excellences will need to presuppose a divided soul – and so on. (These, it has to be said, are the easy cases; there will be others where one has to work rather hard to exempt Plato's Socrates from the charge of mere eristic opportunism. But see further in section 6 below.)

So there are, I claim, times when Plato's Socrates merely appears to be speaking with a different voice, and when actually, on closer analysis, he has simply borrowed it for the occasion. However there are also times when he seems genuinely to change his tune, as, most importantly, when he allows that the soul may come to be in such a condition that it is apparently dragged about, and the behaviour of its possessor – the agent – changed, by irrational desires working in conflict with the agent's own reasoning. This is in marked contrast to what is proposed in some dialogues, mainly but not exclusively the ones labelled 'Socratic', and provides what I take to be the only plausible grounds for a distinction – which I nevertheless still propose generally to reject – between the 'Socratic' and the 'Platonic' in Plato. In the 'Socratic' dialogues, and indeed even in the *Symposium*, one of the traditional immediately post-'Socratic' or 'middle' dialogues, our desires are all, and always, for what is really good for us, so that they cannot in fact conflict, despite appearances to the contrary; what causes us to go wrong – and that means everybody – is our beliefs, i.e. about what is good for us. This extraordinary set of claims is, or so it seems, and has been thought, very deliberately rejected, by Socrates himself, in *Republic* IV, in the course of his argument for the tripartition of the soul (based on the very capacity of our desires to conflict). Plato seems to want to justify this move on Socrates' part through a qualification to tripartition, introduced in Book X, that it does not apply to soul in its essence, only as we observe it in the hurly-burly of life; but it looks nonetheless as if the move is a significant one. For one thing, it means that Socrates will in fact have to take seriously the case of the 'fevered' city (insofar as the 'fever' results from internal conflict in individual souls), and so – it seems – the political structure that is proposed for controlling it. And yet there still are ways in which Plato's conception of the soul and of desire, and his theory of action, remain thoroughly indebted to the model apparently abandoned in *Republic* IV. (Indeed I shall argue that Plato thinks he can *preserve* that model, despite all appearances to the contrary.) Here is a set of issues that will keep on recurring in the following chapters – and necessarily so, given that one of my main claims, as already announced, is precisely that Plato remains throughout essentially a *Socratic*. The idea of the soul as unitary and unconflicted is one of the very marks of the Socratic; if Plato simply decided to set it to one side, that might well be thought enough to put Plato's Socratic credentials in serious jeopardy.

However what I shall claim, and hope to establish, is not only that Plato sees himself, throughout, as a genuine follower of Socrates, but that this view of himself is justified. The usual – 'sceptical' – view is that he both leaves Socrates behind (at some point after the 'Socratic' dialogues) and understands himself as doing so. Thus, according to this more usual kind of approach, there will be a fundamental difference between the earlier Socrates (the Socrates of the 'Socratic' dialogues) and the later one (in the *Republic* and elsewhere); in a more sophisticated version of the same approach, Socrates will be found, in the post-'Socratic' dialogues, saying things whose full import he – unlike the intelligent reader – does not fully understand.[52] My own alternative approach will propose to do entirely without this kind of distancing between Plato and Socrates. Plato *is* Socrates, except, unavoidably, to the extent that Plato as author is also Socrates' creator and manipulator (manipulating him, that is, in a series of moves that he claims ultimately, and, I claim, reasonably, to have derived from *him*). Indeed Plato is Socrates even when he has the latter cede his place as main speaker to someone else. In the *Timaeus*, Timaeus' reservations about the status of central aspects of his account of the cosmos are Plato's – and also Socrates'.[53] The young Socrates whose ideas about forms[54] are criticized by the great Parmenides in the *Parmenides* is meant to be read, not just as an imagined, or possible,[55] immature Plato, but also *as Socrates*: the two march together. And the magisterial demonstrations of the method of 'collection and division' by Parmenides' fellow Eleatic in the *Sophist* and *Politicus* are as little in Plato's style as they are Socrates'.[56] Similarly with the *Laws*, the

---

[52] See especially Sedley 2004 on the *Theaetetus*, treated as Plato's acknowledgement of his debt to Socrates (his 'midwife'). It is not clear to me how this general approach will handle what I have been treating as the central problem case, that of the *Republic*, where it seems that 'Socrates' can scarcely be unaware of the distinctly un-Socratic nature of large parts of what Plato puts in his mouth. However for Sedley it is the *metaphysical* aspect of the *Republic* that particularly takes this dialogue beyond Socrates; and it is at least true that Socrates embarks on the main metaphysical section of the dialogue only with the greatest show of reluctance. (Yet: in the *Parmenides* a younger version of the same Socrates is to be found defending 'Platonic' metaphysics.)

[53] Compare (or: I shall compare) Socrates' claim in the *Apology* and elsewhere not to have concerned himself with inquiring into the physical world.

[54] On Platonic 'forms' see initially section 10 below.

[55] That is, insofar as the ideas criticized are ideas that Plato might have had, or ideas that someone might have had about Plato's ideas.

[56] This is not of course to deny that Parmenides in *Parmenides*, and his *alter ego*, the Visitor from Elea (Parmenides' home city) in *Sophist* and *Politicus*, are also Plato, to the extent that their starting-points are entirely ones that Plato would himself warmly endorse. Indeed they portray the very

only dialogue among them all in which Socrates is neither present nor even mentioned. The main speaker – a visitor to Crete from Athens – delivers himself on the subject of legislation and associated matters as Socrates did in the *Republic*, but without any of his hesitation and indeed almost with a show of authority, at least in relation to his two interlocutors (one of whom actually connects him directly with Athena, goddess of wisdom: 626D). In short, my thesis is that Plato is to be thought of as presenting himself as well as Socrates as a know-nothing.[57]

5   THE SOCRATES OF THE 'SOCRATIC' DIALOGUES, EVEN WHILE CLAIMING TO KNOW NOTHING, POSSESSES A SUBSTANTIVE PHILOSOPHICAL POSITION AND A DISTINCTIVE SET OF PHILOSOPHICAL STARTING-POINTS

What underpins this claim of mine about the identity between Plato and Socrates is a particular view of the so-called 'Socratic' dialogues (and so more generally of this person *Socrates* with whom I am claiming Plato identifies himself). A proper and fuller demonstration of the usefulness of this view of 'Socrates' will need to wait until the main part of this book, but the essential points may be stated here. I have already given a rough indication of how the 'sceptical' and the 'doctrinal' interpreters respectively tend to see the dialogues in question (the 'Socratic' ones): in the one case, as (more or less) open-ended explorations, and in the other as a kind

---

essence of the Platonic philosopher – but with the crucial exception of their *magisterial* stance. Plato in these cases imagines what it would be like for the philosopher to possess at least something of that authority which his Socrates, and (implicitly) he himself, go on disavowing. (These will be the *koruphaioi*, the 'leaders' in philosophy, that Socrates refers to in the *Theaetetus* 'digression': see chapter 7 below.) Examples: at *Phaedrus* 266B Socrates says he would follow someone with expertise in the method of 'collection and division' 'as if in the footsteps of a god'; and just such an expert appears, in the shape of the Eleatic Visitor, in *Sophist* and *Politicus*, to be greeted by Socrates as 'some kind of god' (*Sophist* 216A5, with reference to Homer). Parmenides himself, in his poem, claimed direct inspiration from above: his authority, for the purposes of the fiction, is already given. But any authority that even he has will turn out to be flawed. Again see chapter 7 below.

[57] For a long time I had thought of the Athenian visitor in the *Laws* as a thinly disguised Plato, because of a remark he makes at the very end about his qualifications as a legislator ('I've had a lot of experience in relation to such things, and thought about them a lot': XII, 968B8–9); Malcolm Schofield disabused me of the idea, pointing out that in terms of tone the Athenian is actually much more like the Visitor from Elea in *Sophist* and *Politicus*. The kinds of things he says are not so different from – and in many respects need to be read in the context of – what Socrates has to say about politics and political arrangements in the *Republic*, but unlike Socrates he appears to have few doubts about his fitness for saying them. At the same time he does not claim anything approaching infallibility; he envisages the laws he and his two interlocutors are putting together for the new city of Magnesia as still capable of improvement.

of preparatory exercise, to rid us of false views, or of a false pretence to knowledge. I propose that both of these sorts of readings, while containing elements of the truth, are ultimately mistaken.[58] There is little or nothing that is genuinely open-ended about the 'Socratic' dialogues, and little that is genuinely exploratory either[59] – or at least from the standpoint of the author and his chief character. It is not just that Plato and Socrates are both ahead of the interlocutor; that is, it is not just a matter of control.[60] The essential point is rather that Plato's Socrates *always has a positive, and substantive, agenda.*[61] He addresses his interlocutors from a particular, and philosophically formed, point of view – one which will almost always be fundamentally different from theirs, and to which it is evidently his purpose to try to bring them over; just as, I presume, it is Plato's purpose to try to bring his readers, us, over (except, of course, to whatever extent we may already be with him). This is clearly essential to my thesis: on any account *Plato* had a 'substantive agenda' (however that may be specified); if Socrates had none, it would be nonsensical to suggest that Plato identified with him as completely as I wish to claim.

The 'doctrinal' sort of interpreters will have no problems with the sugges-tion that Socrates – for the moment, the Socrates of the 'Socratic' dialogues – had a substantive agenda; after all, their Socrates is permanently in full possession of the same truths all along, to which *Republic* and other post-'Socratic' dialogues give us whatever access we may be allowed. That of course is not at all the sort of agenda that I have in mind. However the fact that the 'doctrinalists' can claim that their favoured agenda is there at all, under the surface, begins to indicate the size of the problem that my own claim has apparently to face. To all appearances, the Socrates of dialogues

---

[58] The second reading might appear to receive direct support from a passage like *Sophist* 230B–D; but that passage itself gives only a one-sided picture of the dialectical process – one that concentrates on the preparatory and the negative, and leaves out the possibility of progress beyond 'cleansing' from false beliefs (because of an immediate contrast with sophistical refutations).

[59] This is not to deny that there is an element of exploration, and an important one, in the Platonic dialogues as a whole (see especially chapter 8, pp. 237–8 below). My point here is strictly about the 'Socratic' dialogues, which are often thought to be quintessentially exploratory: that, I claim, is an illusion – except to the extent that we may be able to think away the actual results of the conversation, and the actual signs of the author's intentions in terms of substantive content. See below.

[60] Plato, of course, can always see where the argument will go, since he is making it go there; at least fictionally Socrates will have rather less control, since he won't know quite how the interlocutor will behave. This is where the 'sceptical' reading will acquire some purchase on things, as it will in a more general way to the extent that Socrates' exchanges with his interlocutors illustrate what a philosophical conversation looks like.

[61] An agenda, that is, which is still compatible with Socrates' (and Plato's) position as know-nothing. The conditions Plato ultimately sets on the possession of knowledge, i.e. full knowledge or wisdom about the things that matter, are very high indeed (see chapter 7 below).

like *Euthyphro* and *Laches* (which one might think of as archetypal 'Socratic' dialogues) really does seem to have very few positive ideas to push. Leave aside the claims of the 'doctrinalists' about a hidden agenda, and the field at once appears to belong to the 'sceptics'. First, there is that repeated claim of Socrates' that he knows nothing. If he knows nothing, then surely that ought to imply that he has nothing much to bring his interlocutors over *to*, apart perhaps from a few earnestly held beliefs. Those he surely has in any case – about the importance of philosophy, and of virtue. Beyond general claims of that kind, or so interpreters of a 'sceptical' ilk will urge, he really ought to be committed to exploring things with us, not trying to sell us any goods whose value, as a know-nothing, he is in no position to vouch for. Secondly, the 'sceptics' will ask, if Socrates has a positive philosophical agenda to put forward in these dialogues, why is it that so many of them end in *impasse* (*aporia*, a state in which one does not know what do next, where to go next)? Again, doesn't Socrates typically put his questions in an open-ended way – 'what is courage/piety/justice/beauty?'?

Part of what underlies such objections is an often unspoken assumption among such interpreters that by and large Plato will observe what we think of as philosophical propriety, and not smuggle in substantive premisses that have not been acknowledged by both interlocutors. It might be fair enough – they will quietly suppose – to use short-cuts on occasion, but it would be nothing short of a professional foul (to use a different metaphor, this time a footballing one) on Plato's part to have Socrates rely on assumptions to which we, and the interlocutor(s), have not been given access. So, the argument will run, what you see is what you get; Socrates has no substantive philosophical agenda, and my claim must be false.

I begin with this last and in many ways most important objection, based on what might be called the rules of the game. My first response is to repeat a point I made above: written dialogue (in Plato's case) is not the same thing as, and does not follow the rules of, ordinary live philosophical dialectic. Of course in any ideal philosophical conversation both parties would have to put everything on the table in order to make any genuine advance together. But as author and controller of written dialogue, Plato has a freer hand, and his focus is – I suppose – on *our*, the readers', improvement, rather than that of Socrates' interlocutor. My proposal is that, in the 'Socratic' dialogues, Plato has Socrates examine his interlocutors' views (or those they can be induced to take on and defend) against the backdrop of his own rival views, which may not surface fully and explicitly but which will turn out nevertheless – if and when we have recognized them for what they are – to have had an influence on the course of the argument and its outcomes, and indeed on the very choice of subject for the conversation in the first place.[62] This strategy is intelligible, if – as I suppose – (a) Plato tends to think Socrates' starting-points true,[63] and (b) he is aware of how unfamiliar, if not plain implausible, they will seem to most people (a point to which I shall return shortly). So unfamiliar, in fact, as to make any conversation impossible, except perhaps about the implausibility of Socrates' positions – when Plato's real focus, and target, is actually the positions Socrates is attacking.

As to how we recognize what Socrates' starting-points are, my answer is that we shall need – and are intended – to read across from one dialogue to another: from dialogues that are relatively explicit about Socrates' own philosophical perspective, especially *Lysis, Charmides, Euthydemus, Gorgias*, to others that are less explicit, like *Ion, Laches, Euthyphro*.[64] Like others, I believe that we must always begin by trying to understand a dialogue by itself, since almost all of them are presented, fictionally and dramatically, as being or including self-standing conversations. But it is an essential part of the kind of interpretation that I am proposing, and will argue for in the following chapters, that ultimately the full import of any dialogue will not be capable of being grasped without cross-reference to others. This is much more than the general, and plausible, claim that we should be able to deepen our understanding of any philosopher's position by reading his or her works in their totality. My claim is rather that Plato sets things up in such a way that we *have* to read across from one dialogue to another: not just because he wants us to put things together for ourselves, although he will hardly have been averse to such an outcome, but because it is a condition of getting conversations started in the first place – given where he is starting from – that everything is not laid on the interlocutor, and the reader, at once.[65]

---

[62] Thus the reason why so many 'Socratic' dialogues, as well as the *Theaetetus*, start from the question 'what is . . .?' is not just that Socrates has an obsession with finding definitions (though he, and Plato, may very well have had that anyway). It is also, and especially, because he has a particular view of the *definiendum* that he wishes to advocate in place of the one(s) sponsored by Socrates' interlocutors.

[63] And so real *starting*-points. I shall attempt to sketch these in the next section.

[64] It is undoubtedly part of Plato's purpose to make us put things together for ourselves; we have to work hard even when things are done more directly. However this is not the main reason why he works in such a piecemeal way. That is, again (see preceding paragraph), something that is forced on him in any case if he is to get conversations off the ground at all.

[65] It will now be clear how important it is to my case to identify what I called the 'persuasive' function of Plato's writing – and also its ambitions in terms of audience. He could have written treatises, to be read by specialists; instead he writes dialogues, most of which look safe enough for anyone to enter (but which then tend to bite back).

If modern interpreters, particularly those of an analytical bent, have tended to downplay the contribution to the 'Socratic' dialogues of a distinctive, and substantive, Socratic position,[66] that is partly because – in my view – that position has been widely misinterpreted, and then written off as naive, merely optimistic, or otherwise inadequate and limited, and partly also because of a tendency to approach the 'Socratic' dialogues first and foremost in terms of their outward and formal characteristics. Thus these dialogues are described as 'aporetic'; they are typically 'dialogues of definition'; and they are also typically 'elenctic', consisting essentially in the refutation by Socrates of his interlocutors. The first two of these descriptions[67] are the source of the second and third of those imagined objections to my claim that, in the 'Socratic' dialogues, Plato's Socrates already possesses a positive and systematic philosophical agenda. Why, if that is so, does Plato then set things up in so apparently open-ended a way ('what is x?'), and why have the discussion so often end in *aporia*? To the first question, the reply is that Socrates never asks the question 'what is x?' without already knowing what he thinks the answer should be:[68] if x is any of the virtues, that answer will always be the same – 'knowledge of good and bad' (that is, good for the agent, bad for the agent: see further section 6 below). The conversation will be *presented*, to the interlocutor, as an exploration, but in fact it will explore little except the weaknesses of whatever it is Socrates' interlocutor comes up with, or whatever Socrates comes up with for him. There is never any genuine chance that the discussion will be allowed to end anywhere except where Socrates intends; not just because of Plato's foreknowledge as author, but because the author is colluding with his main speaker and allowing him to operate within the bounds of a particular, and predetermined, set of ideas. And equally, there are no genuine cases of *impasse*, or *aporia*: Socrates, that is, is never genuinely at a loss, or at a loss in the way he suggests.[69] The *impasse* – I propose – is always apparent

---

[66] Thus e.g., for Sedley (2004: 9) the Socrates of the 'Socratic' dialogues is 'an open-minded critic and enquirer', albeit one who at the same time 'defend[s] substantive moral theses of his own' (p. 1), and who possesses a considerable list of 'skills and insights' (listed at Sedley 2004: 34–5) – at least according to Plato's account of the matter. (Sedley is here reconstructing Plato's view of Socrates' 'principles of midwifery' from the *Theaetetus* – 'but if it is Plato's retrospective interpretation of his own portrayal of Socrates, it deserves to be treated with the utmost respect', 35.) My own list of the insights of Plato's Socrates will, naturally, be rather more 'considerable', even in relation to the 'Socratic' dialogues.

[67] I have already criticized the third: see text to n. 16 above.   [68] See already n. 62 above.

[69] The qualification is necessary, and important, because there may well be *other* ways in which Socrates and his author might be in *aporia*. They know the way out of the *impasse* as stated, as the interlocutor doesn't; but as know-nothings they won't claim to have any complete and final answers available. See below.

only, deriving from the shortcomings of the interlocutor or of the direction of the argument, or both; reconfigure the argument and/or change the interlocutor or the way he thinks, and *impasse* can be avoided.

Why does Plato write in this way? I have already indicated my answer. It is not because he enjoys putting on a kind of intellectual striptease,[70] or even, again, because he wants us to do the work (although he does want that). It is rather because he knows *he* has a lot of work to do. The truth cannot be given us on a plate, directly: that is one of the main points of the critique of writing in the *Phaedrus*. We have to see things for ourselves. But this is more than just a sound educational principle: seeing the way things are involves, as it may be, having to give up the way we currently see them. A long process of persuasion is involved, of gentle, perhaps – within the 'Socratic' dialogues themselves – progressive, exposure, combined with questioning of our own (Socrates' interlocutors') ideas. (The idea of these dialogues as 'cleansing', then, gives only one half of the picture: Socrates is already putting forward the ideas he wants to replace the ones he is cleaning out.)

That is one, strategic, reason why Plato is always so careful to avoid representing Socrates as the expert, namely because it isn't just a matter of passing things over, rather of getting people to *see*. But there is a more fundamental reason for Socrates' stance, which simultaneously makes it more than a mere stance. The set of ideas, truths, that Plato and his Socrates want to persuade us to accept is no more than a beginning; it provides us with a framework for thinking, and for acting, without actually telling us what we should do here and now. What we need, we are told, is a certain kind of knowledge, a certain expertise or science; but Socrates himself does not have it, even if he has some considerable insights into its subject-matter.

6 WHAT IS THIS 'SUBSTANTIVE PHILOSOPHICAL POSITION' OF SOCRATES', AND WHAT ARE THESE 'DISTINCTIVE PHILOSOPHICAL STARTING-POINTS'?

I have already briefly referred (in section 4 above) to one essential part of what I claim to be the Socratic position. This is his idea that we human beings always, and only, desire what is truly good for us. We cannot, psychologically, desire what is actually bad for us; it is desire for our good that drives us in everything – desire for our *real* good, that is, not merely what appears good. Excellence or virtue is a good thing; if so, then it too

---

[70] I owe this phrasing immediately to Simon Blackburn.

must be a matter of what is good and bad for us. (So, virtue, excellence, is knowledge – of good and bad; and all virtue[71] is one.) If something we think we desire turns out not to be a good thing, then we don't desire it. So, if we go after something that is in fact bad, and desire for good is what always drives us, it must be our understanding, our beliefs, that are at fault; we don't properly understand what is good and bad for us. In other words, we only go wrong through ignorance. No one goes wrong willingly (how could they?).

What we have here is a strict brand of psychological egoism.[72] But the connection with the virtues (which will include justice and courage) already suggests that this is a rather special brand of egoism, one that allows in the kinds of behaviour which on other accounts will be 'for the sake of others'. Even love and friendship, Socrates thinks, will be traceable back to our desire for our *own* good. Our love for our children, our husbands or wives, our teachers: all are ultimately explicable in terms of that same desire, insofar as – it seems – our children, our spouses, our teachers are all bound up with our own good, or happiness. He will be not the slightest bit disturbed by the accusation that this reduces others to mere instrumental means to our own well-being, not least because he refuses to separate means from end: if we desire an end, then we will also desire the means to it, insofar as we cannot have the one without the other. Granted, that entails that the desire for the means (our children, our wife, as it may be) will be derivative from, conditional on, our desire for our good (our happiness), but then is it so bad for them to be loved by us because they make us happy – that is, because they and their happiness form part of our real good, and on condition that our loving them will involve our doing everything we can to promote *their* real good?[73]

To many, of course, the answer will still be yes (it will be 'so bad'). Add to that the suggestion, incredible to most moderns, that we never go wrong because of our desires – or, to put it in a more familiar form, that there is no such thing as 'lack of self-control' (because what we *call* that is actually a matter of intellectual error) – and one begins to see just how far out on a limb Socrates really is. Nor is that the end of it: just as he thinks that our desire is aligned with things that we may never even have had in our minds,

---

[71] I should prefer to use 'excellence' exclusively for the Greek term *aretē*, in preference to 'virtue'; in this kind of context, however, 'virtue' is too deeply embedded to be easily dispensed with.

[72] Absent from Plato generally, I shall claim, is any kind of *moral* good: see especially chapters 1, 4 and 9 below.

[73] The preceding sentences on desire and love represent the briefest of summaries of some of what I claim is to be derived, whether directly or indirectly, from the *Lysis*. See below.

so he also proposes that when we go wrong intellectually, what we really wanted to get hold of was what we actually missed. So what we wanted to be thinking about was, again, something that we never even thought of. But that follows from the claim about desire: if we wanted some particular action other than the action we did (because the first would in fact have been best, while the second turned out to be bad for us), then we wanted that other action to appear best to us, even if it in fact never entered our heads that it was even an option.[74]

How then are we to achieve that real good that we want? Socrates thinks we need a special kind of expertise: expertise about the good, which will enable us to distinguish it from the bad, and from what is neither good nor bad – a large category, which turns out to include a high proportion of the very things that people normally think of as good (not just money, power, and other obvious things like that, but even health itself: according to Socrates, there will be occasions on which we shall be better off dead, and terminal illness or a fatal accident will be a blessing). Talk of this expertise, or 'art', or 'science' (*technē*), is ubiquitous in the 'Socratic' dialogues. It is, he proposes, an art or science that is in all respects but one like others. Like them it will have its own subject-matter (the good, taken universally, which will then need to be applied to particular cases), its own separate aim, its own separate procedures. The one difference, and it is a crucial one, between this art or science and other arts and sciences is that while they can be misused by those who choose to practise them, the art and science of the good cannot be so misused. For *no one* acts contrary to what he believes or knows is his own good. In addition Socrates holds that it will never be the part of a good man – someone who possesses the art and science of the good – to harm anyone else.

These, I propose, are Socrates' starting-points in – what others call – the 'Socratic' dialogues,[75] together with one further work that is generally treated as post-'Socratic': the *Symposium*;[76] and, strikingly, the first book of

---

[74] To be clear: this is not some *sub-conscious*, or mysteriously 'second-order', desire; it is just that what we all of us want on any occasion is not what appears good for us, but what is really good. See under 'Principle of Real Reference' in the index to Penner and Rowe 2005, and, for the handiest passage in Plato, *Republic* VI, 505D.

[75] For the purposes of the argument, the 'Socratic' dialogues will be a baker's dozen: *Apology* (not strictly a dialogue, but no matter), *Charmides, Crito, Euthydemus, Euthyphro, Gorgias, Hippias Minor, Ion, Laches, Lysis, Meno, Menexenus, Protagoras.* (If some wish to quibble about the list, introducing sub-categories, or giving one or other item a later date, I shall not mind: all, I claim, clearly buy in – are best explained as buying in – to the set of ideas described in the preceding paragraphs.)

[76] For the *Symposium* as containing the same theory of action as its close relation, the *Lysis*, see Rowe 2006b.

that (allegedly) quintessentially post-'Socratic' dialogue, the *Republic*.[77] The connected set of ideas described is the one that I claim (a) is demonstrably required for the interpretation of one of that list of 'Socratic' dialogues, the *Lysis*, and (b) provides the best means to the understanding of the rest.[78] As evidence for (a) I offer Penner and Rowe 2005, a painstaking investigation of the *Lysis* which it would be superfluous to reproduce, even in miniature, here, but whose outcomes[79] appear to me secure until a rival and equally detailed interpretation of that tiny piece – a mere ten thousand or so words in English translation – becomes available. *Plato and the Art of Philosophical Writing* is to that extent, as it was always intended to be, a sequel to Penner and Rowe 2005.[80] As for claim (b), I shall leave that to establish itself in the course of the following chapters.[81] The evidence offered along the way will be far short of complete. However the chief aim of the book is to propose, and argue for, a way of understanding Plato, not to try to achieve closure in the discussion of an author whom my own account will represent as one of the most elusive.

7 THE REVOLUTIONARY NATURE OF THIS PERSPECTIVE, AND THE CONSEQUENCES FOR PLATO'S STRATEGIES AS A WRITER[82]

If what I have just sketchily described accurately portrays at least a part of what Socrates wanted to say, one thing will be perfectly clear: Socrates'

---

[77] I provide evidence for this claim in chapter 5 below, with Appendix.

[78] In fact many of its central aspects are not particularly controversial; at any rate there are others who, if asked to come up with a thumbnail sketch of 'Socrates'' ideas, would produce something not unlike the above. See e.g., Taylor 2000: 62–3.

[79] Only roughly, and incompletely, outlined above; my aim at this point is merely to provide a sketch, to be filled out in the course of direct encounters with Plato's text in later chapters.

[80] Others may be, and evidently often are, content with a looser, more impressionistic kind of reading of Plato than the one offered in that volume (or else unconnected, painstaking analysis of individual dialogues in isolation from others). I, in common with Penner, insist that Plato's Socrates is a highly sophisticated philosopher who always thinks in a *connected* way, and that it is our business as readers and interpreters to dig out the connections. There is more to him than the scary but evidently benign fellow with a few paradoxes and a gift for exposing ignorance that some readings of the 'Socratic' dialogues make him. (Would Plato spend *thirteen* dialogues, half of the total, recommending such a person, before branching out on his own – as some suppose? Maybe.)

[81] See especially chapters 1–5, and chapter 9.

[82] To sum up the broad contrast between my interpretation and that of the 'sceptics': a typical 'sceptical' view of the 'Socratic' dialogues is that they represent work in progress. They are a direct reflection of Plato's thinking in his 'Socratic' period, perhaps genuinely Socratic in shape, exploratory, unsystematic, raising questions rather than providing answers; it is left to the mature Plato to complete the Socratic project, if only by radically transforming it. On the account I am proposing, the thinking behind the 'Socratic' dialogues is already connected, constituting a coherent nexus of ideas if not a system; what then comes after and is labelled 'Platonism' *is* that nexus of ideas, but further articulated, tweaked, expanded.

position is, from a modern point of view, distinctly peculiar. No wonder, one might say, that interpreters – the 'sceptical' sort – have wanted to see Plato leaving Socrates behind. (As a matter of fact not many of them have seen just *how* peculiar Socrates really was.[83] But the point still holds.) And it would have been just as peculiar from a fourth-century Athenian perspective, for many of the same reasons. Technical philosophical objections will not have concerned most of Socrates' or Plato's contemporaries overmuch, but what Socrates had to say about goods, about virtue, and about desire would probably have seemed as odd to them as it does to most of us. If they could conceivably be talked into entertaining the notion that money, reputation or power were not goods in themselves, they would surely have baulked at the notion that *health*, or *life*, were not. Again, they would probably have been resistant to, or at least baffled by, the proposal to reduce the virtues to a kind of knowledge of good and bad. (The noble and the admirable – the closest the Greek context comes to our category of the 'moral' good – play a large role in political, rhetorical and social contexts.[84]) And they would surely have greeted Socrates' denial of the possibility of what we have come to call 'weakness of will', *akrasia* (loss of self-control, acting contrary to reason under the influence of passion), with sheer incredulity.

But in the 'Socratic' dialogues – or more generally in what I take to be the pre-*Republic* dialogues (a formulation I shall now generally prefer, and will shortly justify) – this is, for all we can tell, Plato's own position; for, in these dialogues, he is alternately stating, arguing for, and so, apparently, advocating it. Quite where we find Plato at the end of his career, and how much of the Socratic agenda by then still genuinely remains intact,[85] will be one of the central questions that will be addressed in successive parts of the present book. But I have already[86] given notice of the general conclusion for which I shall argue, namely that Plato always 'remained essentially a Socratic'[87] – which means, among other things, that he remains at least as far removed as Socrates ever did from ordinary perceptions and perspectives.

Understanding that distance between Plato and his intended audience, and between Plato and ourselves, is an essential part of understanding how to read his dialogues. Interpreters have on the whole either ignored or underestimated this aspect of Plato, preferring to try to treat Platonic

---

[83] That is, because so many fail to see him as having any sort of theory, just a few paradoxes . . . For those who do see Socrates as having a theory, the theory in question may actually be even more peculiar than the one I have attributed to him: for limited references, see chapter 4, n. 25 below.

[84] See chapter 4 below, on the *Gorgias*, esp. section 2 (c).

[85] Not to exclude the question of what Plato adds to that agenda: not just a large political element, but (for example) a large-scale account of the physical world.

[86] See section 3 above.   [87] This is, again, far from being the ordinary view.

dialogues as if they were open like other texts, or as if reading them were like listening to conversations between people – Socrates/Plato and their immediate audiences – who are basically like ourselves. But one of the partners to the conversations in question, namely Socrates, and his author, are *not* like us, and were not like their immediate audience, whether Socrates' in the dialogues, or Plato's as author; we, generally speaking, are more like his audience than we are like Plato, or his Socrates. (One of the epithets Socrates' friends and associates attach to him in the dialogues is 'odd', 'strange' – *atopos*, literally 'out of place', 'outlandish'.) So different is the Platonic/Socratic view of things that in some respects they might almost be said not to speak the same language as their contemporaries. 'Good', 'bad', 'beneficial', 'harmful', 'admirable', 'shameful': these and other terms (e.g., 'art'/'science', 'knowledge', 'ignorance', 'desire', even 'pleasure') Plato and his Socrates apply in such different ways from the ways in which they are applied in ordinary language and ordinary contexts and conversations that on the face of it even beginning a conversation that involves such terms ought to be difficult. Even more so, when Plato and Socrates think that other people apply them *wrongly*. (Other people feel the same about Socrates, with the difference that they simply assume that the way they apply the terms in question is right, whereas he has a reasoned account of why they're wrong.) This mismatch between the speakers in a dialogue[88] also exists between Socrates and the reader, and it is a matter of common, perhaps universal, experience that reading Plato's dialogues is difficult.[89] The main reason for that, I propose, or one of the main reasons, is that Socrates and we, like Socrates and his interlocutors, will frequently be at cross-purposes. He just doesn't behave in the way we expect him to behave. And that is because what he says tends to be freighted with baggage the true extent and value of which he will usually not have declared to us (any more than we will have declared our assumptions, perhaps taking these to be inevitable).

That, though, may be a misleading way of putting it, since it might suggest that Plato is deliberately withholding information from us: an unlikely seeming tactic for someone whose main aim is, as I think, to persuade.[90] It

---

[88] I refer here to the generality of the dialogues; what I am looking for first is a broad *type* of explanation of Plato's way of writing, after which one can begin to qualify the explanation and identify exceptions.

[89] He is 'weird' (see section 1 above) – odd, like his Socrates?

[90] For members of the 'Tübingen school' (see n. 8 above), 'withholding' or 'holding back' is an essential part of Plato's writing strategy because the reader needs to be prepared for the more important truths, which in any case cannot be conveyed in writing.

seems preferable to think, as I suggested earlier,[91] in terms of a progressive – or, better, cumulative? – introduction to the various parts of Socratic thinking, from dialogue to dialogue, in the context of his examination of others usually as unfamiliar with that thinking as we may be. Plato feeds us that in bits and pieces not only because – he supposes, with good reason – he has a long way to go to bring readers round, but because at the same time he has to introduce us to philosophical ways of thinking (the habit of dialogue).[92]

This introduces an important point of difference between reader and interlocutor. Some interlocutors are portrayed as having heard Socrates before, which might give them the same kind of advantage as readers who have read other Platonic dialogues. But by and large the unfortunate interlocutor will only have whatever Socrates offers him in the course of the immediate conversation. The consequence is that he will typically be at sea, to varying degrees, in a way that the reader in principle need not be. The dialogues generally exhibit at least two levels of understanding, Socrates' and that of the interlocutor,[93] and the reader is in effect invited to ask himself or herself whether to side with the one or with the other.[94] Quite often there will be different ways of reading the same argument, depending on whether one is starting from Socrates' premises or more ordinary ones;[95] these will be the arguments that interpreters, lacking access to Socrates' starting-points, will typically find the weakest. (Or else – I earlier cited some examples from the *Republic* – Socrates will adopt starting-points from his interlocutors, but, as I claimed, without ever finally depending on them.) But more usually the argument will move in ways that are simply baffling until we have worked out the preoccupations, and the general line of thinking, that motivate them.

In the context of these observations, the dialogue form appears perfectly adapted to Plato's purposes, allowing him to use the play between the

---

[91] See section 5 above.

[92] Here is another respect in which Plato is wholly with Socrates: neither can straightforwardly *teach* anybody anything (cf., e.g., *Theaetetus* 150D).

[93] I am assuming here the kind of identification between the author, Plato, and his character Socrates for which I argued earlier (leaving aside the necessary difference that the character will always know less about what is *going* to happen, or why he is where he is, than his author).

[94] The most extravagant set of levels, or layers, of understanding is probably to be found in the *Lysis*: Lysis himself comes closest to Socrates' level, then Menexenus; then there are the bystanders, and finally poor Hippothales, who has clearly not understood a word of what has been said – and the drunken slaves who insist on taking Lysis and Menexenus home to their parents, at the end of the dialogue. See Penner and Rowe 2005.

[95] See especially chapter 4 and Appendix to chapter 5 below (on *Gorgias* and *Republic* 1 respectively).

interlocutors to mediate between him and his readers.[96] On this interpretation, there will be very little that is in the proper sense *dialogical* about Plato's dialogues (with that one exception, that dialectical exchanges within them may serve as static models for the real thing, i.e. live dialectic, and might even accurately portray examples of it; but that is a different matter).[97] However that is a fully intended part of the interpretation I am proposing. Even the 'Socratic' dialogues contain 'doctrines', if one cares to call them by that name, of the value of which Plato means to try to persuade us. Nor is this merely a matter of a few 'substantive moral theses',[98] but rather of what I have called a nexus of ideas[99] – one that I hope to show to be fit to provide what one might call the infrastructure of Platonism itself.

8 THE PROPOSED INTERPRETATION OF PLATO'S USE OF DIALOGUE FORM COMPARED WITH TWO OTHER INTERPRETATIONS

It may at this point be useful to take stock, by way of a brief comparison between the kind of interpretation I have been proposing of Plato's use of dialogue with two rival interpretations.

The first of these, which has gained in favour in recent years, is that Plato wrote dialogues as a way of avoiding the appearance of dictating to his readers,[100] in a way that might appear to absolve them of the hard work that goes with any sort of philosophical enterprise. This might be thought of as the archetypal 'sceptical' interpretation of the use of dialogue form; but it also finds favour among more literary interpreters, not least those who like to think of texts as inherently polyphonous. To this form of interpretation I now find myself totally opposed. While Plato may on occasion want to distance himself from his main speaker, this will be – I

---

96 A partly separate account, then, will be needed for a (virtual) monologue like the *Timaeus*. However I have already indicated something about how that account will run (in such cases Socrates and Plato themselves become auditors/readers).

97 As a consequence, I have found little that is useful in modern discussions of dialogue for the purposes of understanding Plato.

98 See n. 66 above.

99 One that is not explicitly articulated *as* such a nexus; but a distinction is presumably to be drawn between what is articulated to us, or is capable of being so articulated through the medium of independent dialogues/conversations, and what the author and his main character have in fact articulated to and for themselves (and mean us to put together for ourselves). The question how we decide what that is, given that it is not in fact presented as a systematic whole, I regard as rather less than pressing; if a philosophical story can be told that will explain the phenomena of the written dialogues, it will be wasteful and not merely uncharitable to refuse to tell it.

100 E.g., 'Originally, Socrates used the form of the dialogue to test and to expose presumed authority without having himself to adopt a position of authority', etc. (Frede 2000: 151–2).

propose – only when the main speaker is not Socrates. The core of Plato's enterprise is, from beginning to end, the advocacy of positive ideas, even if, paradoxically, he chooses to advocate them for the most part through a know-nothing.[101] It will then only be in a formal sense that Plato is absent. If the question is why he does not appear in person in his own dialogues, the answer is that he is already ubiquitous and controlling;[102] if the question is why he wrote dialogues (and then did not include himself in the *dramatis personae*), there are more satisfying answers available.

One of these is the second alternative type of interpretation I pick out for comparison with my own. I have previously mentioned this way of understanding Plato's use of dialogue form in passing:[103]

Plato's real reason[104] for persisting with the dialogue form is, I think . . . his growing belief – more than once made explicit in his later work [at *Theaetetus* 189E–190A, *Sophist* 263E–264B, *Philebus* 38C–E] – that conversation, in the form of question and answer, is the structure of thought itself. When we think, what we are doing is precisely to ask and answer questions internally, and our judgements are the outcome of that same process. Hence it seems that what Plato dramatises as external conversations can be internalised by us, the readers, as setting the model for our own processes of philosophical reasoning. More important still is the converse, that these same question-and-answer sequences can legitimately be read by us as *Plato thinking aloud*. And that, I suggest, is in the last analysis how Plato maintains the dominating and inescapable presence in his own dialogues that few if any mere dramatists can rival. They are an externalisation of his own thought processes. Plato's very word for philosophical method, 'dialectic', means quite literally the science of conducting a conversation in this question-and-answer form, and it is vital to appreciate that the inter-personal discussion portrayed in the dialogues is not the only mode in which such discussion can occur; internal discussion is another, and perhaps even more fundamental, mode.[105]

I have indicated at length, in section 3 above, the sorts of reasons that lead me to reject this type of explanation for Plato's using, or 'persisting with',[106] the

---

[101] A solution to the paradox will emerge in the following chapters.

[102] One might also ask: if Plato wanted to avoid the appearance of speaking *ex cathedra*, he made a strange decision when he made *Socrates* his protagonist – perhaps the best-known intellectual figure of his time, who single-handedly spawned more philosophical schools or *haireseis* (some of them emerging, or already emerged, during Plato's lifetime) than practically anyone in the western world before or since.

[103] See n. 39 above.

[104] The author of the passage is contrasting his interpretation with the type of reading I have just rejected; he refers to Frede 1992, Wardy 1996, Press 2000, Blondell 2002, Cooper 1997 ('a more nuanced version').

[105] Sedley 2003: 1–2.

[106] 'What for [Plato] no doubt started out as the external imitation of Socratic questioning gave way in time to the conviction that Socratic dialogical conversation *is* philosophy' (Sedley 2003: 2n. 3).

dialogue form: most fundamentally, that it radically understates the extent to which the dialogues are *staged* – by the author, for an audience. The idea that the dialogues show us Plato thinking aloud is not, in my view, anywhere near sufficient to explain the complexities of the artefact that is the Platonic dialogue, with its changes of interlocutors, location, pace, tone and so on (see further section II below).

However there is one particular feature, or consequence, of this type of reading of Plato's use of dialogue form that I especially want to resist. If the dialogues are a kind of record of Plato's internal thought processes, then they will apparently be an accurate guide to his thinking at the time of writing, or indeed, if he revised any of his works (which seems *a priori* likely enough), at the time of revision; and they will also accurately track any *changes* in his thinking. *Aporiai*, failed attempts at finding solutions to specific problems, will tend to be Plato's own, and differences between solutions offered in different dialogues will mark the evolution, and as it may be the maturing, of his thinking in a particular area (given, that is, that we have what looks like a reasonably reliable picture of the relative dating of different parts of the corpus: see section 10 below). By this account, Plato is learning as he goes along, or learning on the job: making mistakes, then going on to correct them, gradually becoming a better philosopher (even though we may actually read him out of order, as it were – not in order of composition). Now there is nothing inherently implausible in this picture; and if it is hard to think of any other philosopher whose intellectual progress is quite so transparent to us as Plato's usually turns out to be, on the sort of interpretation in question, perhaps that is just because no one else wrote in the way Plato did ('thinking aloud'). One might even grant that such a reading obeys the principle of charity, insofar as it allows Plato to get things right, or more right, as well as to get them wrong. However I believe that it also runs a serious risk of *underestimating* Plato.

Or, to put a card on the table that I have already partly shown, I believe that seeing the dialogues as a record of Plato's own intellectual tussles[107] actually *does* underestimate him. This it does in two ways. First, it underestimates the degree of artfulness in Plato's writing; and here I include all those features of the dialogues that flow from Plato's awareness of his relationship with his readers, and his purpose in addressing them – that is, broadly, as I have suggested, to *persuade* them to a different point of view. But in the second place (and this is a new and important point), reading the dialogues as giving direct insight into Plato's development tends to make

---

[107] *Inter alia*, of course.

us underestimate him as a philosopher: not in terms of any final verdict we may pass on him (because, after all, he gets there in the end even on the developmental reading), but rather in the sense that such a reading must lead us to write off, to varying degrees, a large proportion of his output. After all, if he did move on and get better, then his earlier works will apparently be a record of relative failure. These works will be useful, no doubt, for feeding to undergraduates early on in their own philosophical development, and perhaps also insofar as they are[108] examples of philosophical exploration, but ultimately they will be of largely historical interest.

One of the chief drivers of this approach is precisely the sense that Plato had, as it were, to deal with his master – perhaps even to get Socrates out of his system, by writing the 'Socratic' dialogues. This is the view that leads to what I earlier described as 'the single greatest obstacle to a proper understanding of Plato and Platonism', the division of the Platonic *oeuvre* into a Socratic part, on the one hand, and a truly Platonic part on the other. This division in itself involves another kind of underestimation: the underestimation of *Socrates'* contribution, or at least of whatever it was that Plato thought he had got from Socrates. It is around that contribution, of course, that the present book revolves: remove or devalue it, and the bulk of the argument of the book will disappear in a puff of smoke.[109]

For the kind of interpretation with which I am currently contrasting my own,[110] the Socrates of the 'Socratic' dialogues will have the kind of 'maieutic' role Plato has him ascribe to himself at *Theaetetus* 148E–151D: that is, he will serve as a kind of midwife (*maia*) of ideas who helps *others* to 'give birth' while being 'childless' himself. It is hard to disagree with this claim in some form or another, since the *Theaetetus* passage so plainly picks up Socrates' self-presentation in the dialogues in question (and indeed in others), as a know-nothing, and at the same time seems so accurately to describe his practice – especially when he talks about how unusual a midwife he is, possessing as he does the ability to tell the true and substantial offspring from their false and counterfeit counterparts.[111] However everything here depends on how the analogy is to be understood. What Socrates accepts is (1) that he asks other people questions (2) without declaring his own position, (3) because he 'has nothing wise' (sc. to declare). If this is intended

---

[108] I.e. according to the type of interpretation in question.

[109] For grounds for my confidence that it will not thus disappear, see section 6 above. Especially reassuring is the way in which Socrates' (Plato's Socrates') thinking throughout not just the so-called 'Socratic' dialogues but all those that are 'pre-*Republic*' turns out to fit together. Different parts or aspects of this thinking show up in different places, but they all form part of a satisfying philosophical whole.

[110] See Sedley 2004.   [111] I.e. the ones that are merely images or likenesses (*eidōla*).

as a general claim never to make any assertions, it is clearly falsified by the very sentence in which he makes it.[112] It will make better sense to interpret Socrates as saying that he never declares his hand in relation to the sort of question that he has just now put to Theaetetus, so starting off the whole analogy: 'what is this thing knowledge?', which the two of them have evidently been worrying about for some time. And indeed it is typically on questions like that ('what is piety?', 'what is courage?', 'what is *sōphrosunē*?')[113] that Socrates in fact, typically, fails to declare himself in the 'Socratic' dialogues. In other words, when he accepts that he declares himself *about nothing* (*Theaetetus* 150C6), what he is saying is not that he makes no assertions about anything at all, but rather that he makes no assertions *about the chief subjects he inquires into*.[114] One thinks immediately of his prolonged protestations in *Republic* VI about his lack of qualifications for talking about the good: what he has, he implies, is no more than 'opinions without knowledge' (506C6).[115] Here in the *Theaetetus* he explains his position by saying that the god

> compels me to be the midwife, and has prevented me from giving birth – so, as for myself, I am not at all wise, nor is there any discovery of such a sort [sc. a wise one] that has been born to me as offspring of my soul. (150C7–D2)

What others expect from him is an authoritative answer, and that he can't give because he hasn't discovered it.

My own claim is that not only Plato's Socrates but Plato himself permanently retains the role of midwife. By any modern reckoning the passage just discussed will have been written relatively late (because the *Theaetetus* is a relatively late dialogue);[116] nonetheless I take it to be describing how Plato saw the role of the philosopher – that is, of any philosopher who has to live in the real world, including himself as well as Socrates – even at this point, and indeed at any point, in his own writing career.[117] The particular reason why he needs Socrates to disclaim knowledge at this early point in the *Theaetetus* is because there might be a presumption that someone who actually possesses knowledge ought to be able to say what it is that

---

[112] Cf. Sedley 2004: 32.

[113] Traditionally 'temperance' (which nowadays means either nothing or the wrong thing); *sōphrosunē* in ordinary Greek is something like 'self-control', but emerges from *Charmides* as closer to 'soundmindedness'.

[114] Cf. *Clitophon* for what I take to be some Platonist's conceit on this very point in relation to the *Republic*.

[115] More on this context in chapters 8 and 9 below.   [116] See section 10 below.

[117] For most 'developmentalists', of course, Socrates the midwife will need to be separated sharply from Plato, who has a good few 'children' of his own; the portrait of Socrates in the *Theaetetus* will then have a historical ring to it.

he possesses (and the question for discussion, after all, is what knowledge is); just as Socrates in the *Charmides* claims to suppose that the young Charmides will know what 'sound-mindedness'[118] is if, as others have suggested, he is himself 'sound-minded'.[119] Of course it could be, and many have supposed, that the author himself, Plato, actually does claim to have the knowledge that his character disclaims, in which case he might also have a ready answer to the question about the nature of knowledge (or he might not). However it is my thesis that Plato does not think he has the knowledge he has his Socrates represent himself as lacking. I also propose that Socrates has a preferred account of the nature of knowledge to which Plato subscribes.[120] If there are problems about that account, they have to do not so much with Socrates' and/or Plato's failure to answer a straight question ('so what *is* knowledge?') as with the general limitations Plato attributes to the cognitive resources that human beings share *qua* human.

9 SOCRATES AND PLATO ON KNOWLEDGE AND IGNORANCE

On knowledge, in the following chapters,[121] I shall argue that the position of Plato's Socrates, in principle across all the dialogues, is as follows. (a) While he allows that human beings, and even he, may acquire *some* knowledge ('pieces of knowledge'),[122] he does not believe that *full* knowledge (wisdom) about the most important things – the good, the beautiful and the just, to give Socrates' usual list[123] – is accessible to the human mind or soul. This is the basic position from which he begins, and from which he does not shift. However (b) at the same time he envisages the possibility that there will be, and maybe already are, more expert and accomplished philosophers than himself; and (c) within the context of the discussion of a 'best city', to which an actual city might approximate, and perhaps in some other contexts involving ideal conditions, he will sometimes introduce ideal human knowers, possessing the full, synoptic knowledge that is at the same time the unattainable terminus of the philosopher's search, and the only sort of knowledge that, ultimately, deserves to be called knowledge or wisdom.

---

[118] I.e. *sōphrosunē* (see n. 113 above).

[119] Cf. also *Euthyphro*, where Socrates is discussing *hosiotēs*, 'piety', with Euthyphro because he's supposedly pious; *Laches*, which has him discussing courage with soldiers.

[120] For both the thesis and the proposal, see the following section with chapter 8.

[121] See especially chapter 8.   [122] See, e.g., chapter 11, pp. 267, 271.

[123] More generally, the things in question will be those on our understanding of which depends our understanding of ourselves and the world in which we live; and this will include some kind of synoptic view of the structure of things, and how they are good, beautiful and just.

To many modern interpreters, this set of claims is likely to appear implausible. For Plato's Socrates, they will say, *plainly* comes to accept the possibility of knowledge for non-divine beings; he might go on claiming, with whatever degree of plausibility, that he personally remains a know-nothing, but – in dialogues like *Phaedo* or *Republic* – he allows that others, by applying themselves in the right way, can achieve the wisdom he himself lacks. Indeed, such voices will say, the political argument of the *Republic* depends on his allowing just that: the philosopher-rulers will be qualified to rule exactly because of their knowledge, and not otherwise. One of the tasks I shall be setting myself[124] is to show either that such an interpretation fails, or – in case that seems too strong a claim – at least that it fails to explain some important aspects of central Platonic texts. Key to my argument, once again, will be understanding those two overlapping relationships, of Socrates to his interlocutors and of Plato to his readers.

However it will already be clear from the preceding sections that I shall also want to make a further claim, one that will probably strike the same objectors not just as implausible but as preposterous: namely that *Plato shares the position I have attributed to his Socrates*. In other words, he retains the position of know-nothing that he has Socrates adopt, I believe with full seriousness, in the 'Socratic' dialogues – so that, from this perspective as from others, the label 'Socratic' will pick out nothing distinctive about them. On the normal 'sceptical'/'developmental'[125] view, the so-called 'middle'[126] dialogues like the *Phaedo* and *Republic* show Plato proposing through his Socrates that knowledge, of the newly introduced forms,[127] is after all possible. This new Socrates, on the same interpretation, accepts that others, at least, may acquire the knowledge he himself lacks, and even becomes a bit of a metaphysician himself, a friend of Plato's new darlings (the forms) – while also still retaining traces of his old, know-nothing self. One of the eventual outcomes of my overall argument will be to have claimed to remove, or at least mitigate, this apparent contradiction at the heart of such 'normal' views of Plato: Plato keeps Socrates on as main speaker, I shall propose, because Socrates *remains* his *persona*, his mask. However in the meantime it will appear that this argument of mine will have several mountains to climb. Is it not *obvious*, even *uncontroversial* (some will say),

---

[124] See especially chapters 2 and 7.

[125] Once again, I treat these two trends in interpretation, if somewhat crudely, as going together.

[126] For this term see n. 11 above (and *passim* below).

[127] On which see the following section. Quite why a greater optimism about human cognitive capacities should go along with the introduction of a special theory of *transcendent* objects is in my view something of a mystery; but let that pass for the moment.

that the Socrates of the *Phaedo* and the *Republic* has abandoned the position, as stated by his counterpart in the *Apology*, that there is a kind of wisdom that is peculiarly human – to know one's own ignorance; and that the gods alone possess the wisdom that we long for but shall never achieve?[128] By comparison with the difficulty of showing that anything so obvious is actually not the case (so it might be said), any tensions in Plato's portrait of Socrates – as someone who now does, now does not think knowledge possible – will seem like a molehill. We shall see. Meanwhile it should be clear enough that if the 'developmental' interpreters turned out to be right on this point, my own project, for showing that Plato is 'essentially a Socratic' from beginning to end, might well be considered holed below the waterline before leaving port; for it is in his theory of knowledge, and the allegedly revolutionary metaphysics of forms, that Plato is held (by the same interpreters) to have broken most emphatically with Socrates.

10 ON FORMS (AND THE DATING OF THE DIALOGUES)

For those who accept some version of the 'developmental' reading I have been proposing to reject,[129] a crucial factor will, then, usually be – what such interpreters call – the introduction of (Platonic) *forms*. In the preceding parts of this book I have frequently referred to these entities as if they were known and familiar (which is actually how Plato himself typically operates),[130] because to have done otherwise might have appeared as an endorsement of the view that there are some dialogues in which forms do not appear and others in which they do. It would be more accurate, to my mind, to say that there are some dialogues in which a certain kind of *language* – typically references to 'the *eidos* [or *idea*] 'of *x*', or to 'the *x* itself', and to particular things in the ordinary world as 'sharing in' these *eidē* (or *ideai*) – begins to be used about forms, and other dialogues in which, by and large, such language is not used; and that, of course, is an entirely different matter, insofar as it will allow that forms, whatever these are, may still be present even in those dialogues where the language in question is (by and large) not used.

'Whatever forms are': it is a hard task to say quite what a Platonic form is, and indeed it is a task that for the most part Plato himself fails to address, in any single dialogue or set of dialogues or in any systematic way. I myself

---

[128] For the *Apology*, see especially chapter 1 below.

[129] I.e. a reading that in particular sees a significant movement on Plato's part away from Socrates in the so-called 'middle' (post-'Socratic') dialogues.

[130] See n. 136 below.

shall prefer to operate, at least for the moment,[131] with the barest of specifications of what it is to be a (Platonic) form, drawn from the sorts of terms in which Socrates operates in the central books of the *Republic*: the 'form of beauty' (justice, good . . .) will be that real item in which a particular beautiful (just, good . . .) thing 'shares', that 'sharing' being what causes the thing to be beautiful (just, good . . .), insofar as it is beautiful (just, good . . .). The important aspects of a form as seen in this minimal way are, first, that it is something *real*, and so something there to be discovered (or at least in principle to be discovered), and second that it is only by discovering, and as it were 'grasping', this real item that we shall fully understand whatever it is said to be the form 'of' – i.e. beauty (justice, goodness . . .), where the 'of' serves as no more than an identifying mark, insofar as the form actually *is* beauty (justice, goodness . . .), or rather is primarily what it is. As for the question when Plato first began to subscribe to the existence of such entities,[132] my own proposal is that we should accept one or the other of two theses, one weaker and one stronger: (i) that items of the kind in question are actually present even in, or form part of the background even to, dialogues that do not use language like 'the form of *x*' or 'the *x* itself', and 'sharing in' (the stronger thesis); or (ii) that, as he looks back[133] on such dialogues from the vantage-point of the *Republic*, Plato/Socrates sees such items as presupposed or required by their argument, and easily supplied (the weaker thesis).[134]

It is quite difficult to see how one might begin to decide between the two theses; but for my purposes that is hardly of great moment, insofar as my own chief concern is to establish – at least – the continuity *in Plato's mind* between the various parts of his corpus (which at the very least sets limits on the degree of actual discontinuity). If he did not see all the implications of what he was writing when he was composing prior to the *Republic*, and prior to any other dialogue in which form-language occurs,[135] (a) we

---

[131] My overall strategy in the book will be gradually to allow evidence about how 'forms' are to be understood to accumulate, much as Plato does, and without trying to spell things out in the kind of detail that Plato himself omitted to give us. I shall ultimately associate 'forms' with a particular, more general feature of Platonic thinking.

[132] I am assuming that my skeleton description is sufficient to pick out forms as they appear in the so-called 'middle dialogues'; if not, whatever other features are required should be deemed added.

[133] The discussion here is still primarily about the relationship between *Republic* and pre-*Republic* dialogues, though there will also be implications for other, later, dialogues (like *Theaetetus*, or *Laws*), which also allegedly omit reference to forms.

[134] Of course there is also in principle a third option – that the 'new' metaphysics represents a clear break with Socrates. I shall discuss this third option below; meanwhile I naturally exclude it as a real option, given that I have admitted that it would be sufficient to destroy my overall thesis.

[135] Especially when asking that type of question that typically surfaces in the so-called 'Socratic' dialogues, 'what is *x*?'. (I shall shortly be providing a rather fuller justification of that 'so-called' than I have so far given.)

shall never be able to tell if that was the explanation for his failure to use such language (as opposed, for example, to his not having any use for it); and (b) he may as well have seen the implications, since he writes, in the *Phaedo* and the *Republic*, as if 'forms' are already a familiar topic,[136] so in any case projecting them back into the pre-*Republic* dialogues.[137] This will of course mean that the 'developmentalist' interpretation is still in play, and may even – for all we know – have got hold of an interesting truth about Plato's intellectual history.[138] But again, what matters from my own perspective is that even if Plato did move on, philosophically, in the way the 'developmentalists' suppose, *Plato* will have seen the move in a quite different way: not as a momentous shift, one that would make him finally his own man, but rather as a working out of what was already there in any case.[139]

From earlier sections, however, it will be at once clear that the kind of interpretation I am proposing could at best, and most politely, be called controversial. The broad church of interpreters I have called 'doctrinal-ists' might generally be sympathetic to my approach (as tending towards a proper 'unitarianism'), even while being much more lavish in their expectations of Plato's philosopher than I have been, and indeed intend to remain. By contrast, their 'sceptical'/'developmentalist' rivals will tend to see the forms – the, or a, 'theory' of forms – as a peculiarly Platonic construct, and something that divides Plato from the metaphysically innocent Socrates, i.e. the Socrates of the 'Socratic' dialogues. The new metaphysics, according to these interpreters, provides Plato with a stable set of objects, an entire 'intelligible world over and above the sensible',[140] to be accessed, mapped, and explored by the philosopher, escaping from the fluxing world of par-ticulars. The division of the Platonic dialogues into 'early', 'middle', and 'late', now commonly accepted in English-speaking countries and beyond, mainly rests on one version or another of this reading of Plato's intellec-tual progress: 'early' is also 'Socratic', while to the 'middle' dialogue group

---

[136] See chapter 9 below, where I shall argue in particular that the way in which Socrates introduces the crucial topic of the *form of the good* in *Republic* VI is designed to indicate that the topic will be familiar to anyone who has read a range of what we have come to treat as earlier dialogues. (I shall be turning immediately to the justification for such dating.) Similarly with the *Phaedo*.

[137] That is, if they were not there already.

[138] Plato's 'Socratic period', or 'Socrates in (early) Plato' will then – again, for all we know – remain perfectly legitimate objects of study: see, for example, the voluminous work of Thomas Brickhouse and Nicholas Smith, or of Mark McPherran.

[139] I shall now go on, in effect, to discuss whether this latter view of the matter would be plausible – or whether we need, after all (and from my own point of view, disastrously), to let the third option (see n. 134 above) back in.

[140] Sedley 2004: 100.

belong those works in which this allegedly grand new metaphysical theory figures. ('Late' dialogues used to be, typically, those in which Plato retreated from the theory, or resiled from important aspects of it; this part of the narrative is now much less clear than it used to be, largely because it is generally agreed that the *Timaeus*, which makes heavy use of 'middle' form theory, must itself be late, and cannot conveniently be shunted to an earlier position.)

Now I do not for a moment wish to dispute either that the dialogues were written in a certain order (although we certainly cannot rule out the possibility that Plato went in for significant revision, either of parts of dialogues, or of whole works), or that the order proposed by the advocates of the tripartite early-middle-late division is substantially right. Studies of Plato's style have shown that the dialogues do fall into three groups; and what is more, the stylometrists' dating – which starts from the fact, independently confirmed, that the *Laws* was the last work that Plato wrote – generally coincides with the division, quite independently proposed, into 'early', 'middle', and 'late'. This cosy picture is a little disturbed by the fact that according to the results of stylometric analysis three of the 'middle' dialogues, i.e. *Cratylus*, *Phaedo* and *Symposium*, all of them clearly (for those who see things this way) containing the 'new metaphysics', belong to the group that Plato wrote first.[141] However (a) this group is a very large one; (b) the three dialogues in question might have been written late in the early period, and so in effect contiguously with the dialogues in the second group; and (c) in any case there is no particular reason for supposing that changes in a philosopher's thinking should march exactly in parallel with changes in the way he expresses his thinking, or indeed that there should be any connection at all between the first kind of changes and the second.

So, nothing *too* disturbing there, and by and large, there need be no great disagreement about the order of composition of the dialogues, so long as we set aside the complication that any particular dialogue might have been revised more or less substantially, and so may represent a product of different times or periods.[142] What I believe there should be disagreement

---

[141] 'At first sight, the division into three stylistic groups [proposed by a number scholars working mainly in the nineteenth century] seems to confirm [the] theory of Plato's development [in question], since all of his "Socratic" dialogues are firmly located in the earliest group. But this first sight is misleading. The central group does not at all coincide with what are called the "middle" dialogues, since the intermediate group defined stylistically includes both *Parmenides* and *Theaetetus*, which are generally counted as "late" from a developmental point of view. On the other hand, the "early" group includes *Symposium*, *Phaedo*, and *Cratylus*. A traditional developmentalist who recognizes that the stylistic division is chronological must simply accept the fact that Plato's stylistic and philosophical developments do not proceed at the same pace' (Kahn 2002: 96).

[142] See, e.g., Thesleff 1982.

about is the question of what precisely, if anything, should be inferred from that order of composition. I have in earlier sections indicated my strong opposition to the idea that it should be read in terms of the maturing of Plato's thought – the advent of Platonic maturity after a Socratic childhood. This opposition may now be spelled out more precisely: what I oppose, in particular, is the notion that Plato grew up by becoming a metaphysician, one who invented – or, better, saw himself as having invented – a set of entities to whose existence Socrates was oblivious.

Here things become complicated. Presumably no one would want to say that Plato thought of his Socrates as ever having been in the position of the 'sight-lovers' of *Republic* V, who don't recognize the existence of anything beyond particulars.[143] So maybe 'hadn't recognized' forms, in Socrates' case, ought to be taken simply as connoting 'hadn't *fully* recognized' them; in which case, given the fact that I accept the possibility of the weak thesis that Plato might have come to see the Socrates of the 'Socratic' dialogues, or the way he talks there, as presupposing Platonic forms, there would hardly be any room for disagreement. However everything here depends, once more, on what a 'Platonic form' is supposed to be. At the centre of the debate stands Aristotle, who famously declared[144] that the difference between Plato and Socrates was that Socrates did not make the objects of his definitions 'separate' in the way that Plato did. But this is Aristotle's terminology – Plato never says of his forms quite what Aristotle interprets him as saying. So which particular feature of forms is Aristotle referring to? And again, is it our Socrates, the Socrates of the 'Socratic' dialogues, that he has in mind, or the real one? We have no good reason for *assuming* either that the two Socrateses are the same or that Aristotle thought they were (and he doesn't *say* that he is talking about the literary Socrates).[145]

We may take the two questions together. The best guess, in relation to the first, is that Aristotle is referring to that undoubtedly Platonic contrast between forms, as constituting an intelligible 'world' of stable and therefore – in principle, if not actually – knowable entities, and the

---

[143] See chapter 6 below. Briefly, the 'theory' in question is that beauty (or justice, or whatever) is nothing but particular things. The Socrates of the 'Socratic' dialogues plainly doesn't think *that*; he wants to know what *the thing* courage (*Laches*) is.

[144] See *Metaphysics* M, 1078b27–32.

[145] There is a separate argument to be made in relation to Socratic moral psychology: in that case what Aristotle attributes to 'old Socrates' is actually a – much distorted – version of what we find in the 'Socratic' (and generally pre-*Republic*) dialogues. See Rowe 2002a. Whether or not the Socrates of these dialogues knows about forms is a different matter (and up to a point in Plato's own control).

moving, even 'fluxing', world of particular objects familiar to the senses.[146] If this sensible world is in perpetual flux, and forms are stable, then they can't be part of this world; so they must constitute, or be part of, a different one, in some loose usage of the term 'world'. Now it probably would be reasonable enough to say that, if Plato had wanted to claim that all of this was somehow implicit in dialogues like *Euthyphro*, *Laches* or *Lysis*, then it would look implausible in the extreme. It would be hard, at any rate for someone who wasn't already a convinced Platonist, to maintain that this elaborate kind of metaphysical position – crucially including the idea of the ordinary perceptible world as fluxing – was *needed* for understanding what was going on in these little pieces.[147] So far, then, Aristotle's reading of Socrates as a non-separator seems to fit well enough with the Socrates of the 'Socratic' dialogues. However what has come to be called a 'two worlds' interpretation of the post-'Socratic' dialogues is, in my view, in no way inevitable. It is, rather, one of several different ways that Plato has of representing the relationship between forms and the physical world, the world of experience, or more generally between forms and particulars. (Or alternatively, to keep what I have called my 'weaker thesis' in sight: perhaps, to the extent that the Plato of the 'post-Socratic' dialogues was a two-worlder, he came to think of the Socrates, and the Plato, of the 'Socratic' dialogues in the same light.)

That the 'two worlds' view is just one of several Platonic perspectives on things is particularly plain in the context of the *Sophist*, when the Eleatic Visitor criticizes people whom he identifies simply as 'friends of the forms' for failing to recognize that things that change can be *real*, as well as things that are unchanging.[148] For supporters of the early-middle-late division of the dialogues, this will be a case of Plato belatedly correcting himself (*Sophist* is one of the stylistically late group of dialogues) – part of a general rethinking of his 'middle'-period metaphysics. But if we move away, as I propose, we should, from the whole idea of a 'middle' period marked off by a grand metaphysical theory (a theory itself supposedly recognized by a later Plato himself as mistaken, or at any rate needing radical overhaul or restatement), then the *Sophist* context can be seen just as a redressing of

---

[146] See *Timaeus* 27D–28A, 38A–B, 49A–50A.

[147] But note e.g., *Republic* VI, 485B1–3, where the opposition between an eternal being, which 'does not wander as a consequence of coming into being and passing away' is introduced on the back of no more than a distinction between forms and particulars (which are described as 'many and existing in all sorts of ways', and things in which non-philosophers 'wander' (VI, 484B5–6).

[148] The thought is introduced, apparently with firmness, at *Sophist* 249B; this is in the middle of a complex dialectical argument, but one of the final outcomes of that argument appears to be as stated.

the balance.[149] Yes, from one perspective there is a gulf between forms and sensibles: forms are unchanging, sensibles changing; forms are knowable, sensibles unknowable; and so on. So, from this perspective, talk of different 'worlds'[150] is reasonable enough, and in Timaeus' account of the physical universe in the *Timaeus* the contrast between what *is* – the forms – and what merely *becomes* – things in this world – is central.[151] Yet there are other perspectives under which the contrast between forms and sensible things not only goes along with, but is inseparable from, the idea of a connection between them. Thus, as we shall see, in all three of the similes Socrates introduces in *Republic* VI–VII in place of a proper account of the form of the good, the similes of sun, line and cave,[152] it is entirely essential that the lower levels of objects relate to, and are informed by, the highest: the shadows on the wall of the cave are the shadows of the objects being carried along the wall behind the prisoners, and these objects in turn are related to, are copies of, things in the world outside the cave. Again, the argument in Book V addressed to those 'sight-lovers' (see above) itself depends heavily on the idea that even if we can't discover what beauty – for example – is from particular beautiful things or kinds of thing, nevertheless these particulars are capable of telling us *something* about what beauty is or is like. And it could scarcely be otherwise, insofar as particulars are what they are by virtue of their relationship to forms. In *this* sort of context, talk of separate 'worlds' looks considerably less useful than it may do in others (and, one may add, the physical world will no longer be one of flux: it will acquire a modicum of stability from its association with forms).[153] Forms may be – evidently are – capable of existing independently of particulars, but particulars could not conceivably exist independently of forms; and for so long as there is a physical world – which Plato gives every sign of thinking eternal[154] – forms and particulars are irrevocably tied together.[155]

---

[149] See also *Parmenides* (133B–134E) for an argument from another Eleatic philosopher against erecting too strong an opposition between forms and sensible things.

[150] One place where Plato himself probably comes to using the language of 'worlds' is when he has Socrates talk of 'the *noētos topos*', 'the intelligible place', or 'the place of what is intelligible', in his *interpretation* of the image of the cave, and so outside the image itself (*Republic* VII, 517B5).

[151] See n. 146 above.

[152] For the simile of the cave, see the following Introduction.

[153] In the *Sophist* Socrates emphatically rejects an extreme Heracliteanism, and an incomprehensibly fluxing world, as firmly as he does the view of the 'friends of the forms'.

[154] For a modest justification of at least part of this claim (that the world, for Plato, had no beginning), see chapter 10 below.

[155] The *Phaedo* is perhaps *the* primary source, in Plato, for the two-world reading of the relationship between forms and particulars. I address, and arrive at analogous conclusions for, this dialogue in chapter 2 below.

Another important aspect of this connection between forms and particulars is especially prominent in the *Republic*. The reason why we human beings need to gain knowledge of the forms, so Socrates insists there, is to acquire some kind of model or paradigm for organizing our lives in cities: for legislating, in order to enable us to live the best life possible. According to his argument, we all want knowledge of the good; and we want it because we want to be happy. If, as I proposed in the preceding section, the Socrates of the *Republic* thinks knowledge beyond any merely human philosopher, i.e. any human philosopher not somehow in direct communication with the gods, even the philosopher-rulers of Callipolis – if some approximation to Callipolis were ever realized – would in fact have to occupy their off-duty philosophical time investigating forms not just for the sheer pleasure of it but for the sake of what the truth would finally mean for them (and the city) – the fulfilment of that passionate desire, that *erōs*, talked about at *Republic* VI, 490B5–7, which affects every genuine philosopher;[156] the understanding of a good, if only they recognized it, that is desired even by those untouched by philosophy. For the good is that 'which *every* soul pursues, and [she] does everything for the sake of this, surmising that it is something . . .'[157]

In the *Republic* as a whole, the metaphysical and epistemological focus is on two themes: the impossibility of accessing forms from particulars (e.g., particular actions),[158] on the one hand, and on the necessity of gaining access to forms in order to improve the quality of our lives, whether in the private or the public sphere.[159] Philosophers in the *Republic* may reject the political life in favour of the life of the mind, or else they may wish that they could. The current practice, Socrates says, is that philosophy and politics are carried on by different people, and even in the good city philosophers would prefer it if, impossibly, circumstances allowed them not to take on their share of political rule.[160] In other words, the option of a purely philosophical life, under ordinary conditions, is a possible one; and those who live it may feel they 'have been transported to the isles of the blest even when alive'.[161] (One thinks here of the 'leaders in philosophy'

---

[156] At the end of his search, 'having had intercourse with what really is, having engendered intelligence and truth, [he] would know and truly live and be nurtured and so cease from birth-pangs'.

[157] *Republic* VI, 505D11–E1.

[158] Cf. Socrates' application of what he calls the 'vulgar' (*phortika*) tests to the definition of justice in Book IV: our just man will be 'outside', 'beyond' (*ektos*) *actions* like temple-robbery, theft, treachery . . . (442E–443B).

[159] See especially *Republic* VII, 517C4–5.   [160] *Republic* V, 474C–E; VII, 519B–521A.

[161] VII, 519C5–6.

Socrates refers to in the *Theaetetus*:[162] these pure philosophers are in any case, I take it, an imaginative projection – perhaps his idealized Eleatics.)[163]

But however pleasant philosophy may be, indeed the most pleasant thing in the world, pleasure is not itself the good: Plato devoted the best part of a long dialogue, the *Philebus*, to establishing the point. The chief motivation for philosophy, as it is portrayed throughout the dialogues, is not the 'sight' of truth itself, but rather what is to be *derived* from that sight.[164] Thus it is that the philosopher's pleasures, according to Socrates in *Republic* IX, are a matter of his or her being filled up 'with the kind of filling up that belongs to true belief and knowledge[165] and intelligence *and, in short, all of excellence*'.[166] In a dialogue that is formally structured around the subject of the nature of justice, 'all of excellence (*aretē*)' could scarcely exclude justice – and in any case, in the context the philosopher *is* the archetypal just person; that, then, will be part of the source of his pleasures and his happiness. In other words, I take it that what he derives from philosophy will be an understanding about how to live life best; and unless Plato holds that one can be just without actually doing anything except studying,[167] that will mean understanding how to make the right choices in real-life situations involving the real possibility of injustice.[168] (*A fortiori*, the person who devotes himself to philosophy, at least on the Socratic model, will be no hermit or visionary, but a citizen, friend, fellow-soldier, spouse . . . The one thing he will abstain from is politics, except to the extent that being a citizen requires it.)[169]

My claim, then, is that while the 'world' of forms can, in some circumstances, be sharply distinguished from the sensible world, in other contexts the relationship between forms and sensibles requires to be understood differently. In particular, in the *Republic* itself Socrates insists that we need to 'grasp' forms precisely in order to understand things in this world better;

---

[162] See n. 56 above.

[163] Or are they perhaps members of the Academy, and the counterparts of these in the fictional world of the dialogues: serious young men who talk to Socrates instead of going off into politics? ('Eleatics': see text to nn. 55, 56 above.)

[164] In general terms Socrates seems to be undecided quite how to treat those who devote themselves exclusively to philosophy: they – whoever they are – may tend to get further than he does, and they may live a delightful life; but he doesn't himself join them, and perhaps as an able-bodied citizen cannot. So *exclusive* devotion to philosophy has to be for those physically unfit to live a full life as a citizen (cf. the example of Theages: *Republic* VI, 496B).

[165] The appearance of these two things together in the list is interesting; see chapter 6 below.

[166] IX, 585B14–CI.

[167] As Richard Kraut does (Kraut 2003); but see my counter-argument in Rowe 2003a.

[168] I note in passing that this is still a markedly *Socratic* view of things (as I defined this earlier): 585B14–CI, indeed, surely implies the familiar identification of virtue/excellence and knowledge.

[169] See especially *Republic* VI, 496A–E (the passage that mentions the case of Theages: see above).

without forms, we can do no better than a partial understanding, which by itself will lead into error. The reason for this is that what we experience at the level of sense, and of ordinary life, is as it were fragments of beauty, goodness and justice – things that are e.g., only beautiful to _this_ person, good under _these_ circumstances; actions that are only just under _those_ circumstances – when what we need in order to make the right choices is to know what beauty, goodness and justice are, themselves. When Aristotle seizes on stability versus flux as the defining feature of the relation between forms and sensible things,[170] he is picking out only one of many such features, others of which cut across and soften the distinction that his version of the relation implies. The reason why he makes the choice he does is that he tends to regard separation as Plato's big mistake: take that away, and from Aristotle's point of view we should be on the road to perfectly respectable universals, which are merely secondary beings or _ousiai_ (real being, says Aristotle, reversing the Platonic view, belongs to particulars).

But there is no reason why we should follow Aristotelian doxography here. If the opposition stable/fluxing looks un-Socratic, other ways of treating forms in relation to particulars look entirely consistent with the sorts of things that Plato's Socrates is talking about in the so-called 'Socratic' dialogues. (More flesh, and justification, will be added to this proposal in later parts of this book.) From these other perspectives, form-'theory' looks considerably less grand, and significantly less innovative, if indeed it is innovative at all.[171] In that case, the basis for the now traditional division between 'early' (metaphysically innocent) and 'middle' dialogues (those using or referring to forms) will for all practical purposes have disappeared.[172] Aristotle's 'authority' amounts to nothing; instead of giving us some kind of privileged, because close-up, perspective on the history of philosophy, he is merely telling us where he thinks his teacher Plato went wrong, and where – with the greatest respect – he himself will put things right.

Thus while the chronology of the composition of the dialogues ought to be a relatively uncontroversial matter (if as usual we except the possibilities of revision), what has been done with that chronology in the last century

---

[170] See above.

[171] Even the idea of the sensible world as fluxing has at least a close relation in the perfectly ordinary Socratic idea that things said to be, e.g., good will typically turn out actually to be bad; or that actions that are apparently just under some conditions will turn out unjust under others.

[172] There remains that apparent, crucial shift in moral psychology between the Socrates of the pre-_Republic_ dialogues and the Socrates of _Republic_ IV, who divides the soul; much will depend here on the success of my argument in chapter 5, which will attempt to show that Plato thought he had a way of keeping _both_ models of human behaviour.

or so – the division of the dialogues into 'Socratic'– 'middle' (Platonic) – 'late'(Platonic) – needs to be set aside. Or rather: the division in question should be set aside unless and until it is shown to be useful, as opposed to merely constraining and inhibiting our reading.[173] It should no longer be used as a starting-point; for it is, for the most part, based on a perspective (mainly Aristotle's) which is not only one that we need not share,[174] but one that – I claim – Plato himself patently did not share (as well having no reason to share it).[175] There are three groups of dialogues that show significant stylistic differences between them, but (a) these groups do not coincide with the traditional early-middle-late grouping, and (b) we have no reason to suppose in advance that the fact that the dialogues were probably written in this rough order has any consequences in itself for the debate between the 'developmentalists' and those who, like myself, favour a more 'unitarian' reading of Plato's thinking overall.

Chronology comes to matter, if it matters at all, in two connections. Firstly, it will often be useful to know something about the order of composition of the dialogues for the purpose of identifying cross-references, the majority of which are necessarily implicit (given that dialogues are or include localized conversations).[176] Secondly, there remains that one apparently significant shift in Plato's thinking that I have proposed, however reluctantly, to recognize: the shift away from a strictly intellectualist theory of action towards a position that would allow at least some purchase for a rival view, according to which our reason may be besieged and even overthrown by irrational desires. In this one respect my reading of Plato may itself seem to begin to slide over from unitarianism towards developmentalism; and in this one respect I recognize a division between *Republic* and post-*Republic* dialogues, on the one hand, and pre-*Republic* dialogues on the other. It still remains to be established, however, just how significant this shift is, and how significant Plato thinks it to be.

---

[173] I cite an example of such 'inhibition' below (n. 176).

[174] That is, insofar as there are no finally compelling arguments for it, and – as I hope to show – reasonably compelling arguments against it.

[175] The point is not just that he makes Socrates talk about forms in *Republic* and elsewhere (which would be to rely on the assumption – unproven and unprovable, even unlikely – that his Socrates only ever says things he, Plato, thinks Socrates would have been happy to say); it is rather that he has him talk about them *as if they were familiar*, and in contexts where *readers* as well as interlocutors are evidently meant to be familiar with them (because of what I take to be unmistakeable intertextual references). See especially chapter 9 below.

[176] 'Developmentalist' assumptions have naturally inhibited the search for such cross-references: if Plato is perpetually moving on, he will rarely need to look back except to indicate that he is moving on.

11 THE NEED FOR A HOLISTIC INTERPRETATION

There will be many different types of readers of Plato. Some will merely dip into him, picking out a particular dialogue because it looks attractive, or impressive, or puzzling; and some of those will be disappointed, or even repelled, and go no further. Others, perhaps the ones that Plato had in mind, will attempt something more ambitious: one could imagine individuals, back in the fourth century BCE, waiting for each successive dialogue as it appeared, sometimes perhaps announced by a performance by the author himself. And then there are the academic readers, like myself, for whom reading Plato is – by good fortune, or because they have planned it that way – part of what they do for a living. Some of them will be philosophers, some classicists, some both; some will live in comparative literature departments or departments of political theory. It is a presumption of the present book that it is a common task of all of these academic readers to throw light on Plato's texts for those other types of readers: to try to explain what is strange, puzzling, or simply complex. Different kinds of specialists will essay different aspects of this task: philosophers will take a special interest in what they see as the hard arguments, literary experts in aspects of intertextuality, the interplay of character; and so on. Instead of merely allowing the texts to work their effect, such readers typically attempt to say what effect Plato might have *intended* to achieve, by what means, and (in the case of the philosophical specialists) how effective he is in achieving it.[177]

The present book is an example of this kind of activity. It starts from a point that is probably close to being universally agreed: that no account of any part or aspect of Plato will be complete unless it pays attention to all the manifold aspects of his writing, whether philosophical, literary, dramatic, or . . . (however many aspects different interpreters may recognize). However my approach differs from others' especially in the degree of interdependence that I see as existing between the different elements that go to make up Plato's writings. There are very few places, I claim, where Plato's intentions can be read directly from the surface of the text, not because there is uncertainty about who he means to speak for him, but rather because the person who speaks for him – Socrates – is always speaking for him *under particular conditions*, which he himself has created, for purposes of his own, and which help to shape what he says and how

---

[177] Even some academic readers purport to content themselves with relaying their own experiences of a given text, apparently on the grounds that that is the maximum that any interpreter ever achieves, whatever he or she may claim. Such relativism seems peculiarly out of place with philosophical authors: see Rowe 2002b.

he says it. Only when we have fully understood what those particular conditions are, and how they may have affected the shape of what Plato has put into Socrates' mouth, can we begin to understand what it is that he is saying (wants to say). In other words, it is not just that we need to understand the arguments in their literary and dramatic context, and understand how they relate to their 'frames'. That we certainly do need to do. But we must – I propose – also accept that the structure of the arguments themselves may be at least partly determined by extraneous factors like the state of understanding of the addressees (interlocutors, whether individuals or types), and that almost any statement Socrates or other main speakers make may need to be understood as representing a particular perspective, and so may require correction or completion from other contexts. The general picture – the one I wish to promote – is of a largely stable and connected set of fundamental ideas which can be approached from different directions, represented now from one angle, now from another, now partially, now more fully, with corresponding shifts of focus and emphasis; sometimes, no doubt, out of sheer pleasure and inventiveness (for Plato is the wittiest of writers), but more importantly out of a desire to draw in readers whose tolerance he expects to be as lacking as their understanding.[178] To end this preliminary part of the book where I began it: Platonic variety more often reflects variety of strategy than variety of – changes in – thinking.

---

[178] Once again, I should emphasize that I do not mean for a moment to exclude an exploratory, or more generally reflective, moment in Plato's thinking. That, after all, would make me just another 'doctrinalist'. When I talk of 'a largely stable and connected set of fundamental ideas', I am referring specifically to Plato's *fundamental* ideas or starting-points; and those, of course, include as one prominent item that awareness of the limits of human understanding which his Socrates, and I believe he (Plato) himself, have thoroughly internalized. So beyond those fundamental ideas, all is in principle to play for, e.g., in relation to the organization of society, the best kind of individual life, or indeed the fundamental principles of all existence (starting with that as yet elusive item, the form of the good).

THE DIALOGUES

Introduction: the simile of the cave in the Republic

One of the central themes of the present book, and one that will continue to recur, is the importance, for the way in which he writes, of Plato's awareness of the difference between his view of things – what, through Socrates, he calls the philosophical, or the true view – and the way things appear to ordinary non-philosophical folk, whether these are Socrates' interlocutors, or Athenians/Greeks in general; or, by implication, the generality of the readers of the dialogues. Plato's sense of his, and his Socrates', 'out-of-placeness' (their *atopia*), in relation to run-of-the-mill perspectives, and of the barrier to comprehension that this threatens to raise, is one of the chief determining factors shaping the dialogues. And – as I shall go on to argue in the following chapters – nowhere is this clearer than in the *Republic*. In this Introduction, I propose to try to demonstrate the point in relation to a particular context in the dialogue: the simile of the cave. The outcomes of the discussion of this one context will turn out to be unexpectedly wide reaching.[1]

In the simile of the cave, the form of the good is still at the centre of the image that is presented to us, as it has been in the two similes that precede it (the sun and the divided line). However the focus is now not so much on the good itself as on 'our nature in relation to education and lack of education',[2] where 'our' appears to have the most general reference; that is,

---

[1] The simile, in outline, goes like this. Human beings are tied up facing a wall at the bottom of a deep cave, watching flickering shadows on the wall cast by a fire behind them. But they can be freed; and we are then asked to picture one of them making his painful way up past the fire and out blinking into the daylight, where finally he is able to look directly at things in the world above, up to and including the sun: this, he works out, is the ultimate cause of everything. If he then goes back into the cave and sits in his old seat, he won't be able to make sense any longer of what's on the wall in front of him, and he'll become a laughing-stock, and worse; if the remaining prisoners could get their hands on the person trying to free them from their chains in the first place, they'd even try to kill this supposed liberator . . .

[2] 'Well, after this [sc. the simile of the line and its interpretation]', says Socrates, 'think of our nature in relation to education and lack of education as like the following state of affairs. Picture people as if they were in an underground dwelling-place in the shape of a cave . . .' (*Republic* VII, 514A1–3).

the simile is primarily concerned with human receptivity or otherwise to education and enlightenment, and with the nature of education itself as a kind of 'conversion', a turning 'of the whole soul' that Socrates compares to the turning of the prisoner's body when he is released from his chains (518C). It is just such a 'turning' of the soul that Plato is attempting in the *Republic*, as I propose he acknowledges in his usual, necessarily indirect way.

It is a matter of controversy how we are to interpret the two sets of things seen in the cave: the shadows on the wall in front of the chained prisoners, and the objects being carried along the wall behind them, together with the people who carry these objects. However it seems that the world outside the cave can hardly avoid representing things as they really are, while the contents of the cave will represent what we make of those things (including human beings), whether by the ways in which we construct and understand them, or by what they *become* in the familiar world of experience. The mysterious carriers behind the wall, who are compared to puppeteers (514B5–6), I take to be those supposedly authoritative individuals who have interpreted for us the world 'we' inhabit[3] and given us the patterns of life we live by:[4] so perhaps poets, writers, and generally,[5] but, most importantly, those who have established 'our' laws and customs. (It will become clear later, at 517D–E, that *justice* is involved at both of the levels of understanding represented in the cave: this will turn out to be crucial for my argument.) Socrates puts in, as an apparently casual detail, that some of the 'puppeteers' are uttering sounds, while others are silent: the difference, I suggest, represents that between written and unwritten law (custom).[6] The

---

('State of affairs' translates *pathos*: for a similar use of the term see the beginning of the *Politicus* myth: 269B5, with Rowe 2004b (1995) ad loc.)

[3] Hence the fact that 'manufactured objects of all sorts' (*skeuē . . . pantodapa*, 514C1) comes first in the list of the objects carried: these, I take it, are representations of the things that surround us in our daily lives.

[4] 'Statues', *andriantes*, come next in the list after *skeuē* (see preceding note), followed by *alla zōia* 'worked out of wood and stone and all sorts of materials': *andriantes* need not be statues of *andres*, men, but the term suggests men; similarly *zōia*, after *andriantes*, will primarily be 'images' ('other images'), but *suggests* animals – thus 'other animals', or 'animals besides' – or, as Shorey has it, 'shapes of animals as well' (514C1–515A1). The whole expression *andriantas kai alla zōia* thus neatly covers all human and animal existence; but the ambiguity of *alla* ('other'/'besides') may have a further significance in a dialogue which will go on to suggest a continuum between human and other forms of life (this in the myth: see especially Book X, 619E–620D).

[5] Is this why Socrates specifies 'wood and stone and all sorts of materials' (standing for different media and genres)?

[6] Contrast the case of the rulers in Callipolis, who lay down 'what is to be thought down here [sc. in day-to-day life] about fine and just and good things' (VI, 484D1–3) on the basis of a 'clear model in the soul' (484C7–8). In Callipolis, it seems, the puppeteers will be redundant (like middlemen, purveying fake merchandise).

shadows the prisoners then see are the images of images, which they take to be the real thing;[7] they particularly value skill at observing the shadows going past, and the ability to remember 'which of them tended to come before, which after, and which together', allowing them to 'predict what's going to come along next' (516c9–D2). That is, they operate in a wholly empirical fashion, taking things one by one as they come along[8] and trying to establish patterns of behaviour on that basis, without the slightest idea that what they are seeing is no more than the product of the manufactured products of others.[9]

So we, the bulk of humanity, are apparently nature's empiricists – except that, strictly speaking, we're not even that, because what we see in front of us is no more than shadows. (We *think* we're empiricists, if we think about it at all, but that's a different matter.) What about the puppeteer-like people who carry the objects and the statues along behind the wall? The implication is that these people are closer to the truth than the prisoners[10] (even though it won't feel like that to someone coming up to their level for the first time: a point that Socrates heavily emphasizes); but what they carry is still a collection of images, and not the real thing. And this idea has real bite, if the carriers are or include poets and lawgivers: in the case of the poets, the statues will represent exemplars, of courage, say, or justice, while in that of the lawgivers they'll represent examples of unlawful actions ('thou shalt not . . .'),[11] and all the time there must be some connection with the real things – courage and really courageous actions, justice and just actions, and so on – because we are given to believe that the images really are images of what they purport to be images of; but on the other hand they precisely *aren't* the real things. Why not? Presumably because they are still manufactured, and manufactured in the cave, which is devoid of the light (the understanding) that illuminates the real world outside it. Why would the puppeteers go on parading their artificial stuff up and down if they had the real stuff to hand?

---

[7] 515B4–5 (whatever the right text may be here), B7–9.

[8] The prisoners will, then, bear more than a passing resemblance to the 'lovers of sights and sounds' in *Republic* V (see Preliminaries above, especially n. 143, and chapter 6 below: in fact, these 'lovers' have mysteriously transmogrified into 'the many' by the end of the stretch of argument in question, at 479D).

[9] It seems reasonable to suppose, in the absence of any indication to the contrary, that the carriers behind the wall manufacture the things they carry (as puppeteers – at any rate, modern ones – often make their own puppets).

[10] 515D1–7 almost says it, but not quite.

[11] Things carried, *pheromena*, will also be things said; is there a punning connection with those *phortika*, 'vulgar', tests applied to confirm the Book IV definition of justice (the just man as we have defined him will be the last person to commit temple robbery, burglary . . .: IV, 442D–443B; *phortika*, 442EI)?

If we then continue observing the progress of Socrates' imaginary escaped prisoner, we're told he'd be made to look at the light (fire) itself behind the wall, and after that he'd be dragged up forcibly into the blinding sunlight outside the cave. There he would first have to look at shadows and reflections of 'human beings and the rest' (516A7), before he could see the human beings and the other things up there themselves; after that he would observe 'the things in the heaven and the heaven itself at night more easily, looking at the light of the stars and the moon, than the sun and the light of the sun by day' (516A8–B2). But finally he would 'be able to catch sight of, *katidein*, the sun, itself by itself, in its own place, and observe, *theasasthai*, what kind of thing it is' (516B5–7). Now clearly the sun is the form of the good; but does the whole world outside the cave represent nothing but forms? That is a possible reading, insofar as the whole simile is supposed to inform us about 'our nature in relation to education and lack of education', and a direct encounter with the forms of human being 'and the rest' would presumably do that informing (moreover, Socrates clearly implies that the prisoner will have 'seen' 'justice itself' before he goes back down into the cave).[12] And after all, Plato does sometimes use the language of original and copy for the relationship between form and particular;[13] maybe, then, the statues of human beings, animals, and so on that the carriers carry will represent *actual* human beings?

By this point, however, things are surely getting out of hand. If the statues really stand for what they are statues of, then what are we to make of the prisoners themselves? The whole story, I think, will break down if we take things this way. We should rather continue to suppose Socrates' focus to be on degrees of understanding of things:[14] for example, and especially, degrees of understanding of humanity/human beings, who happen to be about the only items specifically named among the things the prisoner gets to see outside apart from the heaven and the bodies in it. He used to see shadows of images of human beings; then he got to see the images of human beings that threw the shadows; now he sees human beings properly, for the first time – illuminated as they are, as soon as he gets over his temporary blindness, by the light of the moon and the stars, and then by the light of the sun. If we take the simile this way, then it is the heavenly bodies

---

[12] 517D–E has him in dispute with those still chained up, who are described as 'those who have never yet seen/caught sight of justice itself (*hoi autēn dikaiosunēn mē pōpote idontōn*)' (E1–2).

[13] See e.g. *Republic* x, 596A–598C.

[14] As it was in the preceding simile, of the divided line, though less exclusively (insofar as it has more to say directly about the objects of different states of mind); the line is for the most part a static version of, and preparation for, the more ambitious and dynamic simile of the cave.

that represent the forms (it is a given, of course, that the sun is a form): in their light, finally, the prisoner is able to see what human beings – such as himself – really are like, after all,[15] and when he gets to see things in the light of the sun/the good, and sees the sun, ever more clearly still. (The same will then apply to everything else; like Socrates, I simply take human beings as the central example.)

The passage under consideration here is another one of the many whose meaning has been hotly contested over the years, if not for millennia, and I cannot pretend that the brief discussion I have just offered is likely to end the contest. Far from it. However I do claim that the outline reading I propose is at least as workable as any other on offer, not least because it seems capable of taking care of many of the details of the text;[16] I also claim that it fits the wider context of the *Republic* (and of Plato).

Other connections and implications of my reading of the cave simile will emerge in subsequent chapters of this book. But there is one particular connection that matters for my immediate purposes: with Socrates' argument against, or with, the 'lovers of sights and sounds' in Book v – those people who think all there is to beauty, or whatever it may be, is what they see and hear. To this connection I now turn.[17]

Having given a summary interpretation of the simile (517A–C), Socrates goes on to draw some morals. It shouldn't be any surprise, he says, to go by the simile, if people arriving from the light above refuse to take part in human affairs. Nor should it be surprising

if someone comes from observations of divine things (*theiai theōriai*) to human ones – bad things, as they now seem to him[18] – and appears thoroughly laughable as, still blinking and as yet insufficiently used to the surrounding darkness, he is forced to compete in the law-courts or somewhere else about the shadows of justice or the statues (*agalmata*) the shadows are of, and to contend (*diamillasthai*) about this – namely how these things are understood ('thought of'? *hupolambanetai*) by those who have never yet seen/caught sight of (*idontōn*) justice itself. (517D4–E2)

---

[15] See e.g. chapter 3, section 4 below ('what sort of creature am I?' asks Socrates in the *Phaedrus*).

[16] Thus for example I see no insuperable obstacles to aligning my treatment of what the prisoner sees outside the cave with the description of the mathematicians operating in the third segment of the line, at VI, 510D–511A (see n. 14 above: some fairly close connection between the two similes is no doubt inevitable). The mathematicians are said to use visible shapes, and to talk about these, but to be thinking all the while not about these but about the forms of the square, the diagonal, etc.; similarly, I suppose, the newly enlightened prisoner will as it were see through the human beings he has before him – in thought, and looking like the very statues he saw before – to the forms that explain them. (This needs more work, but the general direction indicated seems to me plausible enough.)

[17] On the Book v argument itself, see chapter 6 below.

[18] I am grateful to Ingo Gildenhard and George Boys-Stones for helping me to understand the Greek here.

There are some puzzles about this passage. (i) The simile hasn't mentioned justice, or any of the particular excellences (though in his summary Socrates has talked about the form of the good as being 'cause for everything of everything correct and fine'). (ii) If we're still talking about the prisoners, then they actually don't know even that the statues behind them exist; so how can they enter any sort of competition about them? (iii) In 'how these things are understood', what are 'these things'? Apparently they must be the shadows and the statues; but what sort of contention should there be about how *these* are understood? Aren't the shadows straightforwardly taken, by the prisoners, as real, and the statues likewise by the escaped prisoner (for that brief time until the guide takes him further on)?

By way of solving these puzzles, here are some proposals. Having drawn the first moral of the cave simile – escapees won't want to come back to ordinary life in the city – and so secured a connection with the next part of his argument,[19] Socrates now, in 517D–E, establishes the link between the simile and the main topic of the dialogue: justice. The different parts of the simile, it now turns out, each have an application to this particular item: thus justice is one of the items whose shadow appears on the back wall of the cave, or rather there's a *statue* – now an *agalma*, not an *andrias*[20] – of justice throwing shadows of itself onto the wall; and there will be justice itself somewhere located out in the sunlight above. That is the first part of a solution to puzzle (i). As for puzzle (ii), I propose that Plato for the moment has Socrates abandon the subtle distinction between lower and higher forms of human ignorance in favour of a simple opposition between understanding (full sightedness, or something approaching it) and the lack of it (blindness, or something approaching it). This is an opposition that has been in play before; and most notably in that argument with the 'lovers of sights and sounds' at the end of Book v.[21] And a link with that context will provide a solution to puzzle (iii), insofar as the argument of Book v imagined contention (a dispute) of precisely the kind in question between Socrates, on behalf of philosophers, and the 'lovers of sights and sounds', who were identified by Socrates – but not, of course, by themselves – as mistaking 'the many beautifuls' for the real thing, beauty. Of course they *would* disagree with Socrates' diagnosis, since their sort fail even to recognize

---

[19] I.e. that the very people we'll need to rule in the city won't want to do it (519cff.) – which takes us firmly back to the specific theme of the philosopher-rulers.

[20] An *agalma* will normally be an image of a *god* (while *andriantes* are of, or are primarily associated with, *andres*, men); and justice (itself) is surely divine.

[21] Socrates there started by comparing the different states of mind with dreaming and being awake (476c–D), but he changes the metaphor to blindness and seeing (sharply) as he reflects on the outcome of the argument at VI, 484c–D.

the existence of beauty itself, and of other such things: 'beauty, justice, or whatever – nothing more to them except beautiful, or just, or . . . people, things, actions'.[22] In other words, our passage at 517D–E is Socrates' (Plato's) way of recalling that earlier argument, and indicating that the cave simile dovetails with it.

In a way this is obvious and necessary enough; that is, insofar as the conclusion of the Book v argument, or the claim about the need to have philosophers in power[23] that it is designed to support, provides the basis for everything Socrates has said since then, and everything he is about to say. However there is a further aspect to 517D–E, which is my real reason for introducing the passage here. This is that, if Socrates is genuinely referring back at this point to the Book v argument, the Book v argument then itself implicitly becomes an illustration of the experience of the returned escapee. 'Forced to compete in the law-courts or somewhere else . . .': the 'somewhere else' itself constitutes a covert invitation, from Plato, to look back to the earlier context. ('Somewhere else': that is, back in Book v, or just where the conversation was a bit before midday.) So Socrates' conversation, and Plato's text that 'reports' it, turn out to be implicated in the 'competition', and part of the process of education – the 'turning of the soul' – shortly to be described. (If talk about being *'forced . . . to compete'* has a defensive air about it, 'contending' about how the shadows and images are thought of – at least as I have proposed to understand it – looks like a switch to the offensive, and quite different from 'contending' with the permanent prisoners at the old business of picking out one shadow from another: 516E9.)[24]

If this is right, the consequences are not negligible. It means that the *Republic* is not, or not merely, Plato's report ('report') of a discussion by Socrates of a process of conversion that he recommends for some ideal future. Plato is working with Socrates, now, in the written text, to educate humanity at large. Plato's Socrates *is* the prisoners' guide, and we unenlightened humanity are the prisoners (the cave simile was always about 'our nature').[25] Of course Socrates will shortly be laying out a radically new educational programme for the budding rulers of Callipolis, the 'beautiful city' that he, Glaucon, Adimantus and the rest are in the middle of putting

---

[22] See especially v, 476B–D.
[23] Or, more specifically, to have them establishing and maintaining laws 'concerning beautiful and just and good (things)' (vi, 484D1–3).
[24] 'Contend' is the same verb in both cases (*diamillasthai*).
[25] 514A1–2: 'our nature in relation to education and lack of education'. Of course anyone reading the present book will be far too sophisticated still to be among the prisoners.

together. But that is no more than an attempt to put into terms of a draft curriculum,[26] to institutionalize, a process to which we are already being subjected in the very act of reading.[27] Thus when immediately after that key passage at 517D–E Socrates warns 'anyone of intelligence' against laughing at people who are confused and unable to see things properly (518A–B), that is surely intended to recall the moment in Book V (451D–452E) when Socrates anticipates a ribald reaction to his radical proposals for the treatment of women and children: that women should share the same education as men, should exercise with the men, should exercise *naked* with the men, and so on. Read Socrates' tentativeness there as 'inability to see', and a kind of 'confusion' (not too much of a stretch), and then his behaviour there in Book V will be presented retrospectively as the behaviour of someone who is feeling his way, escaping from ignorance into an unaccustomed light (one of the two causes of confusion identified in 518A–B; the other being that someone is unable to see because he's moving from light into darkness). The place outside the cave now becomes the location for Socratic (Platonic) dialectical construction, freed from the shackles of conventional 'wisdom': a true *noētos topos*, 'intelligible place', in which thought may operate on the basis of what things are *really* like, as opposed to the way they appear to be in the confusion of ordinary life and third-hand imaginings.[28]

---

[26] And a strange curriculum it is: aimed at getting the minds of the future rulers *used* to looking at things 'as they are in themselves' (getting their eyes thoroughly familiarized to the light above), and equipping them with the required dialectical skill (equipping them, ultimately, to see the source of the light), while also providing them with political experience in minor offices – and keeping them out of the trouble they could cause by using that skill in the wrong way. Strangest of all is the last part of the draft curriculum, which lays it down that at the age of fifty those who have passed all the necessary tests must be 'compelled' to turn the 'ray of their soul' towards the form of the good – as if the good were just another subject to be picked up from a lecturer (540A–C). Well, perhaps Plato did after all think of it in that way; and indeed there is anecdotal evidence that he himself lectured 'On the Good'. (Here is one of the foundations of one main sort of 'doctrinal' interpretation of Plato: see the Preliminaries above.) But in *Socrates*' mouth, i.e. in the fictional context of the conversation that he is leading in the *Republic*, the very idea sounds bizarrely improbable. The key points, I take it, are (a) that no one should rule until they are mature and experienced enough to take on the responsibility, and (b) that no one should rule unless they have 'seen' the form of the good. So: if our trainees are indeed to take over, that's what they must do – 'see' the good. It is, I suggest, no accident, that the key passage (i.e. 540A–C) reintroduces the language of the cave simile; what is described needs to be part of the curriculum, but there is no way that, in any possible life, the curriculum can guarantee to deliver it.

[27] Cf. the final part of Socrates' summary interpretation of the cave simile in 517A–C: '. . . and that the person who is going to act intelligently (*emphronōs*) *in either a private or a public capacity* must see [the form of the good]' (517C4–5).

[28] Socrates and the two brothers will, all the same, be working on a lower level than the philosopher-rulers themselves: Socrates' little group produce a mere sketch (*hupographē*, 504D6), and are 'mythographers of a city, in speech' (501E4–5), while the philosopher-rulers are thought of as painting a full picture 'with the use of a divine model' (500E3–4).

The *Republic*, I conclude, is written as a living educational text – to the extent that 'living text' can avoid being a contradiction in terms.[29] And the same, I propose, will be true of other dialogues. The aim, or one chief aim, of Platonic writing itself is to bring us out of the cave – to make us turn ourselves round 'to that place . . . in which is the happiest (part) of what is [sc. the form of the good], which in every way the soul must see' (VII, 526E2–4). Socrates is here describing the effect of the proper study of geometry in the philosopher-rulers' curriculum: to force the soul to take notice of (*theasasthai*: 'observe')[30] being (*ousia*) rather than 'becoming', or 'coming-into-being': *genesis* (526E6–7). This latter opposition, between being and becoming, has been prepared for by the sequel to the argument with the 'lovers of sights and sounds' in Book V (see VI, 484B, 485B), by the simile of the cave (a place in which everything seen is manufactured, or a shadow of something manufactured), and by the discussion of the different ways of conceiving of number and unity in the treatment of the arithmetical part of the curriculum (VII, 522E–525B); insofar as Socrates – and Glaucon and Adimantus, his interlocutors – avoid the mistake of the Book V 'sight-lovers', and are talking about things as they really are (forms), then by implication they are themselves already in 'that place[31] . . . in which is [the good]', even if they haven't seen the good (or at least, not properly, yet). And Plato is inviting us in, offering *us* our freedom; we may go there even now – and not have to wait until death, or some promised future existence.[32] Forms may 'transcend' the ordinary world, in the sense of being above and independent of it, but they are in principle graspable by our human intellects.

Plato does not underestimate the size of the task facing him (how to persuade us to *accept* his offer of freedom?). At every point, the cave simile stresses the extraordinary difficulty that any escaped prisoner will experience in switching from one way of seeing things to another. Thus both when he is forced to look in the direction of the fire and the statues, and when

---

[29] See chapter 11 below (on the *Phaedrus*).

[30] My 'take notice of' attempts to do justice to the *aorist* tense of the verb, which will typically be used of an event rather than a process or a state.

[31] I.e. the 'intelligible place', the *noētos topos* (VII, 517B5 again): 'the place of intelligence', 'the place grasped by the intellect' (see *to tou nooumenou genous*, as contrasted with *to tou horōmenou*, at VI, 509D8)?

[32] Even if those who spend all the time there may think that they've been transported to the Isles of the Blest even when alive . . . (519B-C). On the *Phaedo*, which may appear directly to contradict the claim I have just made in the main text, see chapter 2 below. (498C may promise the philosopher-rulers a relocation to some actual equivalent to the Isles of the Blest after death; in the same stretch of purple prose – Adimantus comments on Socrates' enthusiastic tone: C5–8 – he perhaps also refers to his own case, involving merely 'fine hope': 496E1–2.)

he first emerges from the cave, he thinks he's much worse off; the old facility he had with things when chained up he seems to have lost at each new stage. Only when he gets used to the light above does he finally accept that, yes, things *are* better – and then he has no desire at all to be back in his chains.[33] If he did go back and sit in his old seat, then his eyes would be 'filled with darkness' (516E4–5); if he had to contend (*diamillasthai*) with the permanent prisoners at the old business of picking out one shadow from another, he'd be a laughing-stock, at least until he'd got used to the darkness again.[34] (But of course he won't want to – any more than Socrates will want to give up his ideas for the reorganization of society and go back to conventional ways of thinking.)

At the same time, however, the Socratic educator will have two things going for him. In the first place, it is not as if the prisoners have no idea at all of anything. The progress of the escaped prisoner is permanently towards a *truer* and/or *clearer*[35] view of things. Thus when he sees the things that cast the shadows he saw before, he is imagined as being told that 'now, rather closer to what is, and turned towards things that are more [real?], he is seeing more rightly/correctly (*orthoteron*)' (515D2–4) – presumably because he's seeing statues of men (etc.), and not just shadows of statues of them. So the point is that when he was chained up he had some idea of what a man is; now he has a better one, and soon he will have a better one still. And the same will apply to everything, including justice, even goodness. The philosopher's understanding of the world may look, and will be, radically different from the non-philosopher's, but it is not as if one *completely* different, or unrelated, perspective has to be substituted for another. The human beings we see around us are still human beings, even if they're not what human beings – from the philosopher's viewpoint – can and should be, and still less what a human being is (the real nature of a human being); and there will be more than a little overlap between the just actions performed by ordinary people and the just actions performed by the

---

[33] For him it appears now as Hades did to Achilles in Homer – even being a king down *there* would be nothing compared with what it is like up *here* (516D). (Unfortunately poor Achilles is already there.) So being in the cave is now itself a kind of death, as being out of it is another: see preceding note. Here already are some important pointers for the interpretation of the *Phaedo*, and indeed for the interpretation of Platonic eschatology in general: the question will always be whether the story is about the next life, or this one (or both). See further chapter 2.

[34] 516E–517A. As well as laughing at him, the permanent prisoners would say that the ascent had ruined his eyes, and it wasn't 'worth even trying to go up' (517A5); they'd kill the person trying to free them . . .

[35] Truer, 515D6, cf. 516A3; clearer, 515E4.

enlightened philosopher.[36] And (here is the second cause for optimism, or at least for a lesser pessimism, on the part of the Socratic educator) everyone in fact wants to get a truer and a clearer view. At any rate, everyone wants to get a hold on what is truly *good*. 'No one is . . . satisfied with getting the things that appear good; they seek the things that actually are good', declares Socrates in *Republic* VI (505D7–8).

---

[36] In fact Plato probably takes a stronger position than this: if ever people talk about justice, or whatever it may be, they are actually talking about, referring to, the real thing (see Preliminaries, n. 74 above, and chapter 5 below). This stronger position is, however, not strictly relevant in the present context.

CHAPTER I

The Apology: *Socrates' defence,*
Plato's manifesto

The *Apology,* or *Socrates' Defence,* pretends to be the speech, or rather speeches,[1] that Socrates gave at his trial on a charge of 'doing what is unjust by corrupting the young and not believing in gods the city believes in but other new divine entities' (*Apology* 24B8–C1).[2] The main proposal of the present chapter is that even as Plato has Socrates defend his way of life to the jury, he, Plato, is also issuing a kind of manifesto on his own behalf, which tells his readers – in the broadest terms – about his fundamental concerns and aims. (There are no chronological implications to this proposal; Plato might have written the *Apology* at any time during that relatively early part of his career in which the stylometrists place it.)[3] However the route to this destination will be a fairly circuitous one.

I 'NOT EXCELLENCE FROM MONEY, BUT FROM EXCELLENCE MONEY . . .'

Near the end of the *Apology,* Socrates explains to the 501 members of the jury that even in the unlikely event that they should propose to let him go free on condition that he stopped philosophizing and corrupting their sons, he wouldn't stop. He'd go on saying what he always says, to anyone he meets:

---

[1] A main speech is followed by two short ones – one following the vote to condemn or acquit, the other following the vote on the penalty.

[2] The formal charge may have put things in a different way. But my concern here is primarily with Plato's fiction, not with any putative reality to which it may refer.

[3] That is, it is a work which belongs to the first group of Platonic works, which contains some of the ones others call 'middle'. The *Apology* may even be seen as referring implicitly to the politics of the *Republic*; after all, one of Socrates' proposals is that just as people need to concern themselves with the condition of their souls before 'the things that belong to them', so they should concern themselves with the city's condition before they involve themselves in its affairs (36C) – because in its present condition, anybody who did involve himself in politics, and acted as a good man should, would not survive (32E).

66

My good man, when you're an Athenian, belonging to the greatest city and the one with the highest reputation for wisdom (*sophia*) and strength (*ischus*), aren't you ashamed to be caring about how to get as much money, and as much reputation and honour, as you can, while as for getting as much good sense (*phronēsis*) and truth as you can, and getting your soul into the best condition, that you don't care about, and don't give any thought to? (*Apology* 29D7–E2)

Then, a few lines later, he sums up by saying

You see (*gar*), what I'm doing as I go about is just trying to persuade both the younger and the older[4] among you not to care either about bodies or about money before, or as intensely as, you care about getting your soul into the best possible condition; what I say is "*It's not excellence (aretē) that comes from money, but from excellence (be)come money and the other things, all of them, good for human beings, both in the private and in the public sphere.*' If in saying these things I corrupt the young, these things would be harmful; on the other hand if someone claims I say other things than these, he's talking nonsense. (30A7–B7)

The translator has an impossible task with the italicized words.[5] The standard Hackett translation offers, in the main text, 'Wealth does not bring about excellence, but excellence makes wealth and everything else good for men, both individually and collectively', but with a footnote saying 'Alternatively, this sentence may be translated: "Wealth does not bring about excellence, but excellence brings about wealth and all other public and private blessings for men."' However the choice between these two versions[6] is not a straight or easy one. While both ways of taking the Greek are perfectly possible, the structure of the sentence (or more precisely, the order of the first nine words)[7] seems designed to invite the second interpretation; and yet the first appears to fit rather better with the context. It would be more than odd for Socrates to say, on the one hand, that his fellow-citizens shouldn't care about money 'before, or as intensely as' about the state of their souls, and – apparently in the same breath – tell

---

[4] Among other things, Socrates has been charged specifically with corrupting the *young*.

[5] In Greek: *ouk ek chrēmatōn aretē gignetai, all' ex aretēs chrēmata kai ta alla agatha tois anthrōpois hapanta kai idiai kai dēmosiai.* My discussion of this sentence may be seen as largely complementary to that in Burnyeat 2003. In effect, I aim to show that the interpretations of the sentence by Burnyeat, following Burnet et al. (see Burnyeat 2005a) and by his main opponents, De Strycker and Slings (De Strycker and Slings 1994), are both right, and how they can cohabit – while Burnyeat is quite certainly right about what Plato's Socrates seriously intends.

[6] If there is to be a choice; in fact, I shall shortly suggest that the sentence is deliberately ambiguous. Those who object to a Burnet-type reading (see Burnyeat 2005a) on the basis that it would involve a shift in the meaning of *gignesthai* are barking up the wrong tree; it is the whole sentence that is ambiguous, inviting the intelligent reader (hearer), at a certain point, to reconsider what he or she first thought the sentence was about.

[7] 'Not from money excellence comes, but from excellence money (. . .)'.

them, as he would be telling them with the second version, that actually money and all other good things come from having their souls in the best state (if we could make any sense of that claim in the first place);[8] for if they're to make *that* their grounds for going for soul-excellence, wouldn't that exactly be putting money, etc. before caring for their souls?

These are surely grounds enough for saying that the second interpretation is not a real candidate at all; and yet Socrates still seems – because of the word order – to be offering it to us on a plate. Or is he (is Plato) offering it, teasingly, to the *jurors*? That I take to be the right way forward, and indeed I cannot see any alternative. I shall go on later to say how and why the jurors might be teased by this reading of the sentence; for the moment I note merely that this is one place where we, the readers, appear to need to distinguish ourselves from the purported audience of the speech. In any case the serious reader must evidently plump for the first interpretation: '. . . excellence, *aretē*, makes wealth and everything else good for men, both individually and collectively'. And this will have a perfectly respectable point. The only material rewards worth having are those that come from being excellent (i.e. *morally* excellent, 'virtuous'?); get money, power, or whatever it may be by other means, and it will be worth nothing – just because what matters first and foremost is the state of ourselves (our souls: ourselves as moral beings?), and everything else is secondary. (Socrates' advice is 'not to care either about bodies or about money *before, or as intensely as*, you care about getting your soul into the best possible condition'.) Everything, then, is in order: Socrates, fine and upstanding man that he is, is saying not just the sort of thing we might want him to say, but the sort of thing that should have led the jurors to acquit him forthwith, if only enough of them had understood him, and believed him.

Yet there is potentially more to the sentence than this. It is not too much to say that, if we stick with the interpretation of it that I have just given, or some variant of that interpretation, we shall already have made a decisive choice in respect to our understanding of Plato, and, especially, in respect to his relationship to his Socrates. The story, starting from here, will go roughly as follows. Socrates thought justice, and 'moral' virtue/excellence in general, the most important things in human life. So these are the things we need to acquire before anything else. But how can we acquire them if we don't know what they are? *He* certainly doesn't have the relevant knowledge, and is all too aware of the fact; and so he goes off and tries to find out if he can get it from anyone else. But even by the end of his life (as described

---

[8] See further below.

in the *Apology*) he has got nowhere. And so we are left, and Plato was left, with a Socrates who gets certain important things right, e.g., about the need for a thoughtful approach to the moral life, and who has a penchant for the pithy and the paradoxical ('virtue is knowledge', and so on), but all the same a Socrates that even by his own standards failed to come up with solid results. Small wonder, then, that the pupil, Plato, felt he needed to move on. The whole project, in fact, sadly, was always a wild-goose chase. For who would ever want to agree that being just, or courageous, or possessing any of the parts of excellence, is a matter just of *knowing* anything?[9]

It is not, however, inevitable that we should follow this narrative; and the sentence at *Apology* 30B2–4 may serve as the portal, as it were, to an alternative reading. The issue is about the identity of the 'excellence' 'from' which 'money and the rest become good for human beings', and then about the way in which money, etc. 'become good from' it. The first story took excellence as being *moral* excellence ('virtue'), i.e. justice, courage and so on, and the goodness of other things as deriving from this excellence by virtue of being conditional on it. This idea might well seem to be encouraged by a passage like *Meno* 78B–E: Socrates and Meno agree that money and the rest must be acquired justly and piously, or not at all – so that excellence can't after all be the capacity to provide good things for oneself,[10] as Meno has just been induced to accept as what he wants to say. But there are other contexts in the pre-*Republic* dialogues where human excellence is treated in a different way: that is, as itself being a kind of wisdom or knowledge,[11] from which the goodness of other things derives in a rather more direct way. This view of things is most clearly illustrated by the 'first protreptic' in the *Euthydemus*, where Socrates sets out to show how he thinks the young

---

[9] On this account (which is a caricature, but should nevertheless be recognizable enough to those familiar with the last two centuries or so of writing about early Plato), knowledge will be supposed to be important because desire follows belief: our desires are for whatever we believe good (the apparent good), and so if we know what the virtues truly are, which will include knowing that they are truly good, they'll appear good to us and we'll live virtuous and happy lives. The weakest link here will normally be taken to be the account of the relation between belief, or knowledge, and desire – a point on which, allegedly, Plato was rather sounder than Socrates. ('Moral knowledge', at any rate if this is what Aristotelian 'wisdom', *phronēsis*, represents, will apparently presuppose the possession of justice, courage, etc., so not being a purely intellectual matter. Cf. e.g., Vlastos 1994: 116.)

[10] I.e. because failing to get them will turn out to be as much a sign of excellence as succeeding. More on this *Meno* passage below.

[11] I.e. as opposed merely to having wisdom as one of its parts (a kind of moral wisdom/knowledge?), as it will on the other reading. (I shall go on to suggest that the intellectualist account in fact, despite all appearances, survives in the *Republic* itself, and by implication beyond the *Republic*: see chapter 5 below.)

Clinias should 'care about[12] wisdom and excellence (*sophia te kai aretē*)',[13] and ends up showing him that he needs to look for a particular kind of knowledge or wisdom: knowledge or wisdom about how to put things – the things ordinarily called good – to good use, i.e. so as to benefit himself. Without this knowledge (which is presented, in the context, as a superior kind of technical skill, but a technical skill nonetheless),[14] money, physical strength, even courage and (so-called?) good sense, *sōphrosunē*, will in fact be less desirable for anyone than their opposites, insofar as they offer us more opportunities to go wrong. Indeed, concludes Socrates, by this line of argument nothing except wisdom will be a good thing, and nothing except ignorance will be bad (that is, nothing will be good *by itself* except wisdom, nothing bad *by itself* except ignorance: the conclusion is drawn in 281E2–5).

There are some who would have reservations about treating the *Euthydemus* itself as 'pre-*Republic*',[15] and so although I have no such reservations myself, I use this passage in the first instance simply because of the directness with which it spells things out: excellence *is* wisdom or knowledge, i.e. knowledge about good things and bad things, and it is what makes other things good which, in its absence, are neither good nor bad. Appealing to the *Euthydemus* in this way is safe enough, because there is a whole range of dialogues that everyone would accept as predating *Republic* in which Socrates suggests, or apparently moves in the direction of suggesting, or hints, that excellence, or one or more of its parts, is knowledge of good things and bad things:[16] *Charmides*, *Gorgias*, *Hippias Minor*, *Laches*, *Lysis*, *Protagoras* – and *Meno*.

---

[12] I.e. *epimelēthēnai*, part of the same verb Socrates uses in *Apology* 29–30 (see above). For any issues about the dating of the *Euthydemus*, see below.

[13] *Euthydemus* 278D3.

[14] For Vlastos 1994:115–16, it is rather a kind of wisdom that 'would differ . . . radically from . . .the . . . practical crafts'. The *Euthydemus*, he claims, is in this context 'confront[ing] a problem which every moral theory must address: the difference between, on the one hand, the wisdom required for the morally wise choice of ends and, on the other, for devising optimally effective means to morally unweighted ends'. Similarly in the *Laches* 'the wisdom which accounts for the brave man's courage has everything to do with moral insight, *and nothing to do with technical skill*' (117; Vlastos' italics). However Vlastos offers no conclusive evidence to show that the wisdom in question in *Euthydemus*, and ultimately in *Laches*, is not itself seen, by Socrates/Plato, as a technical skill with its own special subject-matter (i.e. good things and bad things). The only difference between this and other technical skills is that someone who possesses it could never go wrong, even by choice: if everyone desires the real good, and no one ever knowingly goes for what he or she even believes to be bad for him or her, then knowledge of what the real good is, other circumstances permitting, will be followed by pursuit of it: this is the main point of the argument of the *Hippias Minor*.

[15] On what I take to be the only serious grounds for treating *Euthydemus* as post-*Republic*, see chapter 9, n. 12 below.

[16] The claim is that *what people are referring to when they talk about excellences* – including wisdom (and so anything that might be called 'moral' knowledge?) – will be identical with this kind of knowledge. The good and bad things in question are clearly meant to be understood as things good or bad for us, i.e. for the agent.

Meno I introduced just now as a likely exhibit for the 'moral' reading of *Apology* 30B (on the strength of 78B–E); in fact it will ultimately count against that reading. For in 87C–89A Socrates introduces what is in effect a copy of the substance of the *Euthydemus* passage – and that in turn will have consequences for any fully considered reading of 78B–E. Here is the way Socrates sets things up in that passage: everyone desires good things, Socrates says (78B3–8), and no one is better than anyone else in this respect, i.e. in respect of their desires (sc. for good things); any superiority of one person over another must be in the capacity for them ('capable of the things that are good': *dunasthai*, B8, sc. *tagatha*, understood from B3–4 *boulesthai te tagatha kai dunasthai*). 'So this, according to your argument/account (*logos*) is excellence, capacity for providing for oneself the things that are good' (B9–C1), which Socrates is easily able to show to be untenable – given Meno's view of what good things are (health, wealth, etc.). But once we get to 87–9, a different take from Meno's on 'the capacity to provide good things for oneself' will retrospectively become available (i.e. *knowledge* about things good and bad, beneficial and harmful), and Meno's retreat from that account of excellence will have proven premature. Admittedly, Socrates will appear to row back, after 87–9, from the equation of excellence with knowledge, on the grounds that if excellence was knowledge, it would be teachable, and if it was teachable, there would be teachers of it, which there are not. But the objection is specious: the reason why there are no teachers of it might just be that no one has yet acquired the relevant knowledge. Since Socrates is as it were on record as believing just that, we are presumably licenced – providing, once more that we have prior licence to read across from one part of Plato to another[17] – to take his apparent readiness to abandon the equation of excellence with knowledge as no more than apparent. In other words, the *Meno* may be treated as ultimately a quite safe piece of evidence in support of taking Plato's Socrates to be quite serious in identifying excellence, not with the 'moral virtues', but with a particular kind of knowledge (which will nevertheless itself involve a commitment to the 'virtues', insofar as these are good things when wisdom is 'added').[18]

Now this of course does not amount to any sort of proof that Plato meant us to read *Apology* 30B along the same lines. Plato might have been trying out different solutions; more generally, the licence to read between dialogues

---

[17] See Preliminaries above, section 5.

[18] The Greek is *prosgenomenēs . . . phronēseōs* (*Meno* 88C7–D1). Truly just actions, for example, will for the most part be the same actions as the ones people currently call just (cf. *Republic* IV, 442D–443B); if they flow from wisdom, then there will indeed be a sense in which wisdom is 'added'.

has to be argued for. However there is no denying that a *Euthydemus*-style[19] reading of the *Apology* sentence is at the very least not ruled out.

To sum up the argument so far, we appear to have not just two but three different ways of taking *Apology* 30B2–4: (1) 'It's not excellence that comes from money, but from excellence come money and all the other things good for human beings, both in the private and in the public sphere' (what I have called the 'teasing' reading – that is, one that is placed there to tease the jurors); (2) 'It's not excellence that comes from money, but from [i.e. if we have and use] (moral) excellence money and the other things, all of them, become good for human beings [sc. and not otherwise] . . .' (the standard modern reading); and (3) 'It's not excellence that comes from money, but from excellence [=a kind of technical knowledge, i.e. knowledge of what's good and what's bad, sc. for human beings] money and the other things, all of them, become good for human beings, both in the private and in the public sphere' (the '*Euthydemus*-style' reading). If we suppose that the first reading is possible but uninteresting, how should we decide between the latter two?[20] Other things being equal, that might depend on which of them gives us the more philosophically fruitful outcome; and I suspect that the majority of modern readers would prefer a Socrates who put the moral good, and moral knowledge, at the centre of his concerns than one who did not.[21]

However it seems to me that other things are not equal.[22] In the first place, it ought to be fairly common ground that the *Apology* and other 'Socratic' works are saying things that are broadly compatible;[23] and I do

---

[19] It perhaps might be better to say '*Meno*-style', insofar as Socrates finally gets into trouble at the end of the 'second proptreptic', and doesn't seem to have provided himself with quite so ready an escape-route as he does in *Meno*. (In the context of the *Euthydemus*, and of the picture that dialogue means to sketch of Socratic activity as compared with that of the 'eristics' Euthydemus and Dionysodorus, it matters that the protreptic should end by emphasizing that Socrates is a *searcher*.)

[20] Some might propose – see n. 14 above – that there is no real choice to be made, and that the third reading is actually identical to the second: if excellence/virtue is knowledge, then it must be *moral* knowledge. In my view, however, 'moral' knowledge is imported by interpreters into Plato mainly on the basis that they would like to find it there, i.e. on the grounds of philosophical charity; misplaced, according to Penner and Rowe 2005. See further chapter 4, below, section 2(c).

[21] As a matter of fact, the kind of life he will end up by recommending on either interpretation will be much the same; but there is nevertheless all the difference in the world, philosophically, between a Socrates driven by notions like morality, duty and obligation and one who sees all of us, including himself, as acting whenever we act out of a passion for what is really good – for ourselves.

[22] I also happen to think that the third reading is the most philosophically satisfying; but in the present context I am more concerned with establishing what Plato wanted to say than with establishing what it would have been better for him to say.

[23] That is, insofar as it is commonly held that the *Apology* gives some kind of thumbnail sketch of Socrates' life and ideas, which is then filled in, in greater detail, at least in the allegedly 'Socratic' items among the pre-*Republic* dialogues (why else call them 'Socratic'?). I distance myself from the

not myself find,[24] in the latter, anything of that focus on *moral* excellence, and *moral* knowledge demanded by the second reading of *Apology* 30B. The only way to defend that reading, so far as I can see, would be to force the *Apology* apart from the dialogues it appears to relate to – the *Apology*, perhaps, being seen as closer to a historical account of the great man, the others treating him more freely. But in that case the trajectory of Plato's Socrates would for most modern interpreters be in the wrong direction: away from a proper concern with the moral good, and towards a concern with what is good for the agent – a kind of *egoism*.[25]

More importantly, there are – in my view – clear signs internal to the *Apology* that a *Euthydemus*-style reading (the third of my list of three) is the one we need, i.e. the one that gives the best explanation of the target sentence in its context. Here we need to take a step back, and look at how Plato has set things up in the *Apology* prior to 30B. In summary, Socrates' defence up to this point has been as follows (I paraphrase):[26]

People like Aristophanes have accused me of investigating things beneath the earth and in the heavens, making the weaker argument the stronger, and teaching others the same things,[27] but I don't discuss these subjects at all. Neither do I undertake to teach people, and charge money for it, in the way that others like Gorgias, Prodicus and Hippias do; I don't claim to be an expert, like Evenus, in human excellence, the sort a citizen needs,[28] and the sort that rich men like Callias seek for their sons – though actually I do seem to have some sort of purely human expertise/wisdom. I have this on the authority of Apollo at Delphi, who when asked whether there was anyone wiser than me, declared that there wasn't. Not being aware of knowing anything at all, I went on to try to refute the oracle's response by looking for someone wiser than I was – and that's how my reputation for wisdom came about, because people assumed I knew the answers to the questions I was asking. But I don't. All the same my search for someone who was actually wiser than me came to nothing, and on reflection I came to the conclusion that I was wiser than others at least in one respect: that I knew that I was ignorant. So this is the

kind of biographical approach in question; but then I find it difficult *not* to treat the 'Socratic' dialogues – and a whole lot of others – together in any case.

[24] Well, the reader might interject, perhaps you should have tried harder; and anyway, don't Greek terms like *kalon* and *aischron* ('fine', 'noble', 'beautiful'; 'shameful', 'ignoble', 'ugly'), which are scattered all over Plato's text, bring in a specifically moral value and the lack of it? So they may do, I respond, in ordinary language contexts; but Plato himself wants to reduce the 'fine and noble', or the 'fine-and-good' (*kalon te kai agathon*), to the good. See further below; and e.g., that first protreptic in the *Euthydemus* (which denies that even the parts of 'virtue' are goods without knowledge, sc. of good and bad); and especially Penner and Rowe 2005, which argues the point with particular reference to the *Lysis* (a 'Socratic' dialogue for most, though not for Vlastos, who treats it as 'transitional' – a category that will only interest 'developmentalists', and only some of them).

[25] But – see n. 21 above – it will in any case be a special kind of egoism: one that resembles the respectable kind of self-love that even Aristotle's good man will have (*Nicomachean Ethics* IX.8).

[26] Starting at 18A.   [27] 19B5–C1.   [28] I.e. *hē aretē hē anthrōpinē te kai politikē*, 20B4–5.

wisdom I have, a kind that's appropriate to mere humans. But I go on looking for someone who really does know something substantial, and when I think they're ignorant I show them they are. This is what I spend all my time doing, and I hardly have any time to do the city's business, let alone mine, so that I live in poverty. The consequence is that people get angry with me instead of themselves, and make up those stories about my corrupting the young, looking into 'the things in the heavens and beneath the earth',[29] not believing in the gods, and so on. The actual charge against me is one of corrupting young people, and not believing in the city's gods but other, new divinities: the first charge is ridiculous, as is the second insofar as it's a mere cloak for the charge that I'm actually an atheist. All that I am doing in my life is following what I take to be the god's command, and if the result is that I run the risk of being executed for it, that's a risk I must take for staying at my post just as I have done as a soldier on service. And in any case, to fear death is to do the one thing I pride myself on not doing, and thinking I'm wise about things I have no knowledge of. I don't know what goes on in Hades, so it would be unreasonable of me to be afraid of it. Even if you said you'd let me go if I stopped doing philosophy, I'd go on doing it . . .

So: Aristophanes got him wrong – he doesn't swing in the air in baskets, or teach rhetoric; he doesn't teach for money, like the sophists; what he does do is go round looking for people with the wisdom he claims to lack; and his awareness of his ignorance actually turns out to help him think about how to behave in the present difficult circumstances. All the emphasis here is on what other people say Socrates does, and teaches, and what *he* says he does, which is not to teach but to philosophize. And (I add the introductory lines to a passage cited a few paragraphs above)

there's no way I'll stop *philosophizing and exhorting you and giving my demonstrations*[30] to anyone I meet, saying the sorts of things it's my habit to say, to this effect – 'My good man, when you're an Athenian, belonging to the greatest city and the one with the highest reputation for wisdom (*sophia*) and strength (*ischus*), aren't you ashamed to be caring about how to get as much money, and as much reputation and honour, as you can, while as for *getting as much good sense (phronēsis) and truth as you can, and getting your soul into the best condition*, that you don't care about, and don't give any thought to?' (29D4–E3)

'I won't stop philosophizing and exhorting you and giving my demonstrations': 'exhorting' them, presumably, to philosophize, i.e. to look for the wisdom or knowledge they lack, and so to 'get as much good sense (*phronēsis*) and truth as you can'. 'Getting your soul into the best condition'

---

[29] 23D5–6.

[30] The verb is *endeiknumenos*, which I take to refer to the way Socrates says he *demonstrates* (*endeiknumai*) people's lack of wisdom to them when he finds they lack it (23B6–7).

will then consist in getting 'good sense (*phronēsis*) and truth';[31] and so it will in 30B too:

> What I'm doing as I go about is just trying to persuade both the younger and the older among you not to care either about bodies or about money before, or as intensely as, you care about *getting your soul into the best possible condition*; what I say is 'It's not excellence (*aretē*) that comes from money, but from excellence money and the other things, all of them, become good for human beings, both in the private and in the public sphere.' (30A7–B4 again)

In which case 'excellence' must be excellence, the best state, of soul; and this must be wisdom or knowledge.[32]

As for what kind of knowledge this is, my hypothesis is that it is the knowledge *of good and bad* that Plato's Socrates talks about elsewhere. I shall return shortly to the question why he doesn't *say*, outright, here in the *Apology*, what kind of knowledge he is so passionately concerned about; but meanwhile I shall argue that my hypothesis nevertheless finds some confirmation in what he does say.

One of the outstanding puzzles about the *Apology* is that even while saying he thinks he has nothing worth calling knowledge, or that he's conscious of knowing practically nothing,[33] it turns out that there are actually things that he is prepared to say he knows, and not inconsiderable things at that, insofar as they determine his behaviour. Thus at 29B7–8 he refers to 'things I know to be bad', the immediate reference being to the badness of 'disobeying one's better (*beltiōn*), both god and man' – *that*, he has just said, he knows to be both bad and shameful (*aischron*). In consequence of this knowledge, he says, he will always stay where the god has stationed him, 'philosophizing . . . and examining myself and others', just as he stayed where he was posted by his human commanders in battle.

So how does he know that it's a bad thing to 'disobey one's better', when there are so many things he doesn't know? The solution depends, I believe, on the way we, and Socrates, take 'better'. The generals in charge at Potidaea,

---

[31] In 36C8, the order is reversed: it's a matter of taking care that one as 'good and wise as possible' (*hōs beltistos kai phronimōtatos*).

[32] That Socrates is identifying excellence with wisdom is in fact clear even before this point. If one of you says he does care for his soul, I'll examine him, and 'if he doesn't seem to me to have acquired excellence, but to say that he has, I'll rebuke him . . .' (29E5–30A1). This process of 'examination' is presumably not to be distinguished from the one he said he practised in response to the oracle; and what he was looking for there was the *wisdom* he lacked.

[33] The first formulation is intended to give the sense of what Socrates concluded about himself at 21D4 (*ouden kalon kagathon eidenai*), the second of 22C9–D1 (*emautōi suneidē . . . ouden epistamenōi hōs epos eipein*).

Amphipolis or Delium could have been the most upstanding gentlemen in the world, but that wouldn't have been of the slightest interest to Socrates the hoplite as he stood awaiting the enemy in the phalanx. What would have interested him is their strategic understanding, insofar as that would lead to a more successful outcome for him and for the army as a whole. The generals would have been 'better' than Socrates, in other words, not because they were decent characters but because they were more expert in generalship,[34] and so more likely to be successful in achieving the appropriate ends; that being so, it would have made no sense for Socrates not to concede strategic decisions to them.[35] *A fortiori*, he should obey divine orders, if gods are wise.[36] Given his awareness of his own, human ignorance, disobeying the god will be even less of an option than disobeying his 'better' in battle. He envisages the jurors inviting him to disobey the god by desisting from philosophy on the grounds that if he goes on he'll die or have something else bad done to him; but that, he suggests, presupposes that he knows that death is a bad thing, and 'I don't have sufficient knowledge about the things in Hades, and not having it I don't think I have it' (29B5–6). Death might even be the greatest of blessings (29A6–8). So he'll carry on doing what he does, according to the god's orders, confident – because the god is wiser than him – that things will turn out well for him even if staying in the ranks leads to his death.

It is not that there aren't plenty of other reasons that can be adduced for people's 'defying death', as we might describe what Socrates is doing.[37] He himself refers to such other reasons: he cites the example of Achilles, who went knowingly to his death because he was more afraid of dying a coward, and without avenging someone he loved, so earning the derision of others (28E9–D4). Moreover Socrates directly applies the consideration of what would be *shameful* (*aischron*) to his own case: drawing on the parallel with Achilles, he claims that one must always stay and take one's chances

---

[34] Plato's *Ion* ends with the rhapsode Ion claiming such knowledge for himself, and Socrates showing him the absurdity of the claim.

[35] Admittedly, Socrates hardly stresses the expert qualifications of the generals who were in charge of him, characterizing them simply as 'the people you chose to command me'; but after all Athens is the city 'with the highest reputation for wisdom' (29D8). In any case, given his own lack of expertise in generalship, even the slightest smidgeon of strategic skill would have been enough to make the generals relevantly 'better'.

[36] As Socrates says they probably are – 'In fact . . . the god is likely to be the one that's wise, and to be saying in this oracular response' (23A5–6). However the 'likely' (*kinduneuei*) applies not so much to the proposal that the god is wise as to Socrates' interpretation of the response as a whole (after all, what does he know?).

[37] Achilles is said to have 'despised' or 'belittled' death (*oligōrein*, 28C9; cf. *tou kindunou katephronēsen* at C2).

wherever one positions oneself in the thought that this is best, or is positioned by a commander . . . not putting thoughts of death or anything else before thoughts of what is shameful. (28D6–10)

And what he actually knows to be 'bad and shameful' at 29B7–8 is *'doing what is unjust (adikein)*[38] and disobeying one's better, both god and man', which should probably be understood as 'doing what is unjust *by* disobeying . . .'; hence 'bad *and shameful*' (injustice being the sort of thing typically thought shameful, along with cowardice). Nonetheless, all the emphasis in the context as a whole is on the badness, not the shamefulness, of disobedience. 'So', concludes Socrates in the next sentence, 'I won't be afraid, or run away from, things that I don't know aren't actually good things before bad things that I know to be bad' (29B7–9). Doing what is best includes avoiding what is shameful, and indeed that above all,[39] but evidently Socrates' avoidance of the shameful is *because* the shameful is bad; he obeys the god's command because he trusts the god to have got the balance of good and bad, for him, right.

Socrates knows that disobeying his better is a bad thing, then, by way of inference from a combination of his awareness of his own general ignorance, and his conviction – which is evidently something he thinks wholly justified – that the god giving him his orders has the knowledge that he lacks; given that, he should clearly obey, and the likelihood is that things will turn out for the best. He doesn't know that they will (any more than the soldier does, in the parallel case), but meanwhile he does know that he's better off *not* doing something that he might otherwise have done, i.e. giving up philosophy for a quiet life. (Right at the end of the *Apology*, he will return to the possibility that death will, after all, be a good thing; one of the signs is that his divine voice has not once tried to hold him back since he left home in the morning and started addressing the jury.)

In short, there will be at least one thing that Socrates can claim to know, i.e. that it's bad and shameful 'to do what is unjust by disobeying one's better'[40] – but only on condition that 'better' is a matter of being 'more

---

[38] Abandoning one's post and running away from battle will be a straightforward case of injustice – there will be rules against that sort of thing, not least because of the damage it does to others; if Socrates 'abandoned his post', and stopped philosophizing, he would at any rate be stopping doing people good (depriving them of wisdom they might otherwise have acquired). (The verb *adikein* here picks up *adikein* at 24B8, in Socrates' statement of the charge against him: what really *would* be a case of 'injustice' would be to disobey someone wiser than me.)

[39] 28D6–10 (cited above).

[40] Even if not, perhaps, still, in the strictest sense; that is, unless it were impossible that what he claims to know could be false, which is clearly not the case, at least on my reconstruction. (And after all, that god is *commanding* him is itself a mere inference on Socrates' part, from the oracle's response.)

expert'. (In battle, generals know what to do; in life, if anyone knows what's good for us humans, it will be a god.) In general, 'good' (*agathos*) in the *Apology*, as applied to personal subjects, needs (*ceteris paribus*)[41] to be read as 'wise', just as 'excellence' (*aretē*, the noun corresponding to the adjective *agathos*) needs to be read as 'wisdom' – that is, as opposed to 'virtue' = 'moral' excellence; and specifically as wisdom in relation to good and bad (for the agent), as opposed to something called 'moral knowledge'. In one way these are all distinctions without a difference, insofar as it is perfectly plain that Socrates' good (wise) man will also be just, courageous and so on. However it is no less plain that his notions both of the nature of these excellences/virtues, and of how they will be motivated, will be utterly different from those implied by that more familiar view that operates in terms of the 'moral'.[42]

If all this is along the right lines, then there are only two, not three, available interpretations of *Apology* 30B2–4, i.e. (a) the first of my list of three: 'It's not excellence that comes from money, but from excellence come money and all the other things good for human beings, both in the private and in the public sphere,' and (b) the third on my list: 'It's not excellence that comes from money, but from excellence [=a kind of technical knowledge, i.e. knowledge of what's good and what's bad, sc. for human beings] money and the other things, all of them, become good for human beings, both in the private and in the public sphere.' But now both of these readings still require further work. Let me begin with the first, which I take it may readily be agreed merely to be something dangled before the jury, or at any rate any member of the jury not quick enough to think through the options in the way that a reader has the leisure to do. How would such a juror take it?

See Preliminaries above, section 9 – which places me in broad sympathy with Burnyeat 1992 (1977) and Santas 1979, both of which see Socrates as settling for true belief to guide his actions. (Vlastos' riposte in his 1994: 67–86, esp. at 72–3, is unpersuasive, insofar as it takes insufficient account of the difference between what Socrates aims at, what he has currently achieved, and what he currently expects to achieve. Vlastos' own proposal, to introduce two different sorts of knowledge, is in my view unhelpful insofar as it makes Socrates' disavowal of knowledge at least in part disingenuous.) In any case, I believe that what Socrates is most of all concerned to deny is that he knows what he's showing other people they don't know (see *Apology* 23A3–5, with Preliminaries, section 8 above); his is always a genuine inquiry, and his ignorance is not a stance (a kind of irony). (But, as I suggested in Preliminaries, section 5 above, when such an inquiry is written up, the investigation is already finished; a report of an investigation is no longer an investigation.)

41 I.e. allowing for context; thus in the context of *generals*, 'better' will indicate the possession of a greater expertise in generalship, not that of wisdom *tout court*.

42 Cf. n. 20 above. In brief, the idea will be that justice, courage, etc. are all identical to knowledge of what is truly good and truly bad; and that since we all desire what is truly good, we shall be just, courageous, etc., and shall act justly, courageously, etc. if and when we can identify the truly good and bad.

Once again, the crucial question is what this 'excellence' is supposed to be. For example, would an ordinary Athenian immediately suppose, given the context of the *Apology* so far, that 'from excellence come money and all the other things good for human beings' amounted to a claim about the power of the 'moral' virtues, justice and the rest? I suspect not. In the first place, it would seem to him too bizarrely unlikely a claim;[43] as we are told first by Thrasymachus and then by Glaucon and Adimantus – on behalf of common opinion – in the *Republic*, justice, at any rate, is the most obvious route to a loss rather than a profit. And if the point is supposed to apply to cities as well as to individuals ('both in the private *and in the public sphere*'),[44] the claim would be merely comic; it's by using their strength that cities become rich and powerful, not by behaving justly towards their neighbours. In short, if this is what is being dangled before the jurors, the invitation being put to them would be to write off Socrates as a mere buffoon, which is not at all the tone of the defence as a whole.

The more likely approach is to suppose that, for the ordinary juror, 'excellence' could be expected to be something rather indeterminate: it will be that set of qualities that best fit a human being and a citizen for the living of a successful life. That is not to say that he would deny that justice, or courage, were excellences, and desirable qualities (up to a point?). He – this imaginary, average juror – might even go so far as to say that they were necessary parts of what goes to make up a good (*agathos*) person, or a 'good-and-fine' (*kaloskagathos*) one. However the question 'what is the excellence needed by a citizen?', which is the one in the air from that moment in the *Apology* when the sophists are introduced,[45] will in principle be an open one. And so it appears in a whole range of Platonic dialogues: thus in the *Protagoras*, Protagoras is found offering[46] to teach 'political

---

[43] Greeks in the fourth century BCE, at any rate, would have been unlikely to share a Protestant optimism that heaven rewards honest toil with material advantage – or if any of them did (harking back, perhaps, somewhat hopefully to Hesiod's ambivalent declarations in the *Works and Days*), it isn't their voice that dominates in the world of the Platonic dialogues. When at the end of Plato's *Republic* Socrates allows himself to assume something of the kind, he openly represents it as a triumph of dialectical argument over experience.

[44] I take it that 'in the public sphere' picks up 'when you're an Athenian, belonging to the greatest city and the one with the highest reputation for wisdom and strength' at 29D7–8. Once again (see n. 3 above), the *Apology* clearly does have a political aspect – one which may also be visible in the weight that Socrates gives in the later parts of the *Apology* to Anytus, as opposed to Meletus, among his prosecutors, despite the fact he represents Meletus as the one who wrote the indictment and put the case for the prosecution.

[45] I.e. at 19D–20C; what is at issue for the sophists, and for rich men like Callias who want to give their sons the best kind of education, is *hē aretē hē anthrōpinē te kai politikē* (20B4–5).

[46] Actually in Callias' house (cf. preceding note).

expertise (*technē*)', and to promise 'to make men good citizens',[47] with justice and a sense of shame (*aidōs*) as part of the formula; Euthydemus and Dionysodorus in the *Euthydemus* identify a training in excellence as training in disputation; in the *Laches*, Laches and Nicias are wondering whether their sons should be taught to fight in heavy armour as part of what will make them grow into responsible adults. From this perspective, what Socrates is doing is to offer one more answer to the question: go to him, and you'll get *his* version of what everyone else is promising. Only, as is demonstrated by Socrates' account here in the *Apology* of the slanders current about him, people are confused about what exactly it is that he is offering: is it science? Rhetoric? The kinds of thing the sophists offer? The one thing that's clear is that the ordinary man (juror) wouldn't expect to do without the normal good things life has to offer.[48] So when Socrates appears to offer an excellence – whatever it is – that will actually *produce* such things, that will seem to put him not only in contention with other providers, but even ahead of the competition.

But this is after all only a tease; Socrates has already said that his way of life has reduced him to extreme poverty (a 'ten-thousand-fold poverty', 23C1). What he is really promising is the excellence, the expertise, about the good and the bad, which alone will make other things good. We get some sort of idea of what Socrates thinks will be the outcome of this brand of excellence or expertise – his version of 'human excellence' – from the things he says on his own account about what is good and what is bad. Whereas other people think death, exile, and loss of citizen rights to be 'great evils/bad things' (*megala kaka*, 30D3), 'I don't think so; I think it's much more of a "great evil" to do what [Anytus] is doing now – to try to kill a man unjustly' (30D3–5). 'Money and the rest' aren't goods, by themselves (our target sentence, which I now call in evidence: 30B2–4). 'This [trying to get you to put the state of your souls before anything else] . . . is what the god tells me to do, I assure you (*eu iste*), and I think myself that no greater good has yet come about in the city than this service of mine to the god' (30A5–7).

2 THE *APOLOGY* AS MANIFESTO

Here at long last the argument of this chapter comes round to the second topic announced in the title: 'The *Apology*: . . . Plato's manifesto'. For his

---

47 This is Socrates' formulation of Protagoras' claim at *Protagoras* 319A3–5, though Protagoras readily accepts it; his own version was that he teaches 'the ability to deliberate well (*euboulia*) about one's domestic affairs, so that one might govern one's own household in the best way, and about the city's affairs, so as to have the highest capacity for acting and speaking in relation to these' (318E5–319A2).

48 That is, his perspective on life will be more like Socrates' accusers' – which decidedly isn't Socrates' (see esp. 30D1–5).

putative audience, the jury, Socrates' words represent an *apologia pro vita sua*; for the readers of the written work, the *Apology*, they are (also), insofar as they look back/forward to the written 'reports' of the conversations – e.g., with the politicians and the poets – that helped to get Socrates into trouble, *a kind of manifesto*. Or, less dramatically, they are Plato's summing up of the principles that drive him, as Socrates' successor. And 30B2–4 may be used – might even have been designed – as the pivotal point of that summing up. 'We are all of us looking', Socrates says, for himself and for Plato, 'for the kind of excellence that will bring success in life'; but what constitutes success? The rest of the world thinks it knows what this is – money, reputation and so on. So it wants the kind of excellence from which these things will flow (the 'teasing' reading). 'But *I* say (the proper reading), and it isn't hard to get any of you to see, if you'll talk to me, that these things are only good if they're put to good use. So what is needed is wisdom about what will constitute good use. Just what is good for us, and what is bad for us? That's the kind of excellence we need – expertise about what is really good and bad.'[49]

While others offer teaching of various kinds, Plato offers his readers an invitation to join him, and (his) Socrates, in investigating a question that everyone else takes for granted. (Not that they will do that merely by reading him; they'll have to follow that up with philosophizing of their own. So – of course – the *Apology* is simultaneously an exhortation to philosophy;[50] but it is an exhortation to philosophy *with Socrates*, which means with Plato, since Socrates is dead.) It is an invitation they – Plato's readers – cannot refuse except at the cost of living a life that is less than truly human: 'the unexamined life', as Socrates famously says at *Apology* 38A5–6, 'is unliveable for a human being'.[51] But the invitation comes with a warning that the answers that will emerge from the investigation are likely to be radical and unsettling; after all, here is Socrates claiming – even as he says he has nothing to teach anyone – that he'd rather die than stop 'examining himself and others', and questioning the status of any other commonly agreed good. 'The unexamined life is unliveable' is actually to be taken *au pied de la lettre*, which is how he takes it himself. What people need more than anything is to be unsettled, and to be made to rethink, because otherwise they will continue to live unsatisfactory, even sub-human, lives. So he is doing nothing but good to his fellow-citizens.

---

[49] Once again I make no apology for leaning heavily on the *Euthydemus*, which merely states a position that can be put together readily enough from elsewhere. For such a putting together, see e.g., Penner and Rowe 2005.

[50] See, e.g., De Strycker and Slings 1994: 13–16.

[51] Will this, then, be part of what it is to see those real human beings in the world outside the cave (see Introduction above, p. 64)?

After the jury have passed a majority vote to condemn him, and Meletus has proposed the punishment of death, Socrates proposes that what he deserves, as a poor benefactor who needs the leisure-time to keep exhorting his fellow-citizens, is to be fed like an Olympic victor in the Prytaneum at public expense. The difference, he says, is that Olympic victors only make people think they're happy, while he actually makes them happy – presumably, insofar as he offers them the route to the wisdom they need for true happiness (36D4–E1). (Since wisdom, as he claims, is actually beyond human capacities, we might have to read that as a claim to make people wis*er*, *more* happy than they are. On the other hand his implicit claim is that they are presently not happy at all; so 'I make you happy' will after all be more than a rhetorical overstatement.)

Earlier on in the *Apology* Socrates has suggested another comparison, though one that he markedly underplays. The search that led him to the politicians and the poets, in response to the Delphic oracle, was a 'wandering . . . as of someone performing labours, in order that the oracle's pronouncement should not go unrefuted' (22A6–8). If we spell this out, as he does not, what he does with the politicians and poets will be compared to what Heracles, or the Athenian Theseus, did when they made the countryside habitable by ridding it of monsters.[52] But the comparison is made very delicately ('as of someone performing labours'). Similarly in the closing lines of the *Apology*, when Socrates imagines himself meeting

the true jurors,[53] the ones who are said to act in this capacity there [sc. in Hades], Minos and Rhadamanthus and Aeacus and Triptolemus and all those other demigods (heroes) who achieved justice in their own lives. (41A2–5)

Once again, for a moment, Socrates seems to associate himself with the heroes/demigods, insofar as the implication is that *these* judges would declare him innocent – which the unwary might take as equivalent to making him another (demigod?) who had 'achieved justice' in his life. But any such fleeting implication is removed by what follows. The great men whom Socrates looks forward to meeting in Hades, apart from the four named in 41A2–5, fall into three groups:[54] poets (Orpheus, Musaeus, Hesiod and Homer), people who died because of unjust judgements (Palamedes, Ajax son of Telamon, and unnamed others), and powerful people (Agamemnon,

---

[52] And if politicians and poets are already living a less than human life (see above), the analogy is perhaps even closer?

[53] I.e. as opposed to 'these people who call themselves jurors' (presumably the ones who voted to condemn him: see e.g., 41D6–7).

[54] 41A6–C4.

Odysseus, Sisyphus, together with myriad others). What Socrates says he looks forward to most is examining these people in Hades – if the stories are true, and he will meet them – as he has examined the living, to see 'which of them is wise and which of them thinks he is, but isn't' (41B7). The upshot is that he clearly distinguishes himself, as well as everyone else,[55] from Minos and the other demigods 'who achieved justice in their own lives' (sc. and therefore are in a position to judge others: the first three named, at any rate, are the standard judges of the dead). This is in line with Socrates' unwillingness at 34E–35A to claim to possess any of the excellences ('virtues') himself, even courage, let alone wisdom. He might do things that people, including himself, call courageous or just, and he may be wis*er*, and so *more* courageous, just and so on; but he will be as chary about claiming that he has courage and justice as he is about claiming that he has wisdom. So Socrates is, and will remain, a man, aware of his human limitations; no 'demigod' he, even though his author and speech-writer may fleetingly suggest it.

Plato has Socrates finish the picture of his future philosophical activity in Hades with a witty flourish. One great difference between there and here, he says, is that people there don't kill you for talking to them and examining them: they're happier than their counterparts here in other respects too,[56] but 'especially because they're deathless for the rest of time, if in fact what is said about them is true' (41C6–7). One can't kill someone if he's already dead.[57] But that presumably means that there's a real danger that he'll upset the dead as he has been upsetting the living – dead poets and politicians (or their equivalent) among them. The parallel with his story of his quest in response to the oracle is clear, and the moral, I take it equally so: that Socrates' quarrel is as much with past generations of the 'wise' as with the present. And Socrates' future in Hades is also his future in Plato's

---

[55] At least, until he has examined them.

[56] What are these respects? Is it that the dead don't have the options available to us, and so also lack the opportunities to go wrong? (What else do they have to do *except* talk – if they can do that?)

[57] 'If in fact what is said about them is true', Socrates adds: this might just be a reminder that he doesn't actually know anything about Hades, but it rather seems to qualify the particular point about deathlessness. My own tentative suggestion is that Plato is deliberately having Socrates keep his options open; in *Phaedo* and elsewhere Socrates will happily introduce the idea that souls will normally be reborn, and won't be 'deathless' even when 'dead'. See the following chapter. Stokes suggests that 'one cannot rule out the possibility that *Plato* had in mind already, whatever he attributed to his Socrates on this occasion, the after-life bliss which awaits the philosopher in the *Phaedo*' (Stokes 1997: 33): the difficulty is that 'all the dead are there', according to 40E6, so that Socrates oughtn't just to be talking about philosophers. (In any case, I shall go on to suggest in the next chapter that this 'after-life bliss' for the philosopher, if it extends much beyond what is suggested here in the *Apology*, is a will-o'-the-wisp.)

dialogues;[58] for Plato will have him, in effect, cross-examining the poets of the past, especially Homer (so most famously in *Republic* II–III), just as he cross-examines contemporary ones,[59] and expressing hardly greater respect for past politicians than he expresses for their present counterparts.[60]

Plato will also confirm the findings of the original quest, by having his Socrates in the *Meno* cross-examine Anytus, the prosecutor said in the *Apology* to be representing the politicians' interests, along with those of the craftsmen,[61] and Ion the rhapsode in the *Ion* – in each case discovering that they don't after all have the wisdom they thought they had. The outcomes of the argument of the *Ion* are particularly close to what Socrates says he concluded from his encounters with poets in *Apology* 22B5–C7; and, strikingly, the Anytus of the *Meno* is found threatening Socrates with trouble, for slandering people too easily – because, Socrates says, Anytus thinks he's insulting accomplished statesmen like Themistocles, Aristides, Pericles, or Thucydides son of Melesias, and counts himself as one of them (*Meno* 94E–95A; in fact, of course, Socrates would claim just to be telling the truth about them).

And the connection between *Meno* and *Apology* may possibly be closer still. Anytus is said in the *Apology* passage to have been representing the *craftsmen* as well as the politicians: why would he do that, as a well-off and successful politician?[62] The answer, I tentatively suggest, may be in the text of the *Meno*. Socrates admits in the *Apology* that the craftsmen certainly did know a lot of fine things that Socrates didn't, i.e. about the subjects of their crafts; but each of these good[63] craftsmen made the mistake of supposing, because of what he could achieve through his craft, that he was also 'wisest in the other things, the most important ones' (*talla ta megista sophōtata einai*: 22D7–8). If we look closely at Anytus' position in the *Meno*, it could be seen – by Socrates – as ending up exactly here. The good (*agathos*) doctor, Anytus says there in the *Meno*, the good shoemaker, and so on are all experts who can teach their own skills to others (90B7–E8). But he aggressively resists the suggestion that the sophists, who profess

---

[58] In the *Protagoras*, Socrates compares his encounter with the sophists in Callias' house directly with Homer's description of Odysseus' visit to the underworld, while still alive, in *Odyssey* XI (*Protagoras* 315C–D).

[59] Notably Agathon and Aristophanes, representing tragedy and comedy respectively, in the *Symposium*.

[60] So e.g., in the *Meno* (see below). Sisyphus is introduced in the *Gorgias* myth as one of those powerful people said (by Homer!) to be suffering eternal punishment for his crimes (*Gorgias* 525D–E).

[61] *Apology* 23E5–24A1.

[62] One might speculate that, as a democratic politician, he saw the craftsmen as his core supporters; but this has the flavour of anachronism.

[63] I.e. expert (but the term used is *agathoi*, 'good').

to be able to teach others the 'wisdom (*sophia*) and excellence (*aretē*) by means of which people (*hoi anthrōpoi*) govern households and cities finely', and so on[64] (91A3–4), should be treated in an analogous way. Who then does teach the wisdom and excellence in question? Who would teach it to Meno, for example? Anytus responds 'any of the Athenians he happens to meet, the upstanding ones (the *kaloi kagathoi*) – there's not one of them who won't make him better than the sophists will, if he's willing to be persuaded to do it' (92E3–6). Admittedly, Anytus seems to want to restrict his list of expert educators to people prominent in political life (these are his *kaloi kagathoi*), but Socrates succeeds in the sequel in showing him that none of his named candidates evidently was able to teach their 'wisdom', because they evidently failed to teach their own sons. In that case, Socrates might have gone on to suggest (had Anytus stayed around to continue the conversation), perhaps it's the craftsmen who're responsible for that superfluity of excellence in Athens, since at least you, Anytus, agree that they have some sort of excellence that they *do* successfully pass on?[65]

This may well seem, and be, a stretch. Yet the links between the relevant parts of the *Apology* and the *Meno* seem to me to be hardly less striking than the similar intertextual links between *Apology* and *Ion*,[66] and in any case are surely too striking to be dismissed.[67] It does not follow, of course, that the connections in question have the significance I am suggesting, i.e. that they support the interpretation of the *Apology* as a kind of manifesto,

---

[64] More specific skills belonging to this 'wisdom' are added.

[65] The unfortunate Meletus, whom Socrates treats with open contempt, is even represented as saying that *all* Athenians 'make [younger people] fine-and-good' except Socrates (*Apology* 25A9–11); *Meno* 92E3–6 (cited in the main text above), while not mentioning Socrates, looks like a more sensible version of the same sort of claim – and might even verbally evoke the *Apology* version?

[66] One might add to the list the question Socrates asks Anytus at *Meno* 92A2–6 'So are we to say, on your account of things, that [not only Protagoras but a whole lot of others, some before him and some still living] knowingly deceive and do damage to the young, or that it's even escaped their own attention that that's what they're doing? And shall we think them so mad, when some people say that they're wisest of men?' This, I suggest, is an abbreviated version of the argument against Meletus at *Apology* 25C5–26A7 ('corrupting the young will bring harm to me; so either I don't corrupt them, or I do so without intending to do so (*akōn*) . . .). On a more general level, the *Meno* context shows Anytus displaying the kind of animosity towards sophists which the Socrates of the *Apology* claims to be part of what underlies the case against him (23C–E); the slogan 'making the weaker case the stronger' (23D6–7; 18B8–C1) was particularly associated with Protagoras.

[67] In general, any puzzles in the *Apology* are more likely to have *literary* rather than historical or biographical solutions; see especially De Strycker and Slings 1994: 1–8. (Thus – another piece of sheer speculation: is Meletus' connection with the poets – Socrates says he represents them, as Anytus represents craftsmen and politicians – a pun on his name? 'Meletus' suggests (a) *melei*, aorist *emelēse* (a pun Socrates himself employs at 26B1–2; cf. 24C4–8), (b) *melos*, 'lyric'. But there was a tragic poet called Meletus, and maybe our Meletus was his son: see De Strycker and Slings 1994: 91. In any case Socrates' statement of all three prosecutors' motives is transparently an invention.)

or prospectus[68] for, or commentary on, other dialogues. But, first, no one denies that the *Apology*, as an account of Socrates' life, will necessarily have some sort of relation to the large number of dialogues which claim to represent moments in that life; and second (apart from other considerations I have introduced along the way), Socrates himself expressly refers – as he addresses those who voted to have him put to death – to a new generation that will carry on his mission and irritate them even more than he has done. Since Plato (a) is younger, (b) is named as one of the young men Socrates is supposed to have corrupted, and (c) appears to endorse, because – in his writing – he goes on repeating, Socrates' (his Socrates') plea to people to review and rethink their ways,[69] the proposal in question – to treat the *Apology* as a Platonic manifesto or prospectus[70] – ought to be unobjectionable.[71]

However it is a peculiar sort of manifesto: not only because it is in the voice of someone else (already dead),[72] but because it is a philosophical document addressed to a non-philosophical audience (the jury), in a form (that of a forensic speech) that is not only alien to the very thing (philosophy or dialectic) it defends but apparently despised both by its actual author and by the speaker. Because of what I take to be the perfect coincidence between the outlook of the speaker and the writer, the speech may in fact serve both the writer's purposes, defence and statement of intent, if it serves either. But the distorting effect of form and audience is considerable. The

---

[68] Again, no chronological implications are intended here; there is nothing to prevent prospectuses from being written during or after what they (pretend to) announce.

[69] It should probably also be noticed in this context that Plato chooses to put his own name first in a list of supporters willing to help pay a large fine (38B6); Socrates says a fine wouldn't have hurt him if he'd been able to pay it (B1–2), and presumably accepts his supporters' offer on the basis that it wouldn't hurt them either. If Plato is serious about Socrates, as he is, he must have agreed that it wouldn't.

[70] I.e. at the same time as respecting its status as a (fictional) defence of Socrates himself.

[71] This is no doubt an optimistic conclusion, insofar as there are many who will still hanker after some sort of historical reading of the *Apology* and/or the 'Socratic' dialogues, and will resist my positioning of the relationship *between Plato and his readers* at the centre of things. One of the most moderate versions of such an objection might be derived from De Strycker: the *Apology*, he writes, as a philosophical work 'is the more interesting because Socrates so frankly expresses his own favourite ideas, whereas when we read the aporetic dialogues we often wonder whether what he says is an expression of deep conviction or only a challenge to elicit a contradiction. In that respect, the *Apology* complements the early works that have so exercised the ingenuity of the interpreters' (De Strycker and Slings 1994: 15). My quarrel with De Strycker is fundamentally that I think he mistakes open *passion* for frankness; in fact, in my view, we learn more about Socrates' thinking from the 'aporetic' dialogues (especially if this category includes the *Lysis*) than we do from the *Apology* – in which Socrates' manner of presenting himself is more heavily limited by the nature of the occasion, and – above all – by the audience.

[72] Though we have no reason to suppose that Plato only started writing after Socrates' death, the *Apology* must be presumed to postdate it.

business of identifying the standard rhetorical features of the *Apology* I may safely leave to others;[73] what is of greater interest for the purposes of the present book is the way in which Plato adapts his account of Socrates, and of himself, to the context of an Athenian lawcourt, and, in effect, to a general audience.

The *Apology* is perhaps the only one of Plato's works that is clearly marked, by virtue of being constructed as for a particular court on a particular occasion, as intended for the public at large. But perhaps this is to put things the wrong way round. Plato – I surmise – chose the genre of the defence speech (both because he wanted to reconstruct the sort of defence the best speech-writer might have put up for Socrates and) because it offered an opportunity to address *the Athenians*, and not just some self-selecting group of educated readers. (This too, of course, fits well with my use of the term *manifesto*.) So the point is not so much that Plato is 'distorting' his message, as that he is putting it in such a way as to allow it to be understood as widely as possible. The very choice of genre might help here: people would have been far more used to forensic speeches than to philosophical dialogue. In short, the *Apology* offered what was perhaps a unique opportunity for Plato to present himself, even if at one remove, to Athens; just as no doubt the actual trial of Socrates would have been the first and only time that many ordinary Athenian citizens would have seen and heard Socrates (as well as the first and only occasion on which he made a public speech, whatever the real speech might have been like).

3 STRATEGY AND CONTENT

I have already indicated what I take to be one crucial element of Plato's strategy, in my earlier discussion of that sentence at 30B2–4: that is, to operate simultaneously on different levels. One might say that this strategy partly surfaces after the second vote, when Socrates begins to address separately those who voted to put him to death and those who voted to acquit him, insofar as he identifies the latter as people he'd like to have a conversation with, now, for as long as the officials are tying up the court business (39E). In fact he has already claimed that if he'd had more time – many days instead of one – to converse (*dialegesthai*) with the jury as a whole, he could have persuaded them, as he himself is persuaded, that 'I never willingly treat any human being unjustly' (37A5–6), putting this as if he's actually been having

---

[73] See, e.g., De Strycker and Slings 1994, Stokes 1997.

a dialectical discussion[74] with them, rather than delivering a monologue. If we put the two passages together, there are perhaps two points being made: that one can achieve less with a speech than with a conversation, and that some people – as it happens, the majority – will be less easy to persuade than others. The latter, perhaps, are the ones Socrates means to tease (as I put it), even while he gets on with saying things that he actually wants to say, for those able to hear it.

But the most important point here is Socrates' (Plato's) awareness of the difficulty of persuading his audience *in general*; if he has managed to persuade some of them, so much the better, but the fact is that he failed with the majority, as he always knew was likely. He began his defence by referring to the old slanders against him, perpetrated by comic poets and others, remarking that he has only a little time to try to change the jury's view of him:

So I'd like this to happen, if it's in any way better, both for you and for me, and I'd like to achieve something by my defence; but I think it's a difficult thing, and I'm not at all unaware what sort of task it is. Still, let it go in the way the god wants it to go, and I must obey the law and make my defence. (18E4–19A7)

So the members of the jury start off with the wrong view of him; somehow or other he has to get them to see him in a different light – his true light, for he has already promised to tell 'all the truth' (17B8). But the fact is that he cannot tell this audience everything, and certainly not in a speech; 'all the truth', taken at face value, would be just too complicated. What he gives them, and us, is for the most part the *outcomes* of the positions he holds, not those positions themselves. Thus he tells the jury that he is looking for wisdom and excellence, but (as we have seen) without telling them directly what the wisdom he seeks is *about*; he tells them what sorts of outcomes the possession of this wisdom will have, but not why it will have them;[75] nor does he tell them why *he* thinks wisdom and excellence are so important.[76] In the last case, he can simply rely on the fact that they are already agreed that excellence is a requirement, for a successful life; if there remains a difference between his idea and theirs of what a successful life is, that is what Socrates wants to put before his audience – rather than the philosophy that lies behind it.

---

[74] The verb *dialegesthai* is of course the standard one for philosophical *conversation* (cf. 'dialectic').

[75] How, for example, will justice always turn out to be a good thing, as he repeatedly indicates that it is, in his view?

[76] I.e. because (on his view) everyone desires the real good, so that – obviously – everyone needs to know what the real good is.

For us, the readers, on the other hand, Plato has larger ambitions: not just to present us with a choice between different lives, but to bring us to a philosophical understanding that will at the same time enable us to make the right choice. For this, we have the time that the jury lacks; and we also have other resources, in the shape of the dialogues to which the *Apology* implicitly refers us, and which it invites us to put together. Not that they will all be much more direct than the *Apology*, since Socrates' interlocutors in these dialogues will not always be noticeably more formed, intellectually, than the jury or the prosecutors in the *Apology*. But they tend to offer complementary perspectives, and, most importantly, they can use a narrower brush than the *Apology*, representing as they do that very thing that the Socrates of the *Apology* misses: one-to-one conversation.

The dialogues are in any case, fictionally, a large part of what the *Apology* summarizes in its account of Socrates' life. That is, they represent the 'reality' that Socrates describes as his quest to refute the oracle, and the life of 'examination', of himself and others, that followed.[77] Of this life he gives us few details: mainly that he doesn't teach, makes himself available to anyone, younger or older, rich or poor, and doesn't charge for his services;[78] the main emphasis is on the quest itself, which is figured as completed by his visits to the craftsmen. Such an arrangement is plainly dictated by the argument of the *Apology* at this point, which requires a strong refutation of the claim that he has wisdom in any recognized sense, together with an explanation of how he acquired a name for wisdom in the first place. This is not to suggest that Chairephon's visit to the oracle is itself a fiction, rather that it is put to strategic use: 'actually, yes, even the Delphic oracle confirmed that I have a certain wisdom, but I then managed to confirm my own view of myself as ignorant . . . and wise at the same time'. I have pointed out the 'real-life' engagements in *Meno*, *Ion* and *Symposium* which – fictionally – provide the basis for the first two parts of this supposed confirmation; if there are no 'recorded' engagements with craftsmen among the dialogues, his examination of them, according to what he says in the *Apology*, was in any case only a last resort – he went to them because he knew they knew

---

[77] For this division into two phases, I rely especially on 23B4–5 'And even now I go around looking . . .', following 22C9 'Finally I went to the craftsmen . . .'

[78] 'As for me, I was never yet a teacher to anyone, but if anyone were to want to listen to me speaking and minding my own business, whether he was older or younger, I never yet begrudged that to anyone, and I don't carry on conversations on condition of getting money for it and otherwise not, but I treat rich and poor in the same way, making myself available for them to ask questions, and if anyone wants it, to answer my questions and listen to whatever I say' (33A5–B3). Add 'citizens and foreigners', 23B5–6 (on which see further below).

'many fine things',[79] even if they were the wrong ones. These three groups, politicians, poets and craftsmen, are chosen just because they 'appeared to be wise',[80] and will allow Socrates to reach the desired, paradoxical conclusion about himself (wise but not wise). Sophists, a group that figures so prominently in the dialogues, have of course to be omitted from the list of interlocutors in the *Apology*: not only do they not 'appear wise' to anyone, except presumably themselves, but Socrates is trying to disassociate himself from them. (How then could he admit to visiting them?) The orators,[81] on the other hand, another well-represented group in the dialogues,[82] and another not previously mentioned by Socrates as among those he examined, do sneak in by the back door: Lycon, he says, the third of the prosecutors, attacked him on behalf of the orators as Meletus and Anytus did on behalf of their clients (23E–24A).

In sum, the *Apology* may be characterized as a literary version of an already literary, or at any rate partly fictionalized, Socrates. This is an important conclusion, for two reasons in particular. In the first place, obviously enough, we shall need to be doubly cautious about treating the *Apology* as any kind of historical source (doubly, because any reading of the piece will already have had to take into account its undoubted rhetorical affiliations).[83] Secondly, any part or aspect of the *Apology* may be wholly or partly determined by the work's own dynamic, making it perilous to cite it, independently of its context within the whole, as documenting even the *literary* Socrates. So for example the predominantly negative take on Socratic 'examination' in the first half of the *Apology* derives from Socrates' need to demonstrate the truth of his claim not to be any sort of teacher; once that task is completed, we are given a distinctly more positive perspective on his activity, as a search for 'good sense and truth'. (The phrase is found at 29E1, in the passage from which this chapter began.) What Socrates *now* says makes it perfectly clear that 'having one's soul in the best condition' isn't just a matter of being

---

[79] 22D2. He suggests, without actually saying, that the poets too say 'many fine things'; what he actually says is that they're like seers and oracle-mongers who say such things – without knowing what they're talking about (a central idea in the *Ion*).

[80] I.e. had a reputation for wisdom in the world at large (21B9; cf. 21D8, 21E6–22A1, 22A3).

[81] Stokes claims that 'orators' are 'politicians' (Stokes 1997 ad loc.); and indeed in normal political usage *rhētores* is a standard term for politicians, as *politikoi* (the term used to represent Anytus' clients) is not. However *Plato* normally distinguishes between *politikoi* and *rhētores*, and I see no reason for supposing that he is doing otherwise here. (My own suspicion is that Lycon, about whom we appear to know virtually nothing with any certainty, knew about nothing much except rhetoric – which in Plato's eyes leaves him pretty low in the food-chain.)

[82] Gorgias and his pupils in *Gorgias*, Meno, by implication another pupil of Gorgias, in *Meno*, Thrasymachus in *Republic*, Phaedrus as admirer of Lysias in *Phaedrus*.

[83] See n. 67 above.

aware of one's ignorance, as he is – which it couldn't be in any case, because Socrates specifically claims *not* to have a soul that's as it should be (that was what the first half of the *Apology* was about).

Thirdly, and for my present purposes more importantly, a literary *Apology*, understood as I have proposed to understand it, and treated with appropriate circumspection, is capable of offering a starting-point for the interpretation of the dialogues. This point builds on what was said in the last paragraph about the ultimately positive perspective the *Apology* offers on Socrates' activity. In his immediate post-oracle phase, he is searching for someone wise in order to be able to show the oracle to be wrong. But then, according to his narrative, he came to the conclusion that the oracle was right. What the Pythia was saying, in her usual riddling way, was that the wisest human being is 'the one who, like Socrates, has recognized that he is, in truth, worthless when it comes to wisdom' (23B3–4).

So for these reasons[84] what I still do, even now, is to go around searching and hunting down, according to the god (*kata ton theon*), among citizens and foreigners alike, anyone I think to be wise [word for word 'going around I search and hunt . . . if ever I think someone to be wise']; and whenever he doesn't seem to be wise, I come to the aid of the god and demonstrate that he isn't wise. (23B4–7)

So, at first sight, he went on in just the same way as before. But there are differences. Instead of 'going to' (21B9, 22A8, C9) those generally thought to be wise, i.e. regarded by the world as such,[85] he now 'hunts down'[86] anyone *he* thinks is wise (and among foreigners as well as his fellow-citizens). Socrates goes hunting now, not because he wants to test the oracle (and always ends up confirming its veracity), but because he wants the wisdom he lacks, and so needs to find someone who does have it (and when he's disappointed, he demonstrates the individual's ignorance to him). This is 'according to the god' in that the god has confirmed that he, Socrates, is, currently, ignorant; if he 'comes to the aid of the god' by showing that his quarry doesn't after all have what he needs, that is now just a by-product of his search, not (as it were) its point. All the succeeding descriptions of what he does suggest the same sense of the priorities.[87] In effect, what Socrates

---

[84] I take it that *tauta* at the beginning of the sentence is employed in its absolute, adverbial use (see LSJ s.v. *houtos* c.viii.i). Others, e.g., the Hackett translator and Stokes 1997, take *tauta* as the object of *zētō* and *ereunō*, but (a) the verbs seem too far away for comfort, and (b) *tauta* would have no clear reference (*what*, exactly, are the plural things Socrates is searching for?).

[85] See n. 77 above.

[86] 'Hunts down': *ereunan*, used of *tracking*, e.g., by dogs (though the verb can also more boringly denote simple exploration).

[87] 'Philosophizing . . . and examining myself and others', 28E5–6; 'spending time on this search, and philosophizing', 29C8; 'philosophizing and exhorting you . . .', 29D5–6 – cited just now (exhorting

does is to present the two sides of his activity, negative and positive, in the form of a diachronic narrative.

Socrates' engagement with his various interlocutors in the dialogues is, I suggest, to be interpreted in the light of the more positive description: what Socrates does is in each case is to 'philosophize . . . and examine'[88] one or more others, these others being people he has some reason or other for thinking wise, or could claim (however transparent the irony might be) to have some reason for thinking of in this way. That is, in each case, Socrates talks to someone who, by his (Socrates') lights, ought to possess the wisdom in question. There are the easy cases, like the politician Anytus, the poets Aristophanes, Agathon, and the rhapsode Ion, all of whom *ought* to have it, in virtue of their profession; in a different way Gorgias, in *Gorgias*.[89] Then there is Meno, in *Meno*, who suggests at once that he can give Gorgias' answer to Socrates' question about what excellence is – because, Socrates says, Gorgias has taught him how to give a ready answer to any question at all. There are the sophists, Hippias in *Hippias Minor*, Protagoras in *Protagoras*, Euthydemus and Dionysodorus in *Euthydemus*, all of whom actually claim to teach excellence. And there's Thrasymachus in *Republic* I, not a sophist (he claims), but someone who has his own idiosyncratic position on justice and excellence which he'll try to bully others into accepting.[90]

And the same kind of analysis, I propose, will be applicable to those archetypal 'Socratic' dialogues, the 'dialogues of definition'. Socrates discusses piety with Euthyphro because Euthyphro's actions suggest a complete certainty – confirmed by his immediate responses to Socrates – about what piety is, and pretty well everyone is agreed that piety is a part of excellence. Laches and Nicias in *Laches* are generals, who belong to the list of fathers concerned about the education of their sons, and ask Socrates about the subject; but as generals, they are also the sort of people who ought to know everything about courage, another agreed part of excellence. Charmides is said to be outstandingly *sōphrōn*, 'temperate', 'self-controlled', 'sound-minded', and the *Charmides* is about *sōphrosunē*. And Socrates has a particular reason for supposing that people who actually are sound-minded, courageous or pious ought to be able to give an account of what they

the Athenians to get as much 'good sense and truth' as possible); 'going round . . . persuading [you] . . . to care for [your souls]', 30A7–B1. etc.
[88] 28E5–6 again (see preceding note).
[89] Socrates shames him into saying that he must give his pupils an understanding of justice (*Gorgias* 459D–461B).
[90] The sophists and orators tend to be from outside Athens: cf. *Apology* 23B5–6 ('I hunt down any of the citizens and foreigners . . .').

possess: if, that is, excellence is *wisdom* (knowledge). Of course Socrates doesn't have this wisdom, which is why he's looking for it. But if there is someone out there who is genuinely sound-minded, or whatever, then they should have at least part of it; indeed, if excellence is all one thing, and the knowledge that constitutes it is knowledge of good and bad *tout court*, they should have it all. Similarly with 'friendship': in the *Lysis*, Lysis and Menexenus are or claim to be friends. But if they are genuinely 'friends', genuinely love each other, then they will know about what is truly loveable (the good). Or if they're too young, at least Socrates isn't, and by the end of the dialogue he hopes to have become their friend – if only he knew what that was about.

Thus, on the interpretation I am proposing, there is always a clear agenda behind any question about what this or that is (a part of excellence, or 'friendship'; or, in *Meno*, excellence as a whole). The question is not open-ended: Socrates is after a particular kind of answer.[91] And this is borne out in practice, because without exception the interlocutor will gradually find himself being steered towards some kind of identification of the *definiendum* with knowledge. Then, since that view of things will normally be quite foreign to the interlocutor, the conversation tends to end in *aporia*: impasse, perplexity. But Socrates himself will scarcely be satisfied either, because '*x* is knowledge of good and bad' will only be a beginning. What *is* the good that *x* will be knowledge of?[92] (*Aporia*, impasse, is thus doubly motivated.)

To sum up: when the Socrates of the dialogues is 'examining others', he is specifically examining people for the expertise he thinks they might, should, or could have, just as when he examines himself he is asking, most of all, how much or how little he knows. (The latter point is fundamental to his defence in the *Apology*.) And that will also mean examining people's lives, because the expertise he is examining them for is expertise in the business of life itself: what one puts first, what one goes for, what one thinks good or bad. However I shall return to this topic, of Socratic 'examination' (*exetasis*), in greater detail in the next chapter but one.

Meanwhile I shall close the present chapter by relating my argument to another piece that interpreters have proposed to treat as a 'dialogue of definition': Book I of the *Republic*. (Some think that it was originally written as a separate dialogue, because of its conformance to the pattern set by *Euthyphro*, *Laches*, etc.; in a later chapter I shall give reasons for rejecting any such idea.) The discussion of the nature of justice that occupies the major

---

[91] So too, I shall suggest, in the *Theaetetus*; see chapter 10 below.
[92] A question that will be central to the *Republic*; see chapter 9 below.

part of the book, and then subsequent books, starts off from Cephalus'
claim that his wealth has helped him to avoid injustice, because he can
always tell the truth and pay what he owes. (So here is someone who really
does think that 'from wealth excellence . . . comes': some expert *he* is.) The
fact that he has Thrasymachus as a house-guest may also have something
to do with his wealth: compare the case of Callias in the *Apology*, who has
invested in Evenus the sophist, for the sake of his sons:[93] Cephalus' son
Polemarchus is now a mature adult, but the presence of Thrasymachus
suggests clearly enough the kind of education his father will have bought
for him and his brothers Lysias and Euthydemus.[94]

If that is part of the point, we may then go on to observe that whereas
Adimantus, one of Plato's brothers, is with Polemarchus when we first
encounter him (327c), the other brother, Glaucon, is in *Socrates'* company
(327A). Glaucon will prove to be someone quite familiar with Socrates, his
ideas and arguments,[95] and is thus marked off as someone who has associated with Socrates – like Plato himself (*Apology* 34A);[96] Adimantus, after
he has helped Glaucon restate the case for injustice, at the beginning of
Book II, will play a significantly less prominent role, is not represented as
having the same familiarity as Glaucon with Socrates, and generally seems
less philosophically engaged.[97] Polemarchus takes over the argument from
Cephalus,[98] elaborating on and defending the kind of view of justice his
father had briefly suggested. The cast of the *Republic*, as Plato sets it up,
illustrates the choices available to fathers when it comes to the education of
their sons: Thrasymachus, or Socrates? Ariston, father of Glaucon and Adimantus (and of Plato, of course) seems to have had mixed success, though
Socrates praises Ariston for both of them;[99] Cephalus did less well. But for
the purposes of Socrates' search, there ought to be plenty of possibilities
here – plenty of people who, in one way or another, he might claim to
'think to be wise'. And what Socrates draws out of the argument by the

---

[93] *Apology* 20A2–C3.
[94] Also named as present at the discussion in the *Republic* (328B).
[95] See chapters 5 and 6 below.
[96] By implication Socrates seems also to treat Glaucon as *rhētorikos*, 'skilled in oratory' (*Republic* VIII,
548E–549A); is that because of his performance at the beginning of Book II, restating the case for
injustice?
[97] For other cases where interlocutors are nicely distinguished, see *Lysis* (with Penner and Rowe 2005:
61–3), and *Phaedo* (with Sedley 1995).
[98] Polemarchus is 'heir' to the argument, as Socrates puts it (331E1), as he is – presumably – to his
father's wealth.
[99] He cites with approbation a line of verse he attributes to Glaucon's lover, celebrating the two brothers'
bravery in battle: 'Sons of Ariston, divine offspring of a famous man' (*Republic* I, 368A4).

end of *Republic* I – before he claims to throw it away again[100] – conforms to what he arrives at in those independent 'dialogues of definition': that justice (like piety, etc.) is a kind of wisdom, and that it will enable a man to live well (350D, 353E).

However what then follows, in Books II–IV, is an apparently quite different approach to justice. Justice, in Book IV, is defined not as wisdom but in a quite different way: as a state of the soul in which the soul's different parts – for Book IV will argue that it is in fact tripartite – each do what belongs to them. How will all *this* fit the Socratic vision, as elaborated in that alleged manifesto of Plato's that is the *Apology*? Or must we rather conclude that the break between *Republic* I and the remaining books – where the discussion is still led by Socrates[101] – marks a departure from his vision? This question will be central in the chapters that follow: most immediately in chapter 3. But before that, in chapter 2, I shall discuss another dialogue, the *Phaedo*, which turns out to have unexpectedly close ties to the *Apology*.[102]

---

[100] One crucial question, of course, will be how serious he is about jettisoning the apparent gains of the argument: see the Appendix to chapter 5 below.

[101] And, curiously, for most of the time in conversation with Glaucon, who knows him well, and with whom he went down to the Piraeus in the first place (to see a torch-race).

[102] Unexpected ties, that is, for anyone who subscribes to the early-middle-late division of Plato's works; for *Phaedo* is a 'middle' dialogue, while the *Apology* is 'early'. (In fact, as I have said, both works belong to the earliest stylistic group: see Preliminaries above, section 10.)

CHAPTER 2

The Phaedo: *Socrates' defence continued*

Even a friendly reader, who knows his or her Plato, might at this point object that my argument has skirted at least one major obstruction that has the potential to wreck it: the *Phaedo* (not to mention the others; more of them in subsequent chapters). It is all very well, such a reader may say, to claim that Socrates and Plato are at one. But doesn't the *Phaedo* contradict this? In the *Apology*, Socrates exhibits a studied agnosticism towards the idea of his surviving after death (does he not?), whereas in the *Phaedo* he enthusiastically supports the idea, even at one point claiming to have proved it, before he is forced to retreat to a more moderate claim.[1] What is more (the objection might continue), he uses the soul's survival as the basis for a picture of philosophy that seems literally a world apart from the one he presents in the *Apology*. Instead of philosophy's being the route to a better life in this world, in the *Phaedo* it becomes a means to a better existence after death, in which the philosopher may perhaps even go to live with the gods, escaping permanently from the cycle of death and rebirth to which, Socrates now suggests, the generality of the human race is condemned.

This is a formidable objection, and all the more formidable insofar as the perspective of the *Phaedo* has, historically, been taken as partly emblematic of Plato and Platonism. It is a dialogue in which Socrates appears ready to reveal his mind, in a way in which he did not in the 'Socratic' dialogues; he also not only refers to Platonic forms, but puts them at the centre of his arguments for the survival of the soul. And the sense of a change in the air – in relation to the *Apology* – is likely to be all the greater insofar as the *Phaedo* is set within the same dramatic context as the *Apology*. How better to explain the differences between the two than by treating the latter as reflecting a Socratic, the former as a Platonic perspective on the event of the old man's death?

---

[1] *Phaedo* 107 A–B.

Formidable although the objection is, I shall argue that it fails to take account of the *uniqueness* of the *Phaedo* within the Platonic corpus. Thus, for example, and centrally, there is no single other dialogue in the whole of the Platonic corpus that comes close to matching the *Phaedo*'s apparent endorsement of a life of asceticism; and Socrates' hint of a permanent escape for the philosopher is not only not followed up elsewhere but comes close to being rejected.[2] Either the *Phaedo* is evidence that we shouldn't, after all, be reading from one dialogue to another; or it is an isolated thought-experiment; or its anomalous features have another explanation that will bring the dialogue into line with others. The last will be my preferred option; much will turn on the difference of audience, as marked by the nature of the people Socrates is addressing, between *Phaedo* and *Apology* – and indeed *Phaedo* and any other dialogue.

I THE MYTH: TWO KINDS OF HADES

These, however, will be issues for the second part of this chapter. In the first part, and by way of beginning the task of comparing the outcomes of the *Phaedo* with what we[3] have found in the *Apology*, I propose to discuss the eschatology of the dialogue.

I begin by noting that despite appearances, or at any rate what has appeared to many interpreters, the attitudes towards death that Socrates expresses in the two works are remarkably similar. In the *Apology*, Socrates offers two possibilities: (a) that the dead person is '*as it were (hoion)*[4] nothing, and has no perception of anything' (40c5–7); (b) that 'in accordance with what is said a certain change takes place, and a change in the place of residence (*metoikēsis . . . tou topou*) for the soul, from here to another place' (c7–9). Option (a) plainly operates with a Homeric model of Hades, and of the soul, which without outside intervention is

---

[2] This in the *Phaedrus* myth (*Phaedrus* 246 A–257 A), which makes any escape (a) contingent on repeated success in living a philosophical life, and (b) in any case only temporary, since the philosophical soul will have to run the gamut like every other soul when its 7,000-year period of parole comes to an end. All this, of course, is subject to the rider that to the extent that in both *Phaedo* and *Phaedrus* the eschatological material is for the most part contained within *myths*, we shall need to reach some general conclusions about how we are to handle Platonic myth-making/story-telling before we can say anything firm about what he actually *believed* in this area (if indeed we can ever say anything firm about it at all). However the present chapter will make some contributions in this direction.

[3] The 'we' here is intended to include any reader inclined to be sympathetic to the reading I have proposed for the *Apology*; absent such sympathy, 'we' signifies 'I'.

[4] Omitted in the Hackett translation.

mindless;[5] the 'soul' – Homer's version of it[6] – can apparently reflect on its condition, and talk, only when given blood to drink.[7] This is to be distinguished from actual extinction (hence '*as it were* nothing'), a possibility that Socrates does not consider at all – and perhaps does not need to, insofar as option (a) is functionally equivalent to it. Option (b), for its part, will fit with any eschatology which is neither of the above (i.e. which neither is (a) nor treats death as extinction): it hints at the promises held out by mystery religion, the Pythagoreans and – possibly – others[8] of a better fate for the initiated, but does so in thoroughly literary terms, shaped by Socrates' own preoccupations – so transforming Odysseus' encounter with the mindless shades into a Socratic philosophical encounter with the great – or not so great – minds of the past, still in full possession of their faculties.

If we then compare this with the situation in the *Phaedo*, we find rather few differences. Cebes at *Phaedo* 70A compares what is plainly option (a) to a state of extinction, using Homer's own conceit of the dead soul as like smoke;[9] Socrates then defends what is equally plainly a version of (b), which he has already offered as his own preferred option. The only obvious difference between *Apology* and *Phaedo* is that in *Apology* Socrates formally offers the jury an open choice between (a) and (b), whereas in *Phaedo* he starts from (b) as his own option. However even this difference is likely to be more apparent than real, if we take into account Socrates' belief, which he declares at *Apology* 41D2, that '(the good man's) affairs are not neglected

---

5 *Iliad* 23.103–4 *ē ra tis esti kai ein Aidao domoisin | psuchē kai eidōlon, atar phrenes ouk eni pampan* ('Alas – there, in the halls of Hades, there is a kind of | soul and shadow, but in it there is no mind at all').

6 Homer's Hades is populated with a rather different kind of 'soul' from the Platonic: one which is insubstantial yet still, to a visitor like Odysseus, looks like the living person whose counterpart it is, as that person was at the time of his/her death.

7 Socrates here counters an objection to his overall stance that might otherwise have been raised by his comparison of himself with Achilles. Achilles in the *Odyssey* notoriously complains to Odysseus how *appalling* it is to be in Hades (quoted by Socrates in *Republic* VII: see Introduction above, p. 64n.33); if so, was his choice of death over life after all so sensible? Socrates anticipates this: if Achilles in Hades is mindless, he can't see his life as miserable.

8 The mention of Triptolemus at 41A4 suggests a link with the Eleusinian mysteries, with which Triptolemus is intimately connected. Pythagoreans: see below, esp. n. 64. Others: Orphics? (However I am for the present content to go along with E. R. Dodds's general scepticism about the demonstrability of 'Orphic' influences on Plato: see Dodds 1959: 297–8, 300, 373–6 – all in reference to the *Gorgias*, but the general conclusions seem to me – for the moment – to be applicable to the Platonic corpus as a whole.)

9 70A4–6: '(people are afraid that the soul) exits like breath or smoke, scattered and gone, flying off, and is no longer anything anywhere', recalling *Iliad* 23.100–1 'and his soul went beneath the earth like smoke', with 16.856, 22.362 'and his soul was gone from his limbs, flying to Hades'.

by (the) gods', coupled with his comparison, just before, of an eternal future of non-perception to a single night of dreamless sleep:

I think that not just a private citizen but the Great King himself would find it easy to count the number of days and nights [that he passed better and more pleasantly than] ones like these; so that if that's the sort of thing death is, I myself count it a gain. (40D7–E1)

and equally a gain, one might add, for everyone. If that were the true outcome, how would *that* cohere with Socrates' belief that the gods care for 'affairs of the good man'?[10]

The connections between the two works, *Phaedo* and *Apology*, are closer still than this. *Phaedo* starts with, and from, *Apology*. When Socrates says at *Phaedo* 63B that he supposes Simmias and Cebes to be saying that he must defend himself 'as if in a lawcourt', and that he'll try to do so 'more persuasively to you than I did to the jury', he is referring not just, or not at all, to the real trial and his real defence, but to the defence he put up in the *Apology*. He starts by picking up part of, and giving a different version of, that literary defence, adapting it to the immediate context:

Come then . . . let me try to defend myself more persuasively to you than I did to the jury. Because if I didn't believe . . . that I shall enter the presence, first, of other gods [i.e. those of the underworld, to be distinguished from their upper world counterparts, just mentioned] that are wise and good, and next of dead people, too, that are better than those in this world, then it would be unjust of me not to be resentful at death; but as it is, be assured that I expect to arrive in the presence of good men – well, *that* I wouldn't at all insist on, but that I shall enter the presence of gods who are entirely good, be assured that if there's anything I should insist on in such things, it's that. So that's why I'm not so resentful, but rather have good hope that there is something for those who've died, and in fact, as we've long been told, something much better for the good than for the bad. *(Phaedo* 63B4–C7)

Compare *Apology* 40E–41C: there is 'much hope' (*pollē elpis*, 40C4), Socrates says, that death is a good thing, because it is either like an endless, dreamless sleep, or it is, 'as we've been told', a change of place:

If . . . what we are told is true and all who have died are there, what greater good could there be, gentlemen of the jury? For if any new arrival in Hades who has got away from those who call themselves judges here will find those true judges who are said to sit in judgement there, Minos and Rhadamanthus and Aeacus and Triptolemus and as many of the other demi-gods who became just in their

---

[10] Cf. *Phaedo* 107C5–8 'if death were a release from everything, it would be a godsend for the bad when they died to be released from their own badness along with their soul'.

own life, would that be a poor kind of change of place? [Socrates then goes on to list Orpheus, Musaeus, Hesiod, Homer; Palamedes and Telamonian Ajax, as examples of those unjustly convicted; Agamemnon, Odysseus, Sisyphus . . .] . . . it would be an extraordinary happiness to converse (*dialegesthai*) with them, to be with them and to examine them. People there certainly don't put one to death for it, I imagine; they're happier than people here in every respect, and especially because for the rest of time they are deathless, if indeed what we are told is true. (40E4–41C7)

If we put these two passages together, as I myself think it clear that Plato intended us to do, the effect is to make the *Phaedo* take up, and develop, the rhetoric of the *Apology* passage. That is the particular point of Socrates' saying that he must 'try to defend myself more persuasively than I did': he must explain just why he thinks philosophers like himself will be better off in Hades, since after all, if there are people who say that there will be 'something far better for the good than for the wicked', there are also plenty of people who say that things are no better for them. If Sisyphus, the last person mentioned in the *Apology* passage, is distinguished for the particularly bad time he is having in Hades,[11] in the Homeric–Hesiodic tradition generally it takes extraordinary favouritism from the gods to ensure that anyone goes anywhere except to Hades, and that is a notoriously dreadful and gloomy place to be in for eternity.[12]

One particularly compelling reason for connecting the *Phaedo* with the *Apology* in this context lies in the way the Socrates of the *Phaedo* links his desire to put on a more persuasive defence with his belief that the good will do better in Hades than the bad (I cite the passage – 63B4–9 – again):

Come then . . . let me try to defend myself more persuasively to you than I did to the jury. Because if I didn't believe . . . that I shall enter the presence, first, of other gods that are wise and good, and next of dead people, too, that are better than those in this world, then it would be unjust of me not to be resentful at death . . .

That is, the defence turns out to be a defence of *this belief*, and not at all of himself in general. It hardly needs to be said that there can be no real reference to that fictional account of what occurred at the trial, so that 'I must defend myself more persuasively than I did to the jurors' is, as it were officially, a comparison of his defence now, before Simmias and Cebes, with his more important defence at the actual trial. Only it cannot avoid also being a literary reference to that statement of belief in the *Apology*.

---

[11] And indeed by Socrates himself, elsewhere: see chapter 1, n. 60 above.

[12] Cf. n. 7 on Achilles – and he was the son of a goddess. By contrast Menelaus received special treatment apparently because he managed to marry a daughter of Zeus; hardly much question of goodness of any sort in his case, except perhaps by association (marriage).

The clinching point is perhaps that apparently heartless suggestion that he'll meet 'better people in Hades than I do here' – softened in a few lines by an 'I wouldn't at all insist on that', and still further at 69E1–2: 'believing that there too, no less than here, I'll encounter good masters and companions'. The reference was always, at least primarily, to that fantasy in the *Apology* of his meeting Homer, Palamedes, Agamemnon and the others (after he has met those 'true jurors').[13] The same reference also lies behind the first softening; because after all what Socrates will do when he meets these allegedly 'better' people is to examine them, and see if they really are better, i.e. wiser.

In general, it has to be said that the *Apology* really does do a poor job of explaining Socrates' cheerfulness at the prospect of death. It's not true, as he claims, that those who fear death behave as if they know death is bad; it's enough that they think it might be – and if he thinks it won't be, even on the worse of the two options he considers, that's evidently just because of what Homer says about the mindless condition of the dead, and Homer's wisdom has yet to be established. (A reliable answer to the question – the dead: mindless or not? – will have to wait, it seems, till Socrates gets to Hades; and on Socrates' own account most of what Homer says about Hades is wrong anyway.) So why is he so cheerful, after all? The *Phaedo* tells us, setting out to show, *by argument*, both that the soul survives death and, importantly, that it has 'some power and good sense (*phronēsis*)'.[14] The one thing it cannot show is that the gods will look after the good man, even after he is dead; as in the *Apology*, that remains a matter of mere conviction. What the *Phaedo* adds, in other words, is a series of arguments for believing at least part of what Socrates has already shown in the *Apology* that he believes – or rather, that, plus a remarkable illustration of the proposal that we humans live in a world that rewards the good for their goodness.

This illustration comes in the shape of the myth at the end of the *Phaedo*, though the myth has been thoroughly prepared for in what precedes it: especially in the second and third arguments for the soul's survival (the arguments from recollection and from the affinity of the soul to the forms respectively), and in the passage traditionally labelled as Socrates' 'autobiography'.[15] In the case of the two arguments, Socrates introduces the idea

---

[13] I.e. Minos, Rhadamanthus, Aeacus, Triptolemus, 'and all those other demigods (heroes) who achieved justice in their own lives' (41A3–5).

[14] *Phaedo* 70B3–4; this is picked up, at the end of the final argument, by Socrates' suggestion that the soul has been shown to go off, when a person dies, 'safe and undestroyed/indestructible' (*sōn kai adiaphthoron*, 106E6–7).

[15] *Phaedo* 73A–76E; 78B–84A; 96A–100A.

of the soul's transmigration, from one body to another, and the possibility of its escaping the cycle of rebirth altogether,[16] while in his 'autobiography' he describes the kind of account of the cause of things that he was looking for (he says) in his youth, but failed to get from the experts in physics like Anaxagoras or anywhere else: a *teleological* account, which showed 'the good that binds, binding and holding' things together.[17] The myth offers just such an account of the earth and its topography, making it provide efficiently for the reward and punishment of the good and bad after their 'death', i.e. their separation, as souls, from their current bodies.[18]

Socrates of course claims in the *Apology*, with his human jurors as audience, that he knows nothing about physics at all (19C); if Meletus suggests otherwise, he must be confusing him with Anaxagoras (26D–E). And he repeats the same claim in the *Phaedo*, albeit in a different form: 'I *used* to concern myself with such things – and hoped to get decent answers from people like Anaxagoras; but no more.' This might seem to make the myth peculiarly un-Socratic: how could someone who says that natural philosophy is nothing to do with him come up with so impressive a piece of speculation about nature, even if he does claim that it isn't his (of course),[19] and isn't something he *knows* about?[20] (Surely this must be *Plato*, then, not Socrates?) However this is to miss the way that Socrates characterizes the account he says persuades him. 'There are many amazing places of the earth,' he says by way of introduction, 'and the earth itself is neither of the sort nor of the size *it's judged (doxazetai) to be by those accustomed to talking about (the) earth*, as someone's persuaded me to believe' (108C5–8). As I take it, Socrates is specifically saying that the account isn't a scientific one at all. His mysterious informer, the 'someone' who persuaded him, is no natural philosopher, or at any rate no geographer. (At least one natural philosopher, Empedocles, was in fact perfectly happy to talk eschatology.) He is, rather, some religious expert, real or imaginary; the same kind of source, perhaps, that lay behind Socrates' earlier reference to the possibility, for the initiated, of permanent escape from the ills of this life.[21]

But this needs a little more precision. What Socrates has heard is hardly something that he could plausibly claim to have heard from any ordinary religious expert, since no such expert would talk about escape through

---

[16] ' . . . truly passing the rest of time with (the) gods, as is said of the initiated' (81A8–10) – but actually Socrates has already talked about *this* idea back at 69C, where it formed part of an 'ancient riddle'.

[17] *Phaedo* 99C5–6 (. . . *to agathon kai deon sundein kai sunechein*).

[18] See Sedley 1990.   [19] It's something he's been 'persuaded' about (108C8).

[20] 108D7–8 ('even if I did know [sc. about what I'm going to describe to you]').

[21] See n. 16 above.

purification *by philosophy* (114C3); unless, that is, he were a Pythagorean (so combining what may crudely be called a 'religious' outlook with a distinctly intellectual one). This is part of the reason why the source of Socrates' story, his brilliant description of the earth and the eschatological narrative which it founds, is left so indeterminate; namely because that description is a *mélange*, an elaboration of elements from Eleusinian religion and from Pythagoreanism (and maybe from elsewhere too). But the chief explanation for Socrates' vagueness about his source – as I shall now argue – is that the story, in the end, owes most to Plato's own imagination, and that it is in large part allegorical. (So it is not something Socrates could have got from anyone, i.e. except Plato. But I shall also argue that there is nothing in the allegory over which Plato would have wished to assert his rights of ownership over Socrates'.)

One of the myth's strangest aspects is the way it allows the victims of some crimes – those their authors have regretted, having committed them e.g., under the influence of passion – to determine the length of the criminals' punishment.[22] Having spent a year in Tartarus, this class of criminals is thrown up by the rivers Cocytus or Pyriphlegethon into the Acherusian lake, and must then supplicate their victims for permission to end their punishment by leaving the lake and the rivers behind them; but if they fail in their supplication, back they go, and the process will not stop until they succeed, 'for this is the penalty ordained by the judges' (113B5–6). Thus, it seems, justice has not merely to be done, but has to be *felt* to be done by the victims, who while having lived only middling lives themselves[23] nevertheless find themselves, instead of the judges, in control of the perpetrators' fates – and this when the perpetrators have already repented. Apparently everything would depend on the whim of souls with somewhat less than perfect judgement; they might even decide to leave the sufferers to suffer in perpetuity. This hardly seems consistent with the kind of rational justice Socrates calls for in the *Apology*; and the setting of the *Phaedo*, after Socrates' trial and in the hours leading up to his execution, seems by itself to demand a degree of continuity between the two works.[24]

There is also something odd about the fate of those 'middling' souls themselves, on the shores of Acheron. They are presumably to be identified with the souls described back in 82A10–B3:

---

[22] 113E6–E6.   [23] See 113D4–E1 for this characterization of the souls at Lake Acheron.

[24] Or, in case this begs the question, I appeal to those references in the *Phaedo* back to the *Apology*, which seem to establish that Plato means us to read them together, as part of the same sequence of events around the same person (Socrates).

'Then happiest', [Socrates] said, 'even of [the bad, i.e. the unpurified, weighed down with body/bodily desire], because they go to a place better than the one the others go to, are those who have practised the demotic sort of excellence, the sort that belongs to a member of a *polis* (*tēn dēmotikēn kai politikēn aretēn*), which they call by the name of sound-mindedness (*sōphrosunē*) and justice, which has come about through habit without philosophy and intelligence?'

'How [asks Cebes] are these happiest?'

'Because it's likely that these arrive back in some such political, cooperative (*hēmeron*) race of creatures, whether of bees or wasps or ants, and indeed back in the same race they once belonged to, the human one, and that moderate men/men of a decent size[25] come out of them.'

'That's likely enough.'

They 'arrive back', of course, after their sojourn in Hades as described in the myth:

And those who have lived middling lives, after they have been brought to the [river] Acheron, and boarded the vessels (*ochēmata*) available to them, arrive at the lake on these, and there they live and are purified, being released from their injustices, if any of them has committed one, by paying penalties, and carrying off honours for their good deeds to each other (euergesiai), each according to his deserts. (113D4–E1)

Now if we look back to what must be the original description of 'demotic', unphilosophical excellence, at 69A–D, we find Socrates saying he fears it is

a kind of shadow-painting . . . truly slave-like, and containing nothing healthy, nor true, and in truth sound-mindedness and justice and courage genuinely (*tōi onti*) are a kind of purification from [the pleasures, pains and fears dominating the calculus behind unphilosophical excellence], and wisdom itself is a kind of purifying rite (*katharmos*). And probably these people who established the rites for us were no mean individuals, and were genuinely (*tōi onti*) riddling all those years ago when they said that whoever arrives in Hades without experience of the rites and uninitiated will lie in the mud, while he who has arrived there purified and initiated will live with (the) gods. (69B6–C7)

How, we may reasonably ask, will the uninitiated be purified in Hades by 'paying penalties', as Socrates suggests in 113D–E, if the cause of their 'impurity' was their lack of philosophy? Shouldn't they be getting some philosophy instead? And Socrates himself ought to be suggesting the same thing, if he's the same Socrates who told off Meletus, in the *Apology*, for

---

[25] The Greek is *metrioi andres*: cf. Herodotus 2.32, where the contrast is with pygmies; here the contrast is with men who have become *insects*.

taking him to court instead of trying to 'teach and admonish' him, because clearly it could only have been *ignorance* that caused him to corrupt the young. (How could he have done it knowingly? By corrupting them he would have made them worse, and everyone knows that bad people damage those near them.)[26]

In other words, while the myth claims to describe a world, and an order of things, which ensures that everyone gets their just deserts, the justice system it actually describes seems importantly flawed. Socrates himself warns us not to trust in the detail of the myth,[27] and the warning seems to have a double point: firstly, and more obviously, that any intelligent person should know not to believe detailed reports without proper evidence, but secondly, that there are aspects of his report that are unbelievable in any case – that is, not even believable by him. If the world really is so structured as to ensure justice, then it shouldn't be as he has described it; that is, the system for dealing with 'sinners' had better be part of what Socrates suggests that 'no intelligent person should insist on' (even while claiming that such a person *should* suppose 'either this or something like it' to be true: *Phaedo* 114D1–3).

So why does Plato have Socrates introduce so flawed a system for delivering justice in a supposedly just cosmos? The solution to the puzzle is suggested by a combination of two observations. We may first observe that the parts of the mythical penal system in question exhibit aspects of *ordinary* Athenian practice. Thus the case of the repentant parricides and matricides readily connects with the fact that, in the absence of public prosecutors, the Athenian system relied heavily on the families of the victims, or the victims themselves, to initiate any prosecution and to carry the process through to completion; the situation envisaged at Lake Acheron just has the advantage that the victim can be involved even in cases of homicide. As for what happens to the middling souls, with 'civic' or 'demotic' excellence, the general rule not just in Athenian but presumably in any criminal justice system one might name is that the criminal would be 'freed' from his crime, and so as it were 'purified', by paying the appropriate penalty.[28] (Contrast the kind

---

[26] *Apology* 25D–26A. See chapter 4 below for similar puzzles about the *Gorgias*.

[27] ' . . . to insist that things are as I have gone through them doesn't befit a man of intelligence; but that either this or something like it is true of our souls and their dwelling-places, given that *deathlessness* is something that evidently belongs to the soul, this seems to befit me and worth the risk to believe that it is so . . .' (114D1–6).

[28] The middling sort receive honours ('each according to his deserts') for 'the good they have done to each other': not having genuine excellence, they wouldn't have performed any genuinely excellent actions – and I wonder whether, from a Socratic point of view, any of them could have done any genuine good to each other either. A similar point may lurk beneath 'if any of them has committed [an injustice]'; if doing injustice is a matter of inflicting genuine harm (one need not add 'unjustifiably',

of case Socrates envisages in the *Apology*, where someone has gone wrong through ignorance; the 'penalty' would take just as much time as it took to teach him what he didn't know.)

The second observation to be made is that the Socrates of the *Phaedo* has already talked about two different kinds of Hades. On the one hand there is the traditional Hades (*Haidēs*), the one we all go to when we die; on the other, there is the *a-ides*, the *unseen*, to which only the philosophical soul has access – and is, for that kind of soul, its goal or destination even during this life.[29] The pun is carefully prepared for, during the argument from affinity, by the division of things into what can be seen (what is *horaton*) and what cannot (the *aïdes* or *aoraton*):[30] the soul is more like the *aïdes* than the body, and 'when it investigates by itself, it goes/it is gone (*oichetai*) to that place [sc. the *aïdēs* one], to what is pure and always is and is deathless and in the same state[31] whereas when it uses the senses 'it is dragged by the body to the things that are never the same'.[32] Socrates then goes on to suggest that at death

the soul . . . , the unseen (*to aïdes*), goes/is gone (*oichetai*) to such a place [i. e. an unseen one], another one [i.e. other than the one it 'went to' in life], noble and pure and unseen, to [the place] of Hades in truth, to the presence of the good and wise god,[33] where if god wishes it my soul too must shortly go (80D5–8):

being what it is (Socrates asks), can we really suppose that the soul is at once blown apart by the wind (when even the body, being what *it* is, may last some considerable time)?

---

if – as Socrates proposes elsewhere, perhaps most explicitly at *Crito* 49C–E – the good man never harms anyone), no 'middling' soul will be able to do that either. Objection: doesn't Socrates' defence in the *Crito* of his decision to abide by the court's verdict amount to, or imply, an acceptance of the Athenian legal system? I respond: *Crito* 49C–E offers the grounds on which *he* might defend his own decision, on the hypothesis, proposed by Crito, that an injustice has been done to him (a hypothesis that will only stand if the court has actually done him any harm – something that *Apology* 30C–D throws into serious doubt); what the personified Laws then offer is *their* version of the kind of defence he should offer, which he finally accepts *faute de mieux* (*Crito* 54D: 'as far as my present beliefs go', *hosa ge ta nun emoi dokounta*). (And undermining the city's legal system while having nothing to put in its place is presumably not something to be undertaken lightly: Socrates may *have* an alternative, i.e. a philosophical one, but Athens is evidently unprepared to accept it.) The *Crito* might be read as Plato's reassurance to the Athenians that the Socratic (Platonic) project both does and does not pose a threat to their institutions.

[29] For the same idea in the *Republic*, see Introduction, p. 63.   [30] 79A7, 9–10, etc.
[31] 79D1–2.   [32] 79C6–7.
[33] I.e. the god Hades. 'To Hades' is typically, as in the present sentence, *eis Haidou*, i.e. 'to [the house/place] of Hades'; hence the easy transition – given Socrates' belief, expressed in that passage, 63B4–C7, cited at the beginning of the present chapter, that after death he will join the company of (other) good and wise gods – to the idea that the philosophical soul after death will be in the presence of 'the good and wise god' (Hades).

So the philosophical soul is in a way in Hades already, before it even goes there[34] – and that, of course, is in line with Socrates' claim at the beginning of his defence, that what genuine philosophers *do*[35] is 'dying and being dead' (64A6). The puzzle about the treatment of non-philosophical souls and their punishment in the myth may, I suggest, be resolved by supposing that these souls too have their own Hades above ground, as it were, as well as one below it. Just as philosophers may enjoy the rewards of death – separation from the body – even in life, so non-philosophers pay the penalty for their lack of intelligence before death as well as after it. The myth, in other words, is *both* an account (however rough and sketchy, and however credible or incredible in its detail) of what awaits us after death, *and* an allegory of life as we live it now. Those middling souls are at their Acherusian lake even now, in life, punishing and rewarding each other (and dealing with serious criminals), in the only way they know how, just as their philosophical counterparts are already in their heaven. And there is a fair chance, I think, that we are also to think of them as already changed into the creatures whose bodies they will inhabit in their next life – whether bees, wasps, ants, or men (82B): that, at any rate, will fit nicely with the comparison in the myth of people round the Mediterranean to 'ants'[36] or frogs around a pond'[37] (109B2),[38] and it might also give point to the detail that the souls in question 'boarded the vessels available to them' to travel down the Acheron river (113D5–6). Men would need boats like Charon's; souls 'boarding' bees and wasps could fly . . . (I say nothing about ants.)[39] If the main point about their 'transmigration' into animals is that their behaviour has come to resemble, and to be no superior to, that of animals, then in a way they will also have been bees, wasps, ants or whatever in life too – only without the appropriate body.[40] As for those 'who seem to have

---

[34] Cf. the reference in 107C2–3 to 'this time . . . in which we do what we call living' – though this is already (or also?) motivated by the Pythagorean idea of the body as a tomb (*sōma/sēma*; see *Gorgias* 493A).

[35] 'Do' here is *epitēdeuein*, for which 'training' (*meletan*) will later be substituted (67E5 with D8); of course the later pun will work better if philosophers are pictured as being, in a sense, actually already dead. (For a similar though less explicit connection between separation from things bodily and one kind of death, see *Republic* VII, 519A–C.)

[36] That Plato puts ants before frogs might perhaps be intended to signal the connection; at any rate – though this is said from a purely northern European standpoint – we might be more likely to expect to find frogs than ants around ponds (or swamps).

[37] Or 'swamp' (*telma*) – which might appropriately recall the idea that the uninitiated will 'lie in the mud' at 69C6.

[38] So they are now (like) ants . . . round a pond, as they will be ants . . . around a lake.

[39] The myth of course treats souls in the way that Homer treats his 'souls' (shades), i.e. as having visible shape, location, etc. For the body as a 'vessel', or *ochēma*, see *Timaeus* 69C7.

[40] See Rowe 2005a, which illustrates the idea in question through Flann O'Brien's *The Third Policeman* (but the point is in any case pretty much spelled out in 81E).

excelled in their progress towards living a pious life', and are rewarded by 'being released and set free from the places in the earth as if from prisons' in order to live on the pure outer surface of the earth (114B6–C2), this is presumably the company to which Socrates belongs: freed from the prison of the earth after death as he has freed himself from the prison of the body in life through philosophy,[41] and as he will be freed from the city's prison by the hemlock. Finally there are those who 'having purified themselves adequately by philosophy live without bodies altogether for the whole of time to come . . .' (114C2–4): not now the know-nothing Socrates and his ilk, but some superior brand of philosophers who will have advanced far enough to be compared to gods, whether in this life or the next.[42]

If this kind of reading is along the right lines, the myth will after all have introduced rather little of substance, on the subject of our fate after death, that is not also contained or implied in the *Apology* (except insofar as Socrates seems to allow, here in the myth, that humans may after all cross the boundary separating them from gods: more on this in the second part of the present chapter). The crucial point is still that the good man – the philosopher[43] – will be rewarded after death. If now, in the myth, we do seem also to be told something about the fate of non-philosophers, *that* description turns out at least in large part to be not so much of the underworld as of the world of the living. What the *Phaedo* provides may fairly be called a colourful, and highly complex, illustration of the limitations to the perspectives of ordinary, non-philosophical people that the Socrates of the *Apology* says he has spent his life combatting: by contrast with the soaring freedom of the philosophical soul, such people live a kind of death, like ants/frogs round a pond. The whole universe is now found to be as philosopher-friendly, *sub specie aeternitatis*, as it presently appears – at least in the tiny portion of it represented by Athens – to be hostile to philosophers. Justice will be done; that is, philosophers will have

---

[41] For the idea of the body as a prison or guard-house (*phroura*), see 62B3–4; though there the image is of a prison from which we are not permitted to release ourselves (our souls) by what might seem the easiest route, i.e. suicide.

[42] Another part of the myth that fits the allegorical reading is the passage where Socrates corrects Aeschylus' character Telephus for saying that there is only a single path leading to Hades (107E–108A). 'It doesn't seem a simple path or just one to me,' he says at 108A1–2 (and this in the middle of a story he claims to have got from elsewhere), because otherwise there wouldn't be a need for guides; 'for I imagine one wouldn't make a mistake in any direction (*oudamose*) if there were only one road . . .' (A2–4). But 'the orderly and wise (*phronimos*) soul follows [his guide] and is not ignorant of the circumstances [*ta paronta*: his surroundings, and/or his ignorance, *Apology*-style?] . . .' (A6–7; cf. e.g., 82D). The context will bear close comparison e.g., with passages in *Republic* and *Symposium* where the philosophical soul is led, by a single if indeterminate guide, towards its goal.

[43] Who will at least be *better*, wiser than others.

the freedom, somewhere and somehow, to ply their trade and urge others to wisdom, and to justice. But again, that is what the *Apology* too predicts, if with a rather simpler vision of Hades, modifying Homer instead of taking flight, like the *Phaedo*, from the motifs provided by mystery religion and by the Pythagoreans.

2 FORMS; BODY AND SOUL

'That is as may be,' someone might interject at this point (no doubt the objector who intervened at the beginning of the chapter); 'but the *Phaedo* still portrays the philosopher, and philosophy itself, in a radically different way from the *Apology*. Most importantly, there is all that talk about forms, a category of object of which there is not the faintest trace in the *Apology*; and what about all that talk about the need to separate the soul from the body, and to assimilate oneself to a state of pure reason? Nothing of that in the *Apology* either. So there is still a large distance between the two works – and that I still choose to call the distance between Socrates and Plato.'

I begin with the first point, about forms; and here the outcome of my argument will be consistent with what I have already said earlier on the subject of forms, in a more general way.[44] Briefly: when Socrates introduces objects like '(the) just itself', '(the) beautiful itself', and '(the) good itself' for the first time in *Phaedo* 65D, he is – I claim – doing no more and no less than (re-)introducing the very sorts of things whose definitions he seeks in the so-called 'Socratic' dialogues, and the search for which preoccupies him in the life he describes in the *Apology*. And when he makes his next move, of establishing that we cannot find out what each such thing is 'most truly' through the body and its senses, and that we'll come closer to knowing what it is, the more, and the more accurately, we apply our thought to *the thing itself* (to paraphrase 65D11–E4), Socrates connects this with the simple fact that we can't see, or grasp with any of the other senses, 'the essence of each thing, what it actually is'. We can't see, or hear . . . justice, or beauty . . . only just things – people and actions – and beautiful things; we can't grasp *size* (another of Socrates' examples) with the senses, only things of a certain size. Socrates implicitly concedes that the senses can give us some sort of hold on justice, beauty, size . . . only 'the truest aspect of them is not observed through the body' (E1–2). He then draws the inference that the soul will

---

[44] See Preliminaries, section 10.

'come closest to knowing' these things (E4) '*most purely*' (*katharōtata*, E6) if someone

'approaches ["goes to"] each thing as much as possible by means of thought (*dianoia*) by itself, neither bringing in any vision to complement one's thinking, nor dragging in any other sense to accompany one's reasoning, but using thought unalloyed, itself by itself, to try to hunt down each of the things that are, unalloyed, itself by itself, freed as much as possible from eyes and ears and so to speak the whole body, as something that brings confusion (*tarattein*) and prevents the soul from acquiring truth and good sense (*phronēsis*)[45] when it shares in the hunt – is it not this person, Simmias, the one who will hit the target in his search for what is, if anyone[46] will?'

'What you say . . . Socrates, is superlatively true.' (65E6–66A8)

What Simmias[47] agrees to here is just a more specific, and philosophical, version of something that a few moments ago Socrates said even the poets knew, that people's sight and hearing tend to mislead (and they're the most accurate of the senses; the others are even worse); if our soul tries to investigate anything with the body, in order to acquire 'good sense', it's deceived, and only in reasoning (or 'calculation': *logizesthai*, 64C2, 5) does any aspect of things become clear (65A9–C9). This, then, Socrates says, is the second context in which 'the philosopher's soul puts a most negative value on (*atimazei*) the body and takes flight from it, and seeks to be itself [alone] by itself' (65C11–D1). (The passage as a whole is explaining Socrates' claim that real philosophers 'practise dying and being dead', death having been defined at 64C4–8 as the release of the soul from the body, so that each, soul and body, now subsists separately from the other.) The first such context in which the philosopher devalues the body was in the ordinary conduct of life: philosophers, as philosophers, have no great interest in 'so-called pleasures'[48] like those of food and drink, nor are they much exercised about sex, or about dressing up (except insofar as they need to).[49] Conclusion: such a person, the philosopher, 'stands back as far as he can

---

45 For this pairing, see *Apology* 29E1 (I translate *phronēsis* here in *Phaedo* as 'good sense' in order to bring out the connection: see chapter 1, pp. 74–5 above).

46 For this translation of the Greek (*eiper . . . tis allos*), see Dover on *Symposium* 211D2–3; see also *Phaedo* 65C2, where the translation of *eiper pou allothi* as 'if anywhere' (not 'if anywhere else') is guaranteed.

47 Who is, to judge from his responses, quite familiar with Socratic ideas and methods; as is his fellow-interlocutor Cebes, who has for example 'often' heard Socrates identifying learning with recollection (72E).

48 64D2.

49 It hardly needs pointing out that the list is based on Socrates' lifestyle (even more so in the detail: for an occasion when he did get dressed up, and put shoes on, see *Symposium*).

from the body, and is turned towards the soul'.[50] From a combination of both examples of the philosopher's rejection (so far as this is possible) of the body Socrates now, in 66B, after the passage introducing forms, constructs an imaginary piece of reasoning on the part of 'genuine philosophers' (B2):

From all of this some such idea as the following must occur to genuine philosophers – they must say some such thing as this to each other: 'Very likely there brings us and our reason out [sc. of here?] in our inquiry, like a path, [the consideration] that[51] so long as we have our body, and our soul us defiled by being in the company of this kind of badness, we'll never adequately acquire what we desire; and we assert that this is the truth.[52] (66B1–7)

'We'll never adequately acquire what we desire': this on two grounds, the 'genuine philosophers' continue: first, that the body is always asserting its needs – it has to be fed and watered, it gets ill, it

'fills us full of passions and desires and all sorts of illusions (*eidōla*) and a whole array of rubbish, so that really and truly it is not possible for us – as the saying goes – even to think at any moment about anything. For wars and civil discord and fighting have no other origin except in the body and its desires . . . ' (66C2–7)

and the second reason (the last straw) is that when we *do* get time off from looking after the body to investigate something, 'it keeps on turning up everywhere in our inquiries and causing uproar and throwing out [our reasoning] so that we can't see the truth' (66D5–7). So, the speakers conclude,

'we've really proved that if we're ever going to know anything in its purity (*katharōs*), we need to be free of our bodies and observe the things themselves with our souls by themselves; and it's then, it seems, that we'll have what we desire and are lovers of, good sense ["wisdom", *phronēsis*], that is, when we die – so the argument indicates – but not while we're alive. For [this, presumably, is "the argument"] if it isn't possible to know anything in the company of the body, then one of two things holds: either knowing isn't possible for us anywhere, or it's possible for us when we've died; for then the soul will be itself by itself, apart from the body, and not before that. And while we're alive this, it seems, is how we'll be closest to knowing – if as much as possible we avoid the company of the body, and don't go into partnership with it, except so far as we cannot avoid it, and we don't fill ourselves up with *its* nature, but purify ourselves from it until the god himself releases us; and when released, pure like this, from the senselessness of the body,

---

[50] 64E5–6.   [51] For the interpretation of this difficult sentence see Rowe 1993 ad loc.
[52] 'This': i.e. that what we desire is the truth; but might 'this' also refer to what has just been said to be 'very likely'?

then probably we'll be in the company of such [pure] people and we'll know, through ourselves, everything that is unalloyed, and this is, we hazard, what is true; for perhaps it is not permitted for what is not pure to grasp what is pure.' (66D7–67B2)

The chief reason for citing this passage at such length is to bring out exactly what is being claimed – not by Socrates directly, but as something 'genuine philosophers' might claim, on the basis of an expanded and more extreme version of what Socrates and Simmias agreed to. Simmias and he, after all, only agreed that the philosopher's 'preoccupation' isn't with the body,[53] a position that is decidedly short of the asceticism recommended by the imaginary 'genuine' philosophers. Socrates thus simultaneously associates himself, and Simmias, with these philosophers, and keeps himself at arm's length from them; for what they recommend for themselves is not *his* way (as described in 64C–E).[54] And these other philosophers do also seem to have higher expectations than does Socrates: 'probably we'll be in the company of [other people such as ourselves] and *we'll know*, through ourselves, *everything that is unalloyed*' (67A8–B1). The first part of this echoes Socrates' own prediction for himself (63B: 'I'll meet better people than there are here'), but the second part goes way beyond it. Socrates nowhere says that *he* expects to acquire knowledge after death. Indeed even these 'genuine philosophers' whose thoughts he is reconstructing hedge their bets ('*if* we're ever going to know anything in its purity'; 'one of two things holds: *either knowing isn't possible for us anywhere, or* it's possible for us when we've died').

And well they might hedge those bets of theirs, since there is nothing whatever to show that merely getting rid of the body will do the trick and give them access to knowledge. The body may get in the way in all sorts of respects, but there is no guarantee that without it the truth will just *show up*, as it were. Nowhere in the *Phaedo* is there any commitment, on Socrates' or anyone else's part, to the idea that the objects of knowledge (the forms) will be available on demand, as it were, after death, even to the 'purified' soul. The myth makes no provision for it, and in fact doesn't

---

[53] 64E4–5: 'Then in general, does it seem to you that the preoccupation (*pragmateia*) of [the philosopher] isn't about the body' (he just 'stands back as far as he can from the body, and is turned towards the soul')?

[54] See n. 49 above, with text. Once again we come to what is beginning to look like a running theme in the dialogues: Socrates sees himself as second-rank even as *a philosopher* (cf. the way he distinguishes himself from the 'leaders' in philosophy in the *Theaetetus*; and, rather closer to home, that distinction he makes in the *Phaedo* myth itself between people – like himself – good enough to live on the real surface of the earth and the superior beings who go off to 'still more beautiful dwelling-places': 114C4–5).

mention forms at all; and Socrates on his own account associates access to, or approaching, true reality – the unseen, *aïdes* – specifically with *this* life, not the next. Thus with 79D1–2:

. . . when it investigates by itself, [the soul] goes/is gone to that [sc. *aïdes*] place, to what is pure and always is and is deathless and in the same state

we may compare 80D5–7:

'The soul . . . , the unseen, goes/is gone [on death] to such a place, another one, noble and pure and unseen, to Hades in truth, to the presence of the good and wise god . . . ,

and then

So being in this state [the soul] goes off to what resembles it, the unseen, what is divine and deathless and wise, and having arrived there may enjoy happiness, freed from wandering and mindlessness and fears . . . (81A4–7),

where 'what . . . is wise' seems to build simply on the previous reference to arriving in the presence of 'the wise god'. The 'genuine philosophers' themselves specify that if they will come to know 'everything that is unalloyed', they'll know it 'through ourselves (*di'hēmōn autōn*', 67A8), i.e., I take it, through their own resources. That is, they'll have to go on working it out for themselves; it won't be a matter of some kind of *revelation*. If Plato wanted to propose any such thing, he had the means immediately to hand, in the shape of the extended metaphor of the philosopher as an initiate in the Mysteries, and a golden opportunity in the shape of the affinity argument; he could have had Socrates say 'just as the philosophical soul "goes to" the unseen (forms), to which it has such affinity, in life, so too it does in death'. But he does not – instead, he has Socrates say that the 'dead' soul goes to another unseen place, Hades proper, where there is wisdom, but only in the shape of a wise god.[55] Perhaps those higher habitations said in the myth to be granted to those who 'have purified themselves adequately by philosophy' do stand for the forms, but the signs are that they rather represent Olympus, or wherever it is that the Platonic gods reside. (At any rate the idea that some privileged souls will come to live with the gods has been mentioned,[56] as living in some form-world has not.)

That there is no mention of direct contact or acquaintance between the (adequately) 'purified' soul and the forms is all the more significant in the light of the fact that, according to the argument from recollection

---

[55] See 79D1–2, 80D5–7, 81A5–7 (passages cited just above).   [56] I.e. at 69C and 81A.

(72E–76E) either some or all of us[57] are supposed to have been born with a latent knowledge of forms. We must have acquired that knowledge somehow; how, exactly? One possibility, suggested by the *Phaedrus* myth, is that our souls have actually 'seen' the forms while in their discarnate state (every 10,000 years, according to Socrates' story in the *Phaedrus*, we get the opportunity to join the gods in their feast, which consists – for them – in passing outside the heavens and gazing on true reality; the best we can do is to catch a glimpse . . .). But the *Phaedo* gives no more sign that we had such direct acquaintance with forms before birth than it does of the prospect of our having it after death; Socrates concentrates on establishing that the phenomena presuppose that we, or some of us, acquired knowledge of forms before we entered our present bodies, and is silent on the question how such knowledge might have been acquired.

We are not, however, left entirely without the resources to speculate on this question, and fruitfully. Cebes introduces the subject of recollection – the idea that this is what learning is – by way of reference to the frequent occasions on which he's heard Socrates talking about it (72E). This, together with certain aspects of Cebes' introduction of the subject, immediately sends us readers scrambling for our text of the *Meno*, one of the (rather few) other places in the Platonic corpus where this particular idea of recollection features – and the only one where it is used in the way Cebes suggests, as grounds for believing the soul to be deathless. (The two crucial *Meno* passages are 81A–D and 85B–86B; no one, I think, seriously doubts that the *Phaedo* is here meant to invoke them.) And the *Meno*, I suggest, contains the clue to Plato's own answer to the question how we acquired knowledge of forms. What Socrates reports there, drawing on the authority of priests and priestesses, and of poets (including Pindar), is that

because the soul is deathless and has been born [sc. into a body] many times, and has seen all things, both the things here and the things in Hades,[58] there is nothing that it has not learned; so, that it should be capable of being reminded of what it actually knew before, about excellence [the main subject of the *Meno*] and other things, is nothing amazing. (*Meno* 81C5–9)

Now *perhaps* we are supposed to identify 'the things in Hades' with the forms; but what then are we to make of 'the things here'? (The claim does not seem to be that we can recollect contingent events and states from our experiences in other bodies.) The overall effect of 'all things, both the things here and the things in Hades' is to say: *everything*, whatever it

---

57 Depending on one's reading of the argument: see Scott 1995.
58 I have taken it that *kai panta ta chrēmata* is epexegetic of *kai ta enthade kai ta en Haidou*.

might be. But why then should it matter that the soul is deathless, and has undergone many births? If it is just a matter of seeing, and contingent things are to be excluded, why should we need more than a single experience of discarnate existence to put alongside our present existence in a body? Maybe two or three, to make it all sink in; but why more than that – even an indeterminately large number of such experiences, as the reference to deathlessness not only allows but suggests? (The soul never dies, but is always born again into a body; the process could in principle have been going on for ever, or for as long as one cares to imagine.)

Or is Socrates' thought rather that, if our souls have had an eternity to think and talk – *philosophize* – about 'excellence and other things', they should by now have come up with the right answers? 'All nature is akin', says Socrates in the *Meno* passage, so that if one thing is recollected, there is nothing to prevent everything else from following (81C9–D2): not just isolated pieces of knowledge, then, but in principle knowledge of – everything.[59] If one asks why Socrates actually puts things in terms of seeing, here in the *Meno*, rather than of philosophizing, the answer is that he is talking the language of the priests and poets whose ideas he claims to be reporting;[60] and does not the metaphor of 'seeing' the truth happily cohabit with dialectic in the *Republic*?[61] In any case no method of acquiring knowledge except philosophy seems to be openly on offer in either the *Meno* or the *Phaedo*, whether in relation to the soul's time in the body or to its time out of it.

This proposal about the source of the soul's original knowledge – forgotten at birth, but available to be 'recollected' – is of course speculative. I venture, however, that it is more secure than any rival proposal of the sort that has the soul somehow coming to know the forms by direct acquaintance; that is, as if it had *only* to be 'purified' by philosophy before leaving the body in order to gain access to the full truth. As I have argued, the Socrates of the *Phaedo* gives no such picture of knowledge-acquisition after death, even when he has provided himself with the perfect opportunity to do so. A philosopher like himself, when dead, will evidently still have to go on searching, even during his sojourn in the imagined (but barely imaginable)

---

[59] That is, everything non-contingent. (The *degree* of knowledge/understanding of everything will, still, I suppose, be whatever is appropriate to a merely human soul – and of course, insofar as every human soul regularly forgets whatever it has learned, this already makes its state inferior to that of divine souls.)

[60] True, at this point Socrates is probably *inferring* from what the priests and poets say; nevertheless he is patently still using their language.

[61] See the Introduction above.

beauty of the surface of the earth, and so he will, too, on his eventual return to a body. Of all the dialogues, it is only in the *Phaedrus* that Plato introduces the idea of the direct vision of the forms by the discarnate soul – and there even the best human souls, dragged down by their earth-bound horses, find it a struggle to catch sight of *some part* of the true.[62] (For gods, it is easy; but we are not gods and, according to the *Phaedrus*, never will be.) The idea of a direct contact with reality, and even that of a *kind* of direct contact, by the eye of the soul, is always in Plato a matter either of metaphor (or simile), as in the case of the *Republic*, or, in the case of the *Phaedrus*, of myth (i.e. extended simile); and there in the *Phaedrus* it is generated by the peculiar and complex machinery of a particular story that Plato has to tell. There is, in sum, no available evidence that direct acquaintance with forms is part of his armoury of beliefs.

My conclusion about forms in the *Phaedo* is that this dialogue does nothing to alter the picture we seem to get from other parts of the corpus: that access to the forms, and to knowledge, for human beings, is by philosophy – dialectic – alone. There are no short cuts, even after death. So far as the *Phaedo* is concerned, the forms are those things, whatever they are, that the philosopher seeks to 'grasp' through dialectic; the very things that Socrates is seeking to grasp in the *Euthyphro*, the *Laches*, the *Meno* . . . That is one reason why Plato can have him, in the *Phaedo*, describe 'beautiful and good and all such being (*ousia*)' (76D8–9) as 'the things we're always chattering about', and then later refer to them just as 'those much-chattered-about (*poluthrulēta*) things' (100B4–5) – the other reason being that from within the fiction of the dialogue, they will have been 'much-chattered-about' in the sorts of conversations that the written dialogues claim to reproduce. (Once again, I insist on the importance of understanding the *intertextuality* of the Platonic corpus.)

It must be conceded, however, that this result – that death is no guarantee of knowledge even for the philosopher – comes as something of a surprise. After all, the main point of the whole exercise was supposed to be for Socrates to come up with good reasons why he should be cheerful at the prospect of death; and his chief, even his only, strategy was to suggest that 'genuine philosophers' would conclude from the facts that cheerfulness was in order because death would bring them the wisdom and knowledge they longed for – that is, if anything would. Now it turns out that while death may bring some advantages, in the shape of an absence of distractions and of misleading sense-impressions, what it has otherwise to offer a Socrates is

---

[62] *Phaedrus* 248C2–3 *hētis an psuchē theōi sunopados genomenē katidēi ti tōn alēthōn* . . .

essentially more of the same (more searching and seeking), except without the impediment of the body.

This, I think, is the point at which it matters to identify the allegorical aspect of the *Phaedo*, not just in the myth itself but in the parts of the argument of the dialogue that look forward to it. The dialogue argues for the superiority of the philosophical life over others in the context of a universe that is for the best and one in which we – as immortal souls – are perpetual players.[63] And it does this by means of borrowing and adapting a discourse from outside Socrates', and Plato's, own repertoire:[64] one whose origins are left largely indeterminate (Eleusis? Pythagoreanism? [Orphism?]) but whose *language* and general direction would have been immediately recognizable to Plato's Athenian audience. What he is doing, as so often, is to translate the unfamiliar (his own ideas) into the more familiar; and our task, as intelligent readers, is to translate them back again, not to be seduced into taking the version before us at face value.

Here is the central example of this phenomenon from the *Phaedo*, which will be crucial for our overall understanding of the dialogue. I start from a phrase in that piece of argument Socrates attributes to his 'genuine philosophers':[65] 'For wars and civil discord and fighting have no other origin except in *the body and its desires . . .*' (kai gar polemous kai staseis kai machas ouden allo parechei ē *to sōma kai hai toutou epithumiai*, 66C2–7).[66] What are we to make of the last, italicized phrase? The natural reaction is to say that Plato can't literally mean that the bodily appetites belong to the body; any half-decent philosopher would have to say that they belong to the soul. So the phrase must just be shorthand for something like 'the desires/appetites that human beings have as a result of their souls' being in bodies, and which they wouldn't have if their souls weren't in bodies'. The

---

[63] Both the latter points – the goodness of the universe and the immortality of the soul – still of course remain matters of *conviction*, even after the arguments of the *Phaedo*.

[64] Some of Plato's ideas – e.g., the immortality of the soul, or its transmigration from one body to another – are obviously in some sense 'Pythagorean'; but it is in general unhelpful to call *him* a Pythagorean, insofar as he is very picky about what he takes from there, and thoroughly transforms what he does take. The *Phaedo* is a brilliant example of such transformation. (For the concept of such 'transformation', or *transposition*, see Diès 1913.)

[65] Who will, presumably, be closely related to the clever 'Sicilian or Italian' who in 'story-telling' mode made up the slogan *sōma* ('body') *sēma* ('tomb'): *Gorgias* 493A. Sicily and southern Italy were Pythagorean strongholds.

[66] Some of what follows had its origin in a paper solicited by Wilfried Kühn for a *journée d'études* on the *Phaedo*, and on Ebert 2004 , at the Sorbonne in 2004. I am grateful for the opportunity provided by the occasion to begin developing my present ideas on the *Phaedo*; my differences from Ebert may, in this written context, be left to speak for themselves.

surrounding text[67] gives some encouragement for this kind of reading; and then 66C5–7 will fit neatly enough into the kind of picture of the relationship between soul and body that we may seem to find elsewhere in Plato, wherever this is spelled out.

So the obvious way of taking the expression 'desires of the body' is as standing for something more precise, and more sensible. (There's nothing wrong with the idea of 'carnal desires', so long as we recognize properly that they really aren't desires the flesh *has*.) But this is by no means a trouble-free way of treating *Phaedo* 66C5–7. For in fact the phrase seems to have been deliberately chosen as part of a whole context designed to give the impression that death will leave true philosophers as purely rational souls, with everything else – not just appetites, but passions, fears . . . – behind them. Thus it is that Socrates can not just portray them as going to live with the gods,[68] but even suggest that they will *become* gods:[69] while other souls pass into the bodies of hawks, or bees, or ants, or men, 'Into the race of gods it is not permitted for one who did not philosophize and depart wholly pure to arrive – [for no one] except the lover of learning' (82B10–C1).[70] And this, then, is presumably also how we should finally read that reference in the myth to the highest grade of souls living 'without bodies altogether for the whole of time to come' (114C2–4).

Now as we have seen, Socrates is in the end careful to distinguish himself from these paragons; while they go off to the heavens, he will merely go off to the real surface of the earth. But he is nevertheless happy to associate himself with them, to the extent of sharing their hopes (for they are, of course, never more than hopes):

So . . . if these things [i.e. what he has imagined the 'genuine philosophers' as saying] are true . . . there is great hope, for one who has arrived where I am journeying, to acquire there if anywhere the thing for which our great preoccupation has been in our past life, so that the change of place that is now ordained for me occurs with great hope, and for any other man who supposes that his thought is prepared as if purified. (67B7–C3)[71]

---

[67] See especially 66C2–4 '[the body] fills *us* full of passions and desires and all sorts of illusions and a whole array of rubbish'.

[68] 69C, 81A.   [69] So, evidently, at 82B–C.

[70] We should note the form of this statement, giving the conditions of something rather than stating it outright – and so avoiding saying it outright. With no class of souls mentioned between those who turn into bees, ants, men and those who may or may not turn into gods, Socrates must be associating himself with the latter; in which case the fact that he doesn't make the statement outright is all-important.

[71] With apologies for the inelegant translation, which is intended to bring out the precise wording of the statement.

Socrates' last words here are important: he is *comparing* his state to that of the philosophers in question, and not actually identifying himself with them. His thought, his mind, is *as if* purified; the language of purification is theirs, and not his. And similarly when he concludes at 67E4–6 that 'those who philosophize correctly really do practise dying, and being dead is for them, of all humans, least frightening', he is at one and the same time both one of these 'correct philosophizers', and also distinct from them.[72]

As I have said, the identity of these people is left indeterminate; but we know roughly where we are with them, given the whole Pythagorean ambience of the dialogue,[73] the grounding of the whole present context in the Pythagorean idea of the body as a tomb, and the recurring references to initiation and purification. Plato's strategy for Socrates is to have him lock into such ideas, elaborate them, build a rhetoric on them – but all the time maintain his distance by talking in the third person. Typical is 69C3–D4:

And probably these people who established the rites for us were no mean individuals, and were genuinely (*tōi onti*) riddling all those years ago when they said that whoever arrives in Hades without experience of the rites and uninitiated will lie in the mud, while he who has arrived there purified and initiated will live with (the) gods. For there are indeed, as those concerned with the mystery rites say, 'many thyrsus-bearers but few Bacchants'; and these, in my judgement, are no other than those who have philosophized correctly. *Of these I too yearned in every way to become one, not weakening at all so far as I could avoid it in my whole life.*

And the same pattern is repeated when Socrates uses the argument from affinity to return to the theme of the necessity for purification: we have the same reference to the mysteries ('. . . truly passing the rest of time with the gods, as is said of the initiated': 81A8–9), and the same third person talk of 'the correct philosophers' (82C2–3), 'the lovers of learning' (82D9, 83A1), 'genuine lovers of learning' (*hoi dikaiōs philomatheis*, 83E5), 'a philosophical man' (84A2). After driving home his theme for more than three Stephanus pages, Socrates falls silent for a long time, because – Phaedo says – he 'was

---

[72] Another small indication in the same direction is provided by the matter-of-fact way in which transmigration into animals (and even gods) is introduced in the aftermath of the affinity argument. (But see further on this below.)

[73] The whole dialogue between Socrates and his interlocutors, Simmias and Cebes, is related by the Socratic Phaedo to one Echecrates and his friends in Phlius in the Peloponnese; it appears that Phaedo's audience has Pythagorean connections – as have Simmias and Cebes, only of a more distant sort (they have simply heard the famous Pythagorean Philolaus lecturing). The framing device in itself may help to distance Socrates from the Pythagoreanism from which he liberally, but not too liberally, borrows (and which, in his borrowing, he transforms).

absorbed in the preceding argument' (84C2–3). But then seeing Cebes and Simmias whispering to each other, he says

What? Surely you don't think there was anything lacking in what was said? There are still very many ways in which it leaves room for misgiving and counter-attack, at any rate if one means to explore [what was said] in an adequate fashion. (84C5–8)

There could scarcely be a clearer sign that Socrates himself has his doubts about what he has just said. ('Surely you don't think . . .?' can hardly avoid being ironic.) Simmias and Cebes, too, are already showing their scepticism,[74] and indeed the main effect on them of Socrates' rhetorical turn seems to have been negative rather than positive. (Phaedo and the rest, on the other hand, have been rather impressed; that's the reason for *their* 'absorption' in the argument. But then Phaedo, at least, may have Pythagorean affiliations of his own.)

There are, then, I suggest, important reasons why we should not understand Socrates' endorsement of an extreme asceticism, leading to assimilation to the divine, as anything more than temporary and opportunistic. (There is opportunism on Plato's part, too, insofar as he chose to give the *Phaedo* as a whole its Pythagorean/quasi-religious setting and tone.) And such a conclusion will happily square with the fact that Socrates actually shows no signs of such an endorsement anywhere else. This is not at all to suggest that he, and Plato, would be prepared to jettison the whole package. Far from it, for it is of course the very resemblance between their position and the one(s) they appropriate and transform that causes the introduction and use of the package in the first place. Just how much of it they keep, it is hard to judge. But the lack of parallels elsewhere in the corpus tends to suggest that the extreme hostility evinced by the 'correct philosophers' towards the body will not be part of what is kept, nor will that hint that humans may escape to become pure, and purely rational, soul.[75] That is, the whole theme of the body as tomb remains Pythagorean rather than Platonic.[76] (The appetites are not, for Plato and for Socrates, 'desires of the body'.)[77] What Plato surely has a use for is the idea of transmigration into animals – or at any rate the idea that souls will have 'practised' in life, i.e. trained

---

[74] Simmias will go on to say specifically that they must examine 'what is said', *ta legomena*, about death and dying (85C4–6); I take it that he is referring primarily to the *legomena* on which Socrates has been relying.

[75] The position implied in a passage like *Republic* VII, 519A–B, or its companion at X, 611E–612A, seems to me, when taken in its context, to be considerably less extreme. See further chapter 5 below.

[76] As indeed *Gorgias* 493A may tend to confirm.

[77] This, however, is a issue to which I shall need to return, especially in the context of the *Republic* (see chapter 5 below).

themselves up in, the 'characters' of animals;[78] but since he is also clearly committed to the idea of the survival of the soul after death, and to the idea of the fundamental goodness of the way the world is structured,[79] we should probably not feel too queasy about supposing that he also believed in transmigration as the fundamental expression of that goodness. Where, in any case, would all those immortal souls go if they were not recycled?[80] Plato's universe is finite and closed, with nothing located outside it; any rewards and punishments must apparently be allocated, and enjoyed or suffered, inside it.

If we then ask the question with which I began this chapter, whether – as is normally supposed – the *Phaedo* shows Plato moving away from the Socrates of the *Apology*, the answer I should propose, based on the argument of the present chapter, is a fairly emphatic *no*. Of course there is no mention of recollection in the *Apology*, and the *Apology* only contains the barest hint of the idea of a deathless (immortal) soul; but then (a), as I have proposed,[81] we should not expect Plato to say everything he has to say about everything on every occasion; and (b) even if it were the case that Plato's Socrates (Plato) had not thought up the theory of recollection, or endorsed the idea of transmigration, at the time (of writing) of the *Apology*, there is nothing in either the theory or the idea that goes against rather than with the grain of what I claim we find in the *Apology*.[82] And if I am asked whether there are *forms* in the *Apology*, I retort, *more Socratico*,[83] that we need to know first what 'forms' are. If forms are things like justice and goodness, understood as non-identical with just things and good things, then the answer is that of course there are forms in the *Apology*. Indeed any decent discussion of justice, goodness, beauty, or whatever it may be must in any case refer to the sorts of items that Plato tends to label as 'forms' (*eidē, ideai*). (So the question 'are there forms in the *Apology*?' will turn out to be not only too hasty but actually malformed.)

---

[78] See 82E1–3, where Socrates says that the souls of inferior people are bound (chained) back again into a body 'by desire; and they are bound, as it's reasonable to suppose, into such characters (*ēthē*) as they happen actually to have practised in their lives'. (The Greek is helped by the fact that *ēthē* can also be used of the *haunts* of animals.)

[79] One of the ideas that he clearly shares with his Timaeus in the *Timaeus*.

[80] The theory of learning as recollection will of course demand some such theory, though it need not include transmigration of human souls into animal bodies.

[81] See the Preliminaries above, section 5.

[82] What is more, the idea of recollection in one of its roles, identified by the *Phaedrus*, will ultimately be presupposed by Socrates' activity as described in the *Apology* and illustrated in the 'Socratic' dialogues: see chapter 6 below. (Briefly: that activity depends on a shared human ability to bring the outcomes of many sensations into one, which the *Phaedrus* 'explains' in terms of 'recollection'.)

[83] And more or less in the mode of section 10 of the Preliminaries above.

CHAPTER 3

'Examining myself and others', 1: knowledge and soul in Charmides, First Alcibiades, Meno, Republic, Euthyphro, Phaedrus

In this chapter I set out to explore the notion of 'examination', *exetazein*, as the central term in Socrates' statement of his philosophical 'mission' in the *Apology*.[1] I shall take as my starting-point the main version of that statement in the *Apology*, pairing it by way of anticipation with a contrasting passage from the *Phaedrus* – which will serve as an introduction to the apparently rather different notion of the self, and the soul, that seems to emerge, and with some radical consequences, in the *Republic*. The *Phaedrus* will be the topic of the fourth, short section of the chapter (the second will be an equally brief digression on learning as recollection); chapter 5 will then, *inter alia*, discuss the degree of difference between the conceptions of soul in the pre-*Republic* dialogues and in the *Republic* and after. (Chapter 4 will discuss related issues in the – pre-*Republic* – *Gorgias*.) The focus throughout will be on what Plato's Socrates understands by *self*-examination, which I take to contain the key to a proper interpretation of what it means for Socrates to 'examine' others.

Here is Socrates' ringing statement of the nature of his life's mission in the *Apology*

Perhaps someone might say 'But Socrates – why shouldn't you be able to leave Athens and keep your mouth shut, living a quiet life?' This is what it's most difficult of all to persuade some of you about. If I say that living a quiet life is disobedience to the god, and that therefore it's impossible to do it, you won't believe me because you'll think I'm being ironical. If on the other hand I say that it really is a good of the highest order for a human being to spend each day *in discussions about excellence* ['goodness', 'virtue': *aretē*] *and the other things you hear me conversing about, and examining myself and others, and that the unexamined life is unliveable for a human being* – if I say that, you'll believe me even less. (*Apology* 37E3–38A6)

---

[1] The first three sections of this chapter adapt and modify the major part of a chapter – on 'Self-examination' – submitted some time ago for a collection edited by Donald Morrison; the eventual shape of that chapter will have been thoroughly improved by the working over of its argument for the present book.

And here is the Socrates of the *Phaedrus*:

> For myself in no way do I have leisure for these things [sc. rationalizing traditional myths like that of Boreas and Oreithuia], and the reason for it, my friend, is this. I am not yet capable, in accordance with the Delphic inscription, of 'knowing myself'; it therefore seems absurd to me that while I am still ignorant of this subject I should inquire into things which do not belong to me. So then saying goodbye to these things, and believing what is commonly thought about them, I inquire . . . not into these but into myself, to see whether I am actually a beast more complex and more violent than Typhon [a hundred-headed dragon, who was the last obstacle to Zeus's ascent to kingship of the gods],[2] or both a tamer and a simpler creature, sharing some divine and un-Typhonic portion by nature. (*Phaedrus* 229E4–230A6)

I 'SELF-EXAMINATION' IN THE *APOLOGY* AND OTHER SELECTED DIALOGUES (I)

What is it, exactly, that Socrates 'examines' when he talks about 'examining myself and others'? The standard view is that what Socrates examines are his own and others' *convictions*.[3] Let us suppose that it is Socrates' typical method to start from an interlocutor's conviction about what one of the excellences is (note that reference in the *Apology* passage to 'discussions about excellence and the other things'), and from there to go on to other things his interlocutors are convinced of, or believe, in order to get them to think about jettisoning that first conviction or belief: in that case it will be natural to suppose that what he is doing is looking for *consistency in people's belief-sets*.[4] Add in the assumptions (a) that everyone has at least some true beliefs or convictions, about the things that really matter, and (b) that Socrates in particular will have succeeded in weeding out all or most of his own false ones, and we shall be well on the way to having a method for discovering actual truths about 'excellence and the other [relevant] things' – provided, of course, that one accepts that crucial assumption about there being truth around in people's, or at any rate Socrates', beliefs (so that all one has to do, in principle, is to get those beliefs straight).[5] And this

---

[2] See Hesiod, *Theogony* 820 ff.

[3] See, e.g., Vlastos 1991: 134 ('elenctic argument is the very process on which [Socrates] depends to test the truth of his own convictions about the right way to live, no less than those of his interlocutor').

[4] 'The method by which Socrates "examines himself and others", which I am calling "the elenchus" . . . involves the form of argument that Aristotle was to call "peirastic": a thesis is refuted when, and only when, its negation is derived *"from the answerer's own beliefs"* (*Soph. El.* 165b3–5)' (Vlastos 1991: 111; italics added).

[5] Some such view of Socratic method is held by Donald Davidson, following Gregory Vlastos; Davidson thinks (what I have called) the 'crucial assumption' stands a good chance of being true in any case. See Rowe 2005b, which discusses Davidson's position.

analysis of Socratic 'self-examination' might well seem to receive indirect confirmation from the introduction, in *Meno*, *Phaedo* and *Phaedrus*, of the theory of learning as a kind of recollection. There may well appear to be a pleasing continuity, and natural kinship, between the proposal that we have only (only!) to interrogate ourselves, and our souls, to get to the truth, and the sort of theory of innate ideas that this account of learning seems to give us.[6]

So on this account self-examination will be a way of getting to the truth, on the basis that the truth is somehow in oneself; but it will also, importantly, be a matter of examining, and coming to know, one*self*, that is, one's true self, as this is revealed by the discarding of false beliefs and the identification of the ones that are true. (These are not just one's true, or deep, beliefs, those that one truly or really holds, but such beliefs that one holds that are really true.) From here it might be only a short step to the kind of view that we find in the *First Alcibiades*[7] (whether or not that dialogue is by Plato, though I myself hold that it is not): that what we need is to get to know ourselves, on the basis that knowing ourselves is a matter of knowing that we are identical with our soul rather than our body or the combination of soul and body.[8] At any rate, Plato's Socrates seems generally to think that caring for our souls, and so for ourselves, has everything to do with getting our beliefs straight. On the interpretation in question (self-examination as the examination of one's belief-sets) this process has to do with examining and sorting *one's own individual* beliefs, keeping some and throwing others away – a kind of individual intellectual therapy (even if everyone would, presumably, end up with exactly the same, true, set of beliefs).[9] That – on the same interpretation – is what Socrates helps others to achieve, but also, and more importantly, aims to achieve for himself: 'Socrates is more concerned with testing his own soul. And he tests it to see if it has true beliefs, assuming that they [sc. beliefs, presumably] determine character . . .'[10] Seen in this way, self-examination is a means of self-improvement, which will – so Socrates hopes – throw up real truths along the way.

---

[6] I shall return specifically to the 'theory' of recollection and its implications in section 2 below.

[7] See Annas 1985.

[8] See *Alcibiades I* 124A, 130E–131B, 132C–133E. However the *First Alcibiades* is probably closer in spirit and substance to the *Phaedrus*: see section 4 below.

[9] That is, on the most important subjects, the ones that affect the quality of one's life (cf. the *Phaedrus* passage above: Socrates will be not much concerned about e.g., the truth or otherwise of the story of Boreas and Oreithuia). See further below.

[10] Irwin 1979: 182, on *Gorgias* 486D.

This way of understanding the *Apology* fits well enough with another feature of Socratic conversation, the demand that the interlocutor should always say what he thinks.[11] How could anyone examine another person's beliefs without knowing what those beliefs actually are? The same understanding also appears – at first sight – to sit rather happily with a well-known context in the *Gorgias*, when Socrates says, extraordinarily, that 'I *and you* [Polus] *and all the rest of mankind consider* that doing injustice is worse than suffering it, and not paying the penalty for injustice worse than paying it' (474B3–5) – when Polus claims actually to believe exactly the opposite, and plausibly suggests into the bargain that everyone except Socrates will agree with him. On the usual interpretation of this interchange, what Socrates proceeds to do is to find something else that Polus believes (namely that doing injustice is more *shameful* than suffering it) – and to derive what he, Socrates, says about injustice from that. In principle, such a procedure might very well be taken as an inquiry into Polus' own deepest beliefs.

Yet there is also good reason to reject this approach (and also the general interpretation which it embodies). The argument that Socrates uses here in the *Gorgias*, to move from 'more shameful' (*aischion*) to 'worse' (*kakion*), is generally considered a transparently poor one, which succeeds in showing nothing at all. If so, Socrates won't believe in his own argument, and any claim to have established what Polus and others really believe, by using such an argument, is likely to seem merely provocative. If that is the best Socrates can do, Polus and everybody else may reasonably brush him aside; they won't need *him* to tell them what they believe.[12] Nor, if we turn to Socrates' motivation for requiring his interlocutors to 'say what you think', need that be connected with any desire to investigate their innermost beliefs. Asking that the other person say what he thinks might, surely, just be an elementary precaution against too easily being taken in by wrong assumptions, making false steps. (Merely to say 'let it be so' will be a matter of seeing which way the argument goes whether this particular premise be true or false – which

---

[11] See, e.g., *Crito* 49D–E, *Gorgias* 495A. Finding out 'what someone really thinks' may itself be taken as involving a sorting of beliefs: '[for Socrates,] to discover the limits of one's knowledge [i.e. by finding out what one knows and does not know] it is necessary first to find out what one really believes. [An] opinion will need to be tested, but to have formulated it and thought through its implications and connections with other beliefs is already a step towards self-knowledge . . .' (Burnyeat 1992 (1977): 59).

[12] I myself suppose that the argument will work on Socrates' own premises: see chapter 4, section 2(c). In general, I would not wish Socrates to be left, even for a moment, completely undefended against the charge of arguing *transparently badly*; I do not believe he ever does that, at least without acknowledging that that is what he is doing. See *Republic* V, 451A for his view about the seriousness of doing any such thing.

is a feature of certain types of discourse, whether rhetorical or 'eristic',[13] against which Plato's Socrates repeatedly sets his face.) And as a matter of fact what Socrates and his interlocutors discuss is not usually marked off as something to which anyone – whether Socrates or the other person – is particularly *committed*.[14] If it often takes Socrates time to work out what people have in mind when they say something, again that need have nothing to do with finding out what they really believe; what they just happen to have come up with in answer to a question – whether or not that answer is connected with what they would recognize as their beliefs – may itself stand in need of qualification, and in fact will usually turn out to do so.[15] Thus, even if what Socrates and his interlocutor end up by deriving from what they first started out with might count in some bare sense as the 'belief' of one or other or both of them, that will be rather far from what would normally count as 'conviction'.

This is not to deny that there are occasions when interlocutors are to be found defending their convictions: what Thrasymachus defends in the first book of the *Republic* is surely something of which he is convinced, indeed is passionate about; and similarly with Callicles in the *Gorgias*. Both men's commitment to their positions is heavily emphasized. But these are the exceptions. Much more common is a situation that Socrates describes in the *Charmides*:

> But, I [Socrates] said, 'Critias, you bear down on me as if I claimed knowledge of the things I'm asking about, and as if I'd agree with you if only I wanted to; but it isn't like that. Rather, *I investigate with you on each occasion what is put forward* (*zētō . . . meta sou aei to protithemenon*) just because I don't know the answer myself.'
> (*Charmides* 165B5–C1)

Socrates, Charmides and Critias have considered a series of different accounts of *sōphrosunē*[16] without their showing, severally or together, any great attachment to any of them: they are just accounts that have been 'put forward' – if Critias is inclined to defend his candidates, that is only because he doesn't like to lose.

---

[13] On 'eristic' see Preliminaries above, n. 51.

[14] Some parts of the *Alcibiades* (i.e. *First Alcibiades*: see above) may seem to suggest some such interest in the individual self, but on closer analysis this turns out to be an illusion. So for example a passage on 'the self itself (*to auto auto*: 130E–131B) is aimed just at sorting out what it is to examine something (anything) in, or by, itself; and the *Alcibiades* shows no more interest in what individual human beings are than it shows in what an individual *anything* is.

[15] The *Charmides* gives numerous illustrations of the point (see below).

[16] The term *sōphrosunē* is here even more untranslatable than usual: traditionally it is 'temperance', presumably because of its association with self-control, i.e. control over one's desires, but it is emphatically not that in the *Charmides*. 'Sound-mindedness', in the context of the *Charmides*, will be a better rendering: see below.

But what, in that case, should we make of the idea of *self*-examination ('examining *myself* and others')? The *Charmides*, again, is revealing. Shortly after the passage just cited, Critias accuses Socrates of trying merely to refute him, Critias, without any regard to the subject in hand – to which Socrates responds

> What a thing to think of me . . . even if I am as much as anything refuting you – to think that I'm refuting you for any other purpose than the one for which I'd be thoroughly investigating what *I* was saying, out of a fear that I'd ever think, without realizing it, that I knew something when I didn't. Just so now: *this* is what I claim to be doing, looking into what's been said mostly for my own sake, though perhaps also for my friends as well; or don't you suppose it to be a good thing for practically the whole human race, that how it is with each of the things that are [sc. the case?][17] should become clear? (*Charmides* 166C7–D6)

What is at issue here is clearly not what people believe, or are convinced about, but rather whether or not they *know* anything. In this light, self-examination is no different in kind from the examination of others;[18] it will be self-examination merely to the extent that it is an examination of how one stands, oneself, in relation to knowledge. That, for Socrates, is the absolutely fundamental question.

Why so? Because, for the Socrates of the *Apology* and the *Charmides*, the only difference between people that matters is whether or not they are wise. 'Virtue', or 'excellence' (or 'goodness': *aretē*) *is* knowledge – that is the theme around which the Socrates of a whole series of dialogues dances, without ever firmly asserting it; but then how could he *assert* it, when he knows nothing? None of us desires anything but the – real – good, as the *Lysis* tells us,[19] and as Diotima told Socrates, according to his story in the *Symposium* (205E–206A);[20] the difficulty for all of us is to establish just what

---

[17] This way of taking the phrase *ta onta*, 'the things that are', would avoid any suggestion (perish the thought!) that *forms* might figure in the *Charmides*. My own view is that 'the things that are' refers to things like 'sound-mindedness', identified as real entities whose nature can be investigated; what exactly these entities will lack, to stop them from being forms, is not presently clear to me. (See further chapter 9 below.)

[18] I am here taking it that examining what Critias says is a case of 'examining others', and that the contrasting case of Socrates' investigating what *he* says can then be treated as a case of self-examination. If we try restricting the description 'examining others' to cases where what the speaker says demonstrably issues from his deep beliefs, as opposed to representing what he thinks in the given argumentative context, 'examination' will – so I have proposed – be a somewhat rare phenomenon in the dialogues; and that, I take it, would be an odd outcome on any analysis except one that, extraordinarily, saw the *Apology* as quite separate from, making no important reference to, the written dialogues that purport to show Socrates strutting his stuff. For after all, examining people is just what he says he does.

[19] This result has to be worked for, from the text of the *Lysis*; the necessary work is done in Penner and Rowe 2005.

[20] See also *Republic* VI, 505D–506A.

that real good is, in any set of circumstances. Socrates is especially careful
not to assume, or suggest, that he will get it right. The only way he, or
anyone, will reliably get it right is if they acquire knowledge; if they do,
they'll be good – 'excellent', 'virtuous' – people, but until then they'll be
no more than neither good nor bad – not good because not wise, i.e. given
that goodness/'virtue' is knowledge, and not bad because not terminally
ignorant. (How could we tell that anyone was like that in advance – or at
all?) So knowledge is all-important; knowledge, that is, of what is really good
(which turns out to be knowledge itself, and the knowledgeable *life*), and
of what is really bad (ignorance, and a life built on ignorance), because only
by having what is really good and avoiding what is really bad can we have
what we all desire (the real good, a.k.a. happiness). If we start from here,
knowing that one knows or does not know will be all one needs to know
about oneself. Nothing else matters.[21] (This too will be compatible with the
treatment of self-knowledge in the *Alcibiades*, insofar as that culminates in
the understanding that the only goods are goods of the soul – and insofar
as goods of the soul reduce to knowledge.)

All of this lies just below the surface of the *Charmides*. Not long before
the first of the two passages from the dialogue cited above, Critias proposed that 'sound-mindedness', *sōphrosunē*, was a matter of 'doing what
belongs to oneself', which in response to Socrates' questioning he soon
emends to 'doing what is good (for oneself)'. But, Socrates asks, mustn't
the person who does what's good for himself know when he's doing that?
Exactly, says Critias – and this is the point where self-knowledge comes
into the discussion: sound-mindedness pretty much (*schedon*) *is* a matter of
knowing oneself, Critias now claims (164D3–4). (Critias takes it that acting

---

[21] I.e. for the pursuit of one's life. If I know I know what is good/bad for me (no matter how), I
can go ahead and act on what I believe/know; if I know I don't know, then I shall be circumspect
about acting on what I believe, and will – if I really am aware of my lack of knowledge about what
really matters to me – start looking for that knowledge (doing philosophy). It might be tempting
to suppose that knowing what is good/bad *for* me should count as knowledge *about* myself. But
that would be to presuppose not only (1) that what is good/bad for me is specific to me, but (2)
that the way for me to be happy may be different from the way(s) in which other people will be
happy; and while Socrates might agree to (1), insofar as what is practically happy-making for a
person in any one set of circumstances may be different from what is practically happy-making for
another person in a different set of circumstances, we have no grounds for supposing, and good
grounds for not supposing, that he would agree to (2). Were he to have accepted (2), it would be
hard to understand, for example, why he should have put so much faith in philosophical argument,
which seems capable of getting rather little purchase on what makes one person happy as opposed
to another – if indeed there is such a thing. (On the notion of 'practicable happiness', see Penner
and Rowe 2005: 90, 263.)

sound-mindedly without knowing it would be a case of self-ignorance.)[22] Socrates now, initially, converts this self-knowledge into a knowledge that is knowledge of itself, i.e. an awareness of the presence or absence of knowledge; and this he claims to find distinctly problematical. It is obvious enough why he should be interested in such an expertise, since it is more or less what he claims for himself in the *Apology*, even while having no (other) knowledge, i.e. no substantive knowledge.

So the question is: is it possible to have a knowledge (*epistēmē*) that is just of itself and of its absence (non-knowledge, nescience: *anepistēmosunē*), without that knowledge requiring knowledge *of* anything apart from itself? Are there seeings, hearings, sensings of any sort that are just of themselves, and not – at all – of the objects of other seeings, hearings, sensings, i.e. objects other than the sensings themselves . . . (and so on with other examples)? Surely not! Nevertheless Socrates is unwilling to give up on this kind of analysis of *sōphrosunē*,[23] and is perfectly clear that if *sōphrosunē* were able to offer a capacity to distinguish knowledge from ignorance, then our lives would all be the happier for it. That is, our lives would be happier if there were such a thing as knowledge of knowledge and ignorance (and we could acquire it) – not knowledge of any old knowledge and ignorance, but knowledge of knowledge and ignorance about the good and the bad (174B–C), which is what actually gives all the other kinds of expertise whatever value they may have. So if *that* is what *sōphrosunē* is, it will be every bit as beneficial for us as Socrates is convinced *sōphrosunē* must be. For, since what we all want is to be happy, in possession of the real good, knowledge of our ignorance must motivate us to that sort of inquiry which alone can lead us to an understanding of what that real good is. (Or, in the unlikely case[24] that we know that we already have that understanding, such knowledge will enable us to act unhesitatingly.)

There is insufficient space here for a full treatment of the *Charmides*, and of the sometimes bewildering twists and turns of its arguments. However it can hardly fail to be significant, for the topic of the present chapter, that

---

[22] He is helped along in this by Socrates' formulation in 164C5–6: 'does a person who has acted beneficially sometimes act sound-mindedly . . . but not know himself, that he is acting sound-mindedly?' – where 'know himself, that . . .' is ordinary Greek idiom just for knowing something about himself.

[23] I.e. 'sound-mindedness'. But by way of alternation, and as a sign of my lack of commitment to this particular translation of the Greek term (even in the absence of anything superior), let me for the moment revert to the Greek.

[24] 'Unlikely', if only because Socrates himself claims ignorance – and he has spent much of his life in the necessary kind of inquiry.

Socrates' (Plato's) most extended discussion of self-knowledge[25] should turn out to be a discussion of the principle, and the possibility, of Socrates' own preferred activity, of examining himself and others; even more significant, what the knowledge which *sōphrosunē* or 'sound-mindedness' would be able to test for, if it really were capable of what Critias claims for it, would be knowledge of good and bad (identified specifically as what makes us happy, *eudaimones*, or unhappy). Here is Socrates' vision of what *sōphrosunē* could do for us:

'... what benefit would we get from *sōphrosunē* if it is of this nature [i.e. a knowledge of knowledge and ignorance]? Well, if . . . the *sōphrōn* man knew what he knew and what he did not know (and that he knows the former but not the latter) and were able to investigate another man who was in the same situation, then it would be of the greatest benefit to us to be *sōphrones*; for those of us who had *sōphrosunē* would live lives free from error and so would all those who were under our rule. Neither would we ourselves be attempting to do things we did not understand – rather we would find those who did understand and turn the matter over to them – nor would we trust those over whom we ruled to do anything except what they would do correctly, and this would be that of which they possessed the knowledge. And thus, by means of *sōphrosunē*, every household would be well run, and every city well governed, and so in every case where *sōphrosunē* reigned. And with error rooted out and correctness in control, men so circumstanced would necessarily fare admirably and well in all their doings and, faring well, they would be happy. Isn't this what we mean about *sōphrosunē*, Critias,' I said, 'when we say what a good thing it would be to know what one knows and what one does not know?' (*Charmides* 171D1–172A5, tr. Sprague in the Hackett translation, but with minor modifications)

Of course at this point in the dialogue, and indeed later on, it still remains to be established that 'knowledge of knowledge' is possible, and what exactly its relationship would be to the substantive knowledge of good and bad. (These are the issues around which the dialectic of the *Charmides*, and the *aporia* or *impasse* in which it at least formally ends, are constructed.) But given what he says in that *Apology* passage from which I began (37E3–38A6), Socrates is scarcely going to give up on either kind of knowledge: what he wants more than anything is the substantive knowledge in question, and a precondition of his getting *that* will be knowing whether and when he, or anyone, has it.

It is not, I think, too much to claim that the *Charmides* is itself a paramount example of Socratic *self*-examination: not just because it shows

---

[25] 'Knowledge of knowledge' in the *Charmides* is rather more than just *self*-knowledge, insofar as it will include knowledge of knowledge in others. But it will at any rate include knowledge of one's own (state of) knowledge.

Socrates asking what he should believe (discussing with Critias 'out of a fear that I'd ever think, without realizing it, that I knew something when I didn't': *Charmides* 166D1–2), but because it has him asking whether his own fundamental claims will stand up, or how and why they do stand up. He does also examine others – Charmides, Critias; but everything in the end comes back to himself – and after all, in the end what *he* ought to believe will be exactly the same as what everybody else ought to believe. '[O]r don't you suppose it to be a good thing for practically the whole human race, that how it is with each of the things that are should become clear?' (166D4–6 again).

2 DIVERSION: LEARNING AS RECOLLECTION

Here we need to pause. In favour of the reading of self-examination, and self-knowledge, that I am proposing to reject – the one that sees it all, roughly, as a matter of making one's beliefs internally consistent, and so finding the truth within oneself[26] – there is one seemingly obvious piece of evidence that has so far been left out of the equation: the 'doctrine' of learning as recollection.[27] At least in the *Meno* version of this idea, Socrates does seem to suggest, more or less directly, that discovering the truth is ultimately a matter of digging down into our souls. Socrates there straightforwardly interprets the latent mathematical knowledge of the slave in the *Meno* as 'true beliefs' (85c6–7, 86A7), waiting to be stirred up (85c9) or 'awoken' (86A7) by questioning, and as showing that 'the truth is in us' (86B1–2). Put that together with the passage like the one on the 'cleansing' of ignorant souls by the noble sophist in the *Sophist* (230B–D), and what Socrates has to say about his activity in the *Theaetetus*, and my opponents' case might well seem open and shut: 'examining' the soul will, after all, be a matter of the sorting of, each individual's beliefs, throwing away the false ones and keeping the true ones.

However there is something here that is not quite right. If the truth really is in us, about everything (and that was what Socrates seemed to derive from the priests and the poets at *Meno* 81c), waiting there below the surface to be 'stirred' and 'awoken', why do Socrates and Meno not get further than they do with the main target of their investigation, the nature of excellence

---

[26] See above, pp. 123–4.

[27] Thus 'in the *Meno* at least, [the doctrine of recollection] was . . . a theory of the Socratic method, designed to explain how the dialectical process of eliciting an interlocutor's beliefs and testing them for consistency need not be wholly negative and destructive; if the discussion is pursued with sincerity and determination, Socratic inquiry can lead to knowledge' (Burnyeat 1992 (1977): 57).

(*aretē*) – about which, Socrates says, there would be 'nothing surprising' in the soul's being able to recollect, along with other things, given that it knew them before (81C7–9)? And in general, why does Socrates have such difficulty in making headway with so many of his interlocutors in other dialogues, on so many other subjects? In short, Socrates' encounters, whether in the *Meno* or elsewhere, tend either to undermine his claim about learning, or at any rate to demonstrate its lack of general application. (I leave out of account the possibility that he is just a bad questioner; questioning is the one thing everyone agrees he is good at.) What may be true of mathematics – that one can be brought to 'see' things, and more and more of them, through questioning – is just not so obviously true in other spheres, and Socrates does not operate as if it is. But then, for the purposes of resolving Meno's dilemma – how to look for something we don't know about, and how to know when we've found it? – the mathematical case, plus the machinery of 'recollection', gives Socrates all he needs: discovery *is* possible (the slave learned something, didn't he?), and it's possible because in a way we do already know the things we're looking for. In the *Phaedo* and the *Phaedrus*, the two other dialogues in which learning as recollection plays a major role, what is represented as successfully 'recollected' is hardly as systematic, or as knowledge-like, as what is recovered by Meno's slave. In the *Phaedo*, while it is agreed by the interlocutors that 'we knew/used to know' (*ēpistametha*) the forms of the equal, the beautiful, the good, and so on (75C–D), that point is derived from no more than 'our' apparent ability to grasp how particulars 'fall short of' them (74A–75C), and Simmias is afraid that when Socrates is dead there will be no one able 'worthily' to give an account of them (76B–C). What is more, the beautiful, good, just and so on are identified as the things Socrates and his circle ask their questions and give their answers about. The mathematical model evidently doesn't work here: 'we' (Socratic philosophers)[28] know that there are such things as the beautiful and the good, and the equal, and we may also know some other unspecified things about them, but our use of question and answer hasn't yet enabled us to arrive at an account of them.[29] (Even Socrates' account will be 'worthy' rather than true – according to Simmias; Socrates is silent on this claim about him.) And in the *Phaedrus* even souls that 'have

---

[28] It is of course philosophers, as opposed to non-philosophers, who recognize (know about) the existence of forms; and the language of 75C–D puts it beyond doubt that the *Phaedo* is taking the same line.

[29] It is clearly the beautiful, good, just etc. that are in question here, rather than the equal; that is, when Socrates asks at 76B8–9 whether everyone, people in general, can 'give an account' of 'the things we were talking about just now', the primary reference will be to these. (Apart from anything else, these rather than the equal are the things Socrates is typically most interested in 'giving an account' of.)

sufficient memory' of the forms to be reminded of them – to be reminded of beauty itself, by the beauty of the beloved – are confused rather than enlightened; 'they do not know what has happened to them, for lack of clear perception' (*Phaedrus* 250A5, A7–B1).[30]

So the idea of learning as recollection offers no quick fix, even in the *Meno*. It nowhere has any effect on philosophical *method* as such. What it does offer – so long as it is true – is some kind of guarantee that it is possible to acquire knowledge (*Meno*), and that we have the potential to access the forms (*Phaedo, Phaedrus*). (The *Phaedo* and *Phaedrus* I take here as explaining the acquisition of knowledge in terms of forms; that in itself will not obviously take us on beyond the vaguer formulation[31] in the *Meno* – that 'there would be nothing surprising about the soul's being able to recollect about excellence and about other things': 81C7–9 again.) If we take *Meno* 81C[32] seriously, as I see no reason to avoid doing, then Socrates (Plato) means to suggest that every soul has in fact learned everything – everything important – that there is to know.[33] By contrast, he seems to leave it entirely indeterminate how much, if anything,[34] any individual soul will in the event be able to 'recollect'; just as indeterminate as he leaves the answer to the question, asked without any reference to recollection, how much intellectual progress any individual soul will make during its (present) existence in a body. (So, once again, knowing that learning is recollection, if it is, will make no difference in practical terms.) But in that case, regardless of what Socrates may say about the 'true opinions' about mathematics that

---

[30] All of this will, of course, be consistent with the conclusion reached in my last chapter, that there is no commitment on Plato's part, whether in the *Phaedo* or anywhere else, to the notion that we can – our souls can – ever acquire direct acquaintance with forms (the possibility of which, if Plato *were* ever committed to it, might suggest that he thought it possible to acquire, and recollect, full knowledge of them; naturally I here exclude metaphors or similes which present cognition of forms *as if* it were a matter of direct acquaintance of some kind).

[31] The vagueness no doubt being determined by the fact that Socrates is there drawing on religious and poetic sources.

[32] 'So since the soul is immortal and has come to be born many times over, and since it has seen all things, both the things here and the things in Hades, there is nothing that it has not learned', 81C5–7. If we read this in the light of the simile of the cave in the *Republic*, it will mean that every soul will have made the journey up as far as the good itself at least once in its past existence in and out of bodies; cf. my suggestion in the previous chapter that the soul's pre-natal knowledge will have been learned *through philosophy* (a suggestion which gains a modicum of support from a passage like *Republic* VI, 498D, in which Socrates imagines himself helping Thrasymachus so that he will be better placed when he encounters similar arguments in a future life in the body).

[33] But see the caveats at chapter 2, n. 59 above.

[34] This is probably to go too far: in the myth of the *Phaedrus*, Socrates specifies that every soul that enters a human body must be able to 'comprehend what is said universally [or "according to (its) form": *kat'eidos*]' (249B6–7), 'and this is a recollection of those things which our soul once saw when it travelled in company with a god . . .' (C1–3). The context is one that has already cropped up in the course of my argument, and will crop up again.

Meno's slave recovers, the truth about beauty, goodness and the rest will be 'in' us in an equally indeterminately potential way; and it will become rather less than plausible to describe us, indiscriminately (and in advance of any investigation of our current intellectual state), as having true beliefs about beauty, goodness, or anything else 'in us'. Indeed it is not entirely clear either how we shall ever know if we harboured them at all: will certain ideas we come across suddenly seem all too familiar, and perhaps lead on to others equally familiar-seeming? In any case Socrates nowhere proposes using any such criterion of truth; his sole such criterion appears to be the ability of a given position or statement to stand up to challenge.[35] I conclude that what we learned before birth and forgot at birth does not form part of our belief-sets, or part of what is *examined* by Socratic method. Whatever the content of such learning, it will be only fitfully accessible.[36]

3 'SELF-EXAMINATION' IN THE *APOLOGY* AND OTHER SELECTED DIALOGUES (II)

Is there then no more to self-knowledge than knowing whether one knows or not (the question raised in the *Charmides*); and no more to self-examination than discovering the answer to that question? The answer is yes; there is more, even on the reading I have proposed. For if self-knowledge, knowing whether one has knowledge or not, is a first priority for human beings, then anyone who actually makes self-knowledge his or her priority will by so doing be valuing soul above body – 'caring for' the soul, rather than for the body, and so *ipso facto*, after the manner of the *Alcibiades*, recognizing that he/she is identical with his/her soul. That, of course, raises the question: just what is this thing, 'soul', for Socrates and Plato? A first pass at this question follows in the next section of this chapter, a second in chapter 5.

The *process* of self-examination, however, and of examining others, is still – I insist – entirely about discovering whether one possesses knowledge oneself, and whether others do. 'Examination', *exetazein*, is not about excavation, but rather about *accumulation*. Part of the problem with previous attempts to understand Socratic method has been a tendency to treat it as

---

[35] See especially chapter 8 below. (Not even the author of the *Seventh Letter* uses *previous* familiarity as a criterion: the 'flame' of understanding at 341C–D is evidently new-born, not reborn.)

[36] I am acutely aware, in this and other parts of the book, of trampling in large-sized boots over territory that has been minutely explored by others: in this particular instance, see especially Scott 1995. Here and elsewhere, however, my interest is not in hand-to-hand fighting with individual scholars; rather it is in setting out a new map, to which the results of their explorations may or may not transfer – whether to their detriment or mine, I leave to others to decide in each case.

essentially a matter of refutation: that then makes it a puzzle how a Socrates can make any positive progress, and do any more than talk about acquiring knowledge. Solution: either he aims just to clear his interlocutors'/our minds of the dross of ignorance, and then leave us to do our own thinking in the pure air of reason; or he supposes that, deep down, we all have the truth in us in any case. The latter proposal I have spent the main part of the present chapter attempting to demolish, while the former – in my view[37] – will hardly survive a few hours' close reading of any allegedly 'Socratic' part of the Platonic corpus. There is just too much around in the way of positive ideas, plainly owned by the know-nothing himself, wherever one looks in the text.

Rather than being about refutation (though that is frequently, even typically, a by-product), Socratic method is about *questioning, challenging* – precisely: *examination*. The issue always is whether this or that idea, whether mine or yours, will stand up to testing. If it does, then it can be the start of a pile of such ideas, or be added to one you or I already have. As we go on, items in our pile may turn out to need junking; and some of them may become apparently permanent possessions ('apparently', because after all Socrates is a know-nothing). We may even build up a sizeable collection – as indeed Socrates has done. That is the basis of his 'mission': he (thinks he) has seen enough, and is sufficiently excited about it, to go off and talk to others about it, passionately. But he needs to do that – talk to others – in any case, because others may have the very items he needs to add to his pile next. Plato, as the writer of the fiction, can of course make up encounters for him at will; so in fact the Socrates of the dialogues meets and feeds off an astonishing range of people, real and imaginary, often identified merely as 'someone', or 'some people'. The one thing that really makes Socrates nervous is the prospect of putting forward conjectures of his own about the most important subjects – something, according to what he says in the *Theaetetus*, he never does): witness his extraordinary wriggling at the beginning of *Republic* V when Adimantus, Glaucon and Thrasymachus try to get him, finally, to explain the radical proposals he has hinted at before for the treatment of women and children. He even expects it to be 'a lesser mistake (*hamartēma*) involuntarily to become someone's killer than [sc. involuntarily] to become a deceiver of fine-and-good people [sc. like Adimantus, etc.] in relation to things just and lawful' (*Republic* V, 451A5–7);[38] or, in other words, he'd rather be someone like Euthyphro's father, in the

---

[37] As already stated (Preliminaries, above, section 5).
[38] I here adopt Slings's text as printed in the new Oxford *Republic* (= Slings 2003).

Euthyphro, arraigned by his son for murder, than someone like Euthyphro, ignorantly proclaiming – to Socrates, and *via* his action – about justice and the law.[39] The example illustrates brilliantly both how important Socrates thinks self-knowledge is, and why he thinks it so important. If you lack it, you may even end up taking your father to court, and that's about as miserable it gets on any ordinary scale (whether or not your father is guilty, and it isn't at all clear that Euthyphro's was).[40]

Mention of the *Euthyphro* is opportune, because this particular little dialogue also exemplifies the other side of the equation: nervous as he may be about making concrete proposals for legislation (what does he know about that sort of thing?), Socrates still does have firm positions of his own.[41] Here, in the following three paragraphs, is a broad-brush reading of the way the *Euthyphro* begins and ends – a reading that will simultaneously give a further illustration of the way in which I propose generally to read the 'Socratic' dialogues.[42]

If he was prepared to go as far as prosecuting *his own father*, Euthyphro clearly must know about 'piety' ('pious', *hosion*, is how he labels what he is doing: the term roughly indicates something the gods would approve of), and Socrates had to talk to him. 'Religious experts' can be added to the list of people Socrates went to, according to the story in the *Apology* in response to what the priestess at Delphi said about him. Only it turns out that Socrates was ahead of the self-proclaimed 'expert' after all; having set out – genuinely, according to the fiction – to get knowledge from Euthyphro, he ends up giving him, and of course us, the readers, a lesson in philosophy and philosophical method, which almost takes Euthyphro to where he, Socrates, began.

How so? At the end of the dialogue, the argument has arrived at the suggestion that 'piety' is some kind of service to the gods. Right, says Socrates; so tell me what fine and good things the gods achieve through our service?

I told you only a little earlier, Socrates, that it's too large a task to understand all these things in detail; I'll say simply this: that if one knows how to say and do things that find favour with the gods, in prayer and at sacrifice – *that's* what pious things are . . . (*Euthyphro* 14A11–B4)

---

[39] Euthyphro's father had had a day-labourer who had knifed and killed someone; he tied him up and left him in a ditch while he consulted the religious authorities about what to do. The man died (but at least Euthyphro's father was *asking* what he should do; no such uncertainty on Euthyphro's part).

[40] I do not insist that *Euthyphro* was in Plato's mind when he wrote *Republic* v; but it might as well have been.

[41] That is, to continue the no doubt by now tiresome metaphor, as part of his 'accumulated heap'.

[42] The *Euthyphro* is paradigmatically 'Socratic', according to the usual view; so too the *Charmides*.

Socrates retorts

You could have given me that summary account I was asking for [sc. of the many fine and good things the gods achieve through us humans] much more briefly than that if you wanted to; but you're not keen to teach me, that's clear. For now you took a diversion when you were at the very point that if you'd given me an answer I'd by now have had a good enough lesson from you about piety. But as it is, since the lover must follow the beloved wherever he leads, what is it – I ask again – you say the pious and piety are? (14B8–C3)

Socrates here pretends to be hauling Euthyphro up for a simple technical infringement – for taking refuge again in generalities, instead of giving a specific answer: what *kind* of fine and good things do the gods achieve through us? If he'd answered that question, Socrates would have from him the knowledge of 'the pious and piety' that he wants. But of course Euthyphro is incapable of giving him the general answer required. He can only list the different prayers and sacrifices appropriate to each occasion, as becomes clear enough in the next and almost final part of the conversation, when he agrees to treating piety, *hosiotēs*, as a kind of expertise in commercial exchange between men and gods. So on one level Socrates is merely indulging in a gentle irony at Euthyphro's expense: the 'beloved', Euthyphro, has what the 'lover', Socrates, wants, and is just refusing to give it to him.

However for the reader – and especially the reader who knows his or her *Apology* – there will be rather more to Socrates' retort in 14B8–C3. There is one very special sort of way in which humans can 'serve' the gods, as their 'slaves' (*Euthyphro* 13D5): that is, by doing philosophy – or rather, by 'doing philosophy and examining [one]self and others' (to quote the *Apology*).[43] And the 'fine and good' thing the gods will achieve through our doing that is to reduce the amount of ignorance in the world, including ignorance of the very sort that Euthyphro is exhibiting: ignorance of his own ignorance, or, in the terms suggested by the *Charmides*, lack of self-knowledge. The truly pious, then, will make people better people[44] (by making them wiser);

---

[43] '(It would have been a terrible thing to do if I'd stayed where I was positioned in battle by the generals,) but when the god gave me my orders, as I thought and understood, that I must live doing philosophy and examining myself and others . . . I left my post' (*Apology* 28E4–29A1). 'Others' here is *hoi alloi* – apparently *the* others, i.e. everyone else – rather than *alloi*; since there is clearly no question of Socrates' examining the total world population, and he evidently has exactly the same thing in mind as in the passage from which this chapter started, and which has *alloi* without the definite article, 28E–29E will be one of those contexts that demonstrate that *hoi alloi* may be indistinguishable, in the right context, from *alloi*.

[44] In the course of trying to establish what kind of service to (of) the gods Euthyphro might want to say piety is, Socrates has raised, only at once to withdraw, the possibility that piety might benefit the

and they will possess at least a Socratic kind of wisdom or expertise, itself founded in self-knowledge. Piety, service to god, *is* on this account a kind of wisdom.[45] But then for Socrates all the excellences are a kind of wisdom, or knowledge: that I take to be the idea, however incompletely worked out, that Plato means us to carry away from the last part of the *Protagoras*,[46] and from the *Meno* – despite the fact that he has Socrates present the equation (excellence = wisdom), in both cases, as no more than part of an argument which, for all that he actually says, leaves him without any clear commitment to it.[47] But that is the way he typically operates, appearing to leave things open while actually wanting to take us, even as he fails to take his interlocutors, down a particular route. (It will be especially clear in this kind of context how important for my thesis the near-identity[48] between Plato and his Socrates is. Of course *Socrates* has no inkling of our – the readers' – existence; but he is nevertheless saying things to us that a Protagoras or a Meno cannot hear.)

There is no sorting, in the *Euthyphro*, of Euthyphro's beliefs,[49] any more than Socrates sorts Charmides' and Critias' beliefs in the *Charmides* – or Laches' and Nicias' in the *Laches*, or Lysis' and Menexenus' in the *Lysis*. Indeed, as I have said, it is not clear to me that such a description fits what Socrates is doing in any Platonic dialogue. (Yes, he may spend a lot of time working with an interlocutor to establish what the interlocutor really has, or might have, in mind; and lots of false notions come to be thrown away. But if Socratic method is really about isolating the true items – whatever they may be – among the things individuals believe, and believed before Socrates got to them, then it can only be said that he does not put his method into practice in the extant dialogues.) The agenda does not even

---

gods by making *them* better, by analogy with looking after horses and dogs (13B–D). The intended outcome of the argument, for the reader (if it is as I suggest), will be the counterpart of this: piety is about making people (not gods!) better.

[45] Cf. also *Phaedo* 60E–61B.   [46] I.e. from 329C to the end.

[47] In the *Protagoras*, he initially introduces the idea by way of clarification of Protagoras' conception of excellence, and ends the dialogue mildly pointing out the irony of a situation in which someone who like Protagoras claims to teach excellence resists its reduction to knowledge/wisdom, while someone like Socrates who is sceptical about the teachability of excellence nevertheless has attempted to demonstrate that all the excellences are knowledge (see especially 361A–C). If excellence is teachable, surely it must be knowledge, and if it is knowledge, it must be teachable (cf. *Meno*)?

[48] 'Near-identity': the qualification will perhaps be more necessary in the case of a dialogue like the *Euthyphro*, where Socrates claims to think he might actually get some knowledge out of Euthyphro, as a religious expert (a claim that we perhaps oughtn't to dismiss quite outright, in the light of his account of his activity in the *Apology*: see chapter 1 above). In the *Protagoras*, Socrates is already in the opening scene warning the young Hippocrates about the dangers of 'retailers' of wisdom like Protagoras.

[49] Cf. text to n. 9 above. By 'beliefs' here, as in the earlier context, I mean convictions, not judgements or 'opinions' adopted for the moment.

fictionally come from the people Socrates talks to;[50] it comes from Socrates. He needs to know, and his interlocutors need to know, whether whatever is being put forward[51] on each occasion (*Charmides* 165B8) is true or not: first, because they all need to know the truth, and second, because if they don't have it to hand now, they need to know that they don't in order to continue the investigation somewhere else.[52] But there is a difference between Socrates and his interlocutors in all the dialogues I have so far been discussing. Socrates is ahead of all of his interlocutors not just in terms of self-knowledge, but in terms of that acquired – accumulated – set of beliefs that have, so far, stood up to testing.[53] A few of those he talks to, like Simmias and Cebes in the *Phaedo*, and Glaucon in the *Republic*, have come some way with him; some, like Lysis and to a lesser extent Menexenus in the *Lysis*, are able to make at least temporary progress with him in the course of the conversation. But most at least begin with little idea even of what he will want to talk about. There will be a similar distribution among those who are there to listen to his defence in the *Apology* – and no doubt, as Plato expects, among his readers.

4 'SELF-EXAMINATION' IN THE *PHAEDRUS*

I inquire . . . not into these things [sc. the myths] but into myself, to see whether I am actually a beast more complex and more violent than Typhon, or both a tamer and a simpler creature, sharing some divine and un-Typhonic portion by nature. (*Phaedrus* 230A3–6; part of a passage quoted at the beginning of this chapter)

This is evidently self-examination of quite a different kind from the self-examination of the *Apology* or the *Charmides*. The idea that the self might be more *complex* than monstrous Typhon is likely to recall – for those who know it – a passage in *Republic* IX, which pictures the human soul as containing three kinds of creatures: a multicoloured (*poikilos*), many-headed beast; a lion; and a human being (588B–589B). These stand for the

---

[50] That is, except to the extent that the agenda fits them (they are the sort of people that ought to be able to participate in an intelligent discussion of the topic in hand, and are chosen – by Socrates, and his author – for that reason).

[51] Usually not directly by Socrates, though he often has a hand in it (if he does put something forward on his own, as at *Lysis* 216C–217A, he makes a song and dance about how unusual that is).

[52] Burnyeat claims that 'Socrates' earlier interlocutors, once they have grasped what is asked of them, are prompt enough to produce a definition', whereas Theaetetus requires Socrates as 'midwife' (1992 (1977): 58); but this seems to be a false antithesis, especially if 'midwifery' can be allowed to extend to helping people to see what they are saying, which covers a large part of what Socrates seems to be doing with his 'earlier interlocutors'.

[53] These will then be strong enough to count as *convictions*, even as knowledge – despite Socrates' reluctance to treat them as such (see further chapter 8 below).

three parts of the soul whose existence has been argued for in *Republic* IV: the human being represents our rational part, the lion the part in us that values honour and the rewards of competition, while the monster stands for the part containing our multifarious appetites, for food, drink, sex and so on. In the *Phaedrus* itself, the three parts are figured differently, and – in the case of the appetitive part – in a rather more kindly way;[54] reason is the charioteer, the other two parts his horses, one white and one black, the second with an inbuilt tendency to go off in the wrong direction, and barely controllable. In any case, what Socrates' question at the beginning of the dialogue seems to amount to is whether he is, himself (and by implication whether we humans are, in general), identifiable with the *appetitive* aspects of the soul, which are deeply irrational, or with its *rational* aspects.

The question is, of course, already answered in the *Republic* image, insofar as this makes reason, and only reason, human. However the Socrates of the *Phaedrus* seems committed to the idea that all human souls necessarily, and irreversibly, combine irrational elements with the rational.[55] So for this Socrates, at any rate, it is not as if we could somehow slough off the irrational in us. He has something rather different in mind: something, perhaps, along the lines of the following passage, from *Republic* x:

That the soul is something immortal, then, both our recent argument and (the) others[56] will compel us to suppose; but as for what sort of thing it is in truth, we must not observe *that* [neuter; i.e. what sort of thing it is][57] in a state of mutilation both from the association of the body and from other bad things,[58] as we[59] observe it now – we must see through, by reasoning, in an adequate fashion (*hikanōs*) to the sort of thing it is when it becomes pure, and then one[60] will find it to be *much* more beautiful, and distinguish more clearly things like justice and injustice and everything we've now gone through. As things are we've said true things about it, as to the kind of thing it appears to be in the present; however, we've observed

---

54 At any rate to the extent that the black horse is no monster, and has only one head; but then the *Phaedrus* is in this context only concerned with one aspect of appetite – lust.

55 See chapter 2, p. 116: no soul, according to the myth of the *Phaedrus*, can guarantee that it won't find itself back at some point in a body, however philosophically it may conduct itself.

56 Which will and won't be the arguments of the *Phaedo* (and the *Meno*).

57 The point is important: Socrates' claim is precisely that we can't observe the soul itself under present conditions.

58 Importantly, the body is not itself implied to be bad (not 'from the association both of the body and of other bad things'); it's the *association* of the body with the soul that's bad, not the body. ('And from other bad things': the Greek, *kai allōn kakōn*, could actually mean 'and from bad things as well', but the context seems to rule that out.)

59 'We' the interlocutors in the *Republic*, or 'we' human beings in ordinary life?

60 By switching from 'we' to an indeterminate third-person subject for this new verb Socrates avoids, as he so often does, any suggestion that he has any privileged insight.

it under similar conditions to those under which people see the briny Glaucus, and wouldn't any longer easily catch sight of his ancient (*archaios*) nature, because some of his former parts have been broken off, while others have been smashed and completely mutilated by the waves, and other things – shells, algae and rocks – have attached themselves to him, so that he looks more like any wild animal than what he was naturally like. It's like that that we observe the soul, too, disposed as it is by countless bad things . . . What we must do, Glaucon, is why we have to look there . . . [namely,] to the soul's love of wisdom [its *philosophia*], and have in mind what it grasps and the sorts of associations it aims for, on the grounds of its affinity to the divine and immortal and to what always is . . .[61] (*Republic* x, 611B9–D8)

According to this perspective, the irrational 'parts' of the soul do not belong to its *essence*.[62] That at first sight might seem to mean that our real selves – despite Book iv's introduction of irrational soul-parts whose desires, unlike those of reason, are not directed towards the good[63] – are identical with our *rational* selves.[64] However, closer examination of the context in *Republic* x suggests that we should not be too quick to make any such inference. The sentence last quoted continues 'and (we must have in mind) of what sort it might come to be once it has followed, all of it (*pasa*), (the divine and immortal and what always is) . . .' (611E3–4). This at once recalls the passage in Book vii (518B–D), which makes education into a 'turning' of '*the whole soul*' (*holē hē psuchē*, 518C8): 'the whole soul', that is, and not just its rational part or element.[65] The Book x passage must, I think, be interpreted in the same way: whatever else might be sloughed off in the process of education, it won't be our capacity to feel hungry or thirsty, for example, or to get angry. It is rather that the energy (as we might put it) that will often be used up in relation to food, drink and in general 'the concerns of the body' will be redirected, in the case of the true philosopher, towards the acquisition of knowledge.[66]

As in the *Phaedrus* myth, we always retain our horses. Where would a charioteer be without any horses?[67] So in its essential, true, nature the

---

[61] Surely a *certain* reference to *Phaedo* (80A–B)?

[62] Interestingly, in the *Timaeus* the irrational parts are treated as mortal: 'another kind of soul . . . the mortal kind' (69C7–8) is given to human beings by the lesser, created gods. See further below.

[63] This at any rate appears to be the outcome of the careful argument at iv, 438A–439B.

[64] This is probably the view of the soul taken by the *Alcibiades* (see section 1, p. 124 above). Gerson 2003 advocates our taking it as *the* Platonic view of the soul; I dissent.

[65] The soul is there envisaged as being freed, not from barnacles, but from the leaden weights 'fastened to it by feastings and gluttonous pleasures in things like that' (519B1–2): same idea, different image.

[66] Thus in the 'hydraulic' image of the soul at *Republic* vi, 485D–E.

[67] Even the *gods* have horses – but only, I suggest, because the mechanics of the myth demand it. Divine horses feed on ambrosia and nectar after their charioteers have feasted on the sights beyond the heavens: Socrates here models on us, and the requirements of our survival – which is precisely the sort of thing he says we shouldn't do (246C–D).

soul *is* a rational entity that loves wisdom; Socrates really is no Typhon, but 'a tamer and a simpler creature', as is each of us. But none of us is entirely 'simple': Socrates in *Republic* x is at first content to leave it open whether there are many kinds of soul in us or only one,[68] but then, in the eschatological myth with which he closes the whole work, he seems to rule out the second option. We shall all be reborn into bodies, and so shall always potentially stand in need of irrational desires – of the sort that Timaeus says are needed 'if indeed there was ever going to be a mortal race' (*Timaeus* 70E5).[69] One of the purposes of the next chapter but one will be to investigate this notion of the 'simpler' soul rather more closely, in the specific context of the project of the *Republic*.

---

[68] 'And then [sc. when one looked to the soul's love of wisdom, etc.] one would see its true nature, whether containing many *eidē* [kinds, sc. of soul] or only one, or in whatever form and however it is' (x, 612A3–5).

[69] Said there specifically of the appetites; but the same will apply to the 'spirited' desires (for victory, etc.). It is in the light of this sentence that we should understand the idea of a 'mortal' soul in the *Timaeus* (see n. 62 above). However there will also be questions to be asked about the status of Timaeus' account of the physical world as a whole: see chapter 10 below.

CHAPTER 4

The moral psychology of the Gorgias

In this chapter, postponing what will essentially be an extended treatment of the *Republic* in chapters 5–9, I discuss three problems in another pre-*Republic* dialogue, *Gorgias*. Each of these problems turns out – I claim – to be resolvable in terms of Plato's writing strategies; the outcome will be a further case study on that topic, but one which at the same time reinforces my so far relatively sketchy account of the positions from which Plato's Socrates starts – and starts, I claim, *as much in the* Republic *as in the dialogues that precede it.*

I PROBLEMS

The *Gorgias*, from most points of view, looks anomalous.[1] For on the one hand the dialogue contains one of the most spectacular applications of the Socratic theory of action, in the shape of Socrates' claim that orators and tyrants *have no power*[2] – a claim from which he not only never retreats, in the rest of the dialogue, but on which he seems to build even more surprising, paradoxical, even (apparently) comical claims. Those supposedly enviable people, who – so Gorgias has claimed – can do whatever they want, in fact – Socrates says – do *nothing* they want, only what seems best to them.

---

[1] Vlastos 1991: ch. 2 treats the *Gorgias* as straightforwardly one of 'the dialogues of Plato's earlier period' (p. 46); evidently he misses the problems that I shall identify (and, I hope, resolve), problems which on the surface suggest at least some kind of *transitional* status for the *Gorgias*. (The dialogue looks 'Socratic' – for those who use such language – but also, simultaneously, *un-*'Socratic'.) Irwin 1979 sees the *Gorgias* as using, and failing to reconcile, two different approaches to 'good-independent' desires: '(1) The unhealthy soul has a faulty conception of its good, and needs to be restrained because otherwise its desires – all good-dependent – will mislead it. (2) Its strong good-independent desires make it incontinent ['weak-willed'], so that it needs control . . . The conclusions of [the] two lines of argument [depending on these different approaches] in the dialogue are never satisfactorily reconciled' (p. 218). What I set out to resist in the present chapter is something very like Irwin's account here; though I differ significantly in the way I state (1), the Socratic position. See n. 5 below.
[2] *Gorgias* 464B–468E.

143

'How ridiculous!'[3] responds Polus. But of course Socrates is perfectly serious: they *don't* do what they want. Why not? Because they don't have the knowledge to enable them to distinguish properly between good and bad, and lacking that, they fail to get what is really good for them – which must be what they want; people don't want what is actually bad (Polus, Socrates' interlocutor at this point, readily agrees).[4] This, surely, is the full Socratic position, which makes our beliefs, not our desires, responsible for our mistakes. We only want what is really good for us; the problem is to know what that is, and here is where we go wrong.[5]

Yet on the other hand – and this is what makes the dialogue seem anomalous – the *Gorgias* is likely, to most readers, to look in significant respects significantly un-Socratic.

(a) In the first place, it seems to have a great deal to say on the subject of, and indeed about the *necessity* for, punishment. People will be worse off if they commit injustice than if they have it done to them, Socrates claims; they will be even worse off if they commit injustice and are not punished for it; any rhetorical skills they have will therefore be most beneficially employed if used to bring themselves and their family and friends to justice, and punishment. And punishment then figures strongly, again, in the chilling myth with which Socrates closes: after death, if we are to believe him (and he claims to believe the story himself), the unjust will be judged, and will suffer appropriately for their injustice; if they are incurable, they will suffer for eternity. But, one may well ask, if it is all supposed to be a matter of intellectual error, what use is it to *punish* anyone?[6] It appears from Socrates' argument that he is seeing punishment as something that improves people, reforms them. But how can making people suffer – fining, imprisoning, flogging, exiling, executing them – how can

---

[3] The adjectives he uses are actually more like 'perverse' (*schetlios*), 'astonishing' (*huperphuēs*: 'beyond the natural'): 467B10.

[4] See especially 468D. In the first part of the *Gorgias* Socrates talks to the famous rhetorician Gorgias, after whom the dialogue is named, in the second to his pupil Polus ('Colt'); Callicles is another, and more formidable, pupil of the great man, whose views somewhat resemble Thrasymachus' in the *Republic*.

[5] See Penner 1991. One absolutely crucial difference between Penner's and Irwin's interpretation – see n. 1 above – of Socrates' position is that Penner sees it as insisting, however paradoxically, that we *only* desire what is *really* good for us. Insofar as Irwin talks – in the passage cited in n. 1 – of ['good-dependent'] desires as potentially '*misleading*' the soul, and so apparently being responsible for its 'faulty conception of its good', he evidently does not take this line. ('Good-dependent', then, will have a distinctly weaker force than in Penner's interpretation: see n. 25 below.) My own interpretation follows Penner's rather than Irwin's.

[6] The problem is seen, and clearly stated, in Brickhouse and Smith 2002 (though the solution proposed there is different: for Brickhouse, Socrates' own position turns out to be actually such as to allow room for, indeed actually to require, punishment).

any of that make them *think* better? It might make them abstain next time the occasion arises, out of fear, or any number of times; but it surely won't give them that better intellectual grasp of things – of what's really good, and what's really bad – that Socrates' claim about those outstanding criminals, orators and tyrants, seems to require. Here the *Gorgias* seems much closer to the alternative view of human nature that he evokes and builds upon in *Republic* II–IV and VIII–IX – a view that gives people a suffi-cient degree of *irrationality* to make them susceptible to the kind of dumb conditioning that the idea of punishment, if it is not seen merely in terms of deterrence, seems necessarily to involve. As I shall argue in the following chapter, the Socrates of the *Republic* will find a way of allowing the two different views of humanity to exist side by side with each other; but at the same time he clearly recognizes the differences between them. The Socrates of the *Gorgias*, by contrast, seems to move from one view to the other as if they were perfectly compatible. His treatment of punishment is one example of this, insofar as he appears to combine ordinary notions of punishment with 'perverse' sorts of ideas that ought to make such notions merely redundant.

(b) The last third of the dialogue, when Callicles takes over the discussion with Socrates, offers another example of the same apparent phenomenon. Socrates there relies heavily on the idea that we need to *control ourselves*, and especially our desires; but again, on the theory that underpins what he says about tyrants and orators (see above), our desires need no such control, since all of them are in any case rightly directed towards the real good. The notion of 'self-control', insofar as that involves the control, by reason or the better parts of ourselves, of our desires and passions, simply has no place in such a context. Once again, two incompatible sets of ideas appear simply to be juxtaposed, even jammed together.

(c) Together with these two problems I propose to discuss a third, dif-ferent but related. Like the first, it arises out of Socrates' encounter with Polus in the second act of the *Gorgias*. Socrates there makes the claim – one that he also says (474B) that *Polus, and everyone else*, accept as well – that doing injustice is worse, for the agent, than would be his having it done to him.[7] What is of special interest here, in the context of a discussion of

---

[7] Vlastos, spells out the claim differently: '*exactly what* [Socrates] *means*' is that '[d]oing wrong is worse *for the wrongdoer* than is suffering it *for the victim*' (Vlastos 1991: 144–5). But Socrates himself, as Vlastos points out on his own account, simply states the claim as 'doing wrong is worse than having it done to one' (so e.g., at 474B), and there seems to me to be no basis in the text for supposing that the doer and the sufferer are meant to be different people – indeed, the text actually tells the other

Socratic and (apparently) un-Socratic elements in the *Gorgias*, is the way in which Socrates is (apparently) content to argue to a conclusion that he himself evidently owns from what *Polus* accepts, and indeed accepts with enthusiasm[8] – and this, against the background of a general context that shows him to be, or at any rate ought to put him, at some distance from the very things that Polus accepts and that he, Socrates, relies on for his conclusion. Polus' position is – or at any rate he *says* it is: see below – that doing injustice is better for the agent than suffering it, but more shameful (*aischion*); by having Polus agree that fineness/beauty (*kallos*, treated as the opposite of *aischos*) is a matter of what is useful (good), pleasant, or useful/good *and* pleasant, and that doing injustice is not more painful (474D ff.), Socrates compels him to change horses and say that after all it is doing injustice that is the worse thing, not suffering it. But now elsewhere in the *Gorgias* Socrates adopts a distinctly radical view of what is good for us: so, for example, at 511C–512C, when he talks about the modest claims that would be made by any truly expert navigator: yes, Socrates says, the navigator saves people's lives, but who is to say – the navigator certainly won't – that he will always have done them a service by saving them? No one else in the dialogue, and certainly not Polus, would even flirt with such a radical view. How, then, can Socrates be content to argue to a conclusion about what is better on the basis of Polus', evidently rather more everyday, notion of what counts as better? Here, one might suppose, is another case of the Socrates of the *Gorgias* carrying his convictions lightly. Again, the Socrates of the *Lysis* and the *Symposium* seems straightforwardly to *identify* the fine/beautiful with the good;[9] what business has he, then, proposing to treat it as *either* the good *or* the pleasant, *or* both (if it is the same Socrates, which is what is currently at issue)?

Now it could be that we should simply say that it is all a piece of bad, or, probably worse, merely opportunistic argument. On this version of events, the end result would be that *Polus* agrees that doing injustice is worse, according to *Socrates'* conception of 'worse', by means of Socrates' playing on *Polus'* (or else, if Polus oughtn't to own up to it, nobody's) notion of good and bad. But the consequences of such a diagnosis look just too unpalatable: if Socrates is prepared to argue like that, one might reasonably

---

way: see e.g., 469B, and esp. 474B7 (Polus to Socrates) 'would *you* prefer to be treated unjustly than to do injustice?' In one way there is no real disagreement here: the issue just is: should one prefer, e.g., to be the one torturing, or the one tortured? Vlastos' introduction of different perspectives appears to be what allows him to accuse Socrates of a fairly uninteresting sort of fallacy.

8 475A2–4 (on which see section 2(c) below).   9 See especially *Lysis* 216C–217A, *Symposium* 204D–E.

ask why we should take him seriously at all.[10] I prefer, then, to set up the problem in the terms suggested above: why is it that – or is it really the case that – the Socrates of the *Gorgias* is so selective in applying what appear to be distinctively his own, radical, beliefs?

2 SOLUTIONS

(a) Punishment

The theme of punishment seems to surface as a distinct topic at 469A, when Socrates declares that the person who *kills someone justly*, while not being miserable, *athlios*, is nevertheless not enviable. We might suppose that killing people justly, i.e. presumably, executing people who deserve to die, is hardly a Socratic thing to do; still, it was not Socrates who brought up the subject of killing, but first Gorgias,[11] and then Polus[12] – and all Socrates wants to do here, at 469A, is to draw up a list of things in rough order of desirability: killing people unjustly makes one miserable, i.e. the opposite of happy, and while being killed unjustly does not contribute to one's happiness, it is less unfortunate either than killing unjustly or being killed justly; similarly with killing justly (if it does not bring 'misery'). At around this point (470A), Socrates gets Polus to agree that being punished is a bad thing; but that is only in order to show him that good and bad are *his*, Polus', own criteria of desirability and undesirability as much as they are Socrates' (470A–B). Then Socrates shows his hand: happiness is a matter of being fine and good, unhappiness a matter of injustice and badness (470E) – which provokes Polus into bringing in his key witness, Archelaus, king of Macedon: supremely unjust and bad, but, Polus claims, supremely happy (471A–D). So the battle-lines are drawn, along with the two men's respective positions on punishment: Socrates thinks it a good thing for people to be punished if they are unjust, on the grounds that that will make them better people (and so happier); Polus thinks punishment simply *bad* (472E).

Thus Polus and Socrates are taking punishment in different ways. Polus takes it merely as involving suffering for the person being punished; Socrates

---

[10] True, some scholars – e.g., Kahn 1983 – are willing to accept a Socrates who merely sets out to fool his interlocutors; but I, for one, would side with Vlastos in preferring a Socrates who merely went wrong to one who cheats. (In this case, I think Socrates actually does neither.) Could Plato really be imagined as making a discussion of how to live our lives – the ultimate subject of the dialogue – hang on a mere sleight of hand, when his own preferred choice, and that of his character Socrates, includes *philosophy*?

[11] 457C.   [12] 466B–C.

sees it as a means to improvement. But there is, nevertheless, nothing so far to stop them having the same kinds of punishment in mind: fines, flogging – and certainly, Socrates is still talking about execution, which seems to put the general point beyond doubt. So punishment seems to be being seen, by both men, primarily in terms of conditioning, and perhaps deterrence. Why else would flogging, imprisonment or execution be thought to help with anything? And this is consistent with the way Socrates argues his case: he builds on Polus' admission, in 473E–475E, that the fine (*to kalon*) is the good or the pleasant (or both), to bring him to agree – or to see? – that just punishment must be beneficial (it is plainly not *pleasant*); and the final move is to use an analogy with medical treatment to suggest that such punishment is beneficial insofar as it 'cures' the 'patient' of his injustice.

However there are several interesting things about the way this move is made. The first is that again Socrates gets Polus to make the running: what, he asks, is the expertise (*technē*) that frees us from badness and injustice, as medicine frees us from sickness?

> 'Or if you can't answer just like that, look at it like this: . . . to whom to we take those that are sick in their bodies?'
> 'To the doctors.'
> 'And where do we take those who are unjust and uncontrolled (*akolastoi*)?'[13]
> 'To the judges, do you mean?' (478A1–5)

To which Socrates simply responds:

> 'In order to pay the penalty for their crimes (*dikēn didonai*)?'
> 'That's what I say.'
> 'So don't those who punish (*kolazein*) correctly punish by employing a sort of justice (*dikaiosunē tis*)?'
> 'Clearly.'
> 'So (the art of) money-making frees us from poverty, medicine frees us from sickness, and justice (*dikē*) frees us from licence (*akolasia*) and injustice.'
> 'It appears so.' (478A5–B2)

What is particularly striking here is the way Socrates actually refrains from endorsing Polus' proposal that judges are like doctors; he then says only that judges punish by using *a sort of* justice. (That itself might be interpreted as a deliberate *refusal* to endorse Polus' suggestion. In any case, Socrates' turn of phrase here needs explanation.) And then, as he moves on from the conclusion about what justice does for those it punishes,

---

[13] A more traditional rendering of *akolastos* (literally 'un-punished'?) is 'licentious'.

we find Socrates combining the language of 'punishment' and 'paying the penalty' with a quite different sort of language: that of *admonition*. Thus at 478E3–4, he talks about the person being relieved of his injustice (*adikia*) as 'being admonished' (*nouthetoumenos*), and 'being rebuked' (*epiplēttomenos*),[14] as well as 'paying the penalty', (*dikēn didous* – and uses these descriptions in that order); then at 478E7–479A1, the same verb for 'admonition', *noutheteisthai*, is combined with 'punishing' (*kolazesthai*) and 'paying the penalty' (*dikēn didonai*). What is significant about this is that the same verb, *nouthetein*, in another famous passage, is *contrasted* with 'punishing', *kolazein*: this at *Apology* 26A, where Socrates says that if he did what he is accused of without meaning to, then he needs someone to teach and admonish, *nouthetein*, him rather than punishment, *kolasis*.

So what, someone might say: look at *Laws* 879D, where there is talk of 'admonition' (*nouthetein*) *by means of a beating* (*plēgais*). That just goes to show – the objector might continue – that we shouldn't read too much into *Gorgias* 478–9. To which I respond that, if we look closely at the *Gorgias* as a whole, there are other clear indications that Socrates holds back from any straightforward acceptance of legal punishment as a means to the improvement of men's souls; or at any rate, *that he has a rival kind of 'justice' and 'punishment' on offer*. (Hence the 'sort of' at 478A; but more of that in a moment.) (1) At 505C, when Callicles proposes to retire from the discussion, Socrates remarks that 'this person won't put up with being helped, and with himself having done to him what we are talking about, being *punished* (*kolazomenos*). So Socratic dialectic is, apparently, a kind of punishment. Mere metaphor, perhaps; but then see (2) 509B–E. Socrates here argues that what we need above all is a defence (*boētheia*, 'means of assistance'), both for oneself and for one's own, against the worst thing of all: injustice. It isn't enough merely to *wish* not to act unjustly, any more than it is enough merely to wish not to be treated unjustly; one must get 'a certain power (*dunamis*) and expertise, *technē* [i.e. I take it, a power that consists in an expertise], since if one doesn't learn whatever it is (*auta*) and practise it, one will act unjustly' (509D8–E2). And finally, Socrates rather puzzlingly refers to a 'previous agreement' (E4) that no one does injustice willingly, or wishing it.[15] All of this surely strongly suggests, and is meant to suggest, that

---

[14] Now *epiplēttein* can be a matter of *beating* (thus the Hackett translator renders *epiplēttomenos* as 'get[ting] *lashed*'); but it can also be 'rebuke' – and the ambiguity, after the use of *nouthetein*, is perhaps particularly acute.

[15] I.e. *boulomenos*. For that 'previous agreement', Irwin 1979 (ad loc.) compares 480A, and comments 'But 467C–468E did not prove this. Socrates must mean that since they have found that injustice is bad for the agent, only people who do not know this will do injustice . . .'

what Socrates thinks we need is what he so often says we need: *knowledge*. So in a climactic passage at 521D–522A, when he claims to be the only person to attempt, aim at (*epicheirein*)[16] the true art of statesmanship (*politikē*),[17] because what he says aims at what is best rather than at what is most pleasant, comparing *himself*, this time, to the – expert, knowledgeable – doctor, who makes his patients suffer to get well (punishes them?).

The contrast here, of course, is with rhetoric; and that, I believe, takes us straight back to a passage at 464B–465C, where Socrates, talking to Gorgias, opposes political expertise, *politikē*, as consisting of the science of legislation, *nomothetikē* and justice, *dikaiosunē*, to 'sophistic' (*sophistikē*) and rhetoric. Exactly how we are intended to take these pairings, and the two contrasts (i.e. *nomothetikē/sophistikē* and *dikaiosunē/rhētorikē*), is not immediately clear, but here is a suggestion which appears to me to do justice to at least most of the phenomena of text and context: the science (art, expertise) of legislation (*nomothetikē*), being to the soul what the science of physical exercise (*gumnastikē*) is to the body, is that expertise (*technē*), whatever it is, that makes people/souls good; and 'justice' (*dikaiosunē*), being to souls what medicine is to the body, is that expertise, whatever it is, that puts souls to rights when they go wrong. Now for Gorgias, and for Polus, the first of these expertises, legislation, will be straightforwardly identifiable with the art of the lawgiver; and maybe that is right. But when Socrates claims to be the only person trying for the politician's/statesman's expertise, he will himself implicitly be setting up in competition with the lawgiver.[18] He will be competing with the lawgiver not just because he appropriates the *name* 'political expert/statesman' (*politikos*), but because what he specifically claims to do, in 521D–522A, is to (try to) make his fellow-citizens into better people.[19] Now admittedly, in 521D–522A he compares himself as statesman/political expert with the *doctor*, which in terms of the pairings and contrasts back in 464–5 ought to make him an expert in justice rather than in legislation. And that, as we have seen, is how he has in fact represented himself, to Callicles (as 'punishing' him, *kolazōn*). But his wording in 521D7–8 perhaps does suggest the wider claim, i.e. to expertise *both* in legislation *and* in justice: he is the only person 'to attempt

---

[16] The Hackett translator's 'take up' for *epicheirein* seems to me to miss Socrates' point.

[17] The 'true' art or science, as opposed to statesmanship, or politics, as it is presently and normally practised; what statesmanship *is*, in itself. True statesmanship, and the true statesman, is the subject of the *Politicus*.

[18] Much, perhaps, as the ideal statesman does in the *Politicus*, with the difference that that ideal person will actually *possess* the relevant expertise.

[19] Which is, again, how I take *nomothetikē* to be understood, because of its pairing with *gumnastikē*.

the true expertise of politics and to practise politics'. The two expertises are, presumably, or involve, the same sort of knowledge.[20]

In short, *that* is why we have that reference to the judges' justice as a 'sort of' justice at 478A: 'punishment', or *kolazein*, for Socrates, is not a matter for the courts but for *philosophical dialectic*. So then, someone might reasonably ask, why on earth should he couch all that long argument with Polus, and then with Callicles, in terms of punishment as normally understood? Well, that perhaps is a question we should have to raise in any case, since Socrates has no reason to believe that punishment as normally understood made anyone any better, and Polus evidently doesn't believe it – if he did, he would hardly treat Socrates' conclusion about the benefits of punishment with quite such incredulity. The reason why Socrates mounts his argument in the terms he does is, I propose, simply because they are the terms his opponents, or interlocutors, can readily understand (even if they scornfully reject the ideas he uses them to frame). Similarly with that basic analysis around which so much in the conversation with Polus turns, of 'fine', *kalon*, into either good or pleasant or both.[21] But at the same time there is also nothing that is not also true when we substitute *Socrates'* conception of punishment for the ordinary one; or rather, to put it strongly, Socrates' argument strictly only *becomes* true once his conception of punishment ('punishment') is substituted for the ordinary one. (Punishment – 'punishment' – of the ordinary kind in fact does not make people better; certainly not, if 'better' is 'more knowledgeable', 'wiser'.) People will be better off if their unhealthy souls submit to the medicine of dialectic; and yes, they should use all their powers of persuasion to get their family and friends, and themselves, to take the same medicine (in which case, of course, those powers of persuasion will themselves have little to do with *rhetoric* as ordinarily understood).[22]

The dialogue as a whole is an illustration of that Socratic, dialectical, counterpart to rhetoric. And the myth of the afterlife in the *Gorgias* is part of that dialectic. What it says is true, Socrates seems to claim (523A). Even Callicles won't take him as wanting to say that it is *literally* true, because

---

[20] And after all, back in 465 we were told that sophists and orators are 'muddled up together in the same territory and on the same subjects . . . and don't know what to make of each other, nor do others know what to make of them' (465C4–7); at 520A6–7, sophist and orator 'are the same thing, or something close to that – the same *sort* of thing'. Perhaps we can suppose a similar 'muddle' , or 'jumbling' (*phuresthai*), between *nomothetikē* and *dikaiosunē*: there *are* two different functions, i.e. making people better people and mending them when they go wrong; but in Socrates' case the two functions merge into one.

[21] This is not, however, to say that Socrates is in either case *merely* relying on what Polus will accept; his argument is not merely *ad hominem* (see following note).

[22] On fine as good or pleasant or both: this too is something Socrates can live with, on his own terms: see section 2(c) below.

after all, at 481A–B Socrates seems to have shown that he thinks injustice dies with its possessor – which is precisely what the myth suggests it doesn't do (he was arguing back then, however jocularly, that if you are going to do harm to anyone, one of things you should do is to make sure, if they are unjust, that they will live as long as possible). Rather, Socrates intends, and Callicles will take him as intending, that what the myth *says* is true; or, as we might put it, its *moral* is true. And its moral is straightforward: that if one removes the apparent material gains the unjust can make, injustice brings misery, and the worst injustice brings the worst misery. For his message, Socrates again borrows the language of punishment, though of course a Callicles would not, in this case, use it himself: for someone intelligent like him, all that talk about our being punished in Hades will be stuff and nonsense (which is part, though not the main part, of the point of Socrates' suggestion that Callicles will think it all a mere story: 522E). Nevertheless, Callicles understands the language of the myth, and the message itself is unmistakeable.[23]

Thus the Socrates of the *Gorgias* does not endorse flogging, imprisonment, or any other vulgar kind of punishment. He continues to think that what people need is *talk*. That, as I propose, is exactly what is behind that arresting claim he makes to be – perhaps – the only person practising the political art: ordinary politics (sc. including its judicial arm) fails to achieve what politics should achieve – making people better; only he, Socrates, properly understands how to do that, and actually sets about doing it. Of course none of his interlocutors is in a position to grasp more than a smidgeon of this; but once again we, the readers, have an advantage over them (if we are prepared to take it) – we can read and re-read the argument. And, of course, we have the further advantage of having witnessed Socrates in action before. The *Gorgias* is a perfect example of the way in which Plato has his main character apparently talk *to* the interlocutors while also talking *past* them; also, and perhaps more importantly, of the way in which the Platonic/Socratic perspective helps to clarify, and sometimes even to give a deeper explanation of, the ways in which people ordinarily talk.[24]

[23] That there are *incurable* criminals in Hades is, I think, itself part of what Socrates is appropriating – Callicles himself, Socrates suggests, will be persuaded eventually – see 513C–D; and if Callicles, why not anybody? Or, just possibly, the 'incurables' are those who, like Archelaus, are never in fact 'cured' of their injustice. *Their* suffering is unmixed and, in a sense, without an end except that brought by death, which is no end. (And of course an Archelaus is as much a supreme exemplar for Socrates as he is for Polus: here is someone who did the worst things, and, from Socrates' perspective, lived the worst kind of life.)

[24] For an essay with conclusions interestingly overlapping with my own, see Sedley forthcoming (sent to me in typescript).

(b) Self-control

What, then, of all that talk about 'ruling oneself' and about the need for 'psychic order' in the conversation with Callicles?[25] The main part of the answer is simple: Socrates specifically introduces the idea of 'ruling oneself' in terms of what *the many* think.

'I'm talking about each [ruler] ruling himself. Or shouldn't he do this at all, rule himself, but only rule the others?'
'What are you talking about, "ruling himself"?'
'Nothing complicated, but just as the many say – self-controlled (*sōphrōn*), master of himself (*enkratēs*), ruling the pleasures and appetites within him.' (491D7–E1)

The effect is to move the debate on to Callicles' territory, for he accepts the same sort of model of human nature as 'the many' (reason on the one side, desires on the other), even though he claims to reject the standards of behaviour they base on it. But there is nothing to prevent Socrates having his

[25] The problem of the juxtaposition in the *Gorgias* of Socratic intellectualism with an emphasis on the need for self-control, and a kind of psychic order, was the subject more than twenty years ago of a useful treatment by John Cooper (Cooper 1982; see also Cooper 1999), in which he claims to show – against Terry Irwin – that the moral psychology of the *Gorgias* is in fact Socratic through and through. Cooper wholeheartedly advocated the need to distinguish between Socrates' perspective and that of his interlocutors, as I have done in the preceding section: they may appear to be saying the same things, but that may hide very different views of the matter. However Cooper's view of the 'Socratic theory' in question is radically different from my own. Here is how Cooper sums up Socrates' position: 'First, [Socrates] maintains that whenever a human being does any action he does it with the idea, and because he thinks, that it is the best thing overall for him to do in the circumstances.' This is agreed ground. But the next part is not. '[Socrates] maintains, secondly, a thesis about desire, apparently counting hunger, thirst, and sexual appetite for these purposes as desires: every desire is for its possessor's overall good (perhaps, of course, on a mistaken conception of what that good consists in).' Irwin calls this second thesis a thesis about the "good-dependence" of all desires. But of course Socrates is not saying that all the desires we experience conform to and derive from ("depend upon") our *considered view* of where our good lies. In fact the dependence runs in the other direction: *whatever* desire we have, in having it we judge that whatever it is the desire for will contribute to our overall good . . .' Cooper 1982: 582–3. Each desire I have, then (on this account) involves – Cooper describes the relation as '*entailing*' – a judgement about my overall good, i.e. 'that whatever it is that the desire is for will contribute to [my] overall good', and there are no 'good-independent' desires. But my 'considered view', which is presumably not 'entailed' by a desire, may, or – if it 'rests on knowledge' – will, trump my desire-entailed judgements about my overall good. In this picture each desire comes as a package, as it were, with a judgement, so that any clashes will be between judgements and not desires, and since these are all judgements about the agent's overall good, they can and will be resolved in a peaceful manner. 'When [potential] conflicts [between desires] threaten to arise they must be immediately settled, by the disappearance of one or other of the competing judgments, and so of the (incipient) desire that entails it' (ibid.). On this interestingly complex view of the Socratic position I make no comment except (1) that it leaves the paradox about tyrants and orators looking at best somewhat flabby (they actually *will* want what they say they want); and (2) that it gives us no clue as to how, if judgements are 'entailed' by desires, we are supposed to manage our desires in consequence of our judgements. For an engagement with Cooper's solution to the present problem, see Rowe 2007b, of which the present section is for the most part a fragment.

own way of seeing what Callicles and the many see in terms of 'controlling one's pleasures and desires' – and something of that special way of seeing things surfaces, I propose, at 499E–500A, when he asks Callicles to agree to the suggestion, originally accepted by Polus in 467–8, that we don't want the actions we do, only the things we do them *for* (a special Socratic idea if ever there was one), and then proposes to apply the principle to *pleasant* things: shouldn't we do these too for the sake of good things? Of course Callicles will have his own way of reading this; but equally, because of the connection with 467–8, Socrates will have *his* way of reading it too, one that integrates it with his general account of the good, and so of human motivation. (The pleasantness of a thing, he will be saying, is never an adequate reason for choosing it; to suppose otherwise will be a mistake about the nature of the good.)

Similarly with the idea of psychic order (*taxis, kosmos*). In 503E–504A, in talking about how craftsmen put their materials in order (*eis taxin*, E6), Socrates speaks of their fitting different parts together ('each . . . compels one thing to be fitting and suitable to another . . .'), and then passes to the soul via the body, where again 'ordering' might be thought of as a matter of fitting parts together (adjusting the proportions of different elements); it is then easy enough to understand his treatment of the *soul* in the same terms, especially when he introduces the 'lawful' and 'law' as what brings about psychic order. (That is, we seem to be, still, on the familiar ground occupied by the many, and by Callicles: reason versus desire.) But even as he does this, he also takes us *away* from the familiar.

'And for the structurings and orderings of the soul the name is "lawful" and "law", from which people become lawful and orderly; and these [?] are justice and temperance (*sōphrosunē*). Do you say so, or not?'
'Let it be so.'
'Then won't that orator, the craftsman, the good one,[26] look to these things when he applies whatever speeches he makes to souls . . . and when he gives whatever gift he gives, and when he takes away whatever he takes away? He'll always have his mind on this; to see that the souls of the citizens acquire justice and get rid of injustice . . .' (504D1–E2)

Here, we are back with the justice which is a part of political expertise, improving people's souls just as the medical doctor heals their bodies, and with Gorgias' orator, who knows about justice and so brings about justice in others.[27] But that is not, of course, what real orators are like. Socrates

---

[26] That is, the *good*, expert orator.
[27] 460A–461B; this view of oratory is one that Gorgias has only proposed belatedly, and under pressure from Socrates.

has suddenly shifted to talking about what orators *should* be; just as he will go on to talk about what political experts should be – that is, like himself, the true 'doctor' of souls, telling people the straightforward truth (521D–522A). And that suggests a different kind of 'justice' altogether, and an altogether different kind of talk: dialectic, not rhetoric. The rest of the argument here in 503–5[28] has its own version of that same analogy as in 521–2: doctors don't give 'lots of food or drink, and the pleasantest' (504E7–8) to their sick patients; they actually prevent them from filling themselves up with what they desire. Just so with the soul: 'as long as it is corrupt, by being senseless [without *nous*: *anoētos*], intemperate, unjust, and impious, we should restrain it from its appetites, and not allow it to do anything else except what will make it better' (505B2–4). Or, to put it another way, 521–2 tells us how *Socrates*, or a Socratic expert, would handle sick souls.

An objection: how will talking to people 'restrain their appetites'? Does Socrates really suppose that people's passions can be controlled by merely *reasoning* with them? These are, I respond, badly formed questions. Socrates' theory just does not allow for appetites getting out of hand, by themselves. If someone has what we are inclined to call an insatiable appetite, Socrates will stay firm, and call even *that* a matter of intellectual error: the person just has the wrong beliefs about the good – he believes passionately, as it were, that the so-called objects of his appetite are the things to go for. This is how he will understand the Calliclean individual. We, and Callicles, will analyse this person's situation in terms of passion, even of passion overcoming reason; and that is why we will talk about the need to 'restrain his desires', and Callicles will applaud him for not restraining them.[29] And these are the terms in which Socrates chooses to frame his argument. But he does not *endorse* those terms. Those people who have souls in bad condition – like those orators and tyrants of *Gorgias* 464–8 – do not, on Socrates' account, desire what they say they desire; what they really desire they don't know at all. They just need to become better, i.e. wiser, people (though it will still be true that they should be stopped, or should stop themselves, from going for what they presently go for, in ignorance).

The moral psychology of the *Gorgias*, then, I claim, is Socratic, and fully intellectualist. The Socrates of this dialogue is the same Socrates who inhabits the *Lysis*, the *Charmides* – a work that examines what *sōphrosunē*

---

[28] The conclusion is at 505B11–12: 'Thus being tempered (or 'punished': *kolazesthai*) is better for the soul than licence (*akolasia*, i.e. not *kolazesthai*, not being punished) . . .'.

[29] Though as a matter of fact Callicles claims that this is the courageous *and intelligent* choice (492A2–3, etc.).

('sound-mindedness'; '*self-control*'?) is without once introducing the idea
of mental conflict into the discussion – or the *Symposium*.[30]

(c) The good and the just[31]

So to our third problem about the *Gorgias*: Socrates' worrying readiness –
or so it seems – to draw a conclusion he believes from premises (Polus')
that he doesn't believe in. (Mere opportunism?)

We may begin with Socrates' initial suggestion, at 474B, that Polus and
everybody else in fact agrees with him (Socrates) that doing injustice is worse
for the agent than suffering it – and this in the face of Polus' emphatic and
repeated assertion of the exact opposite. What Socrates has in mind here
might perhaps be simply that what he says Polus and everyone else agree
about is somehow a consequence, unforeseen by them, of what they do
in fact quite openly say (that is, that doing injustice is more shameful but
better than having it done to one). After all, that is how things seem to
work out. But to read Socrates in this manner is to put ourselves in danger
of reintroducing, in a different form, the very sort of problem I have raised:
after all, unless we have reason for believing what Polus and everybody else
says, we have little reason for being impressed by any alleged consequences
of the things they say, and neither has Socrates. He has himself already
expressed scorn at Polus for relying on witness-statements for the purposes
of refutation (471E–472D). Part of what he is doing is certainly to provide
elucidation of what Polus says: when, in clarifying the latter's claim that
doing injustice is more shameful, *aischion* (less fine, *kalon*), than suffering
it, Socrates proposes that the fine is either the good or the pleasant or both,
Polus agrees enthusiastically – 'you're defining finely, now, Socrates, when
you define the fine by pleasure and good' (475A2–4).[32] But what kind of
move is this; why does Polus agree to it; and should he agree to it?

What is probably the most influential modern kind of answer to these
questions is to say that Socrates believes, perhaps passionately, in his conclusion about the relative merits of doing and suffering injustice, and is
trying to find an argument for it; it is just not a very good argument,
and the proposed analysis of the fine (*kalon*) – into beneficial, pleasant, or

---

[30] On the *Symposium* as a Socratic dialogue, see Rowe 2006b.
[31] This section is a slightly modified version of part of a piece submitted for a *Festschrift* for Jerry
Santas, edited by George Anagnostopoulos. The part is offered to a friend and scholar in the same
spirit as the whole.
[32] The translation here I borrow from Irwin 1979, not being able to improve on it.

both – is its weak point.[33] If so, Polus is duped, and Socrates does not know what he is doing. At best this would be a disappointing outcome. However a different analysis is to hand, which leaves Socrates more like his usual sure-footed self. Only a few pages further back, Socrates has put forward to Polus those rather specific proposals about the good that we have met earlier: that it is the good that we desire; that this good is the end, whatever it – the end – is, for which we do whatever we do; that it is not what we do that we desire, but what we do what we do *for*, and so on (467C–468D). It will, then, I think, be impolite as well as uncharitable not at least to begin by supposing that when the good comes back into the discussion, as it does in the context we are presently considering ('which is *worse*, do you think, Polus, doing injustice or suffering it?', 474C5–6), those previous proposals are meant still to be in play. In other words, Socrates has a *theory* about the good, which – so I am proposing – we should expect to make itself felt, other things being equal, whenever the subject of the good comes up. Just so it will reappear[34] at 499–500, in Socrates' conversation with Callicles: 'for I take it we agreed that we must do everything for the sake of goods, if you remember – Polus and I. Do you [Callicles] agree with us too, that the good is the end of all actions, and that for the sake of it we should do all the other things, not do it for the sake of the other things?' (499E6–500A1).[35] Here as in 467–8, Socrates commits himself to the idea that it is only ends that are goods, at least in the first instance, and, *pari passu*, to the idea that means to those ends are not goods (at least in the same way).[36] The idea perhaps looks bizarre, but – since he recurs to it – it is one that the Socrates of the *Gorgias* evidently sponsors;[37] it is not just something he proposes, out of devilment or to get his own way, and then drops. Why then should we not imagine it also to be presupposed in 474–5?

Grounds for not imagining it presupposed there might be looked for in that initial statement of Socrates' at 474B2–4: 'For I think that I *and you and other men* believe that doing injustice is worse than suffering it.' This

---

[33] So, e.g., Irwin 1979, *ad* 475C: 'Socrates has either a valid argument with an implausible and undefended premise [sc. "*x* is finer (more *kalon*) than *y* if and only if either *x* is pleasanter than *y* or *x* is more beneficial than *y*" *for the subject*, i.e. the agent in action *x*], or a more plausible premise [sc. "*x* is finer (more *kalon*) than *y* if and only if either *x* is pleasanter than *y* or *x* is more beneficial than *y*" *for those concerned*, explained as "those taken to be relevant in any particular case"], and an invalid argument.' Socrates just 'fails to disambiguate' his claim; Polus meanwhile 'accepts Socrates' way of "defining" . . . the *kalon*, presumably because it sounds realistic and down-to-earth, referring to people's pleasure and advantage' (Irwin 1979, *ad* 475A).

[34] See section 2 (b) above. [35] Here too I use Irwin's translation (in Irwin 1979).

[36] For more on this idea, see Penner and Rowe 2005, esp. pp. 54–5.

[37] Like the Socrates of the *Lysis* (see preceding note); I take it to be part of that connected set of ideas with which Plato's Socrates operates on a permanent basis. See Preliminaries, p. 28 above.

after all suggests a common ground for the belief in question, and so – one might propose to infer – the absence of any *special* Socratic elements. But if Socrates does have a special theory of the good up his sleeve, the common ground will apparently not extend very far. Socrates and Polus 'and other men' may all turn out to believe that doing injustice is worse than suffering it, because they all accept that it is more shameful, *aischion*; but if Socrates' argument relies on ordinary notions about what it is to be shameful, then – the old problem – the agreement he trumpets seems hardly very solid or useful.

So we seem to be on the horns of a dilemma: either Socrates is suppressing his own beliefs in order to claim agreement, or claiming agreement while implicitly having Polus and everyone else sign up to *his*, Socrates', account of things. There is, however, a way of avoiding either of these readings of the argument. We should notice that in 482D–483C Callicles will implicitly accept Socrates' argument: where Polus went wrong was just in allowing that doing injustice, rather than suffering it, was more shameful, after rightly claiming that suffering it was worse – for 'everything is more shameful which is also worse'.[38] Callicles, at any rate, has no argument with Socrates' analysis of the fine into good or pleasant or both; it is just that he has a different notion of what is to count as good. This, I propose, is where things stand between Socrates and Polus (and everyone else) too. It is not that Socrates assumes Polus will accept everything he would want to say about the fine (/beautiful/?admirable) and the good. Rather, he proposes to Polus that the fine is the good, the pleasant, or both, whatever account one goes on to give of the good (and the pleasant); meanwhile *he* actually has a developed account of it to give, while Polus does not, though some – different – sort of notion of the good must be implied in his claim that suffering injustice is worse.

At this point, however, we need to make a significant adjustment. In 474–5, Socrates allows Polus the option of treating the pleasant as a separate criterion of choice and action,[39] apart from the good. This is the main basis that Socrates offers him for the distinction, on which he – Polus – insists (474C9–D2), between the fine and the good: the fine is what is good *or* what is pleasant, or both. However later on, in his conversation with Callicles, Socrates will reject that position for himself.

---

[38] This is one salvageable part of the apparently corrupt sentence uttered by Callicles at 483A7–8; see Irwin 1979 ad loc.

[39] This, again (or so I take it), is what the passage is about – the *choice* between doing injustice and having it done to one.

'Do you agree . . . that the good is the end of all actions, and that for the sake of it we should do all the other things . . .?'

'I do.'

'Then for the sake of goods we should do other things, including pleasant things, not good things for the sake of pleasant things?'

'Quite.'

'Now is it for anyone to select which kinds of pleasant things are good and which bad . . .?'[40] (499E7–500A5)

In other words, as I take it, the sensible, technically correct,[41] *wise* thing to do is to consider, before going for something that one thinks will – and even in fact will – prove pleasant, whether it is a *good* thing to go for it or not. ('Wise', because, if it is goods we want, what we 'should', *dei*, do is always to think whether this, now, will give us what we want.) The question that then immediately arises is whether Socrates will want to say, as Polus seems to do, that things can be fine and not good, that is, just because they are pleasant, and that too seems to be ruled out by the conversation with Callicles, part of which turns on the unacceptability, whether to Socrates or even to Callicles, of just such a position.[42] In short, left to himself Socrates would, to all appearances, have been quite content with the move 'And so [doing injustice] is worse [than suffering it] too, if indeed it is more shameful' (474C8–9) – a move which he makes elsewhere,[43] but which Polus emphatically rejects, so forcing him to take a different tack. But in the event no use is actually made of the possibility 'fine because (merely) pleasant' in 474–5, since even on Polus' account doing injustice is not less *pleasant* than suffering it. So in fact, if the fine is the good or the pleasant or both, and doing injustice is less fine than suffering it, it must be worse, whether on Socrates' or on Polus' or on anyone else's view of what the good is. The argument is not the one Socrates would have chosen, but one that is forced on him by the state of Polus' thinking. At the same time, he commits himself to nothing he doesn't believe, and nothing in the argument depends on anything he doesn't believe – and so we escape the horns of the dilemma as outlined.

Or so it seems. However one set of questions still remains – of the very sort with which the present section began. Even granted that anyone (apart from Callicles) will say that doing injustice is the less fine thing, the less

---

[40] I prefer 'bad' here to Irwin's 'evil', for *kakon*.

[41] A reference to 500A5–6 'Or does it need a craftsman [a *technikos*] for each thing?'

[42] 494C–E (what about the pleasures involved in itching and scratching, Socrates asks; the life of the catamite?).

[43] See text to n. 9 above.

admirable (let us finally opt for the latter as a translation of *kalon*, as a way of combining good and pleasant), what compulsion is there on Polus, or on us, to accept Socrates' analysis of the admirable? Even if it is enough to convince Polus, the analogies he uses in 474D3–475A2 to confirm it[44] have generally tended to strike readers as less than impressive. At best they look rather cursory; and from a modern point of view the analysis itself might well seem to come from nowhere – or, again, just too convenient for Socrates. Granted, he makes that addition 'beneficial *or pleasant*' for Polus' sake, and Polus seems to like it well enough (when he approves of the analysis, it is pleasure he mentions first).[45] But why?

Modern scepticism about Socrates' move in this instance is surely connected with the fact that, as we should put it, what he is talking about is, after all, a question of *moral choice*: the *moral* – so our feeling might be – should not, perhaps cannot, be reduced to the (merely) *prudential*. So the induction, the review of instances, is not merely unconvincing, but is evidence of a serious category mistake: we might even put up with Socrates' trying it on in this way, but surely his contemporaries had a clear and distinct notion of the category of the moral? Is it not bound up with the very language of justice and the virtues? Here is the issue: Socrates, and Plato to whatever extent he is here identifying with Socrates, will have their special reasons for denying it,[46] whereas – the objection runs – Plato will have no business foisting the same position on Polus, let alone 'other men', especially if that is supposed to include us the readers.[47]

In response, I point out that on the interpretation I have suggested above, 'foisting' anything on anyone is precisely what Socrates/Plato is trying *not* to do. Having ascertained[48] that Polus (emphatically) does not want to follow him[49] in identifying admirable and useful/good, Socrates gives him an alternative (good *or* pleasant *or* both). So he acknowledges that Polus, and by implication everyone else, do not share his position; and through that alternative he tries to spell out just what Polus' (and the general) position is on the nature of the admirable, and – in effect – how it differs from his own position. This, he suggests, is by virtue of supposing that

---

44 Shapes and colours are admirable because pleasant/good/both; so with musical sounds; and so on.

45 475A2–4 again: 'you're defining finely . . . when you define the fine by pleasure and good'.

46 I.e. whatever reasons lie behind the typical Socratic identification of admirable/fine and good: broadly, that ultimately all our actions, even those we perform 'for others', are motivated by desire for our *own* good. See chapter 1 above .

47 However different Greek assumptions may have been from ours, it is hard to read much, say, of Greek tragedy without supposing that the characters at least broadly share our sense of admiration, shame or revulsion at broadly the same sorts of actions.

48 'Apparently you don't think the same thing is fine and good . . .', 474C9–D2.

49 I.e. again, on my reconstruction of what Socrates' own position is: see above.

the admirable can also involve *pleasure* – as it clearly will do in the case of artefacts, 'practices', and so on, but – and here I speculate, because Socrates does not spell it out – as it will also do in cases of admirable *actions*, or in the case where we have to compare two things in the sphere of action in respect of their admirableness: e.g., doing versus suffering injustice. 'Well,' I imagine Socrates as saying to Polus, 'you say that doing injustice is less admirable than suffering it. As you agree, this means that you will be saying that it is either worse or less pleasant (or both). To the extent that you might even toy with the idea of thinking it less pleasant, that reflects the genuine sense of *distress* (pain) that you feel at the idea of doing injustice. But at the same time you admit that that distress is less than the distress that you think will be caused to you by having that same injustice inflicted on you. So it can't be the distress to you that would be caused by doing injustice that makes you call it less admirable; it must rather be that you think it will be *worse* for you – despite the fact that you actually claim that it's the other thing, having it done to you, that's worse.' When Socrates proposes, and Polus accepts, the addition of the pleasant to the analysis of the admirable ('you're defining finely, now, Socrates, when you define the fine by pleasure and good'),[50] the effect is to mark the difference that at least Polus feels between admirable (fine) and good – the very sort of difference, one might imagine, that we are likely to describe in terms of the moral, or perhaps the aesthetic. Yet the pleasure in question is evidently not any sort of *moral* pleasure, insofar as it is immediately commensurable with grosser kinds: if there is any distress Polus feels at the prospect of doing injustice it is trumped at once – he doesn't even have to think about it – by the greater distress he will feel at being treated unjustly. That might not be a matter of physical pain; it might just be the pain or distress caused by losing face. And *moral* considerations are surely not supposed to be so easily set aside (how, otherwise, will anyone ever be brought to act unselfishly?).

Has Plato short-changed Polus, by not allowing him to decide (what we should call) a moral choice on moral grounds? Probably not, since Polus is not obviously a person of high moral sensitivity. Has Plato short-changed his, and Polus', contemporaries? (After all, the argument is supposed to apply to everyone.) This is a more difficult question to answer. It may be that the Greeks had a relatively unformed notion of the moral; and if we think that notion important (even central), we might conclude that it was Plato's business to shape it better, not to propose abandoning it in the

---

[50] Again, we should notice that Polus mentions pleasure first; as I suggest, it is the addition of pleasure to the good that he approves of.

way that he appears to be doing.[51] Yet we can also see him as *challenging* justifications of the kinds of behaviour we admire in terms of the moral, and replacing such justifications with something he conceives of as stronger: that behaving admirably is simply good *for us*. Callicles will allege that Polus was merely shamed into saying that doing injustice was more shameful than suffering it; it is only convention (*nomos*) that makes people say such things, whereas in fact it is what is worse – suffering injustice – that is shameful (482D–483B). Socrates pays Polus the compliment of supposing that he is saying what he actually believes; he also pays him the further compliment of suggesting that he actually believes something that he, Socrates, thinks philosophically defensible (i.e. along the lines of his own theory).

What is important to note about this is that it is not a matter of mere philosophical charity on Socrates' part. In working out exactly what it is that Polus and 'the others' believe in believing that doing injustice is more shameful, less admirable, than suffering it, he is also, given his theory of desire, pointing to what he thinks it is that drives them, in all their actions and choices: the real good, which is what everyone desires (even orators and tyrants). It is to this that their descriptions – in terms of the admirable and the shameful – really refer.[52] To the extent that they do not realize this, Socrates no doubt over-reaches himself, with a touch of mischievousness, when he proposes that they actually agree with him. 'Agreeing' is hardly something one can be properly said to do without knowing about it. To that degree, Socrates will after all only be inferring 'agreement' to his conclusion (doing injustice is worse), on the basis of premises his interlocutor admits to, without that interlocutor's dreaming for a moment that they lead just *there*. I am claiming, however, that this is not all there is to it. What Socrates gets out of Polus, understood as *Socrates* understands it, is no more than he thinks he would get out of him (and anyone – perhaps even Callicles),[53] with enough dialectic: in Polus' case, as the fully spelled-out version of what he is saying – intends to say – when he uses the words 'doing injustice is more shameful than suffering it'. But that would simply be the moment at

---

[51] I.e. by reducing the admirable to the good (for the agent), and the shameful to the bad (for the agent).

[52] The 'principle of real reference' again: see Preliminaries above, n. 74.

[53] He would, of course, be starting from further back with Callicles, in that Callicles even denies that doing injustice is more shameful (a different dialectical tack would be needed – and in fact Socrates will approach him rather differently). There are signs, however, that Socrates is not prepared to give up even on him; and after all (on Socrates' theory) Callicles wants the same as everyone else. See section 2 (a) above.

which Polus fully understood his own, true, motivation – towards a good (for him as agent) that excludes doing injustice under any conditions.[54]

As for what that good is, Socrates does not say here, or indeed anywhere else in the *Gorgias* (he will raise it in the *Republic*: see especially chapter 9 below). But if the Socrates of the *Gorgias* is, as I propose, a fully intellectualist Socrates, then the answer to that question is bound to have something to do with *knowledge*. For if what we all want is what is good, then everything will depend on our finding out, with as much precision as possible, what that good (for us) is – or, in other words, on our acquiring the kind of expertise possessed by the special 'craftsman' that Socrates proposes, and gets Callicles to agree, will be needed to sort out which pleasures are to count as goods in each sphere (Callicles, of course, will have a rather different view of the expertise involved).

---

[54] For a longer, more fully argued, and more precise treatment of the very complex issues involved here, see Penner and Rowe 2005: Part II.

CHAPTER 5

'Examining myself and others', II: soul, the excellences and the 'longer road' in the Republic

In chapter 9 I shall be discussing the topic of *the good* in the *Republic*. One useful starting-point for that discussion will be the passage at *Republic* VI, 504A–505A, which associates the future philosopher-rulers' study of the good, the 'greatest object of study/learning' (*to megiston mathēma*: 504D2–3, etc.) with their study of the *soul* and of the *excellences* – the latter, themselves, also being among 'the greatest things' (504D6–E3), though the good is ranked higher. Socrates refers back to IV, 435B–D, where he put the crucial question whether the soul too contains the three *eidē*, kinds, that the city had been found – at any rate by the rough and ready sort of method chosen – to contain. Socrates agreed, back there in Book IV, that he and his partners in the conversation should answer the new question by using the same rough methods as before, while insisting that an *accurate* answer would depend on their following 'another, longer and more considerable (*makrotera kai pleiōn*) road' (435D3). Now in Book VI he suggests that such a make-do approach would be unsuitable for any 'guard of city and laws': he or she will need to understand things 'in the finest possible way'. And Socrates reminds Adimantus, his interlocutor at this point, that the accounts of the four excellences agreed to in Book IV were built on that evidently less than accurate answer to the question about the soul (VI, 504A4–6).

It seems, then, that there is something unsatisfactory about the those accounts of the excellences as well as about division of the soul itself, as it was carried out in Book IV. Exactly where we should locate the unsatisfactoriness of the definitions of 'sound-mindedness'/self-control, courage, wisdom and justice in Book IV will be a subject for later in the present chapter. First, however, I shall focus upon the same question about the soul – just how and why was the account of the soul in Book IV unsatisfactory? What would we discover by the 'longer road' that we missed by travelling along the shorter one?

The immediate and obvious answer lies in Book x, in that comparison of the soul, as we observe it in life, to the 'briny' (sea-god) Glaucus.[1] It can hardly be doubted that Socrates is there qualifying what he has said about the soul earlier, not just in Book iv but in the treatment of inferior types of soul and city in Books viii and ix, which directly builds upon Book iv; since the Socrates of Book x claims to be telling us something about the 'truest nature' of the soul, and he has suggested that the Book iv treatment was less than completely satisfactory, then it seems clear enough that Book x[2] will be giving us something that at least approximates to the destination of the 'longer road'.

But now at least three questions arise. (i) In what respects is the Book iv model of the soul less 'true' than the other one? (ii) Why should Socrates need to use this model, in Book iv, rather than the 'truer' one? And (iii) in what does the 'longer way' actually consist? What is the person who is going this way rather than the other actually *doing*, to help him get to the 'truer' destination?

I shall take the third question first. Here is one answer, from among the group of interpreters I have labelled as 'doctrinalists': taking the longer way is simply a matter of *doing dialectic*, where this is a matter of

engagement over many years with numerous subjects: the doctrine [*Lehre*] of soul (which as a theory of the World Soul will include cosmology . . .), the doctrine of Ideas [Forms] with all its implications, and finally . . . the doctrine of the Good as principle of all. (Szlezák 2004: 38)

Here, clearly, is a particular view of the nature of Platonic dialectic: something for the few, the elite, properly prepared inner circle – prepared, that is, to approach, absorb and understand the kinds of doctrines that will make them into perfect dialecticians and philosophers of the sort represented by the fully trained philosopher-rulers of Callipolis. No one without that kind of preparation, and especially the long years of study, will be able to see the truth, whether about the soul or about anything.

Now admittedly this solution has its attractions. What Socrates says in Book vi (to paraphrase) is precisely that any future guardian of city and laws needs to avoid being satisfied with short-cuts, through laziness; he (or she) will have to work as hard at training his intellect as at training his body, or else he'll never get to the goal of the 'greatest and most fitting object of study' (vi, 504D2–3), that is, the good – and shortly Socrates will

---

[1] See chapter 3, pp. 140–1 above.   [2] With vii, 519A–B (see chapter 3, p. 141n.65).

outline the kind of intellectual training that these intending 'guards' should undergo. However this is not the most natural reading of the context that immediately concerns us in Book VI. We have not yet got to the higher education of the philosopher-rulers; for all we know up to this point, we are being told simply that people who are going to take on positions of supreme authority and responsibility can't be allowed to be lazy – for fear that they'll never get to the kind of understanding necessary to underpin their authority, that is, understanding of the good (and the other 'greatest subjects'), because of the huge task it is to acquire it. That is the main point in what Socrates is currently saying, here in VI, 504–5: the sheer size of the intellectual undertaking in question, and the need for accuracy – interpreted as 'not falling short in any way whatever of what is', or incompleteness (504C1–2). Of course the passage (504–5) will gain new resonance once we get to those later, extended discussions of the higher education of the future rulers, so that at least retrospectively, and in the specific case of the rulers, the 'longer road' on any subject might well involve grasping a whole range of high-level ideas ('doctrines'). But for the moment the emphasis falls on rather general requirements: application, accuracy, completeness.

Now it will certainly turn out to be true that any full account of any-thing, or anything important, will for Plato ultimately have to involve grasp of the good as principle of everything. This much of the 'doctrinalist' reading certainly seems right. Yet at the same time such a reading omits the important point that, in the special case of the division of the soul, the Socrates of *Republic* X appears to tell us about at least one very *specific* way in which his treatment of the soul in Book IV (and then in Books VIII and IX) was, or might have been, inaccurate or incomplete. That is, whatever else might have been missed by the taking of the shorter road, there is one particular criticism of the account in Book IV that Plato has Socrates belatedly identify: that it is based on *observation* – observation of the way the soul appears in life.[3] What Socrates now proposes to sub-stitute for that faulty empirical view of the soul is a view of it based on *reasoning*:

we must see through, by reasoning, as best we can to the sort of thing [the soul] is when it becomes pure, and then one will find it to be *much* more beautiful, and distinguish more clearly things like justice and injustice and everything we've now gone through. (X, 611C2–5)

---

[3] 'As for what sort of thing [the soul] is in truth, we must not observe (*theasthai*) *that* in a state of mutilation both from the association of the body and from other bad things, as we observe (*theasthai*) it now – we must see through, by reasoning . . .' (X, 611B10–C4).

And that reasoning, as I have suggested,[4] apart from what can be derived from the immediate context, can be located in a very specific place: the *Phaedo*. The soul of *Republic* x *is* the soul as Socrates, Cebes and Simmias reason about it in the *Phaedo*, and as they understand it on the basis of that reasoning. For what kind of soul this is,[5] I refer back to the closing pages of chapter 3 above.

This outcome has one important corollary, on the nature of dialectic itself. As we have seen, the 'doctrinalist' reading I have been considering identifies dialectic with doctrine, or else with the process of familiarization with doctrine: something, then, for the few, the elite and properly prepared inner circle. My own view is that Platonic/Socratic dialectic is a matter rather of serious philosophical conversation,[6] so that the exchange between Socrates and his interlocutors in the text of the *Republic* will itself count as a perfectly acceptable example of the kind of thing dialectic may be. If so, the longer road can't be dialectic itself, since dialectic is what's already in play; what is at issue is more specific, and especially more *accurate*, arguments, which don't just take their cue from the way things happen to look. Nor is this merely a dispute about a term ('dialectic'). The 'longer road' must on any account be a philosophical one – that is, a *better* philosophical (dialectical) account than the one available in Book IV. I insist merely that that better philosophical account is not to be looked for in decades of discussion between colleagues behind the closed doors of the Academy, but in another text (the *Phaedo*), which claims to represent a single set of arguments that Socrates had with two others on a particular occasion. This, to me, gives more of the flavour of the genuine Socratic/Platonic article: dialectic, 'the art of conversation', of 'talking together'.[7] (Fictionally, of course, the reference will be to a conversation, or conversations, *like* the one 'recorded' in the *Phaedo*.)

I return to the two questions left hanging out of my original three: (i) In what respects is the Book IV model of the soul less 'true' than the other one? (ii) Why should Socrates need to use this model, in Book IV, rather than the 'truer' one? The answers to these questions are closely connected. In Book x Socrates insists that he and his interlocutors should not suppose that 'the soul in its truest nature is such as to be filled to bursting (*gemein*) with

---

[4] See chapter 3, p. 140n.56 above.

[5] What it is *not* is purely rational – a conclusion for which I argued independently in chapter 3 in relation to *Republic* x itself. I owe my original and much of my subsequent attachment to this point to valuable discussions with Xanthippe Bourloyanni.

[6] That is, rather than of the *results* to which such conversation, between ideal dialecticians, might ultimately lead: the 'doctrines' of the 'doctrinalist' interpreters.

[7] See especially chapter 11 below, on the *Phaedrus*.

variety (*poikilia*), and unlikeness and difference, itself in relation to itself (611A10–B3), because something that's put together from many elements and not in the finest way, 'as the soul has appeared to us now to be', won't easily be something eternal (*aidion*). 'As the soul has now appeared to us': once again, the reference must be to Book IV, with Books VIII and IX (or rather, in the context, the other way round: to VIII and IX, with IV);[8] and it is true enough that in Book IV, as in the two later books, VIII and IX, the soul is presented as containing, if not necessarily 'filled to bursting' with, 'variety', 'unlikeness', and 'difference' – for that is the basis of the arguments that Socrates used, and needed to use, in order to show that there are three 'parts' or *eidē* in the individual soul (the 'parts' are distinguishable just because they can somehow be seen as actively opposing each other). What is required for the immortality assigned to the soul by the argument of 608–11[9] is that, whatever our souls become in this life (however distorted they may be as a result of their experiences), they should retain a fundamental unity and internal harmony – whether they are actually composite or incomposite (*polueidēs, monoeidēs*: 612A4 again). So here is an answer to question (i): if soul were quite the rickety contraption Book IV (and VIII and IX) might have made it appear to be, it couldn't be immortal. But it is immortal. So it can't be as Book IV painted it.

However that was, apparently, the kind of soul Socrates needed for his purposes in Book IV: one whose internal 'unlikenesses' and 'differences' would yield 'parts' of the soul. And he needed these to form the basis of his definition/account of justice. He laid out the rationale for his procedure, in effect, when he agreed, in Book II, to move from discussing a simple kind of community – he called it 'the true city' (II, 372E6), but for Glaucon it was a 'city of pigs' (E4) – to its 'luxurious' or 'feverish' counterpart, on the grounds that this will enable him and the others to observe 'how justice and injustice are engendered in cities' (372E5–6).[10] In an analogous way, I presume, Socrates proposes to observe how justice and injustice are engendered in individuals by looking at souls in the sort of condition, and context, in which injustice as well as justice might come about. And the consequence will be exactly as Socrates suggests at IV, 435C–D, as he introduces the discussion that leads to the division of the soul: given the

---

8 Books VIII and IX give a much more vivid picture of the soul than IV, ending in that image of the soul as a human shell containing a man, a lion and a monster.

9 Whatever strengths or weaknesses there may be in that argument; its quality does not concern me directly here.

10 'Luxurious': *truphōsa*, II, 372E2; 'feverish': *phlegmainousa*, E8. For further discussion of this crucial shift in the argument, see below.

methods they're using, what they come up with might be adequate enough from some points of view, but it will lack precision. They won't arrive at a precise account of what soul is, just because they won't be talking about 'the true soul'[11] (as they haven't talked about 'the true city'). The discussion will be of soul as it appears to be, or appears as being in life,[12] not as it really is, i.e. what it can and should be.[13] Nor, as Socrates later confirms, will they reach a precise account of justice;[14] how could they, if the model of the soul on which their account of justice is based will itself be seriously, and relevantly, lacking?[15]

Part of the answer to question (ii), then, is that Socrates chooses the 'shorter way' because that will enable him to explain how it is that justice and injustice come about. But that by itself hardly seems a very satisfactory answer, if the result is that the justice and injustice we'll see being 'engendered' are actually substitutes for the ones we were originally looking for.[16] In order to see why Socrates adopts this strategy, we need to look more closely at the implications of the parallel conclusion that has emerged about his treatment of the soul in Book IV, i.e. that it is not a 'precise' account, and does not describe the soul 'as it really is'.

It is normal to think of Plato as endorsing a tripartite model of the soul, if with severe and largely unspecified reservations about the language of 'parts' (in fact Socrates' preferred term, when he uses one at all,[17] is not 'part', *meros* or *morion*, but *eidos*, 'kind', sc. of thing/soul). The fact that tripartition not only reappears but plays a major role in other dialogues – *Phaedrus* and *Timaeus* – may well seem justification enough for such a view. But in the *Republic*, at least, we are (I claim) quite clearly warned that a more accurate, 'truer', account of the soul may not refer to 'parts', or even

---

[11] Soul 'in its truest nature', X, 611B1 ('its true nature', 612A3–4).

[12] Cf. X, 611C6–7, B6–7; for the two alternative formulations – 'appears to be'/'appears as being in life' – see further below.

[13] I take it that this equation of what a thing should be with what it 'really is' is characteristically Platonic (and, incidentally, Aristotelian).

[14] The future rulers 'mustn't look at a [sc. mere] sketch [of justice and the things we went through], as we are now doing': VI, 504D–E.

[15] The account of justice (and of 'sound-mindedness'/self-control and courage) will after all be in terms of the divided soul; take away the partition of the soul, and we shall evidently need a different kind of account of justice.

[16] The 'longer way', the one that will lead to greater accuracy, would evidently also just be *too* long, *too* great a project for Socrates and his interlocutors to undertake under present conditions. But insofar as the alternative route actually seems to lead to a different place from the one the longer route leads to, it can't *just* be a matter of time, or the qualifications of the interlocutors. The shorter way, in short, isn't a *short cut*.

[17] Greek can operate happily with neuter article and adjective: 'the rational', 'the spirited', 'the appetitive'.

eidē, 'kinds' of soul, at all, insofar as – in the case of the soul that is as it should be/in the case of soul as it really is – there will be none of the divisions that, in the context of ordinary human life, seem to justify talk about 'parts' of the soul: the soul, in such a context, becomes affected in such a way as to make it appear, in commonly occurring circumstances, *as if* it has distinct parts. Otherwise, i.e. outside this context, things will not appear like this; at most, one would have to observe that alongside our rational motivations there were certain others that needed to be attended to, and that we couldn't do without, in order to survive (in a body).

That is very much where my discussion ended in chapter 3. Plato's, and his Socrates', preferred view of the soul is of a unified, rational entity that nevertheless has the capacity for those desires and passions necessary for a bodily existence.[18] However a little more precision is now needed here in my own discussion. When Socrates talks in *Republic* x about how the soul 'appears' in ordinary life, or in the context of a 'fevered' city, is he suggesting that the way it 'appears' to be can be dismissed as a mere illusion? Or is the contrast not so much between the real and the illusory, as between what the soul really *is* and what it actually *becomes*, in life – without, at the same time, losing its real nature, which is merely hidden from view?

The second reading must surely be closer to the truth. The picture of the 'true' soul in *Republic* x is simply incapable of explaining the phenomena – the different types of city and individual – described in Books VIII and IX; and these phenomena are themselves certainly not meant to be taken as illusory. The issue, I believe, is whether or not 'spirit' and appetite ought strictly be treated as (are, 'in truth') separate centres of motivation within us, alongside reason. What Book X, together with the *Phaedo*, tells us is that this is a mistaken idea. But as Books IV, VIII and IX – and the *Phaedrus* – acknowledge, there is at the same time no hiding from the fact that both 'spirit' and appetite regularly appear *as if* they were independent sources of motivation, and of action.[19] Certainly, people think of them as such. Thus when Socrates asks Glaucon whether there are people who sometimes refuse to drink even though they're thirsty, he replies enthusiastically 'many and often' (IV, 439 C2–4). But Book X in effect warns us, retrospectively, to be

---

[18] Many will no doubt object that there is no evidence that the Socrates of the *Apology*, say, or the *Crito* (or of the 'Socratic' dialogues generally), had any such idea of the soul, or indeed any clear idea about it at all (see, e.g., Vlastos 1971: 5); but see chapter 1 above.

[19] 'Spirit' is reason's ally against appetite, IV, 440A–E ('armed' in defence of reason, like the auxiliaries in the city: 440E5–6), but still independent, to the degree that people may be dominated by 'spirit' instead of by reason – that is, they may 'enslave' reason to this 'part' of the soul as well as to appetite (cf. n. 21 below).

wary of an explanation of such phenomena in terms of conflict between different parts.

So how should we explain the phenomena in question – the sort that people like Glaucon, normal people, explain in terms of a divided mind/soul? The pre-*Republic* Socrates would have said simply that what is called being overcome by thirst, or by appetite generally, is really to be explained in terms of intellectual failure. And evidently that explanation would still work perfectly well in the case of the soul observed 'in its truest nature'. However in the *Republic*, and specifically in Book IV (with the argument for tripartition), Socrates seems to give up on supposing that the favoured pre-*Republic* explanation has general application by itself – that it is by itself capable of explaining the phenomena – and instead introduces another level of explanation. This I take to depend on how people – non-philosophical people – actually come to behave in relation to their so-called irrational aspects: having no idea that what we may call their basic physiological impulses and reactions need to be, and can be, kept under perfectly rational control,[20] such people *come to attribute to* such impulses/reactions a power and importance that they don't naturally possess. Eating, drinking, sex: all can be highly attractive things. So people will be drawn to them, and start indulging in them for their own sake, building them into significant elements in their life plans; in the worst case, they actually allow themselves to be completely 'ruled' by them.[21]

In this kind of scenario, our appetites will indeed very often be in conflict with, and maybe even block us from doing, what we seem to desire rationally; and like Leontius, with his pathological obsession with corpses,[22] we may be angry with our appetitive selves, but nonetheless do what our appetites seem to prompt us to do. If, as Socrates proposes, 'the same thing will refuse to do or have done to it both of two opposite things at the same time, at any rate in the same respect and relation to the same thing' (IV, 436 B8–9), then people's souls will be made up of – at least – three parts. But they – people – didn't have to be like that. That isn't how the soul really is,

---

[20] Which I take to be Socrates' line of approach in the *Gorgias*: see chapter 4, section 2(b) above.

[21] I refer here to the case of the tyrant, himself 'tyrannized by Love', which will bring him to do anything, however horrible (IX, 574E2–575A3). Contrast the case of the person who believes in the 'profitability' of justice, and has the man in him treat the monster in him as a farmer would, feeding up its tame heads and stopping the wild ones from growing (X, 589A–B). Here the role of reason in the whole process clearly emerges; similarly in the talk of the person 'who enslaves the best of himself to the worst' (589D7–E1). The dragon in us cannot grow without our help.

[22] *Republic* IV, 439E–440A. To judge from Socrates' language, this was a real and notorious case. A late source explains his behaviour as an expression of a passion for pale young men; I prefer to see Socrates understanding Leontius as clinically ill (see 439D2, which refers to sickness alongside passion as capable of causing reasoning to be worsted).

in its essential ('truest') nature. People just choose to go that way. Appetite may be a monster, but in itself, and properly treated and understood, it is only a *potential* monster. Neither Socrates nor anyone else is destined to be a Typhon. The only trouble is that indulging the appetites is nice, and reason is in short supply.

This is some kind of turning point in the dialogues.[23] To recap: prior to the *Republic* – so long as the *Phaedrus* comes later – Socrates seems to have operated exclusively with a conception of the soul that will make it too, as much as soul 'in its truest nature' in *Republic* x,[24] resist the kind of division introduced in Book IV. Under that pre-*Republic* conception, the soul's desires are always and only for the good. Even hunger, thirst or sexual appetite could be seen in terms of desire to be benefited – at any rate if they were acted upon; otherwise they would be no more than features, whether looming or scarcely perceptible, on one's mental landscape, factors to be taken into consideration by reason as it decided which way to go. On this pre-*Republic* model, conflict between reason and desire is actually ruled out. But now, in *Republic* IV, Socrates allows that embodied souls may, after all, develop in such a way as to generate what looks like genuine internal conflict, of a sort that could only exist between different parts/kinds/sources of motivation: not only between reason and appetite, but between desire and another aspect (part?) of ourselves, labelled 'spirited' or 'angry', acting on behalf of reason.[25] This is a radical change; yet it is not by any means as radical as it is often taken to be.[26] Not only are our souls 'not really' divided into three parts (or more); individual souls may actually not be so divided. Socrates' soul could be a case in point, and even if it is not,[27] he himself is clearly able to envisage – and actually does envisage, in the *Phaedo* and elsewhere – souls that would be, for all that one could tell, in

---

[23] One already signalled in Preliminaries, pp. 18–19 above.

[24] And as much as the 'purified' soul of the *Phaedo*, if *Phaedo* and the *Republic* x context are linked in the way I have suggested (see pp. 166–7 above). (Plato leaves it open that soul 'as it really is' may still be divided – but in other ways: see below.)

[25] Quite how reason is supposed to control the irrational elements in the soul under such conditions, even with 'spirit' to ride shotgun for it, is a mystery. There is no talking to a monster or a dragon; the charioteer in the *Phaedrus* doesn't even have much success with a horse. But that just goes to show how important it is that we don't let the monster grow in the first place. On Socrates' preferred model, there are no such problems; any that exist for the other model he will simply disown (or just propose to send the offending examples out into the country to fend for themselves: *Republic* VII, 540E–541A).

[26] Or indeed (I admit) as radical as I have myself taken it to be in the past.

[27] Much will depend on how we read Socrates' report of the effect on him of what he glimpsed inside Charmides' cloak at *Charmides* 155D, and, perhaps, his readiness to accept Alcibiades' repeated invitations to dine alone with him (*Symposium* 217C–D, though this is perhaps a more straightforward case). Here as elsewhere Plato seems to delight in leaving Socrates' real situation mildly ambiguous.

a state of perfect internal harmony. (Such would be the true philosophers, the philosophical 'leaders' of the *Theaetetus* digression.) Whether even the soul 'in its truest state' should be said to contain plural 'kinds', *eidē*, or not is something that Socrates himself leaves open;[28] but at any rate the arguments for division in *Republic* IV would not be able to get a purchase at all on premier league souls – if there were to be any – who actually managed to realize that 'true' state.

The key point, however, is that Socrates' pre-*Republic* position on desire and actions is actually preserved, even when we take into account the internal conflicts he describes in the *Republic* IV argument; for – I propose – on Socrates' analysis such conflicts, however real they may be perceived as being, or may actually be,[29] constitute only one aspect, and not the most important, of the agent's condition. That is, Socrates' analysis of the situation that Glaucon and others would describe in terms of 'overpowering' of reason by appetite would claim to go deeper than that description. For Socrates, what is supposedly being 'overpowered' will not be reason, or the reasoning 'part' itself, but rather the individual's own particular beliefs about what it is best for him to do. Given that he is divided at all, those beliefs will hardly be in the best shape, even if they might from time to time look respectable enough;[30] and if so, then neither of the directions in which his divided soul is – supposedly – pushing him will be in accord with what he really wants, i.e. what is really good for him. Intellectual error is still at the bottom of it all: the conflicted agent has given the appetites too important a place in his life because he has an insufficiently worked-out view of what is best for him, and now he goes with his appetites even while

---

[28] I.e. in *Republic* X, 612A3–5. Elsewhere in *Republic* X Socrates almost casually divides reason itself – as noticed e.g., by Sedley: 'the clear implication of *toutōi* at [X] 602E4 and *dianoia* at 603B10 . . . that both functions [sc. of measuring and judging by sensory appearances] are carried out by the intellect itself, albeit by different parts of it' (Sedley 2004: 113, n. 40). Some division of reason may in fact also be required by Socrates' pre-*Republic* position: if what we truly desire is always what is really good, and not the merely apparent good, there will be frequent occasions on which our real desires differ from our apparent ones, and the real 'we' from our apparent selves – which are after all going after a different set of objects from the one corresponding to our real desires. But perhaps this would not be an interesting kind of 'division', since in any case it would be unperceived.

[29] My own inclination is to suppose that Plato would prefer to treat internal conflicts as *constructed*, through and through. But in any case, for Plato anyone who thinks such conflicts tell us anything about the soul 'in its truest nature' will be wrong so to think – as wrong as anyone will be who proposes to be able to give an account of the physical universe from the way it *looks* . . . (see chapter 11 below).

[30] The agent in such a case will be no philosopher; he won't have engaged with 'things as they really are' – and that will leave him in a state of *mere* belief, which for Socrates is no way to take on the world.

being aware, however dimly or vividly,[31] that it's not a good thing to do.[32] And this is the reason why Socrates can say at VI, 505DII–EI that the good is 'what every soul pursues, and it does everything for the sake of this'. It doesn't matter how badly people go wrong; what they really and truly want is still what is good for them – that is, what is really good for them.[33]

Nevertheless something has changed in Socrates' approach, and it is an important change. There is, first, a change in the degree of attention he is prepared to pay to the causes of ignorance; secondly, there is a change in his acceptance that any large-scale solution to the problem of ignorance will be political. To an extent he now actually endorses the ordinary view that we are slaves to the passions[34] (that is, to the extent that we have made ourselves slaves);[35] and he sees the city as having to impose wise control on the citizens at large, through education and conditioning and through laws governing behaviour, in place of the internal and effortless harmony that is the soul's true state, under the undisturbed rule of reason. This does seem to be at some distance from the *Apology*,[36] where Socrates' whole emphasis was

---

[31] In Leontius' case, quite vividly; but then the poor man is sick.

[32] We may compare the approach Socrates uses against Protagoras towards the end of the *Protagoras* – yes, there is a phenomenon that the many call being overcome by pleasure, but actually this is a matter of the agent's making mistakes in the calculation of the quantities of pleasure involved (*Protagoras* 351B–357E). The difference is that in the *Republic* Socrates is providing a more elaborate explanation of how the mistake comes about, involving the history and education (or lack of education) of the agent.

[33] The 'un-self-controlled' person (the one resembling Aristotle's 'acratic') has played rather too large a role in the argument of the preceding paragraphs: it is people who *habitually* get things wrong (the person obsessed with his reputation, the gourmand, the philanderer . . .) who are for Plato the more typical cases, as the description of different individual types in Books VIII–IX amply shows. But the latter are perhaps just further along in the downward process, when division has given way to a state in which reason is actually enslaved to, and works for, the irrational.

[34] The crucial verb in the context is *kratein*: we are 'overpowered', 'controlled', 'conquered', 'subjected' by appetite (IV, 439C7, 440AI).

[35] The difference between this view and Socrates' own is clearly marked by the passage at *Republic* IV, 437E7–439B2, in which he carefully separates appetitive desires understood in the context of the agent's overall desire exclusively for good things (which would mean that thirst, e.g., would always be for *good* drink: 438A3–5) from such desires in themselves, which at their most basic are simply for drink/liquid (food/solid, or whatever it may be) without distinction. The whole purpose of the passage is to make room for the kind of opposition between reason and desire that Socrates' own position excludes. However there is no reason to suppose (and VI, 505D–E provides good reason for not supposing) that he is here proposing to abandon that position; 437E–439B certainly gives him no grounds for doing so. (I am keenly aware here of a considerable debt that I owe to conversations with Giorgos Kampalios, and to various written drafts of his, on this controversial part of the *Republic*. It may be that the larger part of my actual conclusions about it were originally his, in which case I here return them to their rightful owner, and refer the reader to the relevant part of his eventual doctoral thesis.)

[36] And so contrary to my generally 'unitarian' reading of Plato. I indicated this particular exception early on in my argument (again see Preliminaries, pp. 18–19 above); I continue to think that it is not sufficient by itself to cause significant upset to my overall reading, for the reasons that I have offered in the two paragraphs preceding in the main text.

on the need not just for the acquisition of wisdom but for its acquisition by every individual, so that even 'caring for the city' seemed to be a matter of making all the citizens wiser.[37] If that was what the Socrates of the *Apology* had in mind, then it is a world apart from the *Republic*, which has him saying that the philosopher-architects of the best city will need to start with a clean slate (VI, 501A), which if they do it themselves will mean sending everyone over the age of ten out into the country so that they can work with a population of children liberated from the attitudes of their parents (VII, 540E–541A).[38] It is the difference, it seems, between Socrates the man with a private mission, and Socrates the political theorist, the legislator, even the statesman.[39] Yet as previous chapters have argued, and as I shall continue to argue, this new Socrates is still recognizably the old one, with the same priorities, the same method, the same epistemology; and despite everything – as I have now tried to show – he even retains his old attachment to the idea of an undivided soul, together with everything that that implies for the understanding of human action and human nature.[40]

Let me take stock for a moment. The question – the second of the original three – was this: why should Socrates need to use the model of the divided soul, in Book IV, rather than the 'truer' model? Why should Plato have him choose to take the shorter route, with the consequential loss of precision? According to the line advocated by the 'doctrinalists', it ought to be because the 'longer road' would just be beyond our capacity to grasp – and beyond the capacity of any written document to contain. My own argument has been that, on the contrary, the *Republic* itself is perfectly adequate to inform us at least about the general direction and destination of this road not taken. That then gives the question even greater urgency: why doesn't Socrates take the longer road, when the shorter road actually

[37] See Socrates' statement of his mission at *Apology* 36C5–8: 'trying to persuade each one of you not to care either for anything that belongs to him before himself, that he should become as good and wise as possible, or for the things that belong to the city before the city itself'. However we should notice that even here Socrates leaves unspecified exactly what 'city-care' would consist in; this is what underlies my suggestion in chapter 1, n. 3 that '[t]he *Apology* may even be seen as referring implicitly to the politics of the *Republic*' (though it remains true that the *Apology* as a whole *appears* to recommend philosophy as a universal solution in the sense that it was for everyone actually to practise it).

[38] They won't even engage with an *individual*, it seems, unless he's a clean slate too (501A5); the equivalent of forcible eviction in this case would presumably mean doing some internal evictions (making the person 'pure': A6), of habits, and especially of beliefs.

[39] For Socrates on himself as the one true practictioner of the art of statesmanship, see *Gorgias* 521D–E (and chapter 4 above). But what he is saying there – that he is the only person doing what statesmen ought but fail to do – would fit equally well in the context of the *Apology*.

[40] In the following chapters, I shall consider whether the old Socrates has taken on new *metaphysical* clothes to go along with his apparently new political ones. (My answer will be firmly in the negative.)

turns out, in a sense, to lead us away from the real and true destination? Part of the answer I have already suggested: that going the shorter way allows him to provide an explanation of actual phenomena – of souls as they appear in 'real' life, and as we cause them to be. However Socrates (Plato) has another, and closely connected, motivation for constructing his argument as he does; one that has to do with his awareness of the needs of his interlocutors (or, in Plato's case, his audience).[41] It is to this aspect that I now turn.

Near the beginning of *Republic* II (368A–C), after Glaucon and Adimantus have restated the case for injustice, Socrates agrees that he must come to justice's aid,[42] despite his not knowing how. An indication of his incapacity, he says, is that the two brothers haven't accepted what he said to Thrasymachus (sc. in Book I), when he, Socrates, thought he had done the job there, and had shown that justice was better than injustice. Still, he must try to help justice in her plight – and the result is a new argument which, with major interruptions and digressions, takes up the next nine books. Now most readers of the *Republic* tend to side with Glaucon and Adimantus rather than Socrates, and find the arguments of Book I distinctly unsatisfying; even Socrates himself, as such readers will point out, ends that first book by saying that he can scarcely know whether justice is an excellence and makes a person happy or not if he doesn't know what it is:

what's happened to me now is that I know nothing from the argument; for when I don't know what the just [sc. justice] is, I shall hardly know whether it really is some sort of excellence or not, and whether its possessor is not happy or happy. (the closing words of Book I, at 354C1–3)

Given that his next move will be to define it, doesn't it follow that his claim about his exchange with Thrasymachus – that he was happy with what came out of it – must at best have been disingenuous?[43]

---

41 This might seem, initially, to take us back to the solution of the 'doctrinalists' just referred to. However (and this is a crucial, perhaps defining, point in my dispute with such interpreters) *their* Plato simply holds back; what *my* Plato holds back with one hand he gives with the other. For those who can follow him, and his Socrates, with due attention to his various nods and winks, at least an outline of the proper story is there to be grasped – and, usually, to be filled out from other dialogues. Even then, we shan't have the complete story, but then, after all, writing is a thoroughly second-rate medium (see especially chapter 11 below); and my Plato will always be missing parts of the story himself, or still busy putting them together.

42 He must *boēthein* her, *epikourein* her (II, 368C1, 3). (The 'auxiliary' guards of Callipolis will be the city's, and the philosophers', *epikouroi*.)

43 I shall return in rather greater detail to the issues raised by the end of Book I/the beginning of Book II in the Appendix to the present chapter.

I myself suggest that the disingenuousness is located rather in the olive-branch Socrates seems to offer Thrasymachus here in 354C. Granted, he doesn't know what justice is. But he has a pretty good idea about it – good enough to allow him to get Thrasymachus' agreement, or at any rate to claim to have got it, about justice's status as an excellence, and as wisdom;[44] good enough, too, to allow him to go on and treat justice not just as one excellence among many but as the excellence of a soul, the one that enables it to fulfil all its functions – 'caring for (things) and ruling and deliberating and all such things' (I, 353D4–6). So it will, if all the excellences are one, and excellence is the same as knowledge or wisdom. Since Thrasymachus has no idea of any of this, and Socrates perhaps wisely omits to enlighten him, he (Thrasymachus) ought to find Socrates' argument distinctly unimpressive; as it is, he seems to suggest that the argument works just so long as Socrates is right and justice is an excellence.[45] And this will be truer than he knows, given what kind of excellence Socrates thinks it is.[46] But Socrates knows perfectly well what he is doing.

The real problem is that Socrates has been talking across rather than to Thrasymachus. He may be satisfied with his own arguments, but he has done little or nothing to persuade his opponent; and indeed, insofar as he is – as I see it – using assumptions that Thrasymachus will never even have dreamed of sharing, one could say that he hasn't even tried. Here is another moment in the dialogues where the course of a discussion is determined by authorial artifice.[47] Book II begins with Socrates thinking the conversation over, as if Book I were just another short dialogue, ending in (apparent) *impasse*. But that conversation turned out after all, he reports, to be a *prŏoimion*, an 'introduction' (II, 357A2), because Glaucon, and Adimantus, wouldn't go along with Thrasymachus' giving up on the argument (and so there occurred the rest of the day's conversation, which would take up

---

[44] 'And so when we had agreed that justice is (an) excellence and wisdom, while injustice is badness and ignorance . . .' (350D4–5). On the argument that leads up to this 'agreement', see Appendix below. We are here in or near the region known in Platonic scholarship by the label 'the Socratic fallacy' (see, e.g., Vlastos 1991) – the idea, often attributed to Plato's Socrates, that we can't know anything about an item until we have fully identified what it is. Since, in the case of the excellences, I take Socrates to be clear enough in his own mind about what they are (knowledge of good and bad), I feel content enough to regard any 'fallacy' involved as being his interlocutors' problem rather than his. So in this case: *Thrasymachus* can't say anything sensible about justice because *he* hasn't correctly identified it.

[45] 'It appears so . . . according to your argument', 353E11.

[46] When Socrates says justice is (an) excellence and wisdom, Thrasymachus must take him to be saying that it's wisdom in the same way that *he* says injustice is, i.e. that it's good policy, because of what the agent will get out of it. Given his, Thrasymachus', own notion of what is worth going for, Socrates' position can only seem silly in the extreme.

[47] A point I shall attempt to drive home further in the Appendix below.

another nine books). This is a set-up. Glaucon starts by asking 'Socrates, which is it – do you want merely to seem to have persuaded us, or really and truly to persuade us that it's in every way better to be just than to be unjust?' (357A5–B1). Why, then, didn't he have a better go at it the first time round? There is a degree of dramatic justification, in that Thrasymachus started by trying to bully everyone and ended by sulking, thus showing himself a less than ideal dialectical partner. That, however, seems a poor excuse for Socrates' behaviour, however dramatically plausible and even defensible from the point of view of any supporter of Socrates. The more important explanation, I suggest, is that Book I is designed exactly as the introduction Socrates calls it (even if he didn't know it in advance): an introduction that imports into the text his own characteristic ideas and patterns of thought, on the model of those other small pieces like *Euthyphro* or *Charmides*, but with the difference that it will lead into something else, far larger and more ambitious. And the introduction neatly ends by identifying the very question with which the new discussion will begin: so what is justice?[48]

Many readers have observed the resemblance between Book I and the 'Socratic' dialogues. Some have taken this as evidence that Plato originally wrote Book I as a separate work, which he decided at a later point to use as the first part – the *prööimion* – of the *Republic*. For those who see a gulf in doctrine between the *Republic* and the 'Socratic' dialogues, the main effect of this decision of Plato's will have been to give a kind of reminder of what the Socrates of the *Republic* was leaving behind. My own reading of the situation is more or less exactly the reverse of this: *Republic* I is there to remind us of what Socrates will retain.[49] The book is a foil to the following ones, in which Socrates will make extensive use of an approach which he clearly marks out as being one he might not choose to employ under different circumstances: discussing a city other than the 'true' one;[50] not

---

[48] Socrates shows no hesitation about treating justice as an excellence anywhere else (that is, justice as he understands it, not as Callicles proposes to understand it in the *Gorgias* (482C–484C), in terms of some 'law of nature' that gives the stronger a larger share of things than the weak); he hesitates – appears to hesitate – only here in *Republic* I and in the following nine books, insofar as these set out to show that justice is a good thing (and so an excellence rather than a form of badness). The terms of the discussion are set by Thrasymachus: his argument has been to deny that justice is an excellence because, given his view of what people's interests are, it is never in the agent's own interests to behave justly. From Socrates' point of view, that will simply mean that Thrasymachus has a faulty notion of justice. To anyone who understood justice properly, as an excellence, it would not even occur to ask whether it was a good or a bad thing.

[49] I thus feel no incentive to engage in any speculations about the possibility that *Republic* I might have been written as a separate dialogue. Apart from its *resemblance* to some 'Socratic' dialogues, there are few or no other signs of its detachability from *Republic* II–X; and my own thesis actually makes it an organic part of the *Republic* as a whole.

[50] The 'true' city (the 'city of pigs'): II, 373E6–7.

discussing the soul in its 'truest nature', but instead taking the shorter rather than the longer road[51] – and as a consequence offering an account of the excellences that will itself fall short (or rather, offering an account of inferior versions of those excellences, which is an inevitable consequence of Plato's decision to treat the soul only 'as it appears': see below).[52] And one reason why he goes this – shorter – way is simply that it will help him do what Glaucon says he failed to do before: persuade his interlocutors.[53] Glaucon and Adimantus themselves will in the event duly declare themselves content with this approach, in a way that Socrates will not be.[54]

So: Socrates argues, after Book I, in relation to city and to soul, and to the excellences, in ways that do not satisfy him, at least in part in order to satisfy others. While Glaucon is by no means a supporter of Thrasymachus, he is not unimpressed by his arguments,[55] and Adimantus is in a similar position. As we have seen,[56] Glaucon is closer to Socrates than Adimantus, and is more philosophically formed. On the other hand, the very fact that Thrasymachus can impress him shows that his philosophical formation still has a long way to go; at any rate he is certainly no Socratic.[57] Because Glaucon, and Adimantus with him, have not been persuaded by the more genuinely Socratic arguments of Book I, Socrates now shifts, in Book II, to territory that will be more familiar to them (and to Thrasymachus); and

---

[51] Socrates clearly expresses his own preference for the longer road at VI, 504B–C. He could, I suspect, have described the shift from the porcine but true to the feverish city, too, in terms of the difference between shorter and longer roads; and indeed when he first starts talking in such terms, at IV, 435C–D, he explicitly treats taking the shorter road as being on the same level as 'the things that have been said and investigated before': D1–5. But that then will already include virtually the whole of the argument of Books II–IV.

[52] We should note in particular that the definition of *justice* in Book IV will be seriously at odds with what Socrates has said or implied about the same excellence in Book I. We shall therefore need some explanation for this discrepancy: either Socrates is junking the Book I account in Book IV, or the plot runs deeper (my vote has already gone to the second option).

[53] Even the *question* he is being made to answer – does justice pay? – is not one that he would put to himself, privately. Of course it pays! How could it not, when it's a matter of knowing what is really worth going for? (Cf. n. 48 above.)

[54] VI, 504B–C again.   [55] And those of others in the same camp: see II, 358C–D.

[56] See chapter I, p. 94 above.

[57] He is thus the counterpart of an intelligent reader who has read some Platonic dialogues before (for the significance of this point, see chapter 9 below). Since Glaucon and Adimantus are Plato's own brothers, the more imaginative reader might start wondering whether one or both mightn't be stand-ins for himself: was he writing, perhaps, in part to persuade *himself*? I see no great virtue in such speculation: Glaucon and Adimantus are representative of a type – decent, courageous and civic-minded (368A–B), intelligent – that Plato (Socrates) might hope most of all to persuade; the fact that Plato chooses his brothers for that role indirectly makes the whole dialogue a conversation between 'friends' (in the Greek sense, which includes one's relatives), who if they really are friends will be looking out for each other – especially, as the argument of the *Lysis* suggests: see Penner and Rowe 2005: 160–70 – by helping them to learn about the things that matter.

after all, the very task he is taking on, at their insistence, is not one that on his own territory would arise at all.[58]

But the world that Glaucon and Adimantus inhabit is in fact the one that Socrates must confront: a world in which the majority of souls are already in a non-ideal condition ('feverish', divided), and in which – he now proposes – only a small minority will be able to do anything, by themselves, to improve their situation. What is offered in Books II–IV, in other words, is not just an explanation of the phenomena, but a solution. Given that people are as they are, and given that most of them will be too far gone for rational treatment and cure,[59] Socrates has to go for the political option – at least so far as the majority are concerned; the rational option will still be there for those who will rule them (even if superimposed on the political), and indeed must be if the city, and the majority, are to be ruled properly. In short, the Socrates of Books II–X is one newly ready to meet the challenges posed by the condition of actual cities and individuals, in which and in whom reason is only uncertainly in control, if it is in control at all. What he will say about the soul and about the city (and about the excellences) is not mere rhetorical opportunism; he is addressing a kind of 'reality', and devising what he takes to be real ways of improving it – even while wishing that it were not like that in the first place. And who better to serve as interlocutors than Glaucon and Adimantus, 'divine offspring of a famous father',[60] who have at least started on the philosophical road?[61]

'Even while wishing that it were not like that in the first place': Socrates' preference, I take it, would be for a city of men and women each of whom would have a soul configured as much like soul 'in its truest nature'[62] as possible. And that, I propose, is what the city which Glaucon dismisses as 'fit for pigs' would be; that is why Socrates is able to call it the 'true', 'healthy' city (372E6). The idea comes and is gone again so swiftly that interpreters tend either to ignore or dismiss it; if it does not recur, that is just because, under actual conditions, it is mere fantasy – or rather, from the perspective of those conditions, it will look like fantasy, even while being, from Socrates' perspective, what a city truly is, just as the undivided soul represents what a human soul truly (is in its true[st] nature).[63]

---

58 See, nn. 46, 53 above.   59 N.b. the 'clean slate' requirement (see above).

60 According to Glaucon's lover, cited by Socrates at 368A4.

61 Socrates perhaps already marks out their philosophical bent by choosing to locate their 'divinity' not – as Glaucon's lover did – in their quality as soldiers but rather in their ability to resist the arguments for injustice even while putting them so forcefully: II, 368A5–7.

62 *Republic* X again.

63 Cf. the picture of the ideal statesman/ideal statesmanship as this emerges from the *Politicus*. This statesman, like the philosopher-rulers of Callipolis in the *Republic*, would have to deal with an

What of the excellences? As we saw at the beginning of the present chapter, Socrates himself suggests that the account given of justice and the rest in *Republic* IV is lacking in precision, for reasons somehow connected with the imprecision of the account of the soul. And the explanation is not hard to find: Book IV defined three of them in terms of the soul's parts, and parts are what the 'true' soul will lack. What 'sound-mindedness',[64] courage and justice will be in the case of the undivided soul is, presumably, what they always were in the pre-*Republic* dialogues: wisdom or knowledge, of the good (for which we may now read: of the form of the good)[65] and the bad. We get a hint of this from the discussion of the qualities that will be looked for in candidates for philosopher-rulership in *Republic* VI (485B–487A), in which Socrates inconspicuously[66] derives a kind of embryo 'sound-mindedness', courage and justice directly from an attachment to learning and wisdom. (So for example with courage: for someone concerned with gazing at[67] 'all of time and all being'[68] his own human life will not count for much; someone like that, then, will not think death anything so terrible.) So what are the excellences Socrates actually describes in Book IV? He comes clean almost casually, at VII, 500D6–8, where he suddenly calls the philosopher-ruler a 'craftsman . . . of *sōphrosunē* and justice and in short all demotic [*dēmotikē*] excellence'. 'Demotic' excellence (excellence as appropriate to the people, the *dēmos*) is what in the *Phaedo* he describes as 'what [people who have it] call *sōphrosunē* and justice, grown from habit and practice without philosophy and intelligence' (82B1–3; cf. 69A–C); the people who have it are the ones who will be reborn as ants, bees, wasps and (sometimes) men.[69] It is not, then, if we have the licence to read between dialogues,[70] something that Socrates is inclined to value highly

---

actual city formed of actual and less than perfect individuals. For a parallel to the 'city of pigs' we might have to look to the state of things in the age of Cronus in the great myth of the *Politicus*: if people at that time didn't need constitutions (*Politicus* 271E8), then, strictly speaking, one might perhaps expect the same to be true of a community of purely rational beings with minimal needs.

[64] Which is what *sōphrosunē* will have to be once more; in the undivided soul, there will be no such thing as 'self-control', on principle, because there is nothing that actually needs to be controlled.

[65] I shall, however, question whether the change makes any substantive difference: see chapter 9 below.

[66] Inconspicuously, because he will not want to undermine the Book IV account too directly; most people will be able to aspire to nothing more than the – splendid, but just not top-grade – kind of excellence described there.

[67] I.e. *theōria* (cf. the *philotheamones*, respectively of plays and of truth, in *Republic* V).

[68] VI, 486A8–9.   [69] See chapter 2 above.

[70] And perhaps even if we do not; in any case we should have to explain what Socrates had in mind with the description 'demotic' (hardly a complimentary term, given just what he has said and will say about the people, the *dēmos*, in the *Republic*).

by comparison with the other, philosophical, sort of excellence; it will be a mere shadow[71] of the real thing.[72]

I do not suggest that Plato is not serious about the definitions he gives of the excellences in *Republic* IV, any more than I wish to suggest that he is unserious in what he says there about the soul; or indeed in what he says about Callipolis. Given what human beings have made of themselves, Callipolis is the best city, and its constitution is the best (VI, 497B7), though it will be a fragile thing (497D), and may itself be no more than a dream. Equally, individuals will be better off with the 'demotic' forms of the excellences – especially, one imagines, if they have been formed by that 'craftsman', the philosopher-ruler – than without them (and the imagined city of Magnesia in the *Laws* will depend on the inculcation of such excellence, however inferior, as much as Callipolis in the *Republic*). But we should not mistake the Book IV excellences for what the excellences are, according to Socrates (and Plato).[73]

The *Republic* ends, as it began, with the individual, not with the city. The great myth with which the work closes, like the *Phaedo* myth, sets human life and the choices it entails within the context of a cosmos ordered to provide the appropriate rewards and punishments – whether in Hades, or in the course of new lives lived in new bodies. Again as in the case of the *Phaedo*, the story is ultimately less about our fate after death – even taking into account that our souls will be reborn – than it is about the here and now; the moral is that our choices have consequences, even in our present lives. The theme of rebirth into different kinds of animals is present but rather less prominent,[74] and understandably so, given that the appetitive part of the soul has been compared to a many headed monster.[75] (The idea in the *Phaedo* is that our choices may actually make us animals rather than humans, despite our human shape; we then naturally pass into the

---

[71] A shadow-painting (*skiagraphia tis*), *Phaedo* 69B6–7.

[72] There is, of course, a sense in which the excellences as possessed by the ruled in Callipolis will be informed by knowledge (see especially VI, 504A–B); that is, insofar as they have been 'crafted' by those possessing the excellences in their true form. (So, e.g., *sōphrosunē* in the ruled will be a settled state, and also not in any way *forced* [see esp. VIII, 547B] – not a kind of Aristotelian *enkrateia*; presumably because it will have become as it were second nature to them, as a result of their training.) But in themselves the excellences of the ruled will remain 'demotic', as Socrates describes them. On the excellences as possessed by the rulers themselves, see n. 82 below.

[73] Except, that is, in the context of the divided soul, i.e. of any soul that lacks the capacity for reflection that would allow it to aspire to something more.

[74] X, 618A3.

[75] *Republic* IX, 588B–589A: 'man' is an outer shell, containing 'three kinds of thing, grown together' (*sumpephukuiai ideai*, 588C4), within it: the monster, a lion representing 'spirit', and a human being representing reason. The whole *looks* like a human being, to anyone incapable of seeing within the shell (588D11–E1).

appropriate animal shapes next time round. Animal monsters, however, will on Socrates' account be in rather shorter supply – except in the traditional myths – than human monsters, i.e. humans that *look* human but are actually monstrous.)[76] Nevertheless the general point is that everyone has a choice[77] between strengthening the monster in him, or the lion ('spirit'), or making what is human in him (reason) the most powerful element, all the time caring for each of the three aspects of ourselves, and making them 'friends to each other and to oneself' (589B5–6).

But this is all still seen from the inferior perspective of ordinary experience, on which in Book X Socrates will superimpose that other perspective, of what the soul is 'in its truest nature'. And this second perspective, I propose, if somewhat speculatively, may itself already be in play even just after the introduction of the Book IX image (man as human, lion and monster). As Book IX ends, Socrates suggests that the person who acts unjustly without anyone's knowing, and without being punished, becomes still worse,[78]

while in the person who is found out, and is punished,[79] the wild element is calmed and tamed while the tame is freed, and the whole soul settles into the best part of its nature and takes on a more valuable[80] condition, acquiring *sōphrosunē* and justice together with wisdom, than if he has a body that takes on strength and beauty together with physical health – more valuable by the same degree that soul has a greater value than body. (IX, 591B1–7)

Here we are still talking about a divided soul: to 'acquire *sōphrosunē* and justice together with wisdom' is still, evidently, a matter of acquiring three separate excellences – because *sōphrosunē* is still being treated, in Book IV mode, as a harmony between different parts or elements (591C8–D3 directly treats *sōphronein* as a kind of 'being in tune' in the soul). Anyone with sense[81] will deport himself in relation to everything with an eye to maintaining this inner harmony, taking on offices and honours, even, only to the extent that he thinks that 'will make him better', and not undermine what harmony he has achieved (592A2–3). So he won't take part in politics, offers Glaucon: no, responds Socrates, except in 'his own city' (*en tēi heautou polei*, 592A7), that is, perhaps, the one that contains the same harmony that exists in him;

---

[76] Indeed part of the message seems to be that humans may be more monstrous than any real animal kind.

[77] Spelled out in IX, 588E–589B.

[78] On this theme as played out in the *Gorgias*, and on Plato's handling of punishment in general, see chapter 4, section 2(a) above.

[79] In a conventional, or at any rate more conventional, way – i.e. not simply involving a talking to (if the 'demotic' excellences can be instilled by a kind of conditioning, as *Republic* II–III suggests)?

[80] I.e. more valuable to him (a condition that brings him more 'profit').

[81] 591C1 *ho noun echōn*.

which, unless he is lucky, will not be the city he was born in.[82] 'You mean, in the city we've just expounded, founding (*oikizein*) it as we went – the city in words; because I don't think it's anywhere on earth' (Glaucon at 592A10–B1). 'But . . . [replies Socrates] perhaps there is a model [sc. of it?] laid up in heaven, for the person willing to see it, and looking to it, found (*katoikizein*) himself' (B2–3) – where 'himself' is and must be the object of 'found'. (The idea is prepared for by 590E3–4, where Socrates talks about 'setting up a constitution' in children 'as if in a city'.)

How exactly are we to take this last idea? The paragon in question will evidently order himself – set up a constitution in himself – as Socrates and the two brothers have ordered a city, if only in words (592A10); and he will do it with his eye on the model on which Callipolis is based. But that, on the interpretation I have been proposing, will be more like the 'city of pigs', the first, 'true' and undivided city of Book II, than Callipolis: itself a model, for emulation, but at the same time, as the present passage confirms,[83] based on a model – as I take it, the model of the 'true' city, to which Callipolis approximates so far as prevailing conditions, including fever and division, allow. Using this model, he would 'found himself' as an undivided entity. We may compare the case of the founders of Callipolis themselves, as they found 'their' city (VII, 540E3), making it their first priority to send away everyone over the age of ten, leaving behind children free from the present ethos (540E5–541A2), and dealing with individuals, private citizens, in the same way (501A5–7): 'cleansing' them, as I took it, in the way any good Socratic would, of their false beliefs,[84] a process that would have as its end result a 'pure' soul after the manner of the *Phaedo* – or *Republic* X.[85]

Or that, I think, will be the sub-text. It will not be the sense that Glaucon will carry away with him; for him, the soul is nothing if not divided.[86] It

---

[82] This harmonious individual resembles the philosopher-ruler in the process of formation. Philosopher-rulers who have completed their education will, I suppose, possess the philosophical/intellectual versions of the excellences to the extent that they are wise (cf. text to nn. 64–7); I shall, however, later bring into question whether Socrates– even in the *Republic*– is disposed to think that any human being can become completely, i.e. divinely, wise (see esp. chapter 8 below), and to this extent the quality of the other excellences, as the rulers possess them, will be in doubt. What is certain in any case is that the rulers won't be just, etc. *merely* as a result of habit and training.

[83] Unless, that is, we try translating Socrates at B2–3 (cited above) as saying 'But . . . perhaps *it* exists *as* a model laid up in heaven.' That would be a quite possible way of rendering the Greek, and indeed a natural one; on the other hand, it would be a little odd for Socrates to suggest that Callipolis *itself* is a model 'in heaven', when he has introduced at least some aspects of it with such hesitation. Of course, on my own interpretation it would actually be ruled out that Callipolis was the 'model in heaven', given its origin as a compromise between the ideal and the actual.

[84] See n. 38 above.   [85] See chapter 2 above.

[86] We should note Socrates' phrase '(a model in heaven) for the person willing to see it' in *Republic* X, 593B3: perhaps an echo of the complaint against the sight-lovers in Book V (there will be some

is Socrates who will point beyond the divided soul, in *Republic* x. (Glaucon is surprised even by the suggestion that the soul 'is deathless and never perishes': 608D. But then he wasn't there for the conversation of the *Phaedo*.)[87] It is for the reader to look beyond Glaucon's vision of things, and 'see' the model intended. Or, alternatively, what I have just proposed, as a reading of IX, 592B, is just too much of a stretch. Even if so, however, the position that I have so extravagantly claimed to be represented in these lines is true to, and the best explanation of, those other passages in the *Republic* that I have discussed in the preceding pages. The 'true' soul and the 'true' city, and (I add) true excellence, lie beyond anything Glaucon, or Adimantus, can so far grasp; by the same sort of distance, in fact, that forms lie beyond sensible particulars, and that what is 'seen' by reason lies beyond what is seen by the eyes.[88]

---

who will not be willing to contemplate a model of the city such as the one Socrates has in mind). Glaucon is in an analogous position to the sight-lovers in relation to the soul, only seeing it as it is, now, not as it can be (and really is).

[87] So any intertextual references to *Phaedo* in *Republic* will go over his head. (But he and Adimantus have heard plenty of other Socratic conversations: see chapter 9 below.)

[88] The question Socrates puts to Glaucon at x, 608D3–4 (see above) is 'Have you not *seen* [perceived: *eisthēsai*] . . . that our soul is deathless and never perishes?' – another case of 'seeing' 'things in themselves'?

Socrates vs Thrasymachus in Republic I

Much of the last chapter has depended on Socrates' being serious when he claims, at the beginning of *Republic* II, that he was satisfied with what he said to Thrasymachus in the preceding book, even if Glaucon and Adimantus quite evidently are not (368B5–7). However so poorly have many of the arguments in the book been received by modern interpreters that it might even appear more charitable to suppose that the remark is just part of a characteristic episode of Socratic self-deprecation. Glaucon and Adimantus have just restated the case for injustice, and Socrates says he is in a quandary:

On the one hand I don't have the resources to come to the aid [of justice] – I think I'm not up to it, and for that I have as evidence the fact that you haven't accepted from me what I said to Thrasymachus and thought showed that justice was a better thing than injustice; on the other hand, there is no way that I can not come to her aid, for I'm afraid that it may even be impious to stand by when witnessing justice being abused and not come to her aid when one can still breathe and utter articulate sounds. (II, 368B4–C3)

Since Book I ended with his apparently volunteering to throw away his case for the greater 'profitability' of justice (on the grounds that he needed to know first what justice is), surely what he says here must be disingenuous? I have suggested in the main part of the present chapter that it is this move, at the end of Book I, rather than the one in 368B–C that we should regard as unserious. But it would help, if that is so, if his case for justice were at least reasonably respectable. The present appendix sets out to show that this is so, taking as a sample a short stretch of argument – 349B1–350C11 – for which hardly any modern commentator has a good word.

What I shall claim is that Socrates is using premises which are perfectly familiar and true to him, but entirely unfamiliar to Thrasymachus, who if told what they were would reject them outright; what he has to make do with, and what he reluctantly goes along with, is a much less satisfactory argument from quite different premises – one that does, nevertheless, work in its own way. Since Socrates believes in his own premises and disbelieves in Thrasymachus' (that is, the general premises from which Thrasymachus will draw the ones he brings to the argument), this is a quite reasonable way for him – for Socrates – to go; and the outcome is that we, the readers, have two different arguments to choose from. If we opt for the one Thrasymachus goes along with (as most modern interpreters do, more or less), than we shall end up about as happy as Thrasymachus, i.e. not very happy. If, on the other hand, we opt for the argument that Socrates has in mind, and that uses his premises, then our degree of contentment will be in proportion to our contentment with the premises, but at least we shall know where Socrates is coming from – and what he thinks is the right way to see things. So, I conclude, he has good reason, from his own perspective (which, again, he thinks true), to be happy with this particular argument; and I propose that the other arguments in Book 1 tend to work in a similar way. There is nothing in what he says in Book 1 that he wants to jettison. Rather, what he says there forms the starting-point for the *Republic*; it is the prelude or preface that sets its very tone – or rather, gives his viewpoint before he dives into the main argument of the book, whose parameters are set, in the way I have suggested in the main body of the chapter (above), by others.

A rough summary of the argument might be: the just person only seeks to outdo the one unlike him (the unjust), not the one like him, whereas the unjust person seeks to outdo both the one unlike him (the just) and the one like him. But in other spheres, e.g., the musical, the medical . . . the 'good and wise person' (the expert) only seeks to outdo those unlike him, not those like him. So the just person, not the unjust, is the one who is good and wise; so justice, not injustice is excellence and wisdom, which both sides agree are good things. Merely from this summary one might already begin to sympathize with those who write it off;[1] but let me try to come to its aid (as Socrates says he must come to justice's aid).[2]

I begin by borrowing a helpful statement of the context of the argument:

The . . . argument [at] 349B1–350C11 begins from the claim that 'the person who is able to do great things [or "the person with great power": *ton megala dunamenon*] overreaches' (343E7–344A1). Thrasymachus said this about the unjust person who uses his opportunities to gain advantages for himself and so to 'overreach'

---

[1] The most dismissive are Cross and Woozley 1966.
[2] The following analysis of the argument is an English version of part of a rather longer paper in French written as a contribution to a *Festschrift* for Monique Dixsaut, edited by Dimitri El Murr and others.

(*pleonektein*) or get the better of other people. This is the person who goes in for 'complete unjust action'. (348D5–9, 351B4–5)[3]

That nicely describes the larger context, but it still misses an important aspect of the exchange between Socrates and Thrasymachus just before 349B (where our argument begins). Socrates has been establishing that Thrasymachus identifies the unjust person – that is, the completely/perfectly unjust person – with the wise and the good (the claim that 349B–350C aims to refute). Such completely unjust people are described as those with the capacity (*dunamenoi*) to make cities and whole peoples (*ethnē*) subject to them, as opposed to cutpurses; 'which isn't to say that such things [as stealing purses] aren't advantageous, if one gets away with them, just that they're not worth talking about' (Thrasymachus at 348D5–9).

The following is what forms the immediate background to the first part of our argument:

SOCRATES 'Does it seem to you that the just person would want to have more than/outdo (*pleon echein*) the just [i.e. another just person]?'

THRASYMACHUS 'Not at all; if he did, he wouldn't be the charming (*asteios*), and simple-minded, individual he in fact is.'

SOCRATES 'What then of the just action? [Sc. does he want to have more than/outdo that?]'

THRASYMACHUS 'Not even the just [sc.action – let alone the unjust action].'

(I, 349B2–7)

The sorts of actions Thrasymachus recommends lead to 'profit', i.e. a disproportionate share of goods as ordinarily recognized (he has just offered power and money as examples: 348D); and the larger the better. Cutting people's purses gives a small profit, but taking over a city or a whole nation gives a much better return. In Thrasymachus' view, by implication, the just person rates even lower than the petty thief because he turns his back on profit of this sort altogether. (Just people think they should get more than the unjust, and think it just that they should;[4] unfortunately, Thrasymachus suggests, they'd never be able to get it: 349B8–10.) This is the point of his response that the just person doesn't *even* want to have more than/outdo the just action. Such an individual is so simple-minded that he doesn't even enter the only competition that matters.[5] By contrast, the unjust individual, the one who is really sensible, and knows how to go about getting

---

[3] Irwin 1995: 177.

[4] Presumably as a reward for their justice – which might be simply a matter of their not suffering the penalties that ought to be meted out to the unjust.

[5] Here Adam's proposal (Adam 1963 (1902), ad loc.) to fill out the text, to give 'And not the just action *either*' (*tēs* <*praxeōs tēs*> *dikaias*), seems particularly unhelpful, insofar as it flattens Thrasymachus'

what life has to offer, will always want to go one better than anybody else, whether just (no competition there) or indeed unjust. That is what Socrates induces Thrasymachus to admit at 349C7–10: 'Then the unjust person will want to have more than/outdo (*pleonektēsei*) an *unjust* person too, and an *unjust* action [sc. as well as a just person and action], and will compete (*hamillēsetai*) to get most of everything for himself?' 'That's so.'

The question most commentators focus upon here is the use of the expressions *pleon echein/pleonektein*: 'having more'/'outdoing'. What receives rather less attention is the position that Socrates wants to defend. The position Socrates is defending is not the same as the one Thrasymachus is attacking, or thinks he is attacking, because their perspectives, as we have discovered even by this stage of the *Republic*, are quite different. Most obviously, Socrates doesn't think the just to be simple-minded, as Thrasymachus does, even despite the fact that they don't want to have more than people like them. They simply have a different idea of what they want out of life, of what is good; and so also of what it is to have more than someone else.[6] The reason why Socrates holds this view hasn't yet been articulated, and won't be in this stretch of argument, but then neither has Thrasymachus told us why he thinks unlimited power and money a good thing. This first part of the argument that we are discussing is, I propose, as important for what it begins to tell us about *Socrates' own* position, and the difference between it and Thrasymachus', as it is for the ammunition it provides for Thrasymachus' dialectical defeat. Far from merely constructing what he needs to see off his opponent, Socrates starts from what he himself believes – and after all, his ultimate aim is, surely (so far as we can tell from the form of the dialogue as a whole), to bring Thrasymachus, and anyone else, round to his own point of view. What our argument tries to do as a whole is to show that, whether he likes it or not, Thrasymachus must accept at least part of Socrates' position (that it's the just person, not the unjust, who's wise). But of course once he has accepted that, a number of other things will follow: if the just are wise, then they're doing the best thing . . . We typically, and perhaps naturally, think of Socrates' task as being to

answer instead of allowing it the kind of forcefulness that his other answers have. (Simon Slings, by printing *oude <tau> tēs [dikaias]*, in the new Oxford text of the *Republic*, most unusually misses the point, following Wilamowitz; see also Slings 2005: 13.) The whole passage is, above all, a conversation *between opposing viewpoints*; and Thrasymachus is at no point a mere patsy.

6 There is surely no doubt that Thrasymachus thinks the unjust person good at getting what is good, or rather what he thinks is good. And there must be even less doubt, in the light of the overall argument of the *Republic*, that Socrates thinks it's the just man who excels at this same thing – getting what is good. It is just that – to repeat the point – he and Thrasymachus have different ideas about what really is good.

undermine Thrasymachus; but actually *Republic* 1 is more accurately described as Socrates' seeing off Thrasymachus' attempt to undermine *him*, and showing why Thrasymachus must after all come over to his side.

As for the alleged differences of meaning in Socrates' uses of the expressions *pleon echein/pleonektein*, I myself claim that these play no significant role in the context. To be sure, having more, or wanting to have more, than someone is not in general the same thing as outdoing or wanting to outdo someone's action; but for the context in which the argument occurs this is hardly relevant, for the simple reason that both protagonists deliberately treat them together, if for different reasons. (1) First, as we have seen, Thrasymachus actually introduced the two things together: the supreme exponent of injustice will seek the maximum gain, and in doing so will not bother with mere purse-stealing; what will interest him will rather be the really big things, like making himself master of cities and whole nations (348D5–6). From this Thrasymachean perspective, *pleon echein* as having more will go together with outdoing someone's action. (2) For Socrates, however, the connection between the two things is even closer: they are actually one and the same thing – that is, if we add in the premise that the present argument will supply – namely that the just person is wise. For, implicitly, the just person will be wise in his choice of *goods*;[7] he will show his wisdom precisely in not going for the sort of profit the unjust person goes for. If he performs a just action, he will already have more than the one person he can 'outdo' in this way, i.e. the unjust person (because he will already have as much good as he can get),[8] and by the same token he will have outdone the one kind of action that he can outdo, i.e. the unjust action[9] (on the assumption that two wise people – two equally, and perfectly, wise ones – will always do the same thing under the same

---

[7] Thrasymachus certainly identifies wisdom and goodness with the ability to acquire goods (as he understands these – see especially 348C5–8 with 349D3–11); and Socrates will be only too ready to go along with this, given *his*, quite different, understanding of goods.

[8] The problem is not at all about what the two expressions – *pleon echein, pleonektein* – *mean*, but rather of what it *is pleon echein / pleonektein*. For Thrasymachus it is to have more of the things ordinarily thought good, such as power and money; for Socrates, it is to have more of what is *really* good. See the question he will raise later in the *Republic* (VI, 505B1–2): 'Do you think it's anything *more* (*pleon*) to have acquired absolutely everything, if what you've acquired isn't *good*?' – and especially the reference to *pleonexia adikos* at *Critias* 121B6, in the context of talk about a mistaken view of happiness.

[9] Should anyone contest that the set of ideas just listed really does follow directly from the idea that the just are wise, I shall not mind. My underlying point is, first, that for Socrates, they do follow, and second, that his present argument is in part designed to announce this elaboration of his position, and its contrast with Thrasymachus'. Once again, the argument is at least as much about what Socrates thinks as it is about what Thrasymachus thinks.

circumstances).[10] Action and outcome come apart, if they come apart at all, in the case of the unjust action.

But I do not wish to press this point here,[11] important though it is for other contexts.[12] In the event Socrates constructs the argument in such a way as to cater for both kinds of *pleonektein* (having more, and outdoing). After rounding off the first part of the argument with a summarizing 'So the just person only tries to outdo (*pleonektei*) the one unlike himself, not the one like him, while the unjust person tries to outdo both' (349C11–D1), Socrates gets Thrasymachus to repeat his claim that the unjust are wise and good, and the just neither (349D3–5). To that, Socrates now responds by suggesting that at any rate[13] in music, and in medicine, things are not like this: you don't find one musical expert trying to outdo (*pleonektein*), or thinking he should have more (*axioun pleon echein*), than another such in the tuning of a lyre, or a medical expert 'wanting somehow to outdo (*ethelein . . . ti . . . pleonektein*) another medical expert, or medical action,[14] in eating or drinking' (350A1–2). In this latter case, I take it, what is being described is self-prescription, not the doctor's prescription for his patient: the point is that the expert doctor doesn't try to get any more for himself than his expertise, and an expertly prescribed regime (action), dictates.[15] If so, then this example drives home the second aspect of the first: the musical expert doesn't expect to have more, i.e. get more, be better rewarded (or regarded?), than another similar expert for getting the tuning of the lyre right. So an expert *neither* tries to outdo another expert's action, *nor* expects to get more than another expert for getting things as they should be, i.e. as their expertise allows both of them to do. (I earlier claimed that any 'differences of meaning' in the uses of *pleonektein/pleon echein* were irrelevant in the context. I now formally add, in the light of the above analysis of the treatment of musicians and

---

[10] That Socrates is assuming just this is shown by 350A6–9.

[11] That is, that for the wise man action and outcome cannot be separated.

[12] See for example *Gorgias* 467–8, 499–500 (discussed in chapter 4 above).

[13] This 'at any rate' is justified – if it is – by the fact that Socrates asks Thrasymachus to look and see if there are any cases where experts behave any differently (350A6–9), to which Thrasymachus replies that he thinks things must be (*anankē . . . echein*) as Socrates proposes (somewhat surprisingly, since he has been claiming up till now that the expert *ruler*, who for him will be the perfectly unjust person, is not like this at all: we must suppose that he is finally conceding the point, without seeing that it will affect his whole claim that the unjust person is wise/expert).

[14] The Greek word here is *pragma* rather than *praxis*, which Socrates used before (349B6, C5), but presumably only because that makes it easier for *iatrikou* to cover both *andros* and *pragmatos*.

[15] Cf. my reconstruction above of (Socrates' perspective on) the case of the just person: the good for the just man consists in acting justly; and the action he will perform in any given set of circumstances will be the same as the one any other just person will perform in (exactly) the same circumstances.

doctors, the claim that Plato knows perfectly well what he is doing[16] with these expressions, and that it is perfectly plain that he does.)

From here on in, given everything he has conceded, Thrasymachus' dialectical defeat is – for the most part – easy enough. If every expert will always do or say the same things as the one like himself 'in relation to the same action',[17] then, given that the expert is wise, and that the wise person is good, then the good and wise person will not wish to outdo (*pleonektein*) the one like him, but only the one unlike and opposite; whereas the bad and ignorant person will wish to outdo both the one like him and his opposite. But that's how the unjust person behaves, while the just man will only try to outdo the one unlike him, not the one like. So the latter resembles the wise and good person, while the former resembles the bad and ignorant.[18] But then, since it was earlier agreed (349D10–12) that just and unjust alike are actually such as those that they resemble, the just will have been shown to be good and wise, the unjust ignorant and bad.

At first sight this last move looks slightly odd; that is, until one sees that 'those that they resemble' applies just to the pairs wise/good and ignorant/bad. Thrasymachus claimed that of course the unjust person *resembles* the wise and good because he actually *is* wise and good, from which Socrates derives the concession (even if Thrasymachus does not yet recognize it as such) that the just and the unjust person will each be of whichever of the two kinds they resemble, wise/good or ignorant/bad. The title wise/good has to go to one or other competitor, and no other title is in question; whichever of them resembles, turns out to have a feature or features of the wise and good sufficient to make him resemble the wise/good, that will settle the matter. Socrates cannot then be accused of moving from a claim about resemblance to one about identity (nor Thrasymachus of colluding in such a move); but perhaps that would be so elementary an error that

---

[16] Nor is what he is doing *equivocating*, as I hope to have shown above; that is, Thrasymachus' defeat doesn't depend on his not understanding some play on meanings. (It depends, rather, on his having an unsustainable view of what *pleon echein*, or *pleonektein*, *is*.)

[17] That is, as I have taken it, in choosing to say and do the same things in the same circumstances (350A).

[18] In view of the way that 'wise' and 'good', and 'ignorant and bad', appear to go around in pairs in the whole context, it is hard to resist the temptation to suppose that the goodness and badness in question are goodness and badness at doing things – i.e. wisdom and ignorance. Thrasymachus seems happy enough to go along with this (see especially 348D, where immediately after asserting that the unjust possess *euboulia*, i.e. roughly, the right policy, he agrees that they're also wise and good – provided that they can get the really big returns). But the identification of goodness and wisdom is something that will be of more immediate interest to Socrates than to Thrasymachus; that is, it's Socrates, not Thrasymachus, who typically claims that goodness *is* knowledge or wisdom. (Well, he regularly does it outside the *Republic*, so that when we find him doing it here, inside the *Republic*, we seem to know where we are.)

anyone would think twice about attributing it to either man.[19] Plato has no interest in making Thrasymachus, let alone Socrates, look merely stupid.

The outcome then is that so far as the argument between the two men has gone, it is the just person and not the unjust one that is wise and good. Socrates can hardly be said to have provided any sort of *demonstration* of this conclusion, given that it in fact depends on an alleged resemblance between the just and the wise – and what is more, on different interpretations of the grounds of that resemblance. Thrasymachus agrees that the just don't try to outdo the just (or the just action), but doesn't understand Socrates' reason for holding that that is the case; Thrasymachus puts it down as illustrating how silly the just are, while for Socrates it flows precisely from the wisdom of the just. For him, though he does not say so, the just resemble the wise because they are wise, the kind of claim that Thrasymachus explicitly makes about the unjust: 349D8–9, with 5–6. Thus from Thrasymachus' point of view the argument turns on what might be called a merely formal point of resemblance, while from Socrates' (even though, again, this does not appear on the surface) the resemblance is real, and genuinely indicative.[20] But at no point, I claim, does Socrates propose anything that he does not himself take seriously. That is, nothing he says is said, or invented, merely for the sake of the argument.

It is true that this defence of Socrates' argument in one way leaves it looking even worse: not only is it rather a weak argument, but it doesn't really address Thrasymachus' position at all.[21] This objection recalls one of the two main objections to the argument that interpreters have standardly raised, and indeed is probably the same objection (the two men have in mind expertise at different kinds of thing).[22] Why is it, such interpreters might ask, and perhaps implicitly do ask, that Thrasymachus isn't allowed to object that as a matter of fact the *perfectly* unjust person won't be in competition with another perfectly unjust person any more than the perfectly just compete with each other, and on the same grounds? Why should there not be supremely, perfectly crafted, acts of injustice performed by experts at the top of their form, acts such that any other expert, however good,

---

[19] Except, that is, anyone who is content to have Socratic dialectic reduced to mere eristic: see above.

[20] And in fact, Socrates might well want to claim that if, as Thrasymachus claims, the unjust man is (a) an expert and (b) someone who seeks the good, he (the unjust man) can scarcely do without expertise *about* the good. See below. (Here, again – at least – from a Socratic point of view, the parallels with music and medicine, which Thrasymachus accepts, have a particular bite.)

[21] The two men are in any case talking across one another, as I suggested in the main body of the present chapter (text to n. 47). The question now is whether there are parts of Thrasymachus' case to which Socrates should have paid more attention.

[22] The other main objection, of course, is that Socrates plays on an ambiguity in *pleonektein/pleon echein*.

could only sit back and admire them (whether in terms of their skill, or more pertinently the resulting profit)? If the just don't compete with each other, that's a merely superficial resemblance to the wise and good/expert. In other words, why shouldn't there be an art or expertise of injustice, parallel to Socrates' *soi-disant* expertise of justice?

But what exactly is this supposed 'art/expertise of injustice'? So far as Thrasymachus sponsors any such thing, it will be the art of getting as much for oneself as one can, whatever the situation. I pass over[23] the fact that it may be impossible to set a limit to the amount of ordinarily recognized goods that could be got from particular situations (so that the experts at injustice might in principle be in eternal competition); injustice might merely be one kind of expertise where even ideal practitioners *will* sometimes compete with each other. But what Thrasymachus treats the unjust as being good at is not injustice. The unjust, for him, are good *at getting the most for themselves*; they are wise because they have the right policy, that is, because they opt for injustice, which gives the greatest returns. And the just are simple-minded because they opt for the wrong policy (even while wanting the same thing). The 'art of injustice' is something introduced by interpreters, not by Thrasymachus, let alone by Socrates. For Socrates, there could hardly be any sort of expertise that was involved in going for the wrong things, unless it was some sort of ratlike, misdirected, cunning. (We may compare the *Gorgias*, where he denies that even rhetoric is a true expertise.) What he takes the unjust man to be claiming to be good at is the same as Thrasymachus thinks him good at: getting the most of the things worth having.[24]

Now it might be that Plato should have allowed Thrasymachus to introduce an art of injustice, in the way suggested above. I am not myself clear that it would be an art worth anyone's having, if its supreme practitioners are to be large-scale crooks and dictators. But in any case Plato will spend the better part of another nine books discussing the attractiveness or otherwise of that sort of option. It will be enough in the present context to point out that his failure to have Socrates develop the argument along the lines in question (that is, in terms of an art of injustice) is at any rate consistent with the general tenor of the whole context under discussion: that

---

[23] As Plato, perhaps, may not have been content to do: see, e.g., the discussion of pleasure in *Republic* IX, or the *Philebus*.

[24] Thus another plausible-seeming criticism of the argument, that – surely? – not all unjust people are like Thrasymachus' perfectly unjust man, seems in danger of missing the point (i.e. Socrates' point). All unjust people will lack proper judgement about what is good.

is, with its generally *Socratic* tenor. As I have suggested, Socrates at every turn begins from positions that he himself holds; and this will be nowhere truer than here, if indeed he declines even to discuss – if Plato chooses not to have him discuss – the possibility of a science of getting what, as he sees it, only the ignorant person should choose. This is not the kind of neutral, open-ended discussion we might have expected, and perhaps hoped for; it is rather, as I have portrayed it (I believe with good reason), a confrontation between two opposing perspectives. The Socrates we find here is no more open-minded on the main point at issue than is Thrasymachus: going for what Thrasymachus says we should all go for just isn't, for Socrates, the right policy, and anyone who says it is has failed to understand what really is good. What the unjust person exhibits, then, has no chance of being any sort of *expertise*, or *wisdom*; how could it, if it derives simply from a lack of understanding? It is the just man who understands, and may be said to be expert (about goods).

*

The immediate purpose of the preceding analysis has been to show that even what appears to be the worst argument in *Republic* I is actually rather decent, and why. There is, in general (so I claim) nothing in this first book of his major work to date that Plato would wish to throw overboard – least of all the premises on which the argument is based; that is, the argument as Socrates reads it. But the analysis may also serve as a worked-out example of what Socratic dialectic, in its written version, is like. Plato's Socrates begins, to use a baseball metaphor, with the bases loaded; even when he is genuinely exploring – as I think he is, for example, in the case of the politics of the *Republic* – he sets out with a collection of ideas that are sufficiently interconnected even to be said to constitute a theory. He is still, at the same time, a know-nothing; he above all is aware of the perils of claiming to know anything. But that does not prevent him from having a thoroughly developed point of view, and one to which he is deeply committed. So deeply committed, in fact, that he devotes a considerable part of his available energy to trying to persuade others to come to share his point of view.[25] (And as usual, I take it that what goes for his Socrates goes for Plato too.) And that is why *Republic* I has to end in *aporia* – *impasse*, entirely constructed by Socrates,[26] to prepare the way for the massive argument that will follow, for

---

[25] 'A considerable part': the other, presumably even more considerable part, must be supposed to be devoted to thinking. Socrates has many more conversations than he 'reports' (and especially with himself) – and Plato hardly thinks only what he writes.

[26] By this stage Thrasymachus has in any case more or less withdrawn from the discussion.

a position (that justice 'pays') about which he surely has not the slightest doubt except to the extent that he is perpetually aware of the dangers of asserting that any important issue is finally and completely closed. The ending of the book is in this respect a kind of play on the endings of the so-called 'aporetic' dialogues (*Euthyphro*, *Lysis*, etc.). Yet in a way it is just like those other endings. The *aporia* in such cases, as I have argued,[27] derives more from the situation of the interlocutor than from Socrates' – and so too, perhaps, in the case of *Republic* I. Thrasymachus may have agreed, verbally, that it is justice and not injustice that is excellence and wisdom, but he has hardly been persuaded of it (any more than most people would be: that is the burden of Glaucon's and Adimantus' interventions at the beginning of Book II). To this extent, that is, in terms of the actual situation between the interlocutors, the question about the nature of justice really still is at issue, and so long as it is, the further question about whether it is justice or injustice that is the more 'profitable' cannot count as closed – even if, from Socrates' own point of view, is it as close to being closed as any important question ever is.

The 'outdoing' argument also beautifully illustrates that special strategy that I have more than once attributed to Socrates (Plato), of arguing on more than one level at once – at the level of the interlocutor, but also, and simultaneously, at a deeper and Socratic level. The rationale for this strategy deserves repeating. Socrates and Plato simply have a different view of the world from other people, although they use the same language: like everybody else, they talk about desire, things good and bad, having more, outdoing . . . but they use them to refer to different things. That is, they use them to refer to what they think are the right things. The question then is, if they are interested in changing other people's ways of thinking, and of using language, how to effect those changes; and one solution – as in the present case – is to appear to use an interlocutor's terms, find ways of unsettling him and drawing him away from his stated position in the direction of Socrates',[28] and all the while avoid committing to the interlocutor's terms or conceding anything to his position that doesn't cohere with Socrates' own. The apparent oddness of the 'outdoing' argument, and the sense that most readers have that Thrasymachus has been short-changed, derive chiefly from reading it exclusively from a Thrasymachean perspective, or at least from a neutral perspective, one that declares that here, as in every

---

[27] See Preliminaries, section 5 above.

[28] 'Him', i.e. the interlocutor: and the readers (us), to the extent that we too might not be able to see through his case.

case, there are two sides to be heard. That will be Glaucon's view, and Adimantus', at the beginning of Book II; it is not Socrates' view, or Plato's plan for Socrates, here. Socrates accepts only that he has, evidently, not done enough to persuade the others; as for himself, he is content enough with the case he presents in Book I. So he says, and I believe him.

A schedule of the genuine dialogues

It may help readers of this book to have before them, for the purposes of orientation, a list of all the certainly genuine works[1] with a note of what I take to be their real main subjects.

1 *Apology*:[2] introduction/manifesto.
2 *Crito*: the implications of Socrates' 'mission' for the city of Athens and its institutions.
3 *Euthyphro*: on piety and wisdom/knowledge/expertise (Socrates consults a religious expert).
4 *Charmides*: on 'sound-mindedness' (*sōphrosunē*) and wisdom/knowledge/expertise (Socrates talks to someone *said* to be 'sound-minded').
5 *Laches*: on courage and wisdom/knowledge/expertise (Socrates consults two generals).
6 *Meno*: on excellence and wisdom/knowledge/expertise (Socrates talks to a Thessalian aristocrat – and, briefly, an Athenian democrat, who is also one of his accusers: Anytus).
7 *Ion*: on excellence and wisdom/knowledge/expertise (Socrates consults an expert on the poets).
8 *Protagoras*: on excellence and wisdom/knowledge/expertise (Socrates confronts sophists).
9 *Euthydemus*: on excellence and wisdom/knowledge/expertise (Socrates confronts eristics).
10 *Gorgias*: on excellence and wisdom/knowledge/expertise (Socrates confronts orators/rhetoricians).
11 *Hippias Minor*: on the difference between excellence and other kinds of knowledge/expertise (Socrates talks to another sophist).

[1] Missing from the list are *Alcibiades I, Clitophon*, and *Hippias Major* (and one or more of the *Letters*) which in the view of some stand a fair chance of being genuine (not in my view), and numerous certainly spurious dialogues and other works that somehow found their way into the corpus.
[2] Not, strictly, a dialogue, but it becomes merely tiresome to keep recording the fact.

12 *Lysis*: on 'friendship', desire and the (real) good (Socrates talks to two friends).

13 *Symposium*: desire and the (real) good (Socrates confronts ordinary views of love and desire).

14 *Phaedo*: on the nature of philosophy (the love of/search for wisdom); life, death and the cosmos (Socrates talks to two members of his circle).

15 *Cratylus*: on language and reality (Socrates talks to representatives of two rival positions).

16 *Menexenus*: on rhetoric and Athens (the Athenians and their perception of themselves: Socrates talks to a young aspiring politician).

17 *Republic* I: on justice and wisdom/knowledge/expertise (Socrates confronts a rhetorician); *Republic* II–X: on 'caring for' oneself and the city itself[3] (Socrates talks to two sons of a noble father: Plato's brothers).

18 *Phaedrus*: on love, and on writing and rhetoric (Socrates talks to a rhetorical enthusiast).

19 *Parmenides*: on forms (Socrates talks to the great philosopher Parmenides).

20 *Theaetetus*: on knowledge (Socrates talks to a young but promising philosopher).

21 *Sophist*: on the nature of sophists and sophistry (a visitor from Elea talks to Theaetetus; Socrates is present – it is supposedly the day after the conversation of the *Theaetetus*).

22 *Politicus*: on the nature of statesmen and statesmanship (the Eleatic visitor talks to a young namesake of Socrates').

23 *Philebus*: on the human good (Socrates talks to another good dialectical partner).

24 *Timaeus-Critias*: a monologue (delivered by one Timaeus) on the physical universe, sandwiched inside a description (by Critias) of an ideal society resembling that constructed in the *Republic* (summarized briefly by Socrates, in the guise of a conversation that took place the day before), presented as a primitive and long-lost Athens.

25 *Laws*: on law, and the kind of legal system that might be put together for an (imaginary) real city (a visitor from Athens talks to a Cretan and a Spartan: no sign of Socrates).

The order given is not intended to be chronological, except that items 17–20 are apparently, in stylistic terms, later than items 1–16, and items 21–5 later still (with item 25 last of all).

---

[3] For the pairing see *Apology* 36c.

CHAPTER 6

Knowledge and the philosopher-rulers of the Republic, 1: knowledge and belief in Book v

There is a short argument at the end of *Republic* v (474B–480A) that demands a chapter to itself, so pivotal is it for the interpretation of Plato. One common reading has the argument making knowledge (*epistēmē*, *gnōsis*) and belief (or 'judgement', 'opinion': *doxa*) into two distinct faculties, with two distinct sets of objects: forms, on the one hand, and particular things that 'share in' forms on the other. On this reading, the person at the level of belief has no contact at all with the objects of knowledge, and the knower's knowledge relates entirely to forms; there will be no knowledge, properly speaking, of particulars, and perhaps there will even be no mere beliefs about forms (either one fully grasps such objects or one is not grasping them at all).[1] A whole range of different versions of this set of ideas – usually labelled the 'two-world' view – is attributed to Plato; however, following my usual practice, I shall dispense with lengthy discussion of others' views and pass directly to the business of presenting and arguing for my own.

The reading I shall offer in this case will not in its general outlines be particularly original (my route to it will be more so); my aim is chiefly to show that and how my overall reading of Plato will negotiate a passage to which interpreters have accorded such importance – rather more, I suspect, than Plato would have accorded it himself, and more than it possesses for Socrates in the context in which he unfolds it. The main burden of my rival interpretation will be that we must pay attention to the *persuasive* function of the argument, and to the fact that it sets out with a very limited goal – to persuade people who have one view of their cognitive state to see that they need to take a different view of it.[2] That is, Socrates does not set out

---

[1] For a version of this interpretation, and an illustration of its possible consequences, see Gerson 2003.

[2] It is here, in particular, that any originality in my interpretation lies. As usual, my focus is not so much on how particular passages may be read in themselves as in how they will fit into a larger context (including the largest context of all: Plato's mindset, to whatever extent we may be able to reconstruct a likely story about that).

to give an exposition on epistemology or metaphysics, and if we read it as such we are liable to convict him of saying things he doesn't want to say at all. My claim, as in all such cases, is not so much that he does not believe what he says as that the form in which he says what he says is influenced, even distorted, by his immediate rhetorical purpose. Above all, he is limited in his choice of where to *start*, because of the need to make contact with addressees whose outlook is different from his own.

I shall begin with what is intended to be a neutral account of the passage, which will on the face of it tend to support the 'common' reading; I shall then present and justify my own, alternative reading. (Sometimes my 'neutral' account will make controversial choices, but these will not, I hope, be in places that directly bear on the main outcomes of the argument.)

For the context of the argument, we need to go back to 471C. Socrates has repeatedly put off the question whether the fine city that he has been constructing with the others is a practical possibility; now he is forced to answer it. Yes, he says, the city is practicable, at least up to a point. Why do things go wrong in cities as they are, and what is the 'smallest' change that would allow the new city to be brought about? What causes trouble is the lack of *philosophy* in government, and in our rulers. The only way to salvation, whether for cities or for mankind in general, is to unite political power and philosophy: either philosophers must become kings or those now called kings must become philosophers. Glaucon responds by saying that lots of people will want to give Socrates a thorough beating for saying such a thing, and he'll have to put up a defensive argument if he's to get away safely.

This begins at 474B. Socrates says he needs to distinguish whom exactly he has in mind when he proposes with such apparent abandon that 'philosophers' should take charge. Some people are naturally fitted both to be philosophers and to lead, others to do neither, but only to follow (474B4–C4). Now lovers of anything love the whole of that thing, not just parts or aspects of it: thus lovers of boys are affected by all boys of the right age, and none is disqualified; wine-lovers welcome (*aspazesthai*, 'embrace') any and every wine, honour-lovers any kind of office or recognition.[3] So philosophers, as lovers of wisdom, will desire all wisdom; they are ready

---

[3] Socrates suggests that Glaucon should remember the general principle (though he doesn't); the reference can only be to IV, 437E–439B, where Socrates established – at any rate to his satisfaction, and Glaucon's – that any desire is itself 'of that thing of which it is by nature, and it is the things added that are of *such* or *such* a thing' (437E7–8). That is, as we discover from what follows, thirst (e.g.) is for drink, *simpliciter*; if we want a cold drink, that's because we are hot as well as thirsty, and if we want a hot drink, that's because we're cold as well as thirsty. 437E–439B made, or at least claimed to make a serious point about the grammar of desire (see chapter 5, n. 35 above); I suspect that the

and willing to taste any kind of learning, indeed are even insatiable for it (474C8–475C8). Glaucon objects that this seems to let in some strange-looking 'philosophers': what about people addicted to theatrical perfor-mances, who love gazing at spectacles and listening, not to discussions, but to a quite different sort of sounds – don't they show exactly the passion for learning Socrates is talking about? These are *like* philosophers, Socrates replies, but the real philosopher is someone who loves gazing at the truth,[4] not plays in the theatre (475D1–E5).

How so? Glaucon asks. It'd be a difficult thing to explain to some-one other than you, replies Socrates – a point that will be immediately exemplified: the lovers of sights and sounds (let them be 'sight-lovers' from here on) turn out to differ from lovers of wisdom (let them be 'philoso-phers') precisely insofar as they wouldn't understand his explanation. Glau-con agrees that things like beautiful, ugly, just, unjust, good, bad are each of them *one*, but nevertheless appear to be many 'by virtue of being in part-nership with actions and bodies and each other' (476A6); and it's just in this respect, Socrates says, that he distinguishes sight-lovers from philoso-phers, because the mind of the former is incapable of 'seeing the nature of the beautiful itself and embracing it' (476B6–8), and so, presumably, of 'gazing at the truth', like those rare birds 'who are capable of going to the beautiful itself [sc. as the sight-lovers go to the theatre] and seeing it by itself' (476B10–11). The sight-lovers believe that there are beautiful things, but not that there is such a thing as beauty itself, and they can't even follow if someone leads them to the knowledge of it; they are like people who are dreaming, who confuse something that is like something else with that thing itself. Contrast the person who does believe in such a thing as beauty itself, is able to see both it and the many things sharing in it, and doesn't confuse these with it or it with these: he'll be like someone awake, seeing things as they are. This one we may correctly say has knowledge, while the other has belief (475E5–476D7).

If the sight-lover is cross at the suggestion that he only has belief, and claims that it is untrue, Socrates suggests that he may be comforted by being

___

present passage is less serious, and the connection with 437–9 merely superficial (which is why Plato has Glaucon not succeed in making it). The point Socrates wants to get to is that the philosopher is insatiable for learning (475C7; he won't want to *miss* anything), and he gets to it via other, apparently more obvious examples of insatiable desire: obsessive boy-lovers, people who 'embrace' wine at every opportunity (475A6) – all the time pretending to cloak himself in philosophical respectability (and a joke at Glaucon's expense: Glaucon is supposed to know all about how erotic obsessives behave [474D2–475A3; cf. Socrates' reference to Glaucon's own lover at II, 368A2–3]). The passage provides a preview of three types of individual who will play starring roles in Book IX: those in whom respectively reason, 'spirit' and appetite predominate.

4 He is *philotheamōn tēs alētheias* (475E4).

gently persuaded, in a way that will conceal from him that his condition is unhealthy (476D8–E2).[5]

The one who has knowledge – i.e. in the particular case in question, and any analogous case – knows something that is, because something that isn't couldn't be known.[6] What is completely is completely knowable, whereas something that in no way is, is wholly unknowable. If there is anything such as both to be and not to be,[7] it would lie in the middle between what purely (i.e. completely) is and what in no way is. Then: if knowledge is over[8] what is, and unknowing,[9] necessarily, is over what is not, what's over this thing in the middle must be something in the middle between unknowing and knowledge (476E7–477B2). Next: there is something that is belief, which is, like knowledge,[10] a capacity, but a different capacity, because what is unerring couldn't be the same as what is capable of error.[11] Now it belongs to knowledge and belief to be assigned to (sc. and so to be 'over') different things, because capacities are a kind of thing by virtue of which we, and anything else that has capacities, are capable of whatever it is we/it are capable of, and they (capacities) are marked off from one another not by their colour, shape, etc. but by reference to 'that alone, both what they are over and what they do':[12] if a capacity is assigned to the same thing and does the same thing as another, they are the same, and if not they are different. Since it belongs by nature to knowledge to be over what is, so as to 'know how what is, is/know what is, as it is',[13] while it belongs to belief to believe – but not, given what has already been agreed, the same thing that knowledge knows. On the other hand neither does belief believe (is belief 'over') what is not, because the one believing refers his belief to *something*, not to what is not (nothing), to which we assigned

---

[5] Evidently, then, Socrates does not expect to achieve more with his hearers – who will ultimately be identified with the majority: see below – than the limited aim he has set out: to persuade them that they only have belief, not knowledge; he won't expect them to go on to *do* anything about it.

[6] Glaucon starts playing the role of the sight-lovers at this point; once again he is clearly distinguished as being on a higher level than theirs. The dialogue form is suppressed in my summary – without loss, on this occasion, because Glaucon/the sight-lovers prove compliant respondents, going along with everything Socrates suggests and merely asking for extra help where necessary.

[7] I shall omit the question that is usually put to Plato's text at this and other points in the argument: 'do you mean is in the sense of "exists", or in the predicative sense, or . . .?', because it will turn out that the question is irrelevant to Socrates' intentions.

[8] 'Over', here and elsewhere in the argument, is *epi* + dative. I shall discuss later what Socrates intends with this idiom.

[9] The noun in the Greek, usually translated 'ignorance', is formed from the root for 'knowledge' with negative prefix; 'unknowing' seems better, not just because it mimics the Greek, but because what is in question is a state of non-cognition (one in which there is no object before the mind at all).

[10] 477D7–8: the most powerful of all capacities, D9.   [11] 477E7–8.   [12] 477D1.

[13] These are alternative translations of two apparently equivalent formulations: *gnōnai to on hōs esti* (477B10–11), and *to on gnōnai hōs echei* (478 A6), on which see further below.

unknowing, as we assigned knowledge to what is. Belief does not have a greater clarity than knowledge, or a greater lack of clarity than unknowing; rather it is a darker state than the first, a more illuminated one than the second, lying in between them. We said before that if anything turned up of a sort both to be and not to be, it would be between what purely is and what wholly was not, and that whatever state of mind turned up between unknowing and knowledge would be over it (i.e. over whatever was of a sort both to be and not to be); now belief has turned up between the two of them, sc. and so it will be over whatever 'shares in both being and not-being' (478E1–2). It remains to find what shares in both being and not-being – but we already have such a set of things, in the shape of what sight-lovers believe in (the many beautiful, just, pious . . . things), since each of them will as much not be as be what they say it is, and will be no more identifiable with that than with its opposite: thus any of the many beautiful things will as much appear ugly as beautiful, any of the many just things as much appear unjust, any of the many pious things as much appear impious, any of the many double things as much appear half, any of the many large things as much appear small, any of the many light things as much appear heavy . . . The things – the many things the many[14] believe in, 'in relation to beauty and the rest' (479D4) – are also in the middle between pure being and pure not being, because they will not appear either darker than not being or more illuminating than being. *So:* those who gaze at (*theasthai,* sc. are *philotheamones* of, 'lovers of gazing' at)[15] many beautiful things (just things, and so on) but don't see beauty itself (justice itself, and so on) and can't follow another person who is leading them to it – their state of mind in relation to everything should be said to be one of belief, and they should be said not to know any of the things they believe, because we agreed that if there was anything 'wandering' (479D9) between being and not being, that would be assigned to belief and not knowledge (and we have found that what our sight-lovers believe in is of this sort). By contrast, those who gaze at (*theasthai,* sc. are *philotheamones* of, 'lovers

---

[14] That the sight-lovers should now be identified with 'the many' (the majority of people) is something of a surprise; but it has already been prepared for by Socrates' suggestion that those who can 'go to beauty itself' will be rare exceptions (476B10–11). The shift is important insofar as the present argument is in part designed – as I argued in the Introduction – to provide the basis for the simile of the cave in Book VII, in which humanity generally is represented as benighted, and watching the shadows of puppets and the voices of puppeteers (so being in a situation rather like that of the sight-lovers – except that the cave–dwellers are *permanently* watching a performance).

[15] The supplement, here and in the contrasting case of the philosophers (below), is justified by 475D–E: it was Glaucon's need for an explanation of Socrates' description of true philosophers as '*philotheamones* of truth', by contrast with the sight-lovers' obsession with gazing at spectacles in the theatre, that helped to set up the present argument.

of gazing' at) things in themselves, things that are always constantly in the same state, should be said to have knowledge and not belief. *So*: the first group should be said to 'embrace and love the things knowledge is over', and be called wisdom-lovers (*philosophoi*), while the second should be said to have the same relationship to the things belief is over, and be called belief-lovers (*philodoxoi*) – and if we tell them that now, after they've heard our argument, we won't be doing them any injustice, and they won't be too cross with us (476E5–480A13).

I make no apologies for presenting a fairly indigestible, and initially opaque (and highly controversial), argument in some detail, because it is on the detail that everything hangs. First point: the contrast between knowledge and belief is worked out primarily in order to *persuade* the sight-lovers that their state of mind (their *dianoia*, 476D5–6) is one of belief, only, without actually telling them too much about the deep reason why this is so. The key concession, which Glaucon makes on their behalf, and which allows Socrates his way in, is that knowledge and belief are different (477E4–7). The strategy of his argument is, fundamentally, to get the sight-lovers to agree to a particular way of spelling out of that difference, namely that knowledge and belief are capacities that are 'over' different things, and have different functions: knowledge is 'over' what is, and knows it (how/as it is), while belief is 'over' what both is and is not; as for what it 'does', well, that's just a matter of having beliefs (478A6, 8). What the sight-lovers aren't told, and are too limp to ask, is what this 'what is' is. When it is first introduced, presumably, they'll need to understand 'what is' as 'what is (whatever that may be, and so far as we can see, so far, that will simply be particular things)', and that will cover beauty, the example everything started off with, justice, and the rest. But even by the end of the argument, when they have been forced to admit that particular things can't be all there is, i.e. because knowledge must be over something else, the sight-lovers are hardly any closer to seeing what Glaucon agreed to back in 475E–476A, namely that each of beautiful, just, and so on is *one* (and something that can be investigated in itself).

Of course, *we* know, and Glaucon knows, what they don't know, and can give a rather fuller account than they can of exactly what is going on in the argument; in particular, we know, or will think we know, what Socrates really has in mind when he talks about the things knowledge is 'over' (one thing in each case – a 'form', in fact), though we have to supply this. The sight-lovers, by contrast, are incapable of following even if someone leads them to knowledge of beauty itself (476C3, 479E2), and in fact won't put up with it if anyone says that beauty, or justice, . . . is one thing (479A4–5,

480A3–4).[16] ('Is there any way a mass of people will put up with the beautiful itself and not the many beautifuls, or the anything itself and not the many each of them, or believe in them?', Socrates asks Glaucon at VI, 493E2–494A2.) So even though we may be able to read more into the argument than Socrates makes explicit, it is not directly addressed to us (unless, of course, we ourselves won't 'put up' with being told that beauty, etc. are each one thing), and it seems that we shall need to be rather careful about what we take *from* it. The one thing it certainly is not is a straight statement of Socratic epistemology and metaphysics, even if – as usual – I hesitate to say that there is anything in it to which in one way or another, and appropriately filled out, Socrates (Plato) would not subscribe. Its chief effect, in fact, if not its purpose, seems to be to provide for the kind of harmony between rulers and ruled – philosophers and non-philosophers – that Callipolis, as a good city, will require. Socrates is admitting in advance that most of the prisoners in the cave won't escape, indeed will resist escaping; but his project is still on track; the non-philosophical majority could be persuaded to go along, even if they will never properly understand the full justification for their being excluded from power.

All this needs to be borne in mind when we ask the crucial question about what, exactly, belief is 'over'; and indeed how this expression, 'being over' something, is to be cashed in. On the face of it the question 'what belief is over' (or 'assigned to') is a question about the objects of belief. Certainly when *knowledge* is said to be over 'what is', i.e. – as we know – beauty itself, and so on, it looks as if this should be taken straightforwardly as saying that these are the objects of knowledge.[17] However if we take particulars, to which belief is 'assigned', as the objects of belief in the same straightforward way, then the only (only!) thing the sight-lovers will be getting wrong is that they don't recognize the 'things in themselves'; and this isn't what Socrates identifies as their problem. The mistake they make, as he puts it, is to misidentify beautiful things, for example, with beauty; and it's just because of this misidentification that Socrates says that they (only) have belief. What confronts us here is two different perspectives on the same set of affairs: what the sight-lovers see as recognizing the existence of particulars and rejecting the idea of 'things in themselves' (not 'putting up' with it), Socrates – and Glaucon, when he's not answering for the sight-lovers – see as misidentifying one thing with another, namely particular beautiful things with beauty, and indeed with *beauty itself* (since that is what beauty

---

[16] They perhaps resemble Socrates' jury at his trial – or those of them who voted against him (resolutely, even lethally, non-philosophical, rather like the prosecutors).

[17] I shall later call this presumption into question.

is). And in this case it won't be at all straightforward to take the particulars as the objects of their belief. Their belief now seems to be as much about beauty as about the particulars themselves.

We clearly need to look at the situation first from the perpective of the sight-lovers, or rather from the (limited) perspective that Socrates wants to persuade them to take. What he gets them to agree to is that knowledge is a matter of 'knowing how what is, is/knowing what is, as it is',[18] whereas belief is 'over' things that both are and are not – which are also the kind of things that the sight-lovers themselves recognize and identify with (or, better, as) beauty (etc.). Substitute the values of beauty, justice, etc. in the relevant places, and the result is that knowledge about beauty, justice, etc. will pick out whatever it is that beauty, etc. are, while the sight-lovers will only be picking out things that are, or appear to be, ugly as well as beautiful, unjust as well as just, etc. So they don't have knowledge about beauty, but only belief – about what? Not about particulars, surely, as many have concluded.[19] Not even the 'limp' sight-lovers would need to feel any compulsion to agree that their state of mind, in identifying – misidentifying, Socrates says – beauty (etc.) with/as beautiful things, was one of mere belief on the meagre grounds that those beautiful things, which are all they recognize in the sphere of beauty, always are – or appear to be[20] – ugly as well as beautiful. Why shouldn't that be just how beauty is?[21] To insist that the argument goes this way is, in effect, to have Socrates simply overpowering his opponents, when he is supposed to be persuading them – and we are, after all, presently trying to see things from their point of view (even benighted sight-lovers deserve better than this).

So what does Socrates offer that should persuade them? The real core of his argument must be about the capacity of particulars to provide evidence about beauty (etc.); after all, his implicit first question to the sight-lovers is 'what *is* beauty?' (Their answer to which is 'particular beautiful things'.) If the sight-lovers were to rouse themselves from passivity to ask why one should suppose that any better evidence was available, or indeed any other evidence at all, Socrates' response will be to say that if the sight-lovers agree,

---

[18] See n. 13 above.   [19] See, e.g., Sedley 2004: 179 (cited in chapter 8 below, text to n. 4).

[20] 'Appear to be' – or 'appear as being [sc. as they actually are]', 479A7, B2, 4; 'are', B9, etc. 'Appears' merely brings in the perspective of viewer/observer, and is not intended to suggest any kind of illusion. Just to the extent that things really do share in whatever it is, they are/appear as whatever it is.

[21] The sight-lover, being a lover of *beautiful* sights, sounds, etc., has particular reason to want to keep beauty and ugliness apart; but he can easily do that even if the same beautiful things will also appear/be ugly – from some angle, at another time, etc. He just appreciates ('embraces') them when they are beautiful.

as they do, that beautiful things are also ugly things, then when they run eagerly to see them, as beautiful things, they must already be identifying them *as* beautiful, rather than as ugly, and so be separating off their beauty from their ugliness. So beauty is something beautiful things *have*, not what they are.[22] And that is as far as Socrates expects to get the sight-lovers. In brief, they do something – seeing things as beautiful – that their 'theory', that beauty is particular beautiful things, shouldn't allow them to do. So their 'theory' is mistaken. As they themselves should now accept, they are identifying things with each other that shouldn't be so identified; and Socrates' description of them, as being like dreamers, and having only belief – about beauty – was correct.

Socrates' perspective on the argument is easier to state. It is that if we direct our attention to particulars we shall end up with only a partial and incomplete view of what beauty, justice and the rest are; for a more complete view, we need to pay attention to what things are in themselves – their real natures. The 'partial and incomplete' view he labels as (mere) belief; and it is the fact that it is directed towards particulars that he expresses by saying that belief is 'over', 'assigned to', 'referred to' (478B7) particulars. The real object of the sight-lovers' belief, from Socrates' point of view,[23] is beauty, justice, or whatever – they think particular things *are* beauty, justice . . . What beauty is, what justice is, and so on: these, ultimately, are the things the sight-lovers have belief about, and the reason that they have belief about it, and no more than belief ('mere' belief), is because the things they 'embrace', the things they direct their attention to, are incapable of giving them any more than belief. The assumption here is, of course, that they have genuinely beautiful things in sight, things that genuinely 'share in' beauty: if so, they will have some kind of conception, even one that might count as a true – if only partially true – conception, of the thing itself.

We should probably also, then, hesitate before concluding even that 'knowledge is "over" what is' translates without remainder, in the argument, into 'knowledge has what is as its object'. Undoubtedly Socrates (Plato)

---

[22] In this respect the argument will have a general application, rather than being tied to specifically Platonic notions: forms are in the background, but no more than that. And this is how it must be in any case, unless we are to suppose that Plato (Socrates) is proposing, unusually, to recognize forms of ugliness, badness, etc. What he is insisting on is the need to try to grasp things as they are in themselves; it will take further argument to limit the list of things that will count as *forms* so as to exclude negative properties (argument either or both in the direction (i) of treating such negative properties as mere privations of positive ones, and (ii) of treating forms in teleological terms, i.e. as real natures to which particulars approximate).

[23] And even, in a different way, from their own. See further below.

does think that things in themselves – ultimately forms, real natures – are the objects of knowledge. If the sight-lovers' belief is[24] about things in themselves, but is 'over', is directed to, particulars, then equally, from the standpoint of the argument with the sight-lovers, we should probably take knowledge's being 'over' what is in the same way: knowledge is directed to what is. This then raises the question about what exactly knowledge 'does': when Socrates describes this as 'knowing *how* what is, is', or knowing it '*as it is*',[25] what, precisely, does he have in mind? What he intends, I suggest, is a general truth, but one that he introduces for the sake of a very specific application. What knowledge 'does', in general, is to grasp the truth about things, which in the important cases – as those of us in the know will be able to supply – will be a matter of understanding things in themselves (forms). (To these it will be 'directed', as I have put it [it will be 'over' these], in contrast to mere belief, which makes such contact with 'what is', if it makes any, via the medium of particulars.) However, the relevance of this general truth, for the argument in hand, and the reason why Socrates introduces it, is that it grounds the specific claim about philosophers that they have knowledge in contrast to the sight-lovers' mere belief *insofar as (and just insofar as) they recognize the existence of a beauty itself*. That is: Socrates is arguing that the philosopher fulfils the criteria for knowing just by virtue of his recognizing that there is such a thing as beauty 'in itself'. Recognizing this will itself be an example, if at a basic level, of knowing what is as it is (or how it is – but we may now settle for the less inelegant version).

This is of some considerable importance, for it is tempting to suppose that insofar as the philosopher is said to have knowledge, and knowledge is said to 'know what is, as it is' apparently without restriction, the philosopher himself is being said to have knowledge without restriction. But this is not the case. Whatever may be being said of knowledge in itself, the only knowledge that is directly and explicitly attributed to philosophers, in this particular context, is by virtue of their ability to tell beauty apart from the things that share in it. To rehearse the details briefly again: the sight-lover's not recognizing a beauty itself (476c2), and his tendency to treat 'what is similar to something not as similar to it but as the thing itself' are compared to a state of dreaming (476c5–7), and contrasted with the philosopher's 'thinking that there is some beautiful itself and being able to see both it and the things that share in it', which is like living in a state of

---

[24] Again, of course, unbeknownst to themselves.
[25] These are the two alternative renderings of the interchangeable Greek phrases *hōs esti* and *hōs echei* that I have been carefully keeping in play, for fear of prejudging any issues of substance.

waking (476C9–D3).[26] The latter's state, just on this basis, is said to be one of knowledge, the former's, again just on the basis given (identifying what is merely like something with that thing itself), a state of mere belief – and the argument sets out to convince him that he has belief, and not knowledge, just in relation to the same state of affairs (his not recognizing beauty itself, etc.). Philosophers have the capacity to see things in themselves, and to grasp 'what is always in the same respects in the same state' (VI, 484B4), but Socrates makes no commitment to their being knowers (that is, of course, beyond their knowing that there are things in themselves to be known). Rather the reverse: the philosopher is introduced as a lover of wisdom, and then a lover of *learning* (*philomathēs*);[27] and the sight-lovers similarly rush everywhere to theatrical performances because of their attachment to *learning*.[28] One of the problems about the sight-lovers is that they are picky about what they want to learn; they actively resist (won't put up with) being told that there are things like beauty in itself, so that they can't be called real lovers. Philosophers have the same enthusiasm as the sight-lovers, but don't share their pickiness: *they* embrace beauty itself. Thus is the ground laid for the three similes which will follow in *Republic* VI–VII to illustrate the nature of the form of the good: all based on the metaphor of sight, and on what people are willing to 'see'. 'Seeing' the objects of knowledge is a precondition of learning about them; it does not by itself imply knowing them, *having* learned about them.[29] So much, at any rate, is true in relation to the argument that we have been considering, at the end of Book V, and insofar as this argument prepares the way for the similes of sun, divided line and cave, the presumption must be – I propose – that the same will be true in that context too.[30]

---

[26] The capacity 'to see both it [beauty] and the things sharing in it' is *explained* – if the 'and', *kai*, may be taken as epexegetic, which in the context seems entirely natural and reasonable – in terms of a person's 'thinking neither that the sharers are it nor that it is the sharers' (D2–3).

[27] V, 475C2; 'lover of wisdom' – all of it, not just of some of it, 475B8–9.

[28] V, 475E1 *mathētikoi*.

[29] The closest that Socrates comes, in the general context of the *Republic* V argument, to saying that his philosopher will have knowledge of what is, i.e. of the *content* (as one might put it) of what is, is at VI, 484D5–6, in the aftermath of the Book V argument, when Socrates asks Glaucon whether they'll prefer to establish as 'guards' people like the sight-lovers, or rather 'those who have come to know, *gignōskein*, each thing that is'. However (a) this recalls the language of 476C–D, which only attributed knowledge (*gignōskein*) to the philosopher in one narrow respect, and (b) no guarantee has yet been given, or will be given, that the philosopher will in fact ever 'come to know' each of the 'things that are'. But then the whole sequence of Books V–VII is introduced with a caution against supposing that things can be realized exactly in the way or to the standard described: 472B–473B. See further chapters 7–8 below.

[30] See further the following two chapters. Readers of Plato do often suppose that 'seeing' forms implies knowledge. That might partly be because of the links Plato sometimes makes – though not, as it

I cautioned against attempting to draw too directly, for Socrates' epistemological and metaphysical commitments, on the *Republic* v argument, insofar as it addresses a specific audience and is partly shaped as well as motivated by that audience's limited grasp. But some things we do appear licenced to draw from it. Thus: knowledge and belief are different capacities, 'over' different things and 'doing' different things. Knowledge, of which philosophers will have a lesser or a greater share, 'is by nature over what is, to know it as it is', while belief is 'over' particular things, and offers a grasp of a limited kind – limited, that is, by virtue of what it is 'over' – of what is. 'Belief' will perhaps be a somewhat unusual capacity, insofar as it is one that people will apparently outgrow, as and when they philosophize, and so begin to get a better hold on things.[31] At the same time, and in a different context, belief will be capable of being described more positively, as something that every human being must share in, and also as something that is *true*; and after all, on the reading of the *Republic* v argument that I have proposed, the special capacity labelled 'belief' does get *a* hold on reality, even if only an inferior one.

The more positive treatment of the capacity of belief[32] is to be found in the *Timaeus*, a dialogue closely linked with the *Republic*,[33] especially at *Timaeus* 51–2; thus for example 'belief together with perception' is said to be what comprehends – 'is by nature over', in the terms of *Republic* v?[34] – the sphere of becoming, that is,[35] of particulars (52A7). This will be consistent with the *Republic* on condition that the sphere of particulars is

---

happens, or not so clearly, in the *Republic* – between the philosopher's 'vision' of truth and what is 'revealed' in religious contexts (especially those connected with Eleusis). However ancient Greek 'revelations' differ somewhat from those in other, e.g., Christian, contexts, insofar as what is revealed is not some truth, exactly (which is surely what Christian 'revelation' *is* supposed to be), as much as some still deeply mysterious object. And outside such religious contexts, sight and the senses generally do not rate highly in Plato's estimation as means to truth; any sort of claim that perception might have to incorrigibility is roundly rebutted in the *Theaetetus* and elsewhere.

[31] There may also be some spheres in which human beings can in fact do no better than mere belief: see chapter 10 below, on the implications of *Timaeus* 29C–D.

[32] This special capacity of 'belief' (i.e. of *mere* belief, as contrasted with knowledge) is to be distinguished sharply from ordinary common or garden cases of believing; see n. 40 below.

[33] See chapter 10 below.

[34] 'Belief together with perception': that is, true belief, insofar as there is successful 'comprehension' (*perilēpsis*). The context as a whole revolves around a distinction between *nous*, 'intelligence' (or *noēsis*, 50A4, which is the state of mind assigned to, or 'over' [*epi*] the highest part of the line at *Republic* VI, 511D8; or, apparently, over both the top two parts: VII, 534A2), and true belief (first, in this particular context, at 51D3–4). The connection with the *Republic* context is cemented by the way Timaeus derives the very existence of forms from the difference between these two states of mind – for which he himself enthusiastically casts his vote, while acknowledging that others see no difference between them: exactly the position of the sight-lovers of the *Republic*, as described from the Socratic (Platonic) perspective.

[35] For the connection, see e.g., *Republic* VI, 484B.

comprehensible only insofar as it 'partakes in' what is, that is, real natures or forms: in grasping, and insofar as it grasps, this sphere, the soul or mind will *ipso facto* grasp something of the way true reality is. This particular connection is made directly by Socrates in the *Phaedrus*.[36] Talking of human destiny after death, in the context of the great myth that figures the soul as a charioteer and his two horses, he introduces the subject of the soul's transmigration, perhaps from a human to an animal or back into a human from an animal:

For a soul that has never seen the truth will never enter this [human] shape. A human being must comprehend (*sunienai*) what is said universally (*kat'eidos legomenon*), arising from many sensations and being collected together into one through reasoning; and this is a recollection of those things that our soul once saw when it travelled in company with a god [sc. to the divine feast, which allows any charioteer lucky enough to catch sight of part of true reality, pictured as located outside the borders of the universe] and treated with contempt the things we now [sc. in ordinary life] say are, and when it rose up into what really is. (*Phaedrus* 249B5–C4)[37]

The capacity to organize things according to types, or classes, is a requirement for human living; and that capacity is itself a trace of a previous 'sight' or 'sights' of 'what really is'. Whether they realize it or not, what any human being is doing when he or she hears, or talks, of things 'said universally' is *referring to real existents*. The trouble is – so runs Socrates' diagnosis in the *Republic* and the *Timaeus* – that most people (non-philosophers) think that there is nothing beyond the things that give rise to their 'many sensations', and that it is these things themselves that they 'collect together into one

---

[36] As I have suggested, it is also implied in the *Timaeus* passage (in being what allows Timaeus to introduce a state of mind labelled *true* belief: what makes it true is its connection, however remote, with truth, i.e. what is: 'forms').

[37] See also 249E4–250A3: 'For as has been said, every human soul has by the law of its nature observed the things that are, or else it would not have entered this creature [man]; but it is not easy for every soul to gain from things here a recollection of those other things, either for those which only briefly saw the things there at that earlier time, or for those which fall to earth . . .' This is how I translated the passage in Rowe 1988; I now rather incline to think that it should read '. . . but *for every soul, it is not easy* to gain . . . either for those that only briefly saw the things there, or for those that fall to earth', because in fact *no* human soul seems to get more than a glimpse of 'what is'. See 248A1–5: 'This is the life of gods [i.e. one involving untroubled feasting on reality]; of the other souls, the one that follows a god best and has come to resemble him most raises the head of its charioteer into the region outside, and is carried round with the revolution, disturbed by its horses and scarcely catching sight of (*mogis kathorōsa*) the things that are; while another now rises, now sinks . . .'; and 248C2–4: 'And this is the ordinance of Necessity: that whichever soul follows in the train of a god and catches sight of part of what is true (*katidēi ti tōn alēthōn*) shall remain free from sorrow until the next circuit . . .' This, by the way, provides some sort of confirmation of the interpretation I have proposed of the metaphor of 'seeing' the truth in the context of the *Republic*; 'seeing' does not imply knowledge (except to the limited extent specified by v, 476C–D).

through reasoning'. They are in fact muddled, and unconscious, nominal-ists, resisting any attempt by philosophers like Socrates to help them ascend from nominalism[38] to realism.

In place, then, of a Plato who thinks that 'knowledge and [belief] are two entirely separate states of mind or faculties, each dealing with its own distinct set of objects',[39] we have two states of mind – knowledge and *mere* belief[40] – that ultimately 'deal with' the *same* set of objects, only with one of them doing it more successfully than the other. The twin ideas of the importance of understanding true reality, and of particulars as both revealing and unrevealing of that reality, are quite central to Plato's – and, I claim, his Socrates' – ways of thinking. We have already met several applications of such ideas in the context of the *Republic*, for example[41] in the shape of Socrates' treatment of the soul, and his distinction between soul as seen 'in its truest nature' and soul as it appears in the hurly-burly of ordinary, non-philosophical life.[42] If we want to know what soul truly is (so ran Socrates' message), we shall not observe it as it appears, but rather as it can and should be – which is something we can discover by reasoning alone. And that we should discover it is of vital importance to us, because it will provide a model for us to live by. At the same time, as the present chapter has confirmed, every soul – apparently, however depraved and distorted – is connected, as a condition of its humanity, to that very reality the recognition of which it may forcibly resist.

---

[38] Many will, sadly, miss the plodding reference here to the unjustly neglected, if difficult, Penner 1987. (For the sort of 'nominalism' in question here, see Penner 1987: 20–4.)

[39] Sedley again (n. 19 above; I quote from the same passage reprinted in chapter 8), standing, as usual, as a moderate representative of a reading that has in my view received rather more support than it deserves.

[40] I see no justification in the text for supposing that Socrates is talking, in the *Republic* v argument or anywhere else, about any and every belief. This is not only because I fail to see any philosophical profit that he might have thought would be got from denying the possibility of holding beliefs about forms (and indeed having certain limited bits of knowledge about particulars, e.g., that they are distinct from and share in the relevant forms/real natures), or because he will openly express his own beliefs e.g., about the form of the good (see especially the reference at vi, 506c6 to 'beliefs without knowledge'), but because in my view an appropriately close reading of *Republic* v and other relevant texts will show absolutely no interest on his part in denying such a possibility. To demonstrate this fully would take many pages; the analysis of the *Republic* v argument offered in the present chapter may, however, be allowed to count as a first and important step towards such a demonstration.

[41] Other examples were in the treatments of the excellences, and of the city. There will be more: in the treatment of knowledge/wisdom; of astronomy (and of the other mathematical 'sciences'), in *Republic* vii; and above all in the *Timaeus*. See chapter 10 below.

[42] See chapter 5 above.

CHAPTER 7

Knowledge and the philosopher-rulers of the Republic, II: the limits of knowledge

Socrates proposes in *Republic* v–vi that political rule should be put in the hands of philosophers,[1] provided that they also 'in no way fall short of [non-philosophers] in experience, nor rank after them in any other part of excellence' (vi, 481D6–7). The question, especially for Glaucon,[2] is what philosophers will bring to the task of ruling that non-philosophers cannot; and that will also be the question for the present chapter. It will turn out that there are two answers, one more sophisticated, one less so; the latter is nearer the surface, and more immediately persuasive for Socrates' (Plato's) immediate audience, while the former is truer to his real position – which will be the subject of a separate chapter (chapter 8).

Socrates begins his answer to Glaucon's question – why *philosophers*? – in that argument which I discussed in the preceding chapter, at the end of Book v. As we saw, his starting-point is that philosophers, lovers of wisdom, are distinguished as such by the fact that they love all aspects of wisdom, something which sets them apart from others who seem to love every aspect of something, like the 'sight-lovers', who are actually quite picky about what *they* love. The latter don't even recognize the very thing they should really be loving (beauty itself); they only recognize the many beautiful particulars, which they misidentify *as* beauty. Socrates' argument then sets out to convince this latter sort of lover that their state of mind, by contrast with that of philosophers, was one of (mere) belief,[3] which is indeed his conclusion: those who observe many beautiful things (watch them in the theatre), or many whatever it may be, and neither see the beautiful itself nor have the capacity to follow anyone who tries to lead them to it (476C3–4, 479E1–2), are indeed in a state of mere belief, while

---

[1] Originally at v, 473C–E.
[2] I refer here to his outburst at the original proposal (v, 473E–474A).
[3] As I shall continue to render the Greek work *doxa*, in the absence of any better alternative.

those who 'observe' things in themselves are in a state of knowledge rather than in one of belief, *so that* the latter group 'embrace'[4] and love what knowledge is 'over', the former what belief is 'over', *so that* the latter are lovers of wisdom, the former lovers of (mere) belief.

Up to this point, even if we have been told something about what knowledge, or wisdom, is (and especially that it is 'over' what is), there has been no suggestion that philosophers actually possess knowledge of things like beauty itself; they know that there *are* such things,[5] and they 'embrace and love' the objects of knowledge, which they can 'see', and tell apart from the many particular things that 'share in' them, but they are still as it were running after them, as the other sort of lovers run to the theatre, and, presumably, following anyone who can lead them there (as the other sort of lovers cannot). But that is exactly what we should expect of philosophers: philosophers are searchers rather than knowers. So it is that Socrates needs another step before his argument – for saying that rulers must be philosophers – is complete.

Given that philosophers are those who are capable of (*dunamenoi*) laying hold of/grasping (*ephaptesthai*) what is always in the same state in the same respects, while those who don't [have this capacity], but wander about among many things that are in all sorts of states, which should be leaders of a city? (VI, 484B3–7)

To which Glaucon replies 'What would be a reasonable response?', thus acknowledging that the choice is so far unclear.

Socrates now goes on to claim that we should choose whichever would be better at guarding 'cities' laws and practices' (*nomoi te kai epitēdeumata poleōn*, 484B9–10), and that we'd prefer guards with keen sight rather than blind ones; he asks whether Glaucon thinks any different from the blind

those who are truly (*tōi onti*) deprived of knowledge (*gnōsis*) of what each thing truly is (*tou ontos hekastou*), and have no clear model in their soul, and lack the capacity to look, like painters, to what most truly is (*to alēthestaton*), and – referring always to that and observing (*theōmenoi*) that as accurately as possible – on this basis to establish what people should think[6] in respect to beautiful and just and good things, if called upon, and to guard and preserve what has been established? (VI, 484C6–D3)

---

[4] As boy-lovers embrace boys (474D7).
[5] This, as I argued, will itself be a case, however basic, of 'knowing what is, as it is'.
[6] Or (or additionally) what is lawful (the term is *nomimos*); the text is in any case suspect here, though the main sense is probably not in doubt.

No, says Glaucon (D4), there's not much difference.

'So shall we set these up as guards rather than those who have come to know (*egnōkotas*) each thing that is, and are not inferior to the others in experience, nor are behind them in any other part of excellence?'
'It would be outlandish (*atopon*)', [Glaucon] said, 'to choose any other people, so long as they weren't lacking in those other respects; for in being ahead in this very respect [sc. recognition/knowledge of each thing that is], they'd be ahead in what is pretty much (*schedon ti*) the most important respect.' (VI, 484D5–10)

Non-philosophers, then, the ones 'truly deprived of knowledge of what each thing truly is', are like blind people, because they have no model before them on which to act in relation to beauty and the rest. So we won't make them rulers; instead, we'll have as rulers those who have come to know each thing as it is, and therefore (we must apparently infer) do have the requisite models in sight, and legislate, etc., by reference to them – just as Socrates and his interlocutors were earlier looking for 'justice, the thing by itself, what sort of thing it is, and the perfectly just man, if he could come into being',[7] 'for the sake of having a model' to refer to (V, 472C4–6). Socrates will later call into question whether he and the others actually did find the models they were searching for (VI, 504D–E), and as he remarks, 'a guard of city and laws' will need to do better than they themselves have done (504C6–7). Evidently, then, these new philosopher-rulers will have gone all the way, and found what they 'embrace and love', the things 'over' which knowledge is. Ideal rulers, ideal knowers.

Next question: can the same people have all the necessary qualities – the other excellences as well as wisdom?[8] To show this Socrates takes a step back and asks what it will be like to have a philosophical *nature*. Natural philosophers 'are always in love with any kind of learning that shows them something of that being that always is . . .' (VI, 485B1–2) – and are in love with the whole of what is, as was previously agreed (if they are true lovers); in which case their desires will have flowed towards intellectual pursuits, leaving them no energy for pleasures experienced through the body, so that they'll be *sōphrones*, 'sound-minded'[9] and not at all lovers

---

7 Injustice too, and the most unjust man.
8 The requirement for *experience* is here quietly, but only temporarily, shelved (see 539E).
9 To translate *sōphrosunē* here as 'self-control' seems particularly inappropriate, insofar as Socrates' description seems to leave nothing to be controlled. See n. 11 below. (The case of this particular excellence is an especially interesting one: it really *is* 'sound-mindedness', not 'self-control', for which there is no room in Socrates' theory; what other people *call*, and think of, as 'self-control' is in fact a matter of knowledge and understanding. But at the same time *sōphrosunē*, even in ordinary language contexts, *includes* both 'self-control' and something more intellectual – 'sound-mindedness'.)

of money (485D–E). Then again, 'a soul that is going to yearn after the whole and the all, always' (486A5–6) will scarcely be mean-spirited, and 'a mind that has grandeur (*megaloprepeia*) and a vision of all time and all being' (A8–9) will not attach any great importance to human life, so that a cowardly and mean-spirited nature won't be philosophical (486B3–4). Two of the four excellences down (*sōphrosunē* and courage), two to go: justice and wisdom. Well, someone with all the qualities listed – orderly, no love of money, and so on – won't be unjust (B6–8), so if we're looking for a philosophical nature we'll look for one that's just and 'tame' even from an early age (B10–12). Finally, there will be certain qualities like readiness to learn, retentiveness, and so on that will need to be looked for in a mind that 'its natural disposition will render easily led to the sight of what is' (D10–11), and will be required by 'the soul that is going to partake adequately and [sc. even] perfectly[10] in what is' (E2–3).[11] It is 'to people like this, once they have been perfected by education and age', Adimantus agrees, and only to them, that the city should be entrusted (487A7–8).

It seems, then, that what philosophers can offer the city is wisdom, in combination with the other excellences: *full*, because '*perfect*', wisdom. But there are one or two features of the context as a whole that should make us pause before concluding that Socrates is proposing that any earthly, realized version of the best city (Callipolis, the beautiful city: VII, 527C2) would be ruled by full knowers. In the first place, we should remember that Socrates prefaced his original proposal for the union of political power and philosophy, itself a response to the challenge to show that Callipolis was possible, with a double warning: not only (i) that he and the others had up till now only been looking for models, and shouldn't be criticized if they couldn't show that the model they'd described of a good city couldn't be realized in practice (V, 472D9–E1), but (ii) that when it came to 'demonstrating how most of all and in what respect most possibly it might be' (472E7–8), it had to be borne in mind that 'things done touch on truth less than things said, even if some disagree' (473A2–3). Plato here marks out the peculiarity of his general position, that things in the 'real' world of experience,

---

[10] Socrates has just talked about souls or natures that are 'adequately' (*hikanōs*) philosophical (486D1); now he goes a step further.

[11] At least the first two of the excellences (*sōphrosunē* and courage) are described in terms that are not wholly reconcilable with the accounts Socrates gave of them in Book IV – that is, insofar as they are derived directly from the nature of the mature philosopher as thinker; and the same will be true of justice too, to the extent that it is derived e.g., from the absence of a love of money, which itself has been derived from the philosopher's preoccupation with learning. For the implications of this, see chapter 9 below; meanwhile I note that the present context comes close to reducing – or at least hints at a reduction of – all four excellences to wisdom.

which merely 'share in' *really* real things, must be further from those real things than a certain kind of talking or thinking. And we have no reason to suppose that the case of knowledge will be an exception: that is, that any examples of actual knowing will be truly perfect, and perfected, and not somehow falling short. Socrates' example illustrating point (i) might have been designed to make just that point:

> So do you think a painter would be any less good a painter if after painting a model of what sort of thing the most beautiful human being would be, and having put everything into the picture sufficiently well, he can't demonstrate how such a man could actually come into being? (v, 472D4–7)

True, none of this *need* be applicable – so far – to Socrates' conclusion at vi, 487A7–8, to the effect that the city should be entrusted only to those with perfect excellence and wisdom. Perhaps in this case he actually does think the ideal attainable. However the immediate sequel provides another reason for doubting this.

Adimantus is not convinced by Socrates' argument. He describes how those who listen to Socrates feel every time he says what he's saying now[12] – that because of their inexperience in the business of question and answer they're progressively led astray, until they find themselves having agreed to something that contradicts what they first said. In the present case, the conclusion reached is patently at odds with the facts: philosophers are strange birds, if not completely unscrupulous, and even the ones that seem the most respectable are quite useless.[13] How *can* we put them in power? Socrates' reply to the objection is in the form of a parable, of a ship, the members of whose crew fail to recognize the need for an expert navigator: they call the navigator 'a stargazer and a babbler'[14] (and so useless for anything, when in fact they need him more than anything). This is the sort of language Socrates borrows from Aristophanes and repeatedly applies to himself.[15]

But *he* says he knows nothing; if *he*, Socrates, is the (or a possible) model of the philosopher, then his proposal for philosophical rule takes on a rather

---

[12] This perhaps should not be taken as suggesting that Socrates has talked about Callipolis before, merely that he's talked often enough before about the need to give power to philosophers: one thinks of a passage like *Protagoras* 319C–D (government should be in the hands of experts), or *Gorgias* 521D ('I am perhaps the only true statesman . . .').

[13] One wonders into which category Socrates falls; perhaps the first (a war veteran of Socrates' distinction could hardly be classed as useless, by anyone).

[14] vi, 488E4–489A1.

[15] See *Apology* 19B–C, with Aristophanes, *Clouds* (Socrates is *adoleschēs* at *Clouds* 1485; he appears on stage in a basket to be nearer the heavens), then *Phaedo* 70C, *Phaedrus* 269E, *Parmenides* 135D, *Sophist* 225D, and *Politicus* 299B – where, significantly, Socrates is a navigational expert who does *research* into the winds and the tides.

different complexion. Not only, in that case, will it apparently not be full knowers that rule, but power will be entrusted even to people who are ignorant – or rather, people who are wise in the way that Socrates says he is wise, in recognizing his own ignorance (and then trying to do something about it): true *philosophers*, in fact. These – or, as I shall go on to suggest, some superior versions of Socrates that he himself conjures up – will be the best kind of approximation to the ideal that mere human beings can achieve; and that in itself will be enough to make Callipolis a possibility, in the terms suggested in that passage at v, 472–3. Full knowledge is something philosophers aim at, not a destination they actually reach.

If this is right, it is understandable that Socrates should not rush to admit it in so many words. He is having difficulty enough already in persuading Adimantus of his proposal for philosophical rule, without also having to convince him that everyone would be better off being ruled by people who hadn't, actually, quite got to the truth of things, yet. (Perhaps he might have had better luck with Glaucon; but evidently he wants to bring Adimantus along too.) And in any case, it remains his position that, *ideally*, the city would be ruled by people with full knowledge. But that it is an ideal (and no more) is, I think, plainly reflected in Socrates' choice of language in those famous similes, at the end of Book vi and the beginning of vii, that centre on the form of the good, represented as the key to the knowledge of everything else.[16] Thus the divided line (the second of the three similes),[17] for its part, says only that reason itself will 'grasp' the uppermost of the four segments of the line

through its capacity for dialectic, treating its hypotheses not as beginnings [sc. as sciences like mathematics do in the next segment down] but actually as hypotheses, *with the purpose that* (*hina*), going as far as the unhypothetical, to the beginning ['first principle', *archē*] of the whole], and having grasped it . . . (*Republic* vi, 511b4–7)

Likewise with the simile of the cave, in which the final phase of the released prisoner's journey upwards – his sight of the sun itself – is clearly marked as no more than a projection. After completing the whole simile, Socrates gives Glaucon some pointers as to how to interpret it: 'the location (*hedra*) that appears to us through the faculty of sight' is represented by the prison

---

[16] On which (the good) see chapter 9 below. Before the grand introduction of the form of the good – though in fact it has already been referred to rather more quietly, indeed almost nonchalantly, in 493c – and after the parable of the ship Socrates gives a long and somewhat pessimistic disquisition of the vulnerability of the philosophical natures he has described, which itself, perhaps, tends to make the ideal of the perfected knower seem ever more remote from 'real' life.

[17] The function of the line is, in effect, to build on the outcomes of the argument with the sight-lovers in Book v, giving a more complete list of different states of mind and what they are 'over'.

where humanity dwells, and the light of the fire in it represents the power of the sun;

and if you posit (*tithenai*) the ascent above and sight of the things above as the journey of the soul into the intelligible realm (*topos*), you'll hit on what I, at least, expect to be the case (*ouch hamartēsēi tēs g'emēs elpidos*), since this is what you long to hear. God knows, I imagine, whether my expectation is true. But at any rate what appears to me appears like this . . . (VII, 517B5–8)

There could hardly be a clearer indication that he, Socrates, has not himself got as far as he would have wished, and got a proper sight of the sun itself;[18] that part he too can only imagine. But after all, if he *had* got a decent view, his hearers might ask, why should he be so reluctant to describe the sun – the good – directly? (He has resorted to images just because of his lack of knowledge about the good, which he has protested, in emphatic terms, in 504E–507A.)

Still, Socrates is proposing that others might get as far as seeing the sun itself, even if he hasn't (or hasn't properly). What will they 'grasp', or 'see' when they arrive? The divided line gives us the wish-list: the aim, for the faculty of reason, will be to climb 'as far as the unhypothetical, to the beginning of the whole' (VI, 511B6–7), and then move down again, with that in its grasp, until – let us suppose – it has mapped the whole of 'what is' (the forms).[19] And, up to a point, the cave leaves the prospect of the satisfactory fulfilment of that whole process dangling before Adimantus, and before us. However when we look more closely at the detail of the text, the freed prisoner doesn't seem to get anywhere near this kind of achievement. All he is envisaged as being able to do is to catch sight of (*katidein*, aorist) the sun outside, 'observe (*theasasthai*, another aorist)[20] what sort of thing it is' (*hoios estin*), and reach the reasoned conclusion – of the sort that, as he will go on to say, Socrates imagines one would have to reach[21] – that it is cause of things both outside and, in a way, inside the cave;[22] after which the

---

[18] For the idea of a *partial* sight of 'what is true', see the passages from the *Phaedrus* cited in n. 37 to the preceding chapter; and for this central part of the *Phaedrus* – Socrates' second speech, with the soul as charioteer and horses careering through the heavens – as drawing on and developing texts like the *Republic*, see chapter 11 below. (Socrates' tone in *Republic* VII, 517B is much the same as the one he uses in, 533A1–6, a difficult passage I shall discuss below in chapter 9 (text to n. 53).)

[19] VI, 511B is a highly controversial context; but what I have suggested ought to be unobjectionable to most, even while it ignores the difficulties of detail.

[20] If Plato were thinking of single actions (looking as opposed to gazing, contemplating), the aorist tense would be what he would choose.

[21] At 516B9–C2, the prisoner is imagined as doing the necessary bit of reasoning ('he would conclude', *sullogizoito an*); at 517C1 Socrates says he imagines 'one would have to conclude', *sullogistea*, the same kind of thing. 'Observing what sort of thing it is' would, I imagine, amount to having some sort of workable account, or definition.

[22] VI, 516B6; B6–7; B9–C2.

ex-prisoner goes down again to the prison. What is said about the fifty-year-old trainee rulers in 540A–B, in relation to their encounter with the good, is much the same.[23] In both cases, what seems to be in question is something considerably less than the kind of extended episode of contemplation and investigation, from all sides and aspects,[24] that might be thought necessary for full understanding. Enough will have been 'seen' to give rise to further reasoning, both about the bright object itself and about other things in its light;[25] but that is all (and, I propose, all that Socrates actually needs for his real, and more sophisticated argument).[26] The phrase 'observe *what sort of thing it* [the good] *is*' (at 516B6–7) may in itself be significant, because it recalls the way Socrates himself set aside 'for now' the question 'what on earth the good is, itself', in favour of a description of something 'very like it' (VI, 506D8–E1, E3–4). The philosopher-rulers will 'see' the good, as the prisoner will see the sun outside the cave – and as Socrates, it seems, has not, or not well enough; but even the philosopher-rulers will fall short of full knowledge, and so, properly speaking, of knowledge altogether.

'And if [the other prisoners] could somehow get (*lambanein*) in their hands (*cheires*) the person who was trying (*epicheirein*) to free them and lead them upwards, and could kill him, wouldn't they kill him?',[27] asks Socrates, at the end of the cave simile (VII, 517A4–6): while this has a banal

---

[23] With aorists throughout (cf. n. 20 above), and most importantly in the case of the infinitive *apoblepsai* at 540A8.

[24] Hardly suggested, in any event, by the case of the prisoner and the *sun* – not the sort of thing one gazes at for long: see *Phaedo* 99D, where Socrates refers to the damage people do to their eyes by 'gazing at and looking into' (*theōrountes kai skopoumenoi*: present tenses rather than aorists) the sun when in eclipse.

[25] The metaphor of sight does not in general seem suggestive of any sort of complete familiarity, nor is that how Socrates has used it before the similes of VI–VII: see chapter 6 above, and especially V, 476D1 (the philosopher can 'see' beauty well enough to distinguish it from particular beautiful objects); VI, 493C5–6 (sophists haven't 'seen' how much 'the nature of the just and good differ, in reality' from 'necessary' and 'just' as the great beast of the assembled people understands them). The notion of completeness is imported by interpreters into the metaphor from the surrounding contexts: see, e.g., VI, 487A7–8, or 490A8–B7, which substitutes a sexual metaphor – the soul 'has intercourse with' true being and 'begets' intelligence and truth. (The latter passage, however, is another that I take to be couched in the language of *aspiration*: see n. 36 below.) As Linda Woodward suggests to me, we might connect the passage with the idea of Socrates as midwife: truth emerges, if at all, in a *dialectical* context.

[26] I.e. the one that would articulate fully his considered position on knowledge/wisdom and humanity.

[27] The text here has been suspected, not least because of the unexpected infinitive at the end of the sentence; however Slings is surely right in proposing that we are to understand an underlying 'don't you think' from earlier on in the passage. The identity of 'the person' in question is also not certain: I have taken it that he is the rather shadowy figure, referred to merely as 'someone' (*tis*: VII, 515D1,E6), who acts as the prisoner's guide on the way up (we may compare the similarly shadowy guide helping the lover to correct loving in the 'ascent passage' in the *Symposium*) – and may guide others. This must in my view be the right interpretation, because the passage is ultimately about *education* (see especially 518B–D, which draws from the cave simile the moral about what education is), and the freed prisoner is the pupil, not the teacher (as we leave him he is scarcely in a position to teach anyone: he's in a state of confusion). He is also, importantly, a pupil who is forced to plunge back

meaning in the context of prisoners who are chained up and so actually unable to see anyone behind them, no one can possibly doubt that it is intended to bring to mind his own trial and execution.[28] So the guide *is* Socrates. But he's a guide[29] who only takes the prisoner so far. The 'person' responsible for the prisoner's escape in fact disappears from the scene as soon as he has hauled his charge out of the cave (515E6–8), and after that the prisoner is on his own. Nevertheless this is as it should be, if we are to take at all seriously[30] those lengthy protestations our Socrates makes at VI, 506B–507A, that is, as the very subject of the form of the good is introduced, to the effect that he cannot speak from knowledge about the new subject, but can only say what he thinks about it[31] – protestations which he then recalls in the passage cited a page or so above:

and if you posit the ascent above and sight of the things above as the journey of the soul into the intelligible realm, you'll hit on what I, at least, expect to be the case, since this is what you long to hear. God knows, I imagine, whether my expectation is true. But at any rate what appears to me appears like this . . . (VII, 517B5–8)[32]

The best Socrates can do, then, as a guide, is to show the way to a place from where others – he hopes and expects – may discover for themselves what they, and he, most need to know about. Other philosophers, he supposes, may be able to do better than he can, but – so I have argued – he also holds, as he always did, that there is a limit to what *any* human being can discover, unless he or she has some kind of privileged access to

into the ordinary world of experience ('in the lawcourts or somewhere else', 517D8, where – to give a very rough paraphrase of what Socrates says – he'll have to dispute about justice with people who've never seen justice itself). His progress will then map as it should onto the succeeding description of the education of the philosopher-rulers in the good city, with the difference that it will then be *his* way of understanding and talking about justice that, in such a city, will be the dominant discourse.

[28] If not also his (half-)joking response to the question in the *Phaedo* as to how he should be buried 'As you like – if you can catch [*lambanein*] me and I don't escape you' (*Phaedo* 115C4–5), sc. because you can't bury an incorporeal soul. Of course Socrates doesn't yet know that people will want to kill him: here is another obvious way in which Plato is ahead of his character.

[29] And a fairly brutal one: in the cave, the prisoner has to be forced (*anankazein*) to look directly at the light of the fire (515E1), and dragged by force (515E6: *helkein . . . biai*) through the exit.

[30] And I see no reason at all not to take them quite seriously; there is no sign of insincerity, and none, either, of his (or Plato's) holding anything back. Quite the reverse: if anything were being held back, Plato would be making Socrates lie. (The 'doctrinal' interpreters who prefer the second option tend to suppose that Socrates speaks for Plato. So, if Plato is holding back, so is Socrates; but he says he is not.)

[31] And '[d]on't you recognize that all beliefs without knowledge are ugly things – the best of them blind? Or do you think those who have some true belief without understanding are any different from blind people who travel on the right road?' (*Republic* VI, 506C6–9).

[32] Once again, I see no reason at all not to take Socrates seriously here; what he says fits snugly with the general, and consistent, stance that he adopts throughout the *Republic* (as this and other chapters aim to establish).

the truth; and perhaps even then.[33] So it is that Plato has Socrates report his encounters with the fictional seer in the *Symposium*, Diotima, who by implication has an understanding of things bestowed on her directly by the gods. Someone else who claimed divine inspiration was Parmenides,[34] and it may have been that claim of his that underlies Plato's decision to introduce him as Socrates' philosophical mentor, and as a model of philosophical expertise, in the *Parmenides*. But even Parmenides is fallible; his fellow-countryman, the Visitor from Elea in the *Sophist*, openly corrects him. It is only mythical humans who come anywhere close to divine knowledge in the full sense – precisely because of their proximity to the gods, guaranteed by the story-teller.[35]

There are, then, I suggest, two rather different views of philosophy, and of the philosopher, in play in the part of the *Republic* under discussion. On the one hand there is the philosopher as he or she might be and would wish to be: someone who has arrived as close as any human being could to the goal Socrates describes for the genuine 'lover of learning' at *Republic* VI, 490B2–7, who

> would advance and not be dulled, or cease from his passion until he had grasped the nature of each thing that is with that in the soul which it befits to grasp such a thing . . . , and having had intercourse with what really is, having engendered intelligence and truth, would know and truly live and be nurtured and so cease from birth-pangs . . .[36]

Diotima in the *Symposium* knows all about this kind of thing, and might be supposed actually to have reached the goal herself: after all, even if she is

---

[33] The problem, for Plato, I take to be not so much that we can't know when we've got something right ('a certain disposition to one's own knowledge'/'a second-order certainty about one's own states', as Thomas Johansen put it in one of his trenchant comments), but that there is too much to learn – which then, in turn, tends to become expressed in terms of self-knowledge or the lack of it, insofar as it is appropriate to us human beings to recognize that we *are* human, time-limited, and so on. We can get some things right – acquire 'pieces of knowledge': see text to n. 42 below – but the whole picture is a different matter. (This was, roughly, Socrates' position in the *Apology*, and is still part of his position in the *Republic*.) Skill at 'seeing things together' is an essential ingredient in dialectic; but can anyone see *everything* together, *perfectly*?

[34] Parmenides, fragment I (Diels–Kranz), e.g., lines 1–4.

[35] So with the original kings of Atlantis, in the *Timaeus-Critias*, who are actually descended from the gods; and in a way, too, with the primitive Athenians who opposed them (insofar as the latter seem to be in direct contact with Athena and Hephaestus in their temples). But such imaginary figures ought strictly not to be called philosophers at all: one who already has knowledge, as the gods do, according to Socrates in the *Lysis* (218A) and the *Symposium* (204A), no longer needs to seek for it, as a mere *lover* of wisdom/knowledge (*philosophos*) does.

[36] This passage I assimilate to that part of the simile of the divided line which I took to describe the philosopher's *aspirations*, not what philosophers typically achieve: '*with the purpose that* (*hina*), going as far as the unhypothetical, to the beginning ['first principle', *archē*, of the whole], and having grasped it . . .' (VI, 511B4–7).

human, she is imaginary. But if so, she will have reached it through divine dispensation. Anyone else, including Parmenides (for all that he claimed about his goddess), will have had to work at it[37] – and even so will never get there. At the same time Socrates seems to imagine the possibility that exceptional individuals, like Parmenides himself, and the unnamed visitor from Elea,[38] might get far enough to carry a degree of authority in the way that he claims that he himself does not.

That is one of the two views of the philosopher I see Plato as proposing: a kind of Socrates perfected, to the extent that perfection is possible for human beings, and philosophers.[39] But then there is Socrates himself, still so far lagging behind that he refuses to claim any sort of authority at all. And Plato, I propose, sees himself as being with Socrates; for actually neither Parmenides nor his fellow Eleatic, nor any other authority-figure in the dialogues, has much to offer, beyond what might have been put in Socrates' mouth,[40] *except* (a degree of) authority and assurance, plus exceptional and special kinds of expertise that Socrates in any case disclaims or is presented as lacking: expertise in special sorts of dialectical method (Parmenides, the Eleatic Visitor), astronomy (Timaeus),[41] legislation (the visitor from Athens in *Laws*).

So where does all this leave us in relation to the argument for philosophical rule in the *Republic*? That argument, I have proposed, does not ultimately depend on the philosopher-rulers' full possession of ultimate truth (fortunately, if that belongs only to beings superior to humans), but

---

37 One thinks of those dialectical exercises he recommends to Socrates in the second part of the *Parmenides*.

38 Whose critique of 'father Parmenides' in the *Sophist* shows that dialectic is alive and well at least in Plato's version of Elea. (In *Sophist* and *Politicus* Socrates is himself a mature philosopher, not a beginner as in *Parmenides*.)

39 I shall attempt to give further precision to this idea in the following chapter, using an important passage at VII, 534B–D.

40 Or what he could have claimed, in a typical Platonic trope, to have heard from somewhere/someone.

41 Glaucon volunteers at *Republic* VII, 531E2–3 that there are 'precious few' experts he's met in the mathematical sciences (including astronomy) who are dialectical experts. Quite how I take this to bear on Timaeus will become clear in the course of chapter 10 below (Timaeus is no dialectician). Thomas Johansen reminds me that Timaeus will portray astronomy as central to our philosophical development (astronomy has in a way actually given us philosophy [*Timaeus* 47A–B], and is a way of nourishing our rationality [90C–D]); he also justly observes that my account generally gives little sense of the usefulness – and, I think he means to imply, the *importance* – of mathematics as a whole in the dialectical enterprise. I am largely unrepentant: it seems to me that whatever glorious future mathematics may have within Plato's Academy, for the Plato of the dialogues it retains a purely auxiliary status. Or so it does, at any rate, in *Republic* and *Timaeus*: the *Philebus* may be a different case (which, given my generally 'unitarian' stance, might have repercussions for my overall interpretation of 'the Plato of the dialogues'). But the kind of mathematics that may begin to come into play there in *Philebus*, and later on in the Academy, is not, it appears to me, the reformed/idealized mathematics of *Republic* and *Timaeus*, but a horse of a different colour.

merely on their having some significant sort of cognitive advantage over non-philosophers – and a lesser such advantage over Socrates. In other words, they will have the kind of grasp of things that will, somehow, give them authority to act as legislators, and to maintain the laws, even while they lack full, perfect knowledge; that is, knowledge of the sort that belongs to gods. (What they have may even be called knowledge; 'pieces of knowledge', perhaps, which is what the *Phaedrus* attributes to the ideal writer/dialectician.)[42] The kind of philosopher Socrates is recommending as helmsman of the good city is another version of himself, as it were: the one who is able to go, or be taken/forced, all the way to the good,[43] and who will – we must presume – be familiar enough with beauty, justice and the good to be able to use them as models for legislation. This is the philosopher who will approximate to the ideal human ruler (VII, 540A–B). No wonder Socrates was so extraordinarily hesitant[44] when he suggested those various radical kinds of legislation in Book V ('in a state of uncertainty, and as someone who is searching': V, 450E1–2) – about how women should be treated, about children, and about the conduct of war. He argued that all his proposals were *beneficial* (good), as well as possible; but his state-educated counterparts will be in a better position to judge that, not only because they are philosophically further on than he is, but they will have practical experience too (VI, 484D6–7).

To sum up: Socrates may insist that no one is in a position to act wisely, *emphronōs*, whether in the public sphere or in private life unless he or she has 'seen' the good.[45] But he is always careful to avoid suggesting that he has seen it (*really* seen it) himself. If he has been out of the cave and in the world above, nevertheless he is still ignorant. And insofar as I claim that he and Plato march together, what goes for Socrates will go for Plato.[46] Neither of them claims to be one of the 'leaders' in philosophy described in

---

[42] *Phaedrus* 276C3–4 (cf. chapter 11 below). See the following chapter.

[43] In the terms of the picture of Socrates in the *Politicus* (see n. 15 above), he will be someone whose research has had some positive and transferrable outcomes.

[44] V, 450A–451C. The resistance he puts up here to being made to reveal his own ideas is particularly marked.

[45] '(But at any rate what appears to me appears like this . . .:) that anyone who means to act wisely (*emphronōs*) in either the public or the private sphere must see [the form of the good]' (*Republic* VII, 517C4–5). (But again, there is no warrant for interpreting 'seeing the good' as implying the acquisition of full knowledge about it.)

[46] If Plato actually lectured 'On the good', as later sources tell us, this might be another place in which one could propose drawing a line between Socrates and Plato (with Plato self-consciously moving beyond his Socrates). But we have no indication as to the status Plato would have accorded what he said about the good when he lectured, and as to how far he might have thought he had genuinely moved on from the *Republic*.

the *Theaetetus*; they are rather among the 'inferior practitioners' contrasted with these 'leaders'.[47] The 'leaders' are philosophers who somehow always avoided the fate of the prisoners in the cave, and manage to spend their whole time in the clear light outside; only their bodies are resident in the city, and their souls or minds live elsewhere.[48] Ordinary non-philosophical people, Socrates says, find such paragons funny. Seen from his own perspective in the *Republic*, they are the philosopher-rulers living the kind of life they would have if there were no requirement on them either to rule or to acquire the experience needed for ruling.[49] By contrast a second-division player like Socrates is a real citizen who lives – both body and soul – in his city, engaging with his fellows, even going to war and sitting on the Council with them, and acting as their intellectual midwife, or (if we prefer the imagery of the *Republic*) as their part-qualified guide. (And Plato, perhaps, as the person who allows that Socratic engagement to continue through his written dialogues, would see himself in the same role.) Being still himself – as *he* sees it[50] – so far removed from knowledge, he can do no better than that. But he is also generally unclear how any human being can get further than true belief with the sort of justification that, strictly speaking, will leave the truth of the belief itself at least in principle open to question.[51] Still, this does not make him inclined to give up the *search* for knowledge. The philosopher may apparently move forward, under the

---

[47] 'Leaders': *hoi koruphaioi* (173C6–7); 'inferior practitioners': *hoi phaulōs diatribontes en philosophiai* (C7–8). This is at the beginning of the digression (as Socrates calls it at 177C1) in the argument about knowledge, which Socrates uses to complete his case against Protagorean relativism (see Sedley 2004: 62–5).

[48] Why shouldn't we suppose Plato to intend himself as one of *these* – given that he, unlike Socrates, has left no trace of a mark on the political and civil life of the Athens of his time? Simply because what the dialogues offer us is so consistently the other, the Socratic, perspective, with anything beyond that – or so I claim – as mere projection.

[49] After the age of fifty the philosopher-rulers will only have to 'engage' with ordinary people when their time comes to rule; for the rest they will be able to philosophize. One of the consequences of my interpretation of the cognitive state of Plato's philosopher/Socrates is that the philosopher-rulers may actually *need* to go on philosophizing, for the good of the city, and not just for the sake of their own happiness. Still lacking knowledge, but in love with it, they will continue to be passionate seekers; but equally, the moment they stop philosophizing, they will be implying that their incomplete state of 'knowledge' is good enough – which may involve a lack of *self*-knowledge (see chapter 3 above), that will be dangerous to the city as well as themselves. If so, then there is no straight trade-off between what makes them happiest – doing philosophy – and doing what it's just for them to do – ruling; it will also be just for them to do philosophy, if that is a condition of their *continuing* to rule well as they were trained to do.

[50] Others see him differently: thus Simmias at *Phaedo* 76B–E, and perhaps Timaeus at *Timaeus* 51E5–6.

[51] To this extent, after all, the (Academic) sceptical reading of Plato will get real purchase (see Preliminaries, n. 7 above). But no sceptic ever talked as much, and so positively, about truth and knowledge as Plato does.

best conditions, in the direction of truth, with dialectic – questioning and challenge – as control.[52]

An advantage of the proposed interpretation is that it goes a long way towards explaining why Plato retains Socrates as main speaker in the *Republic*. Not only is the Socrates of the *Republic* still recognizably the Socrates of the pre-*Republic* dialogues, but the kingdom of philosophy that he imagines would, extraordinarily, be a Socratic kind of kingdom:[53] not one ruled by Socrates himself, because he lacks both the understanding and the experience, but all the same a kingdom ruled by people formed and tested by his methods, and applying – to whatever extent should prove realizable – the sorts of proposals that he has so hesitantly put forward, nevertheless thinking them defensible. (Indeed he appears to think, when he is done, that he has defended them satisfactorily enough: I refer again, primarily, to Book v.) And if philosophy, from this perspective, might still look at best elitist and at worst an instrument of repression (and so thoroughly un-Socratic, as the charge goes),[54] still we should remember the qualification Socrates introduced about the difference between theory and practice. At bottom, project Callipolis is a plea for more rational government – government

---

[52] The two visions of philosophy may be seen as interestingly juxtaposed in *Theaetetus* and *Sophist*. At the beginning of the latter Socrates talks about genuine philosophers as appearing in all sorts of guises, thanks to people's ignorance, 'as they look down from above on life below, seeming to some to be worth nothing, to others worth everything in the world: now they appear as statesmen [*politikoi*, 'experts in the art of politics'], now as sophists; now to some they'd give the impression of being in a state of complete madness' (*Sophist* 216c6–D2). Did the Eleatic Visitor's countrymen think of sophist, statesman and philosopher as belonging to different categories, or as being one and the same thing? Easy, replies the visitor: as belonging to different categories. Yet in the ensuing discussion of the sophist, one of the types identified is the *noble* sophist, whose activity is indistinguishable from a part of Socrates' – who led the discussion on the previous day (as reported in *Theaetetus*), when the Eleatic Visitor wasn't there. So from the latter's point of view it seems as if Socrates resembles a sophist, while he also thinks – presumably, in common with other Eleatics – that sophists and philosophers are different things (as he would, if Eleatic philosophers have got – or are figured as having got – beyond the point of having to insist on their ignorance; though as a matter of fact there is no mention of any disavowal of knowledge on the part of the 'noble sophist'). If *Theaetetus* is genuinely aporetic, of course, it will be natural to treat *Sophist* as showing Plato in a different and more positive mode – and *Theaetetus* as showing Socrates trailing behind him (in particular, on falsity; thus Sedley talks of 'the *Sophist* account [of falsity as] succeed[ing] where the *Theaetetus* account failed', and the Socrates of the *Theaetetus* as not having 'take[n] the final leap': Sedley 2004: 132). I myself prefer to see the difference between the two dialogues as a difference of styles of writing philosophy: the Eleatic in *Sophist* brings out directly, and authoritatively, what Socrates does by indirection in *Theaetetus*. (It is part of the *fiction* that he fails to take that 'final leap'.) At the beginning of the *Politicus* – the third in the trilogy begun with *Theaetetus* and continued in *Sophist* – it is Theodorus and the Eleatic Visitor who agree that statesman *and* philosopher still remain to be covered; Socrates is less clear on the point, and well he might be, having already himself given his account of the philosopher in the *Theaetetus* (i.e. in the 'digression') as well as an extended demonstration of the kind of thing his brand of philosopher does. (But the Eleatic wasn't there to witness it.)

[53] Cf. chapter 10, n. 2 below.   [54] See Preliminaries above, pp. 1–2.

based on the same basic understanding of things (of the good, the just and the beautiful) that Socrates thinks should rule our private lives. That will still be a long way away from the kind of 'populism' that has been attributed, somewhat optimistically,[55] to the Socrates of the 'Socratic' dialogues; but it is even further away from the despotism that the *Republic* is often alleged to be advocating.

I have spent so much time in discussing the Socratic-Platonic view of philosophy and the philosopher for one particular reason, among several. This is that almost everything, for one major aspect of my own enterprise, turns on this single topic. Suppose that the Socrates of the pre-*Republic* dialogues (broadly speaking) is genuine about his claims to know nothing, which is something most 'sceptical' interpreters will readily accept. Then, if his counterpart in the *Republic* turned out to think that philosophy could actually discover once and for all the kinds of fundamental truths that previously, in his pre-*Republic* incarnation, he had appeared to treat as lying beyond not only his own reach but that of any human being, a really significant change would have taken place: from exploration and *impasse*, and from honest and mainly good-natured but apparently unproductive intellectual endeavour, to a presumption of the possibility not just of progress but even of *closure* in the philosophical process, and a vision of a society frozen in its moment of perfection. It has been one of my purposes in the present chapter to demonstrate that such a reading of Plato is unnecessary. Plato's notion of the philosopher remains firmly attached to a self-confessedly ignorant Socrates who, despite his ignorance, nevertheless – whether in the pre-*Republic* dialogues, or in the *Republic* itself and post-*Republic* – has more than enough in the way of resources to want, and to try, to unsettle existing preconceptions, and replace them with others that he has understanding enough to recognize as better. So my proposal, that Plato remains – sees himself as remaining – at one with Socrates, is still alive.

[55] The term is Vlastos' (see Vlastos 1991: 48). The judgement seems primarily to rest on Socrates' willingness to talk to anyone, including skilled workers (the craftsmen of the *Apology*) and slaves (*Meno*); but he certainly puts a low valuation on people's opinions (*inter alia*, see his criticism of democracy in the *Protagoras*). As for Socratic intellectualism itself, this when properly understood is in principle neither inclusive nor exclusive: we may all desire the same thing (the real good), but we presumably need not be equally good at working out what that is. The difference between the *Republic* and what comes before it is in essence that Socrates now engages, at least theoretically, with the political process in a way in which he did not before. But, as we have seen, that engagement is somewhat less than complete; it is not he but his protégés, thoroughly immersed *both* in philosophy *and* in the everyday business of practical administration, that would rule in the good city.

CHAPTER 8

The Theaetetus, *and the preferred Socratic–Platonic account of knowledge*

I wrote in the Preliminaries, at the end of section 8, of a 'preferred [Socratic] account of the nature of knowledge to which Plato subscribes'. This 'preferred account' of knowledge is – unexcitingly – the one that Socrates and Theaetetus reach at the end of the *Theaetetus*: that knowledge is true belief together with a *logos* (a definition, or more generally a description, or a list of features) which will somehow definitively mark off the thing known from other things. This account is itself a close relation of the one Socrates offers in the *Meno* (knowledge as true belief 'bound' by calculation, *logismos*, of the cause), and is equally, and similarly, problematical.[1] How exactly will the 'account', the *logos*, be able to add anything definitive to the belief, which if true must already be successfully referring to whatever it claims to be about?

Not a few interpreters have taken this problem to be fatal to the account, so that for them the *Theaetetus* will end with no solution at all: either because the dialogue was designed as a dialectical exercise,[2] or alternatively, on the more standard view, because it was designed to show that there is no way forward without Platonic forms – to which, allegedly, there is no overt reference in the *Theaetetus*. In one specific version of the latter interpretation, the failure of Socrates' and Theaetetus' last attempt at a definition is meant to teach us

to abandon . . . the [sc. Socratic] idea that true judgement [i.e. what I have called 'belief': *doxa*] could ever be converted into knowledge by [the] power to differentiate;[3]

---

[1] *Meno* 98A. For the similarity between the problems raised, in the texts themselves, about both accounts, see Sedley 2004: 176–8.
[2] A truly 'sceptical' interpretation; see, e.g., Burnyeat 1990.
[3] Though according to Sedley this power is itself to be 'retained as the basis of knowledge'.

for

[a]s in *Republic* v–vii, generally agreed to pre-date the *Theaetetus*, so still in the *Timaeus*, thought to be a considerably later production, the fully articulated Platonic position remains that knowledge and judgement (or 'opinion') are two entirely separate states of mind or faculties, each dealing with its own distinct set of objects. Knowledge is of what-is, the unchanging Forms, while mere judgement is of the sensible world, of items which 'become' without ever 'being'.[4]

In chapter 6, however, I argued that while it is true in an important way that knowledge and 'judgement', i.e. 'belief', *doxa*, in the *Republic* (and the *Timaeus*) are 'two . . . separate states of mind or faculties', they are not *entirely* separate, and while each, in a way, 'deal[s] with its own distinct set of objects', they also 'deal with' the *same* objects. This is the chief reason why the one state of mind can be called 'knowledge' and the other (mere) 'belief' or 'opinion',[5] and also helps to explain how the latter can be true.[6] If this is right, then there will after all be no obstacle to Plato's accepting – continuing to accept – true belief as an element in his account of knowledge, i.e. in the sort of role in which it appears in the last part of the *Theaetetus*.

And this is probably just as well, because it is hard to see how Socratic dialectic – itself touted as a means to the acquisition of knowledge – can function at all without true belief as an element.[7] Some of the mental offspring to which Socrates' interlocutors will give birth, according to the midwife image in the *Theaetetus*, will apparently be true, or at least it is not ruled out in advance that they might be true, and they will certainly be beliefs; and if Socrates goes on maintaining his own ignorance, it looks unlikely that his interlocutors, when and if they get something right, should be understood as leap-frogging him to truth and knowledge.[8] But in any

---

[4] Sedley 2004: 179. So, again, according to Sedley, the *Theaetetus* shows Plato looking back at Socrates while having moved on; for Socrates has no special set of objects for knowledge to refer to – no 'unchanging Forms'.

[5] After all, if in any normal context A was said to *know* while B merely *believed* that what he thought was true, one would naturally assume – if the contrast were to be at all interesting, or worth even mentioning in the first place – that their knowledge and belief were at least somehow about the same things, not completely different ones. (In any case, in the *Republic* context the issue must ultimately be about whether we should give power to those who recognize and inquire into beauty, justice and other important things, or to people who merely have beliefs about such things.)

[6] See chapter 6, pp. 211–12 above, on *Timaeus* 51–2.

[7] In principle dialectic might involve true belief but itself be about something other than the objects of knowledge. In fact, however, the *Republic*, at least, firmly identifies dialectic with talking and thinking about *forms*.

[8] Socrates might at first sight seem to suggest something of the sort at *Theaetetus* 150D, with his talk about the 'amazing progress' people sometimes make with him, without his ever having taught them anything. But closer examination shows that he means nothing of the sort: the progress these people make is only relative to their previous ignorance (which is sometimes complete: 150D3).

case the whole model of intellectual advance through question and answer, and through the challenging of ideas, seems ultimately to depend on the possibility that one way of thinking and talking about things may be better, i.e. closer to the truth, than another. Such an assumption is – I claim – clearly visible behind all those conversations in the 'Socratic' dialogues;[9] it will also underlie and underpin the various sorts of dialectical *method* that Plato's Socrates recommends, whether hypothetical[10] or otherwise. This is surely most plainly the case with the method of definition by 'collection and division' which Socrates praises in the *Phaedrus* and observes the Visitor from Elea actually applying at length in the *Sophist* and the *Politicus*; for it seems reasonable to suppose that any instance of 'collection', i.e. of the preliminary identification of the genus to which the *definiendum* belongs, will be – if successful – a classic case of true belief, based on some kind of inspired guesswork,[11] which is then in the best case confirmed by the division of the genus and the final capture of the *definiendum*.

But how, exactly, is the hunter to know when he has caught what he was looking for? The most fundamental question, for anyone attempting to assess Plato's take on knowledge, is this: how is it that he supposes the philosophical searcher to be able to pass from the process of dialectic, involving the successive challenging of *logoi*, 'statements' or 'accounts'[12] (whether in the context of 'collection and division' or of the application of any other method), to the state of *knowing*? How to be sure that the account, or definition, of a thing – say, beauty – really does capture the

---

[9] That is, on the basis that these are not sceptical documents in the strict sense (Preliminaries, n. 7 above), and that the so-called 'aporetic' dialogues among them are not genuinely aporetic (Preliminaries, section 5).

[10] One might think here especially of the hypothetical method talked about at the end of *Republic* VI, which has the dialectician moving to ever 'higher' hypotheses, i.e. presumably, hypotheses that progressively improve on each other: I understand this as being in principle at least compatible with ordinary dialectical progress as described in *Phaedrus* (276E–277A: cf. chapter 11 below) and illustrated – perhaps – in a dialogue like *Lysis*. (The problem about mathematicians is that they don't move on from their hypotheses, instead treating them as starting-points: see also VII, 533B–C, and text to nn. 27–8 below. Mathematics then, interestingly, for Plato offers no model of certainty; rather the reverse – at least until the dialectician has completed *his* task. But then if no actual human dialectician will or can actually go the whole distance, there will never be a perfected mathematics, and no such thing, ever, except in the divine mind, as mathematical certainty to act as a model, except as a projection.)

[11] As we might put it (and as Plato himself might, using a more literal notion of 'inspiration'?). I am presupposing here that 'collection and division' is meant to be an instrument for discovery, even if the Eleatic Visitor himself, as I suspect, is to be thought of as beginning his demonstrations from a position of at least some greater authority than Socrates himself claims to possess: see further below, and Preliminaries, n. 56 above. (My suggestion is not that what he *says* has greater authority, just that he is *presented as* a figure of greater authority – for whom the first step of the process, 'collection', will be less of a leap in the dark.)

[12] I.e. what I called the 'stripped-down' version of dialectic in Preliminaries, section 3 above.

whole of beauty, that is, the whole of beauty in itself? Let us suppose that two interlocutors, or a single dialectician thinking to himself, gets closer and closer – as he supposes – to the truth; at any rate, things seem to be getting clearer all the time. What is it that will make the crucial difference, and convert all that apparent progress into a clear view of the subject under consideration?

The answer that Plato gives to this question is, I now think, quite clear.[13] Here is Socrates in *Republic* VII, talking about what we might demand of someone who claims to know 'the good itself':

'Do you also call "expert in dialectic" the person who gets hold of the account of the being of each thing? And the person who doesn't have it, to the extent that he isn't able to give an account to himself and another, to that extent you won't say that he is in an intelligent state of mind about the thing in question?'
'How [else] would I put it?', he said.
'So it's the same with the good too: whoever isn't able to distinguish the form of the good by separating it from all the other things, and as if in battle coming through all challenges (*elenchoi*), eager to test (*elenchein*) [sc. it = his *logos*?] not by reference to belief but by reference to being, makes his way through all of this with his account (*logos*) intact [literally 'not having been thrown': *aptōs* (as in wrestling)] – you'll not say that the person in this condition [i.e. the one without the ability described] knows either the good itself or any other good, but if somehow he does have a hold on some shadowy image [of the good],[14] it's through [the faculty of] belief that he has it, not through knowledge, and so sleep-walking as he is through this life . . .' (*Republic* VII, 534B3–C6)

Socrates here puts his recommendation in negative form: we *shouldn't* (won't) say that a person has knowledge of the form of the good *unless*

---

[13] For some time I had thought that the problem that preoccupied Plato was how to bridge the gap between cognitive subject and object, in the light of his insistence that the ultimate objects of knowledge, while 'shared in' by things in the world of ordinary sense-experience, cannot ultimately be accessed from them. I now recognize – largely thanks to the readers for the Press – that this was a mistake; for on my own interpretation, all human beings are *in any case* already guaranteed at least a minimal access to forms (see chapter 6 above, and that passage at *Phaedrus* 249B–C on the role of recollection).

[14] The Greek is *eidōlon ti* [*tou agathou*]. Socrates is talking about grasping things that merely masquerade as the good and treating them as if they were the real thing: compare the mistake made by the 'lovers of sights and sounds' in the argument at the end of Book V, the connection with which seems guaranteed by the next part of the sentence, especially by the reference to 'sleep-walking', *oneiropolein* (*kai hupnōttein*): cf. 476C5 *oneirōttein*, of the sight-lovers. The 'images' of the good that Socrates himself has used in Book VI and at the beginning of VII, of the sun, the divided line and the cave (I shall shortly discuss aspects of this last), are 'images' of a totally different kind: *eikones*, 'likenesses' (as e.g., at 517C8), which he introduced specifically to throw light on the good itself, and are therefore *about* the good itself. They therefore belong to the upper half of the divided line, not the lower half, despite the fact that Socrates originally said, or implied, that he could do no better than *aneu epistēmēs doxai*, beliefs without knowledge (VI, 506B6), and that it is the lower half of the line that is labelled as *doxa*, 'belief'.

he or she fulfils the conditions in question. If he doesn't actually say that someone who fulfils them will have knowledge, that is presumably the implication. The passage clearly looks back to the argument with the sight-lovers in Book v:[15] the sight-lover is still sleep-walking, as ever, but the philosopher has actually acquired part of the knowledge he was looking for, and an extremely important part. And he has found it through dialectic, that is, by submitting his account, his *logos*, to repeated challenge, and coming off victorious, like a successful wrestler, every time. Anyone who can do that will rightly be said to have knowledge; and if they can do it in relation to the form of the good, then they can be said to have knowledge of the good. Then they'll be able to start on the process described at the end of the simile of the line, and then in the cave simile, of interpreting the rest of 'what is' in the light of the form of the good – so fleshing out Socrates' own basic intuition (if that is what it is) that it is the good that gives other objects of knowledge not just their intelligibility but also, somehow, their *being*: VI, 509B6–8.

So: philosopher becomes knower, and through a clearly defined process. We have now moved beyond the metaphor of 'seeing', which suggests some kind of sudden and magic bridging of the gap between philosopher and knowledge of forms, to a recognition of the hard work that will be required to get to the goal.[16] Translate all this into the context of Callipolis, and we have the same result as before, but in a slightly more developed form: the rulers of this new best city will approximate as closely as possible to the state of the perfected dialectician,[17] and to the extent that they have met the criteria for success of the dialectician as wrestler, they may still be counted as having knowledge (pieces of it, at least). Socrates could in principle be pressed about this: even the most successful dialectician, surely, could never be certain that there wouldn't be another, more effective challenge waiting round the corner. When exactly would he declare himself champion – this year, or next year? This month, or after Christmas? But the objection probably should not, and evidently would not, disturb him unduly. We may compare the situation towards the end of the *Phaedo*,

---

[15] See preceding note, with chapter 6 above.

[16] The *Seventh Letter* puts the two things together: 'this knowledge is not expressible like other things that can be learned; but after much intercourse (*sunousia*) in relation to the thing itself, and cohabitation (*suzēn*: 'living together'), like light kindled from a fire that has leapt into flame, once born in the soul it now nourishes itself' (341C5–D2). (The Hackett translator has 'after long-continued intercourse *between teacher and pupil, in joint pursuit* of the subject, suddenly . . .', which may be right; however I prefer to suppose that the writer is referring to a passage like *Republic* 490B5–7, where Socrates talks of 'intercourse' [*migēnai*] directly with 'what really is', in an extension of the fantasy of direct confrontation with the objects of knowledge.)

[17] VII, 521B7–10: the rulers will be 'wisest about the things through which a city is governed best'.

where he is forced – in the light of the importance of the subject and 'human weakness' (107B1) – to abandon his claim to have *proven* what he wanted to prove about the soul's survival, in favour of a more modest claim; even so, he finally reasserts his conviction that he is right, and that his argument has been proceeding along the right lines.[18]

The *Phaedo* also provides other useful material for our understanding of *Republic* VII. At the start of the passage cited just above (VII, 534B–C), Socrates has talked of 'getting hold of' the *account* of the good:

Do you also call 'expert in dialectic' the person who gets hold (*lambanein*) of the *logos* of the being of each thing? And the person who doesn't have [it], to the extent that he isn't able to give a *logos* to himself and another, to that extent you won't say that he is in an intelligent state of mind about this [sc. the being of each thing?]? (VII, 534B3–6)

This 'getting hold' of a thing's *logos* appears to be the functional equivalent of 'grasping' or 'seeing' the thing in itself, since shortly Socrates will talk of the trainee philosopher-rulers again in the same visual terms.[19] The two things hardly seem the same: an account of something reached through reasoning will always be something rather less immediate than a direct visual encounter, or some mysterious sort of mental equivalent. Nevertheless, if we go by what Socrates says to Simmias and Cebes in the *Phaedo*, he has every confidence in reasoned accounts as a way forward. This is at the end of Socrates' 'autobiography', when he has just described his disappointment with Anaxagoras:[20] he had failed in his inquiry using the direct approach to things, and so for fear of being blinded (like people who gaze at the sun in eclipse), he retreated to looking into things by means of *logoi*, 'words' or 'accounts'. But then he adds that of course 'I don't agree at all that the person who looks into things by means of *logoi* is investigating what is (*ta onta*) in images to a greater extent than the person who looks into them by reference to the facts of experience (*erga*)' (100A1–3). No indeed; looking at 'what is' by means of *logoi* is actually the only resource we have.

However the passage at *Republic* 534, along with the general context in which it appears, lacks one feature that, so far as I know, recurs or

---

18 'Right . . . I agree about that, and what's more, our original hypotheses, even if they carry conviction with you, still, they must be examined more closely; and if you analyse them adequately, I suppose, you'll follow out the argument as far as it's possible for any human being; and if this very thing [the outcome of the argument?] becomes clear, you'll search no further' (*Phaedo* 107B4–9). It seems, then, that there will be closure (Socrates thinks).

19 They must be forced to turn 'the radiance of their soul' to the good, at the age of fifty, apparently by dialectical means (540A; 'the radiance of their soul', A7).

20 See chapter 2 above.

needs to be supplied in all other contexts in Plato where knowledge or wisdom is discussed: a rider reminding us of the limitations imposed on us by our humanity.[21] I argued in the last chapter that Socrates consistently stopped short of attributing full knowledge to the Callipolitan rulers, and that he presented the goals of the expert dialectician as aspirations rather than as realistic aims. How should we understand *Republic* 534 (the passage comparing dialectician to wrestler) within this general framework? There are, I suggest, two sides to Socrates' position. On the one hand, he believes that we can make genuine intellectual progress, and even acquire what can from one perspective even be called (pieces of) knowledge. This is what gives Callipolis its point: we *will* be better off if we are governed by people with knowledge. On the other hand, he also holds that our knowledge will always fall short of the real thing; we shall never achieve the complete picture that the gods have (the god's eye view). In *Republic* 534, and the *Republic* generally, it is the former perspective that dominates, because of the requirements of the argument. What we all need, and what cities need, is more of that commodity, knowledge, that is currently so lacking, and as much of it as is humanly possible. The question about what exactly is humanly possible, in this respect, tends to be played down, even while it is raised repeatedly in other respects (especially in relation to political reform).

In the *Timaeus*, by contrast, the *Republic*'s sister dialogue, where there are no such constraints, the same account of knowledge in terms of dialectical robustness is introduced together with the expected rider – and in language that might have been designed to recall *Republic* 534.

So of what is lasting and stable and accompanied by clear intelligence [accounts will be] lasting and unchanging (*ametaptōtoi*) – *to the extent that it belongs to logoi to be unrefutable (anexelenktoi) and undefeatable (anikētoi)*,[22] they must in no respect [i.e. must aim in no respect to?] fall short of this . . .' (*Timaeus* 29B5–C1)

If we are allowed to keep *anikētoi*,[23] these lines contain several of the ingredients of the *Republic* passage, including the somewhat mixed metaphor of battle and wrestling[24] – insofar as *ametaptōtoi* recalls *aptōs*, 'not *thrown*'

---

[21] The passage lacks this feature, that is, except to the extent that its negative formulation ('we won't say that someone has knowledge unless . . .') still leaves it open that other conditions will need to be fulfilled.

[22] The Greek words could in principle be translated as 'unrefuted'/'undefeated', but the modal forms seem to fit better in the context.

[23] Not unexpectedly, given the context, some manuscripts read *akinētoi*, 'unmovable'; but *anikētoi* appears to have the better pedigree.

[24] For comparison, the *Republic* passage went 'whoever isn't able to distinguish the form of the good by separating it from all the other things, and as if in battle coming through all challenges (*elenchoi*), eager to test (*elenchein*) it . . . [and] makes his way through all of this with his account intact . . .'

(by one's opponent); and they precisely raise the issue that was lacking in the *Republic* – just how reliable, finally, are our 'accounts'?

What I propose is that Socrates (Plato) holds back from asserting is that anyone can, through dialectic, and in the span of a human life, achieve that perfect, synoptic grasp of everything that would properly and strictly be called knowledge: the sort of grasp that gods, perhaps, can achieve effortlessly.[25] It is from this perspective, and from this perspective alone, that the reliability of the results of any actual dialectician, however skilled and experienced, may always, in principle, be called into question. But it will be enough to justify that distinction of Socrates' in the *Apology* between divine and merely human wisdom.[26] Not just Socrates, but even philosophers – dialecticians – much better than he is, even those as good as any (human ones) could possibly be: all, in the final analysis, would still need to acknowledge that distinction.

Objection. According to the simile of the line in *Republic* VI, the dialectician will differ from the mathematician in that he or she will no longer use hypotheses as starting-points for investigation.[27] Because they fail to go beyond their hypotheses, mathematicians can't get a proper handle on their subject-matter; dialecticians, by contrast, use hypotheses as mere steps on an upward path, using and then discarding them,[28] 'in order to go as far as the unhypothetical, to the beginning of everything' (VI, 511B6–7), and grasp it (i.e. the beginning) before going on to use that grasp to map out the rest of the intelligible 'world'. Now for the objection: if that 'unhypothetical' something is never in fact *fully* reached, won't the dialectician, as he turns from the (supposed) 'beginning' to map out the other forms, be using hypotheses as starting-points as much as the mathematician? Reasonable though this objection looks, it may be readily met. There are two differences between my dialectician/ruler and the mathematician: first, the dialectician is closer to the source of understanding than the mathematician; second, he or she will already have shown his superiority to the mathematician by the fact that his very method consists in questioning his hypotheses. And even as he uses such knowledge as he has, he recognizes that what he has is still lacking. In that respect too he is a true Socratic – recognizing that, even now, after all that work, from a higher perspective he actually *knows* nothing, and must do better.

[25] And – being gods, and not subject to the factors that cause us humans to forget – have never lost.
[26] *Apology* 23A–C, with chapter 1, pp. 73–8 above. From the perspective I am proposing, *Apology* becomes a key text for Platonic epistemology, along with *Meno* and *Theaetetus*.
[27] See especially VI, 511B–D.
[28] Or 'destroying' them (*anairein*: VII, 533C8), which I take to refer to their having been successfully challenged, to be superseded by another 'higher' hypothesis (i.e. one closer to the real starting-point).

We may now return to the end of the *Theaetetus*, and the alleged flaw in its final definition of knowledge: that the account to be added to true belief, if it is to turn it into knowledge, will have itself to be something known. If, as I have proposed, Plato himself shares the view that both (i) arriving at a definitive, complete and final account of anything, and (ii) achieving knowledge, are beyond human capacities (at least, in the most important single case, that of the good), then so far from being fatal, the alleged flaw in the definition will actually help to confirm its genuineness; that is, that it is the kind of definition Plato will need. Yes, it is indeed hard to see how any *logos* can guarantee to represent true reality in all its aspects; but that just reflects the way in which we human beings fall short. Knowledge *is* true belief plus an account, only an account that we, unlike gods, cannot guarantee to have caught hold of. As in the case of other 'aporetic' dialogues, the *aporia* turns out to be manufactured – and its solution consists just in our seeing that it is.

A final point: the position on knowledge that I propose Socrates to hold will fit very nicely with the way he himself operates. I laid out in the Preliminaries above[29] some aspects of the substantive position that I think underpins much of the argument of the so-called 'Socratic' dialogues (and not just of these), and that skeleton account has been to some degree fleshed out in successive chapters. If we ask what it is that allows Plato to have his Socrates not only begin from, but even – more often than not – presuppose, this substantive position of his (i.e. while remaining an avowed know-nothing), the answer I propose is that, like the *logoi* of the dialectician of *Republic* VII, it has so far survived all challenge; only, being further back than that expert person,[30] he will be even more reluctant to call it knowledge. So, while admitting – on two distinct grounds – that he knows nothing, Socrates still has plenty to talk about, plenty that he can confidently commend to his interlocutors (and Plato to us). However in relation to the most important subjects, the good, the beautiful and the just, he has no confidence in himself, and not much to say except about the importance these subjects have, and about what *cannot* be true of them.[31] It is as he begins, however hesitantly, to introduce fundamental discussion of such subjects – in the *Republic* and later dialogues – that one might, paradoxically, look for that element of 'open-ended exploration'

---

[29] Preliminaries, section 6.

[30] As indeed he must be; he's still in the business of challenging and being challenged, as the dialogues fictionally show us.

[31] Hence his need for training, of the sort that Parmenides offers him in the second half of the *Parmenides*.

that I earlier suggested might be lacking from the 'Socratic' dialogues.[32]
Socrates' essay on the treatment of women and children in *Republic* v is an
example of such exploration, and explicitly so.[33]

---

[32] 'Paradoxically', because it is precisely the 'Socratic' dialogues that appear to be, and are usually
thought to be, open-ended in this way, and the 'middle' dialogues that appear to be less so (see
above).

[33] The reference is above all to v, 450E1–2 (cited above: he is expressing himself 'in a state of uncertainty,
and as someone who is searching').

CHAPTER 9

The form of the good and the good: the Republic in conversation with other ('pre-Republic') dialogues

Last in the order of exposition, in the *Republic*, of what the true lover of wisdom will want to learn, and of what the imagined philosopher-rulers will be brought to 'see', comes the 'greatest' subject of all, the 'greatest object for learning' (*to megiston mathēma*, VI, 504D2–3, etc.). Adimantus expresses surprise that there could be any greater subject to be learned about than the ones they've already treated, i.e. justice and the other excellences – to which Socrates retorts that Adimantus already pretty well knows[1] what this new subject is, because he's heard about it often enough (a point that will be repeatedly reinforced): it's *the form of the good* (*hē tou agathou idea*, 505A2),[2] which is what makes just things and the rest useful and beneficial[3] (sc. so that it really is a more important subject than justice and the other excellences). Adimantus also knows that 'we' (humanity in general?) don't have adequate knowledge of the good – and if we don't have knowledge of *it*, then even the most complete knowledge of the rest will be of no use to us, any more than if we merely possess something without its also being good for us. 'Or do you think it's any advantage to possess everything one could possess, but not possess it as something good? Or to be wise (*phronein*) about everything else without the good, and to have wisdom (*phronein*) about nothing beautiful and good?'[4] Socrates' next move is to remind Adimantus of other things he knows: that the majority of people think the good is pleasure, while subtler people think it is wisdom (*phronēsis*) – and that the latter sort 'aren't able to show *what* wisdom it is, but are forced in the end to say that it's wisdom about [of] the good' (505B8–10). 'Highly comical', says Adimantus. Right, agrees Socrates: they reproach us for not

---

[1] 505A4 *schedon oistha.*

[2] Or, more neutrally, 'the kind/type of thing that the good is' (given that Socrates will go on to say that different people identify 'the good' in different ways)?

[3] It's that 'by having come to stand, in addition, in a relation to (*proschrēsamena*) which just things and the rest come to be useful and beneficial' (505A3–4).

[4] 505B1–3.

knowing the good, and then turn round and talk to us as if we do know it after all, and understand what they're saying when they utter the word 'good'! (505B11–C4)

And what about those who define pleasure as something good? Surely they aren't full of any lesser loss of direction ['wandering', *planē*] than the other lot? Are these people too forced to [sc. do something they don't want and] agree that there are bad pleasures? (VI, 505C6–8)

The shift in the description of the view of 'the many' from 'they think the good is pleasure' to 'they think pleasure is something good' is important, insofar as the second formulation, unlike the first, maintains the character-ization of the many in Book V as unwilling to recognize beauty, etc., each as one thing; they will see pleasure on each occasion as a good thing, and perhaps even pleasures in general as good things, but they won't be able and won't want to answer questions about *the* good.[5] So it is, we may note for the moment in passing, that Socrates in the *Protagoras* has to *persuade* the many that they believe the good to be pleasure, on the basis that they think pleasures good and pains bad, and don't have any other criterion of goodness and badness.[6] By contrast the 'subtler' sort of people – who, incidentally (for the moment), look remarkably like the Socrates of a bunch of 'Socratic' dialogues – don't seem to have any problem talking about the good; in fact that *is* what they talk about ('they reproach us for not knowing the good', 505C1–2), only they don't succeed in saying anything very useful about it. Socrates will refer explicitly back to Book V[7] a couple of pages later, to remind Glaucon (who has at this point taken on the role of interlocutor from Adimantus) of the distinction between two sorts of things: the many beautiful things and the many good things, on the one hand –

And [on the other] beautiful itself and good itself, and so in relation to all the things we posited on that occasion as many, in turn positing [sc. beautiful itself, good itself, and so on] in accordance with one form [or 'kind of thing': *idea* again][8] belonging to each, as being, each, one form [kind], we address each of them as 'what is'. (VI, 507B5–7)

The task, then, in relation to the good is to understand it as a thing in itself (a 'real nature'), and, by implication, to improve on what those 'subtler people' managed to say about it. And it is an absolutely fundamental task: not only does 'every soul pursue [the good], and do everything for the sake of this' (505D11–E1), while being unable even to form stable convictions

---

[5] See chapter 6 above.   [6] *Protagoras* 352D–355E.
[7] 'The things said earlier', 507A8.   [8] See n. 2 above.

about it,[9] but it would be a worthless sort of guard of justice and beauty who didn't know what makes just and beautiful things good.[10]

What is needed, then, is an account of the good that will be more informative than the one offered by those 'subtler' people. Who are these people? I noticed their resemblance to the Socrates of the 'Socratic' dialogues; now is the time to document this. In fact the whole of 505B5–CII is a kind of patchwork of elements from pre-*Republic* dialogues: the connection with the *Protagoras*, and Socrates' discussion there with the many, I have already remarked on, but there are also clear links with *Charmides*,[11] *Euthydemus*[12] and *Gorgias*.[13] This, I suggest, is the basis for Socrates' insistence that Adimantus has 'heard' what he is talking about often enough before – and of course Adimantus could scarcely have heard it from anyone except Socrates.

[9] This (505E2–3) I take to be a reference to the state of the 'fevered' and conflicted soul: see chapter 5, p. 180 above.

[10] I.e. 'useful and beneficial' (504A3–4).

[11] 'You know that subtler people think the good is wisdom, but when asked to say what wisdom *about*, they are forced to say it's wisdom about good and bad': in the *Charmides* Critias ends up sponsoring the view that *sōphrosunē* is a matter of knowledge of knowledges; if we're *sōphrones*, we'll be able to live knowledgeably, because we'll always be able to hand things over to the appropriate expert – and to live knowledgeably will be to live happily. But (Socrates insists) which of the many knowledges makes us happy? None except knowledge of good and bad. (So we'll be happy, have what's good, when we know what's good and bad.)

[12] See the first 'protreptic' passage (*Euthydemus* 278E–282E), which ends with the conclusion that wisdom (*phronēsis* and *sophia*) is all that is needed for a good and happy life; together with the second (288D–290D), which ends with the young Clinias supposedly looking for some special skill beyond (even) generalship to identify with this wisdom – a skill which, apparently, will have something to do with dialectic . . . (290B–C). And then (291B–292E) Socrates and Crito get into a real *aporia* about the identity of this skill: it's not any existing, recognized skill, producing any of the recognized goods (e.g., kingly or political skills). Or rather Crito is in real *aporia*, at a real *impasse*: we surely only have to go back to the first protreptic passage to establish what the skill in question is, i.e. a *technē* of the good and the bad. But if the original question was about the identity of the *good* – and that was how the first passage started – this isn't much help. The *Republic* sketch of the 'confusion' that the 'more subtle' sort of person gets himself into is a fair summary, or caricature, of this whole *Euthydemus* context. – Someone might raise the bogey that *Euthydemus* 290B–C, with its talk of 'geometers and astronomers and calculators' handing over their discoveries to 'the dialecticians', must be a reference back to the treatment of the mathematicians in the simile of the line in *Republic* VI (so that it will be *Euthydemus* that recalls *Republic*, not the other way round). I respond (a) that such an objection presupposes the very 'developmentalist' approach that I am at pains to undermine; and (b) that the reference in the *Euthydemus* seems to be to any case where experts really do discover things (diameters, stellar movements, numbers and their properties) but don't – from Plato's point of view – know what to do with them. This description will apply not only to the mathematicians of the line, or to the geometers and astronomers of *Republic* VII (526C–530C), or the astronomers who turn into birds in *Timaeus* 91D–E, but to ordinary mortals who 'recollect' equality and other such properties in the *Phaedo* and/or the *Phaedrus* (249B–C). All sorts of people, indeed all of us, have *some* sort of grasp of things, but without the dialectician's help we have no real use for what we are grasping: this is the point that the *Euthydemus* is picking out, and it seems to be a rather general one, present in 'pre-*Republic*' dialogues as well as in the *Republic*.

[13] 'You know that those who define pleasure as [the] good are forced to admit that there are bad pleasures': see Callicles at *Gorgias* 499B.

The list should be extended to include the *Phaedo*, where Socrates offers precisely the kind of account of the relation between form and particulars, and by extension, of that between the form of the good and other good things, that Socrates evokes here at *Republic* V, 505A3–4 ('[it is] by having come to stand, in addition, in a relation to [the good that just things and the rest come to be useful and beneficial');[14] and for good measure we should add that the argument of the *Charmides* gives us a close parallel for 'if we don't know [the form of the good], and if we were as much as possible to know the rest, without it, you know that there's no benefit to us' (*Republic* VI, 505A5–7).[15]

But the immediate question was about the identity of the 'subtler people' who identify the good with wisdom. Given those echoes of *Charmides* (that is, the first of the two mentioned in the previous paragraph)[16] and *Euthydemus*,[17] it begins to look as if they might be a front for Socrates himself.[18] And if so, this would be an important moment: Socrates is laughing, and has Adimantus laughing, at these people's 'subtlety'; would he not, then, be laughing at the inadequacy of his older self, and implicitly giving himself a

---

[14] See especially *Phaedo* 100D4–6 'nothing else makes it (whatever it may be) beautiful except the presence of that beautiful [the form], or its [?] being associated with it, or in whatever way and manner [it makes it beautiful] by having come to be added to it' (*ouk allo ti poiei auto* [sc. *hotioun*] *kalon ē hē ekeinou tou kalou eite parousia eite koinōnia eite hopēi dē kai hopōs prosgenomenou*), where the notion that the beautiful makes beautiful things beautiful by 'coming to be/having come to be [there, somehow] in addition [sc. to whatever other features the object has] seems precisely parallel to, indeed the converse of, the proposal, here in the *Republic*, that things (just things, etc.) come to be good (useful, beneficial) 'by standing in/having come to stand, in addition, in a relation to' the good. The presence of the 'in addition' (*pros*), and the use of the aorist tense, in both contexts (*proschrēsamena* in the *Republic* passage being a kind of mirror image of *progenomenou* in the *Phaedo*) in my view is part of what makes it at least plausible to suppose that a cross-reference is intended; another significant point is the *Phaedo*'s description of the forms as *poluthrulēta*, 'much talked about' (see n. 20 below), which parallels Socrates' 'you've often heard' here in the *Republic*. (In common with other editors, I read *prosgenomenou* in *Phaedo* 100D6 in place of the MSS reading *prosgenomenē*, which if it makes any sense at all must give us the same general sense as *prosgenomenou*. See Rowe 1993 ad loc.) – For further intertextuality with the *Phaedo*, see *Republic* VI, 507B2–C6, where Socrates reminds his interlocutors (a) of things already said earlier in the conversation (i.e. in the *Republic*), which (b) are things that 'have been said on many other occasions' (507A7–9), and (c) are highly reminiscent of things said in the *Phaedo* (in particular: see e.g. 78C10 ff.).

[15] I refer here to that part of the *Charmides* that issues in the conclusion 'But my dear Critias, we shall have missed out on each of these sorts of things [sc. the supposedly beneficial outcomes of the other sciences] happening well and beneficially, if this one science [sc. of good and bad] is absent': 174C9–D1.

[16] See n. 11 above.   [17] See n. 12 above.

[18] As it happens, Adimantus is not among the *dramatis personae* of any 'pre-*Republic*' dialogues, though his brother may be (and I myself suspect he is) the Glaucon who is one of those responsible for passing on the story of the great dinner-party that provides the framework for the *Symposium* (172C3). But that hardly matters; the point, presumably, given the patent intertextuality with other dialogues, is that the set of ideas in question will be familiar enough to anyone who has heard, or *read* about, Socrates before.

new (Platonic?) *persona*? I suggest that the inference is far from necessary, for at least three reasons. First, the references to *Charmides* and *Euthydemus* in question are only two among a whole list of such cross-references, the majority of which involve *positive* ideas about the subject of the good, not failed arguments; and these are ideas that the allegedly 'new' Socrates will evidently be building on. So he will just be laughing at isolated failures. But – this will be the second reason for resisting the inference – I have already argued that the *aporiai* (*impasses*) of dialogues like *Charmides* and *Euthydemus* are manufactured;[19] if anyone is in a state of perplexity in such contexts, it is not Socrates but rather his interlocutors. If so, my provisional conclusion about the identity of the 'subtler people' will need to be revised: not Socrates, but his partners in conversation – Critias in the *Charmides*, Crito in the *Euthydemus*. And thirdly, as it immediately turns out in our *Republic* context, Socrates himself emphatically claims not to possess knowledge about the good (VI, 506C–E), despite the positive things he has said about it, i.e. the positive things he reckons Adimantus has heard before. Nothing much new, then, after all – or so it seems, thus far; just the old Socrates, with quite a lot he's confident enough to assert, but still saying he's a know-nothing.

So, apparently, Socrates keeps his old skin. And that will itself be a pretty striking outcome, insofar as it entails that the pre-*Republic* Socrates, including the Socrates of the 'Socratic' dialogues, will have been talking about the form of the good all along – at least from Plato's stand-point as he looks backwards from the *Republic*. The intertextual references are there, I speculate, just in order to mark that continuity.

Now as any reader will remember from earlier parts of this book, this will be a controversial suggestion, since for the overwhelming majority of modern, Anglophone interpreters it is the so-called 'middle' dialogues themselves, including *Republic*, that introduce forms, and indeed *are* 'middle' (or 'Platonic' rather than Socratic) at least in large part for that very reason. On the face of it, such interpreters may feel that there is little in my suggestion that need upset them unduly, given that rider of mine: 'at least from Plato's stand-point as he look backwards from the *Republic*'. If these interpreters accept the existence of the backward references that I have identified,[20] they will presumably treat these as part of Plato's *new*

---

[19] See Preliminaries above, section 5.

[20] In the *Phaedo* too the forms are things 'we're always talking/chattering about', 76D7 (then *poluthrulēta*, 'much chattered about': 100B5). In case some readers should – in my view, impossibly – deny the reality of the connections with other dialogues that I allege, then the reference would have to be to other conversations of which we have no 'report', perhaps standing for discussions within the Academy.

take on his earlier, 'Socratic' essays: '*this*, after all, is how those earlier pieces should be taken – as involving my new metaphysical darlings, the forms, and my absolute favourite, the form of the good'. But this move will be bought at a considerable cost, because the good in the 'Socratic' dialogues always seems to have to do with practicable ends, or, more generally, good in the sphere of life and action; the knowledge of good and bad whose importance Socrates stresses, from the *Apology* onwards, is knowledge of what is good and bad for us human beings. So whatever there is that is new about that new favourite of his (the *form* of the good), it will actually slot quite neatly into the broad outlook of the 'Socratic' dialogues. It will be something familiar (Socrates seems to go out of his way to stress that), but apparently dressed up in new clothes. And as a matter of fact these new clothes, up to the point we have reached, don't seem to extend much beyond a new, or at any rate partly different, vocabulary for describing this thing, the good. The main part of what Socrates has to say about it is, of course, still to come, in the shape of the three great similes of the sun, the divided line and the cave, so that there is plenty of time for the situation to change. At least up to 507B, however, when Socrates starts on the first of his similes, not only are we on what appears to be homely territory, but Socrates has carefully told us, reassured us, that this is so. For all we know, until this point, the much trumpeted ('much chattered about') form of the good more or less *is* the human good,[21] something we can investigate in and by itself and to which we may succeed in approximating (in which we may succeed in partaking) to a greater or lesser extent.[22]

This will turn out to create a puzzle, at least given the way I have so far painted the situation, since perhaps the most significant outcome of the three similes will be to convert the form of the good into something much grander: nothing less, it seems, than a cosmic principle – explanatory, yes, of things human, but also of the universe as a whole. However before I turn to that puzzle, I propose to add to it by pointing out the essential

---

[21] Or rather, the (form of the) 'useful and beneficial', insofar as it gives other things those properties – and this will immediately open up new and wider possibilities, since presumably there will be use and benefit for things other than humans.

[22] It will, then, in a way be practicable and achievable, despite being something intelligible (*noēton*). 'The intelligible sphere is paradigmatically non-*prakton* [practicable, doable]', objected one of the readers for the Press; but for example justice, for Plato, is something *prakton*, and is also a form (and so in the intelligible sphere). There is no more difficulty in principle about the idea of forms as *prakta* than there is about universals being such – except that the relationship between the two sets of things and particular actions (*praxeis*) will need to be stated differently, insofar as forms are not (just) universals. Aristotle famously objects just that the form of the good isn't anything *prakton* (*Nicomachean Ethics* 1096b 31–5); but that is not an observation but an objection, and in my view a mistaken one.

continuity between 504–7, Socrates' introduction to the form of the good, and the similes themselves.[23] In the course of 504–7, he has claimed not only that 'just and other things' become good (useful and beneficial) by virtue of their relationship with the form of the good, but that – well, so far he was merely 'divining' this: 506A6–7 – no one will recognize (*gignōskein*) them before he knows the good. One of the primary aims of the similes, as I shall now argue, and especially of the first, is to restate, illustrate and develop these claims – while actually providing us with rather less help in properly understanding them than we have had before, and especially in 504–7 itself, with all its echoes of pre-*Republic* dialogues. As much as the similes may add to the two brothers', and our, grasp on the kind of thing the form of the good is, we still need what precedes them to understand *them*.[24]

Even after 505A, and the introduction of the *form*,[25] Adimantus is still to be found asking Socrates whether he says the good is knowledge or pleasure, or something else besides these (506B2–3).[26] Glaucon is of course being provocative – trying to sting Socrates into giving his own view of the subject instead of merely retailing what others think. ('No, Socrates, and it doesn't seem appropriate[27] for one to be able[28] to say what other people think, and not what one thinks oneself, especially when one has occupied oneself for so long with these things', 506B8–C1). But the idea is not after all so out of place. Pleasure might be able to overcome the objection just raised to its candidacy for the title of the good, and then it would be the pleasant, presumably, that made other things 'useful and beneficial'; and the *Apology* had Socrates himself making excellence, *aretē*, cause of goodness in other things (but if *aretē* is 'virtue', still 'virtue is knowledge', and so *knowledge* will be cause).[29] If the good isn't either of these two things, then Socrates ought to come up with something better, shouldn't he? And one of the outcomes of the sun simile is to distinguish the good from knowledge: just

---

[23] We should note Glaucon's deflating remark at 509A: 'an astonishing beauty it has, if it provides knowledge and truth, while being above these itself; evidently *you*'re not saying it's pleasure!' He for one is evidently not carried away by Socrates' language. (There is perhaps a kind of analogy here with the plot in the *Philebus*, with knowledge and pleasure competing in the contest to be recognized as the good; so far, however, I am unsure that the analogy is more than superficial.)

[24] This is by way of a certain redressing of the hermeneutical balance: most interpreters start from the similes and read backwards. I do not deny that Plato's Socrates frequently anticipates himself; I merely suggest that on this particular occasion his exposition works in a carefully *cumulative* way.

[25] If it is, quite, yet the form that is at issue there: see n. 2 and text to n. 8 above.

[26] Cf. Glaucon at 509A. Neither Adimantus nor Glaucon, at any rate, has any inkling that the form is not *prakton* (see n. 22 above).

[27] I.e. *dikaion*: 'just', 'fair'?   [28] The verb is *echein*: 'to be allowed to'?

[29] See *Apology* 30B2–4, with chapter 1, pp. 69–70 above.

as the sun is not the same as sight, or light (or the eye), but provides the conditions for sight, so the good provides the conditions for knowledge without itself being knowledge, or truth.[30] So: the good isn't knowledge, as such (and it certainly isn't pleasure: 509A again), but it is what makes other things, like the just and the beautiful, knowable.

What is intended here may perhaps be illustrated by the case of the madman and his weapons in Book I (331C). Giving back what one owes will in general be just, but not always – not, for example, where giving something back will result in harm, to oneself or others (cf. 332B–C). Whether or not Socrates would accept this example as it stands, given his special notion of what it is to harm someone,[31] matters less than that it gives us the *type* of instance where knowing how something is good will allow it to be recognized as being what, as it were, it sets out to be. Someone who just has the rule 'give back what you owe' clearly won't have a proper grasp on what's just – given the cases where the rule fails to apply. He will have that grasp when he understands why it fails to apply, when it fails; which is (I suppose), because following the rule will lead to harm. So: the real criterion of justice is *goodness*. An action will be just only if it is good (but not all good actions will be just, justice being something that has to do peculiarly with our actions in relation to others: or so let us say, *more Aristotelico*).

But now it is only a short step from here to saying that it is that same action's being good that *makes* it just – which will give special point to the claim made in 505A2–4, that it is by virtue of their relation to the form of the good that 'just things and the rest come to be useful and beneficial'. Things *are* only just, etc., if they are good. Socrates couldn't say this, of course, earlier on, given that the goodness of justice – that is, of justice as ordinarily, vulgarly, understood – is precisely what was under challenge. But now that the good has been introduced, he can now at last say what he wanted to say earlier but couldn't. Given that Book VI, with Book VII, is framed by the argument about the advantageousness of justice, I find it hard to suppose that this essential relationship between justice and goodness is not at least a large part of what Socrates has in mind when summing up the moral of the sun simile in 509B7–10:

---

[30] This seems an uncontroversial enough, if partial, summary of 507C–509A. See 506A6–7: the future rulers of the best city won't have an adequate grasp of just and fine/beautiful things until they know the good. (Their case, until then, will be a counterpart of that of Socrates and his interlocutors, who don't have a proper handle on the just and the beautiful as a result of the merely provisional treatment of them down to the end of Book IV.)

[31] *Republic* I, 334D–335E.

[And then I think you'll also say that not only does their being known come to them from the good,] but also that both their being [sc. whatever they are?] and their *being* [sc. at all, as whatever they are?] come to them in addition [*proseinai*] from it, where the good is not being, but still [sc. higher than that,] the other side of being, superior to it in authority and power.

That is to say, if we take the example of justice, which is the one from which everything began and around which the whole dialogue pivots, a thing will be just, and *there in the world*, as a just thing, by virtue of the addition of goodness (sc. by addition to whatever it was already: a particular action in a particular context, etc.). But that, of course, does not mean that the form of goodness is the same as being – because, after all, by the rule that the attributes of particulars derive from their relationship to the relevant form, things ought to *be* by virtue of the form of being. No: here something's being (something) derives – also? – from its goodness, and so (by the same rule) from the form of the good.

But now we need to get to our puzzle, for the sun simile throws it in our face: the *sun itself* is, Socrates says, an 'offspring' of the good (507A3, 508B12–13). The language of 509B7–10 – the indented passage cited just above – in any case surely suggests that the 'power' of the good extends to making knowable *anything* that can in principle be known, and giving it its being.[32] And in the simile of the line, Socrates pictures the dialectician arriving at 'the starting-point (*archē*) of the all', i.e. presumably, of the *universe* (511B6–7); and in case anyone doubted that that was what Socrates meant, such doubts must be swept away by 517B–C, where Socrates completes his summing up of the outcomes of the image of the cave ('cause for everything of all things correct and beautiful, having given birth in the visible sphere to light and the lord of light, and in the intelligible sphere . . .': C2–3). All this being so, Socrates has obviously moved up a register. The good he is talking about now is the principle of everything. But how can it be that, when it was originally introduced in a way that suggested it was a purely *human* good? Here is the puzzle.

---

[32] We shall, I think, need to set some limits on the generative powers of the good. The basic idea is that justice, beauty and the rest (?) won't be present unless goodness is too, i.e. unless the relevant items or actions are beneficial – see especially the *Lysis* and the idea of the 'first friend' (on which see Penner and Rowe 2005, esp. 143–53, 273–9) and, for more direct testimony, *Gorgias* 468B8–C7 (with Penner and Rowe 2005: 251–68). But clearly the good won't actually bring the items and actions themselves into existence, except perhaps at a distant remove, i.e. insofar as the sun is its 'offspring', the sun provides the conditions of existence, etc. (These *Lysis* and *Gorgias* contexts may then be added to the list of what lies behind that 'you've heard it many times before' in the *Republic* VI context.)

There seems to be only a limited number of solutions available; indeed, so far as I can see, there are only two, apart from the wholly unpalatable suggestion that the divine Plato has momentarily nodded off. The first solution would be that Plato is having Socrates make the move which so many modern interpreters think he makes in any case, from one, more restricted and parochial, idea of the good (the 'Socratic' one) to a more generous and ambitious one (the 'Platonic'). And this will perhaps satisfy some – and may indeed need to satisfy others, who find themselves unable to move away from that version of a developmentalist model of interpretation that divides the dialogues between Socratic and Platonic, early and middle (and late). However so far as I can see Socrates gives not the slightest sign that he is shifting positions at all; on the contrary, as I have argued, he gives every indication that he thinks the content of the similes not only consistent but continuous both with what precedes them in the immediate context of the *Republic* and with the pre-*Republic* dialogues.[33]

The second solution, which my rejection of the first already indicates that I shall prefer, is that the alleged 'Platonic' (cosmic) view of the good is in essence an application or extension of the 'Socratic' (human, or humanist) view to a broader context (in fact, the broadest context possible);[34] Plato himself just does not distinguish them, and so feels at liberty to use either or both as the context demands. If *Republic* VI, 504–7 looks as if it is written from the standpoint of an exclusively human good, that is because the immediate context is restricted to the merely human – and similarly with all those contexts in pre-*Republic* dialogues to which it is connected. The idea that the good somehow 'binds together' everything in the universe, as Socrates puts it in the *Phaedo*,[35] is in my view a constant in Plato, emerging if and when it is relevant to his topic at any given moment. Before the *Republic*, this cosmic dimension of the good emerges mostly in the context of myths, which are the only occasions when Socrates tends to stray outside the city and human concerns; but it also surfaces outside the framework of myth, as in the *Apology*,[36] and in the *Gorgias*.[37] And there is also another limiting factor at work (which itself accounts for the general connection between the cosmic perspective and *myth*): Socrates' determined separation

---

[33] And with *Republic* I: see chapter 5 above, with Appendix.

[34] This, of course, puts things back to front: properly speaking, the human good will be an 'application' of a wider principle to the human sphere. (Equally obviously, I am not myself proposing that the narrower view is the Socratic one; that is what I am at pains to reject.)

[35] 99C5–6.

[36] That is, by virtue of Socrates' blithe *assumption* that he needn't consider the possibility that the universe is not philosopher-friendly.

[37] See *Gorgias* 507D–508A.

of himself from the scientists. This is one of the reasons that he concedes – Plato has him concede – that massive and explicit exposition of the role of the good in the cosmos in the *Timaeus* to someone else;[38] it is also part of the explanation of the brief and allusive nature of the reference to the good as the first principle of 'the all' in *Republic* VI–VII – though again, myth provides an opportunity for an expansion of the theme at the very end of the work.[39]

So how is the cosmic view of the good an extension – or 'application' – of the human view of it? I have nothing too complicated in mind. (There is also another pressing question that is raised by my preferred 'solution': how could the *cosmic* good be 'approachable', let alone something 'achievable' or 'doable' (*prakton*), even in the limited way I sketched in the context of *Republic* VII, 534–7? I shall turn to this question shortly.) The essential work is done in the *Phaedo*, a dialogue with which the *Republic* already has considerable connections, in a passage[40] where Socrates is giving an account of his intellectual development. He recounts how he once heard Anaxagoras, the famous scientist, reading from a book of his and saying that it was actually mind, or intelligence, that ordered everything and was the universal cause. He was delighted at this, he says;

and it seemed to me to be in a way excellent that mind should be responsible for everything, and I thought that, if this is so, then mind in its capacity as ordering orders everything and arranges each thing in whatever way was best for it to be; so if one wanted to discover the cause in relation to each thing, in what way it comes into being, or passes out of it, or is, what one needs to do is to discover how it is best for it to be or to do or have done to it anything else. So by this reasoning, I thought, it's fitting for a human being to investigate both in relation to that very thing [sc. human beings][41] and in relation to other things what is best and finest, and nothing else, though I also thought the same person needed to know what is worse, too, because the same knowledge was involved in both cases . . . I didn't for a moment think that, when he claimed that things were ordered by mind, he'd bring in some other cause for them, other than that it was best that they should be as they are; so I thought that, in assigning the cause to each of them [i.e. each thing] and to all of them in common, he would go on to explain what was best for each and what was the good common to all. (97C2–98D6)

---

[38] I.e. Timaeus. See the following chapter.

[39] I refer here, of course, to the myth of Er with which the *Republic* closes, which includes another sketch – rivalling that in the *Phaedo* – of the universe and of the way humanity fits within it.

[40] *Phaedo* 97B–99D.

[41] See Rowe 1993 ad loc.; the interpretation is Burnet's. My comment is '"Knowing oneself", then (the kind of knowledge that Plato's Socrates normally most desires: see e.g. *Phaedrus* 230A), becomes a matter of knowing what is best for oneself.'

But when he read what Anaxagoras had written, all Socrates' hopes were dashed, as he found him introducing all sorts of merely mechanical causes – just like other scientists. They all disregard the way in which 'the good and "binding" truly binds and holds things together' (99C5–6).

It is this last sentence, I believe, that explains the otherwise mysterious reference at *Republic* VI, 493C5 to 'the [true] nature of the necessary and good'. Socrates is there talking about how the sophist, with his version of 'wisdom', learns to understand and respond to the moods of the people as if of some monstrous beast, 'calling the things he's forced into [sc. accepting: *tanankaia*] just and beautiful, and as for how the nature of the necessary (*to anankaion*) and good differs from that, in reality, he neither will have seen nor be able to demonstrate to another' (493C4–6). Things that are truly just and beautiful will be identified only by someone who has 'seen' (and can give an account of) the – truly – good; what just and beautiful things are will flow, *necessarily*, from that.[42] If this is right – and I admit that it is no more than a possible explanation of the passage – then what I have called the 'cosmic' view of the good will already be in operation even before it is formally introduced; but then in a way that must be true in any case insofar as the passage is already, uncontroversially, slipping in a reference to the form of the good, which will then retrospectively carry all the baggage that will be loaded on to it after its formal introduction. And, of course, if the similes do implicitly refer to the *Phaedo* context, then the cosmic view will be – for those of us who have read the *Phaedo* – already built in to Socrates' life story; it forms part of a piece of self-conscious autobiography, a fact that is all the more significant in that the autobiography is constructed, for its subject, by his author. Plato *wants* us to associate that more ample view of the good with Socrates.

How, then, will any sort of cosmic good be 'doable', or however we put it; how on earth will such a thing be relevant to a *human* life, and indeed to a Socrates who claims that his preoccupation is with the human above, and even to the exclusion of, everything else?[43] How, to make the question seem even more difficult, could anyone suggest that 'every soul pursues' that sort of good (*Republic* VI, 505DII)? (This, of course, will be a problem for every interpretation, and not just for mine.) My response is simply to point to that *Phaedo* passage, and especially to the last part of the text cited: 'so I thought that, in assigning the cause to each thing and to all of them in common he would go on to explain what was best for each and what was the good common to all' (97B1–3). Socrates makes it as clear as he could

---

[42] Or they would, from a projected ideal grasp of the good.
[43] This was the important question I left hanging.

that he thinks that the same explanation will be applicable universally to everything, including human beings,[44] and that the explanation will be in terms of what is best for each thing. It will follow, then, that a true lover of wisdom, one who loves all wisdom,[45] will need to investigate *both* what is best for himself or herself, or human beings generally, *and* what is best for everything else, both severally and together ('to explain what was best for each and what was the good common to all'); only so will he or she be able to live a wise and happy life. The form of the good will be a kind of form of the 'best', i.e. best *for* things, a common something in all cases; and in seeking to realize it, we, in common with everything else, will be seeking to partake in whatever that best may be, in whatever form it is appropriate for each kind to partake in it.

That may sound rudimentary, even crude, and in desperate need of spelling out. In particular: what on earth could that 'common good' consist in? Plato no doubt had his own ideas, some of which may themselves surface from time to time in the dialogues;[46] but it will suffice for my present purposes if some general kind of sense can be attached to what – on my analysis of his text – he actually has Socrates present to us, and to his interlocutors. What Plato does not supply, it is not my business, in this book, to try to supply for him. And what his Socrates does say, in *Republic* and *Phaedo* taken together, seems to me to be exactly what, by implication, he presents it as being: clear so far as it goes, but in need of further explanation. That will go, particularly, for his suggestion that we *all* pursue the good, now understood as the principle of 'the all'. Construe this 'form' as a special kind of object, accessible only to reason, perhaps existing in some kind of imaginary space; then the notion that we pursue and desire it will look bizarre, even comic. But now suppose that what Socrates has in mind is something more like an Aristotelian universal, something like the happiness that even Aristotle is prepared to say that we all desire (even though 'happiness' will here be a universal); and suppose that other kinds, besides human beings, were capable of something – structurally? – so similar to happiness that it made sense to treat human happiness in tandem with the 'happiness' of other kinds. In that case, there would presumably be no problem about saying that individual human beings wanted happiness (universal) in this newly extended form. That is not to say that the form of the good is just a universal; I would claim, however, that the features that make it different from a universal – the very ones that allow those other

---

[44] See n. 41 above with text. Human *actions* will be part of what is to be explained: thus Socrates uses his own behaviour, and its causes, in order to make fun of mechanical explanations (*Phaedo* 98c–99A).

[45] *Republic* v, 474C–475C.

[46] The *Philebus* has seemed to many one promising place to begin looking; I leave the task to them.

notions of it, as a special kind of object, accessible only to reason . . . –
fail to disqualify it from being an object of pursuit and desire in the same
sort of way in which a universal may be pursued and desired.[47] And that, I
think, is amply demonstrated by what Socrates says in his 'autobiography'
in the *Phaedo*.

In any case, one of the chief outcomes of my analysis of that crucial
argument with the sight-lovers at the end of *Republic* v was that no one is
so benighted as to have *no inkling at all* about 'things in themselves'; and
that, I think, will apply to the form of the good as well as to other forms.
(In the language of the simile of the cave, even the most ignorant will have
before them images which relate to those originals in the pure air above; the
light reflected on the wall in front of them is itself somehow the product
of the sun.) However elevated an item the good is, still every soul has some
kind of contact with it – 'divining that it is something, but being at a loss
about it, and unable to grasp adequately what it might be', as Socrates puts
it (*Republic* vi, 505E1–2).

Of course we shall now need a clearer account of what a form really is, if
it isn't, exactly, a universal. That task I shall again postpone,[48] preferring to
round off the present chapter with a belated mention of two representative
interpretations of the form of the good in *Republic* vi–vii with which my
own has to compete.

These are (1) that the good in these books is some sort of impersonal, or
non-personal – or a 'non-self-referential' good;[49] (2) that the good is not
itself, after all, some separate item – some separate 'being' – alongside justice,
wisdom, etc., but the system represented by the excellences themselves,
each being a constituent part of the good.[50] (1) seems to me ruled out by
the connection of goodness with usefulness and benefit in 505A: 'by their
relation to the good just things and the rest *become useful and beneficial* –
how would a 'non-self-referential' good have such an effect? For its part,
interpretation (2) appears to rest, for its textual justification, primarily on
a single phrase: *ouk ousias ontos tou agathou* (vi, 509B9–10: briefly discussed
earlier in the present chapter), read as 'where the good is not a being'. Even

---

47 Another, blander way of putting it might be to say that we all desire our own end or *telos* (say, a
kind of flourishing), but that because of the interconnectedness of things in the universe we shall
not understand what that *telos* is apart from a general understanding of teleology, of the ends of all
kinds.
48 See the Epilogue below – though even there I shall have little more to offer beyond a few suggestive
remarks (again, much in the manner of Socrates himself).
49 See White 2002. White's position may be taken as representative of a certain type of approach, common among modern (again mainly Anglophone) interpreters, which has strong Kantian allegiances –
allegiances that are in my view already disabling enough, for the interpretation of any Platonic
context.
50 See Irwin 1995: 272–3.

if such an idea might make sense, it would come from nowhere; and 'not *a* being' is by no means the most natural reading of the Greek. What Socrates has said is that the form of the good is that by virtue of which just things, etc., become *good*. Now he says that it is responsible for things' *being*, which we might have expected to be the business of the form of being; is the good, then (we might ask) the same as being? No, says Socrates, they're two separate things. The form of being will be implicated, one imagines, but (I supply the underlying argument) it cannot work its effect on its own; it requires the good as co-worker. The good, then, has greater authority, is a higher and more powerful cause.[51]

However the second type of interpretation does, I think, have something important to offer. Plato's (Socrates') thinking focuses on 'things in themselves', or 'real natures' ('forms': *eidē, ideai*), and these in turn have fundamentally to do with the way things would ideally be – which Plato would have Socrates express as 'the way things really are'. If there is a good for everything, i.e. for every kind, and every individual member of every kind, and those goods are somehow reducible to a single 'thing in itself' or 'real nature', then there might be a way in which this single good could be seen as containing those separate goods in embryo – or as what generates those goods, as it is applied in different spheres or to different material (as it were). In that case, the 'form' of the good would be not just the principle of the system but, insofar as it was 'present', or 'shared in', by every part of reality, also in a way the system itself. And it is one of the requirements of the dialectician, who will 'see' the good, to be 'capable of seeing things together': 'for the person who can see things together has the skill of the dialectician, while the one who cannot, does not' (*ho . . . gar sunoptikos dialektikos, ho de mē ou: Republic* VII, 537C6–7). But exactly how all this would work, in detail, is unclear. Socrates is open about this; *he* doesn't know.[52] When Glaucon presses him to be more specific about

---

[51] It is not, then, 'beyond being', either, in the sense of being higher than existing things – too grand, even, to take the trouble (as it were) to exist.

[52] And, I add, we have no reason for thinking Plato would claim to know, either. The 'doctrinalist' sort of interpreter, obviously, will think he would; but their arguments – mainly readings of particular texts, like the one just cited, fail to convince me. In general, I believe that Plato consistently represents Socrates as a know-nothing, and it is not clear to me why what disqualifies Socrates from counting as a knower – fundamentally, the weaknesses of the only means available to humans for discovering the truth – should not also disqualify his author. And that leads to the stronger view that I have also consistently attributed to Plato, that knowledge lies beyond any human mind, insofar as any conclusions reached are only as good as the arguments supporting them, and there is no absolute guarantee of the strength of any argument. (The only alternative seems to be to rely on *self-evidence*; but Plato's/Socrates' practice shows little evidence of eagerness to go in that direction; argument is the thing.) But exploration, a research programme – that is quite another thing . . .

the manner of power that dialectic has, and what sorts of kinds it falls into [?], and again what roads it will follow – for these, now, it seems, would be the ones leading to the destination arrival at which would offer respite to the traveller, as if from the road, and an end to his journeying (532D8–E3: that is, 'enough with the preliminaries – cut to the chase!')

Socrates responds, in strikingly halting style that

You'll no longer be able to follow . . . . my dear Glaucon, though for my part there would be no lack of eagerness [sc. to help you?], nor would you any longer be seeing an image of what we're talking about, but the truth itself, as it appears to me – but whether genuinely so or not, it isn't worth insisting on going that far; but that there is such a thing to be seen, that one must insist on – right? (533A1–6)

This is a difficult passage to interpret, and I think Plato has deliberately made it so.[53] The most pressing question is what Socrates is saying 'appears to him'. Is he saying (i) 'if you could follow, you'd see the truth as it [the truth] appears to me', or (ii) 'you'd see the truth, or at any rate it appears to me that you would'? The balance must be in favour of (i), though I think it is a close-run thing, and meant to be – because Plato needs Socrates to preserve his implicit claim that he only has '*beliefs without knowledge*' (VI, 506C6). Such beliefs Socrates described as 'all ugly', 'and the best of them are blind – or do you think that those who believe something true without intelligence [i.e., knowledge?] are any different from blind people going down a road in the correct direction?' (506C7–9). Socrates, then, is at best a blind person on the right road, and so he won't even know that he's on the right one, i.e. the one leading to the truth; still less will he know that his view of what's at the end of the road he's travelling (even if it's the right one) is correct. But that there is a destination like the one he has been describing, albeit through images, *that* he will insist on. The net effect of the passage, as I see it, is to throw cold water on Glaucon's naive optimism – very cold water, if I am right that Socrates is (also) claiming not even to be in a position to assert that anyone who followed the correct dialectical path – or paths? – would see 'the truth itself'.[54] Once again, he stops short of committing himself to saying that anyone (anyone who is merely human) will achieve full knowledge of the good, even if that is what we all passionately desire.

---

[53] See Rowe 2002c.

[54] So (of course) not everything is already familiar and known, from the pre-*Republic* dialogues. What is important to my case is only that the cosmic aspect of the good is not unknown to the Socrates of these dialogues; he just does not talk about it much (as, in many contexts, he doesn't talk about many things he *could* talk about).

CHAPTER 10

Republic *and* Timaeus: *the status of Timaeus' account of the physical universe*

Of the small but elite group of Plato's latest dialogues the *Timaeus* is the only one to which I shall devote a chapter – and it will be a short chapter, dealing with a single but quite crucial aspect of the dialogue: the status of the account that Plato has the main speaker, Timaeus, give of the cosmos and its origins, together with the closely connected question of Plato's, and Socrates', relationship to this Timaeus. (What I present here, as in the previous chapter, will be a sketch, on outline of an idea, but one that is not only consistent with but grows directly from the argument of the book as a whole.) My brief treatment of this dialogue is intended to show the application to the *Timaeus* of my special thesis[1] about the reasons why Plato chooses, in his late dialogues, not to use Socrates in the leading role that he reserved almost exclusively for him in the first two dialogue groups. Given my larger thesis about the closeness, even virtual identity, of Plato to his character Socrates, the question why, in the latest group, he should promote others to this role, in five out of six cases,[2] is clearly pressing. Before, he has

---

[1] First announced in the Preliminaries, section 3.

[2] *Timaeus, Critias* (short and unfinished: a fragment), *Sophist, Politicus,* and *Laws; Philebus* alone has Socrates in his customary role. In *Laws* Socrates neither appears nor is referred to; but his presence nonetheless is assured through the close links of the dialogue not only with the *Republic – Laws* constructs another imaginary city, Magnesia, which is at least a distant cousin of Callipolis – but with a whole range of other dialogues; and also through a curious passage in which the Nocturnal Council, the body ultimately charged with maintaining the founding principles of the city, is envisaged as rooting its activity in what looks for all the world like a recreation of Socratic conversation (the Visitor from Athens tries to initiate such a conversation with one of his interlocutors, on the familiar subject of the unity of excellence, but has to abort it because his partner is not up to it: *Laws* XII, 962–6). But the evidence for Socrates' presence is perhaps strongest in the moral psychology of the *Laws*: while he lays heavy stress on the need for *training* in the excellences, of the sort Socrates describes in *Republic* II–III, his reassertion of the old Socratic maxim 'no one goes wrong willingly' (*Laws* V, 731C, 734B; IX, 860D; cf. *Timaeus* 86D–E) means that the Visitor's diagnosis of human error is still fundamentally intellectual. We need training early on, for example in the context of drinking-parties (which figure prominently in the early parts of the *Laws*), not so much for the purposes of a kind of Aristotelian habituation in the excellences, but because it helps us to make the right choices in relation to our desires, and the place we are to give them in our lives. The Visitor's intellectualist leanings may also be visible in his proposal for persuasive preambles to the laws of the city.

only done this once, in the *Parmenides*, and even there, in a way, Socrates is fully himself: certainly not leading the discussion, but then he is, in this dialogue, still a young man, who could scarcely be represented as anything but a mature student to the great Parmenides. The Eleatic philosopher raises some incisive questions about the way the young Socrates thinks about forms, and gives him some exercises to develop his dialectical fitness; the overall effect is to present him as a good philosopher, but not yet one of the first rank. (This is much as he presents himself in the *Theaetetus*, now as an old man; as far as he is concerned, evidently, he has not fulfilled the promise Parmenides saw in him. Now that *is* the familiar Socrates, indeed the Socrates of the *Apology*.) But in that case the question why Plato so regularly demotes Socrates in the last group becomes all the more urgent – certainly from the point of view of my own argument. Indeed, it might even seem to constitute a *prima facie* case for cutting back what I have called my larger thesis, and saying that the last period of his writing marked Plato's finally breaking away from his master.

However this would be an over-reaction. The continuities between the last group of dialogues and the earlier ones run deep;[3] nor are there are any shared features among the members of the last group, apart from their lateness and their treatment of Socrates (with the notable exception of the *Philebus*),[4] that would justify our treating them separately from the generality of the dialogues – and so as a 'group' in any sense other than the chronological one. *If* my thesis holds for the earlier groups of dialogues, then it should in principle also hold for the latest group:[5] Socrates, and

---

[3] For the *Laws*, see preceding note. On the alleged development of Plato's political thinking after the *Republic*, see especially Laks 1990, Schofield 2006: 60–2, and e.g., Rowe 2007; the case for such a development will have to be made afresh, if it can be made at all, which I myself doubt.

[4] For some preliminary ideas about the *Philebus* (some of which will require modification in the light of the present book), see Rowe 1999.

[5] This may well seem, at least to some, an extraordinarily cavalier way of dismissing one of the longest-standing (modern) views of the later Plato, as the period in which – if we tack on the *Theaetetus* as at least an honorary late dialogue, because of its connection with *Sophist* and *Politicus* as well as because of its philosophical quality – Plato came to his senses and junked the excesses, especially metaphysical, of his 'middle' period (having already moved on from his 'Socratic' period). I make only the most muted apology for my behaviour here, because the kind of narrative just sketched was always poorly supported by the evidence. (Most, indeed, would now claim to regard it as largely discredited, but vestiges of it regularly reappear in the literature.) Everything depends (a) on how we reconstruct Platonic metaphysics (and other relevant aspects of his thinking), and especially on the degree of respectability with which it emerges from our analysis (which should have at least some bearing on Plato's willingness to junk it, and to the degree to which we may hope and expect him to do so), and (b) on whether there is actually any evidence for his having junked it. On (b), I observe merely that the fact that Plato does not directly mention an idea that was previously in his head – as, in the latest dialogue group, he allegedly fails to mention forms – in no way shows that he has ceased to hold it; differences of language, context, perspective, and above all of audience may be

what he represents, are as important in this new context as they were in the old (and after all, he is actually still *there*, except in the *Laws*, either as one of the interlocutors, or in the *Philebus* as main speaker). So the choice not to have him leading is a tactical one. What is behind this tactical shift? For *Sophist, Politicus* and *Laws* I have already indicated my answer. In each case the design of the dialogue demands a figure of some authority: in the first two, to provide illustrations of the application of a new kind of method, and in the third to help put together, and justify, a whole body of legislation. For such roles Plato's Socrates is obviously unsuited, and his place is taken by individuals to whom their author gives only a provenance, not a name – and whose provenance gives a hint about the source of their authority (the Visitor from Elea is in the tradition of Parmenides,[6] the visitor from Athens in the tradition of Solon).[7] If that already seems to imply *Plato's* taking on the same authority (and so, after all, separating himself from Socrates), the answer is that these anonymous figures are themselves, as inventions, also projections, like the philosopher-rulers of the *Republic*; in any case, if we follow out the implications of Socrates' critique in the *Phaedrus* of writing as a medium,[8] Plato would be too sensible a writer to claim for himself the kind of authority that his shadowy characters project.

What then of the *Timaeus*? This seems to be a different case, for if Timaeus is an authority, he also, in relation to some subjects, offers a kind

---

involved, in ways that I hope to have illustrated sufficiently in earlier parts of this book. And these same factors will also be relevant to (a). There is astonishingly little agreement even now between interpreters about what a Platonic form is, not least because of the flexibility of the writing on which we depend for understanding whatever it was that Plato had in mind. Nor can we assume that he felt that *he* had fully understood what was in his mind; certainly not if he was as genuine a Socratic as I suppose him to have been. And insofar as I myself think I have grasped any of what he did have in mind, I confess that I myself find it not only philosophically defensible but attractive: see especially Penner and Rowe 2005: ch. 11. So I, for one, would be disappointed to find that he had let it go. I say nothing about the fact that the *Parmenides*, which is usually treated, by those who think Plato rethought his 'middle' thinking, as the best evidence for such rethinking, is not itself one of the latest group of dialogues – which itself tends to reinforce the general point that there is nothing that unifies that group, in itself, except its lateness, and (with one major exception) its treatment of Socrates.

[6] So in the tradition of a philosopher who has already fictionally encountered Socrates (in the *Parmenides*), and taught him a thing or two.

[7] The large overlap between the actual laws of Magnesia and Athenian law is documented by Morrow in Morrow 1993. The *justification* behind the two systems is of course entirely different; there is no suggestion that Plato thought Solon, or any other Athenian legislator, to be a philosopher. In fact the *Timaeus* could be taken as suggesting that he was a better *poet* – even while making him an intermediate source for the history/fantasy of a primitive Athens after the model of Callipolis (the Athens of the *Timaeus-Critias*, which defeated Atlantis), and so in a thoroughly indirect and remote way linking him with Plato's own political projects (*Timaeus* 20D–21D).

[8] On which see the following chapter.

of disclaimer of authority, saying that he can offer only a 'likely story', or 'likely account' (*eikōs muthos*):[9]

'If, then, Socrates, in many respects on many subjects, on gods and the coming into being of the whole (*tou pantos*), we turn out to be incapable totally and wholly (*pantēi pantōs*) to deliver accounts (*logoi*) that are in agreement themselves with themselves, and made precise, don't be surprised; but if, in that case, the accounts we render are less likely than none [i.e. than no other account that has or could be offered?], one must be content, remembering that I who speak and you the judges possess a nature that is human, so that in relation to these things it is fitting to accept the likely account and seek for nothing further beyond that (*prepei toutou mēden pera zētein*). (*Timaeus* 29C4–D3)

The closing words of the cited passage hold a particular interest, because we have met a similar phrasing before, and in a key context. This was at *Republic* VI, 504C, which saw Socrates contrasting his own dissatisfaction at anything less than the 'longer road' with the attitude of some others, who 'think that [not to have gone the whole way] is already good enough, and that there is no need to look any further' (*ouden dein peraiterō zētein*).[10] The category includes Glaucon and Adimantus, who were perfectly happy – Glaucon has just confirmed that they still are (504B8) – with the account of the excellences in Book IV, and the account of the soul on which it was based, even though both were obtained by just the corner-cutting methods that Socrates now says won't do (either for him or for the future rulers of the best city). Now as it turned out, the chief failing of the methods in question was that they started from the way things appear; in particular, from the soul as it appears in the context of 'the life of a human being' (*Republic* X, 612A5),[11] i.e. – as I proposed to take it – (a) in its embodied state, and (b) in a typically 'fevered' version of that state,[12] as opposed to starting from the 'true' state of the soul. The backward reference to the *Republic* that Plato

---

[9] Timaeus generally treats *eikōs muthos* as interchangeable with *eikōs logos* (see Morgan 2000: 272 n. 52); Timaeus is not, then, claiming to tell a story, or a 'myth' (as is frequently claimed). On the other hand he is claiming that part of what he says amounts to no more than a 'likely', or 'plausible', account. Cf. Burnyeat 2005.

[10] VI, 504C2–4. For a very different kind of 'you'll seek for nothing further', see *Phaedo* 107B9 ('you'll seek for nothing further' – sc. because you'll have reached the end of the *argument*, and the conclusion will have been established).

[11] 'As it is, we have gone through its [the soul's] experiences, and its kinds, in its human life', i.e. as part of the composite, soul + body, that we call a human being. With that approach Socrates contrasts seeing the soul as it is in itself – one way of doing which is to picture it after death, when it leaves the body behind; but the object of inquiry is still the soul as it really is, even during its sojourn in the body (as the immediate context in Book X clearly shows).

[12] Where 'fever' was associated particularly with the enjoyment of luxuries (the verb was *truphan* (II, 372E3), used of the city; but then, for the city-soul analogy to work, the starting-point in both cases – that of soul as well as of city – must have been the same).

puts into Timaeus' mouth[13] – that is, in 29D2–3: 'seek for nothing further' – is designed, I suggest, to recall precisely the contrast which is ultimately in question in the original context, i.e. between approaching things from their surface appearance, and approaching them as they are 'in themselves'.

In short, my proposal will be that when Timaeus says that he will be unable to give wholly accurate accounts of many subjects (citing 'gods and the coming into being of the whole'), and that 'it is fitting to accept the likely account and seek for nothing further beyond that', at least part of the reason for his inability to do better is that the *kind of things* he is basing his accounts on, in the case of these 'many things', is itself incapable of offering any more (more than a 'likely account/story') – because, in such cases, he will be basing his accounts on *the way things appear*. I say carefully 'at least part of the reason' because, of course, the immediate explanation Timaeus offers for his incapacity is that he himself, like the others who will judge him, is no more than human. But that cannot be the whole explanation. In the sentence under discussion Timaeus is building on a contrast that he has just introduced between two kinds of accounts, *logoi*: if they deal with stable and lasting things, they will themselves be 'lasting and unchanging – to the extent that it belongs to *logoi* to be unrefutable and undefeatable, they must in no respect fall short of this' (29B7–C1);[14] whereas if they deal with what is merely modelled on that first sort of thing, and is an *eikōn* (an 'image'), sc. as they will do if we are talking about the sensible world, then our *logoi*, 'being of what is an image (*eikōn*), will be [merely] likely (*eikotes*) and in proportion to those others: what being is to coming into being, this truth is to conviction' (C2–3).[15] So, it seems, Timaeus' account, 'of gods and the coming into being of the whole' (and no doubt of other things), will apparently be merely 'likely' – also[16] – because of the nature of the objects it deals with, that is, sensible, physical things, which are 'modelled after', 'images' of, the stable reality of forms.[17]

---

[13] Timaeus was not one of those present on the occasion of the conversation represented by the *Republic*; in fact Socrates is the only one of the interlocutors in the *Timaeus* who was there. The city that Socrates describes at the beginning of the *Timaeus*, and says they discussed 'the day before' (17A2), is nevertheless unmistakeably a version of Callipolis, albeit with its main feature – the union of political power and philosophy – suppressed, or rather *almost* suppressed (see further below); that there is a close relationship between the two texts is therefore already a given, and references between the two, in whichever direction (see below) should not be surprising.

[14] For this passage see chapter 8, pp. 235–6 above.

[15] 'Conviction' is *pistis*, the term assigned to the third rather than the lowest part of the divided line in *Republic* VI (511E1). See further below.

[16] I.e. in addition to the explanation based on human weakness (if that is a separate explanation: could the point be just that, being human, Timaeus and the others sometimes have nothing better than sensible things to work with?).

[17] The identity of the 'stable reality' Timaeus is referring to is guaranteed by other parts of his treatment.

But this already looks pretty odd. In the first place, Timaeus will apparently be suggesting that the *gods* are themselves 'images', modelled after an original; and while it is true that Timaeus' account represents the visible gods (the heavenly bodies, the earth and the universe itself) and other gods besides as created, the same cannot be said of the god – the divine craftsman or 'demiurge' – who created them.[18] Again, why should the fact that accounts of 'images' are of 'images' by itself tend to make them merely likely accounts (of those same 'images')? There might be an answer to that question, but Timaeus does not provide it; instead he seems to leave us, and his interlocutors, with a mere pun: accounts will be merely likely, *eikotes*, because they are of images, *eikones*.

And perhaps that is all there is to it: accounts, *logoi*, will be of a kind with, related (*suggeneis*) to, the things they are accounts of (of which they are *exhēgētai*, 29B4–5), and that is that. Or perhaps that is as far as Timaeus can go. There is circumstantial evidence that his capacities are limited: at any rate *Plato* has, and perhaps will have, plenty more to say than Timaeus says about both the subjects specified, gods and the beginning of things,[19] and the fact that Timaeus actually recommends not looking any further than what he will be offering seems on the face of it to put him in implicit conflict both with Socrates generally and, in particular, with the Socrates of *Republic* VI, 504. So long as there actually is more to be said, as Plato seems to demonstrate that he himself thinks there is, Timaeus looks like one of those people whom – with Glaucon and Adimantus immediately in mind – Socrates disapprovingly describes as thinking the incomplete 'already good enough'.

I shall return a little later to the question of Timaeus' own standing, and how Plato locates him in relation to himself (and Socrates). For the

---

[18] Taylor 1928: 74 claims, extraordinarily, that in Timaeus' phrase 'on gods and the coming into being of the whole' the reference is exclusively to the coming into being of gods – as if Plato had written 'on the coming into being of gods and the whole' (with *theōn* depending on *geneseōs*, as – from the word-order – it plainly cannot).

[19] Actually, according to what Plato/Socrates says, the universe had *no* beginning; that, at any rate, is the implication of the argument for the immortality of the soul in *Phaedrus*; immortality is derived from the nature of the soul as first and ungenerated cause – and the same position, I believe (without being able to demonstrate my belief), lurks behind the rhetoric of the Athenian Visitor's case against the atheist in *Laws* x (a book which in any case has quite a lot to say about gods that Timaeus doesn't say). Fleeting references like that at *Republic* VII, 530A6 to the 'craftsman of the heavens' (where Socrates is talking about what the 'true' astronomer will think), or at *Politicus* 273B2 to 'the craftsman and father' of the universe (cf. 'maker and father' at *Timaeus* 28C3) do rather little to suggest that Plato's views had settled around the scheme of the *Timaeus* and its account of a divine creation – given, that is, that there is another and better qualified candidate available for the role of 'father': see main text below.

moment, what matters is that *Plato* has more in mind than a mere pun,[20] and presumably expects us to look beyond it. Timaeus does not know it, but the whole passage is redolent of, and builds on, Socrates' argument in *Republic* v–vii, beginning with the conversation at the end of Book v with the 'sight-lovers'.[21] Things in the visible world are 'modelled on', 'images of', 'what is', and if one sets out to give an account of the 'images' themselves, rather than of the originals, then the result will be no more than likely; so says Timaeus. Compare with this what Socrates said to the sight-lovers (I give a highly selective version): knowledge is a matter of grasping what is (beauty); if you think particulars (particular beautiful things), which are only like what is, are all there is, then you won't have more than belief – that is, as I argued, belief *about what is* (about what beauty is), which is what, unbeknownst to themselves, the sight-lovers are actually referring to when they say or think that any particular thing is beautiful.

To be more precise, and to focus more closely on the *Timaeus* passage: if the play on *eikōn/eikōs* is to be more than a mere play, then there must be a likeness between (decent) accounts of the 'images' and (decent) accounts of the originals; let us say that the former sort must approximate to the latter, just as images are approximations of originals. But we know in any case that the originals are what provide the proper explanation of the images. The point is exemplified, I think, by the treatment of soul and the excellences in the *Republic*. There is on the one hand the soul as it appears in the world as it is, and there are the excellences as they appear in such a world; and one can give an account of them as such (Socrates actually does). But on the other hand there is the 'true' soul, and there are the philosophical, non-demotic excellences (Socrates does not give an account of them, and indeed implies that he cannot, insofar as he cannot give a satisfactory account of the good, which makes them what they are); and just as this kind of soul, and of excellence, resembles, and is an approximation to, the other, so the account of this kind of soul and of excellence merely resembles, and is an approximation to, the other.

This appears to me to make good sense of the *Timaeus* passage. The upshot will be that insofar as Timaeus' account is directed towards 'this' cosmos,[22] that is, the 'image' fashioned after the eternal model, then it

---

[20] Something that ought to be objectionable in a passage that pretends to be meticulously, even pedantically, argued.

[21] That the *Timaeus* recognizes (as it were) the *Republic* v passage is guaranteed by 51–2, on which see chapter 6 above.

[22] And does not look beyond it – thus being an account *of* it, in its own terms, as opposed to being an account of 'stable being'.

will be merely likely, *just because he will be substituting a necessarily less true account for a truer one* – the one substituted being, still, in a way, an account *of* the model, only of the model as realized in the 'image'. A proper, truer, account of what the cosmos *is* (a 'true' cosmos) would be in terms of the original. But then of course that would miss out much of the detail, namely the part of it that derived from the difference between image and original, the fact that an image can't be an exact copy, that it will involve some kind of substrate, and so on. The account that takes care of all this detail will be only 'likely' because it will present the cosmos as it appears; to get the true account, one would have to go behind these appearances, to 'what things really are'.[23] But since the appearances[24] would be left out in the *true* account, then there will be a necessary limit to the degree to which the 'likely' account that includes them will be able to claim to represent the truth. So, in this case, Timaeus will be perfectly correct to recommend that we should 'look for nothing further' than his account, that is, on the basis of the approach it uses: that kind of approach is capable of offering us no more (providing only, as Timaeus adds, that his account is no less 'likely' than any other, sc. any other that uses the same approach).[25]

[23] For a further, and important, application of the same idea, see the contrast Socrates draws in the *Republic* (VII, 528D–530C) between astronomy as it is currently practised, i.e. observational astronomy, and a reformed astronomy that would study 'true' motions, etc. (fine though the things in the heavens and their movements are, they 'fall far short of the true movements . . . ', 529D1–2).

[24] These would belong firmly to that segment of the divided line to which 'conviction', *pistis*, is allocated (cf. n. 15 above); there would be no 'understanding' (*nous, noēsis*) of them.

[25] For an example of one kind of interpretation that I am proposing to reject (and that is now almost universally rejected), see Taylor 1928: 'When all possible precautions have been taken, the measurements of physical magnitudes are necessarily approximate and would remain so even if we had not to allow for the possible modifications of every hypothesis in natural science by the discovery of new "appearances". We are dependent for the simplest actual measurements on the evidence of our senses. The senses are not infinitely acute and they only testify to what is given at this or that place and time, and Plato rightly insists on the point' (Taylor 1928: 73). It is of course also the case, for Timaeus (as no doubt for Plato), that no satisfactory account may be given of phenomenal objects, by themselves: he has made this point in 27D–28A, in distinguishing – much in the mode used by Socrates in the divided line simile – between 'what is graspable by understanding together with *logos* [i.e. which can give an account of itself], always being in the same way', and 'what for its part is the object of belief together with perception that lacks a *logos* [i.e. which cannot give an account of itself]' (28A1–3). But by the time we have reached 29C–D, and the introduction of the notion of the 'likely account/story', we have moved on to a new stage in the argument, introduced by 29B1–5 (cf. Johansen 2004: 161–2): 'and given all this, there is every necessity that this cosmos is an image of something. It is most important, with every subject, to begin at its natural beginning. [In the present case, by implication, the 'beginning' is to establish what the status of the account of the cosmos, just begun, will be.] Well (*oun*), in relation to an image and its original, one must make a distinction of this kind: that accounts are of a kind with [share the features of] the things they are accounts of . . .' Thus accounts of what is stable will be stable, while accounts of what has been modelled on something else, and so is an image, will be merely likely (and so on). What we might have expected is some reference to the nature of the image as shifting, moving ('becoming'), to contrast with the

But what of the examples that Timaeus actually cites, among the 'many things' on which he claims it will be 'fitting' to stop with the 'likely account' – 'gods and the coming into being of the whole'? It seems scarcely conceivable that the phrase is not intended to include the most powerful and significant god of all, the creator, and his role in the coming into being of the universe, since these are the very things Timaeus is in the middle of talking about.[26] Since, given Timaeus' scheme, the creator is definitely not part of the 'image' represented by the physical cosmos, I suggest that the phrase must be taken as a hendiadys: what he intends is 'the role of gods in the coming into being of the whole'. Now that *is* a part of the 'image', insofar as it relates to the history of this cosmos; and Timaeus handles it precisely by reasoning from the way the cosmos actually appears. 'Did it come into being?' he asked at 28B: 'yes', he says, on the grounds that it is perceptible, and perceptible things are things that come into being and 'are begotten' (*gennēta*, 28B2). But the last move, on which everything else depends, is justified only by analogy with things as we now see them; there is nothing to prevent there being things that 'come into being', by continually changing and moving, but have no beginning in time – of which the cosmos might be one.[27]

So according to Timaeus, to say that the cosmos was created by a divine craftsman will be part of an account that is – at least – no less likely than any rival account (29C7–8), but still only *likely*. Whether Plato's position is any different from Timaeus' will depend on whether he thinks that the true account of the cosmos, in terms of 'what is', will make room for a creation, exclude it, or leave it as an open possibility. My own preference is for saying that he thinks he can do without a creation. He already has a 'father' for the cosmos, in the shape of the form of the good – which somehow, according

---

stability of the original, and the corresponding changeability of accounts of the image; for that, we have to wait until 51E4 ('[understanding] is immovable by persuasion, while persuasion can change [belief]'). Timaeus for the moment leaves us to make this and other connections, while elaborating his pun. (Sensible things, the 'images', move around, as it were; as Socrates puts it in the *Republic* (VI, 484B5–6), they make people 'wander' by 'being in all sorts of conditions'.) – For what I take to be the mildly ironic tone in which Socrates responds to Timaeus' instructions about how his account is to be received ('Splendid . . . and one must absolutely receive your account as you urge': 29D4–5), Ingo Gildenhard nicely compares Cicero's (?) 'Macte virtute!' at *Tusculan Disputations* 1.40.1 (*q.v.* in its context).

[26] What is more, the first item that is said to be 'in accordance with the likely account (*logos*)' is that 'this cosmos did in truth come into being as a living creature with soul and intelligence through the forethought of the god' (30B8–C1) – a conclusion that is derived from, among other things, reasoning from the analogy of things in the visible world (30B1–3).

[27] As Plato, or his characters, are prepared to envisage in other contexts. It would have been good to identify Timaeus as one of the originators of the argument from design; sadly, it is the goodness of the creator rather than his existence that is derived from the goodness of creation (29D7–30C1).

to Socrates in *Republic* VI, has the sun as its 'offspring' (507A3, together with its sequel), and has other, fairly unspecified, generative powers (509B); and the form is not something that could act at all, let alone at some particular moment. It will, then, be a sustaining cause. But meanwhile Plato as author can make hay with the image of a benevolent divine creator, which he duly does: the 'story' of the *Timaeus* can now unfold.[28]

This last part of my own account is not in the least original; but my route to it, *via* an alleged distinction between Timaeus' perspective and Plato's own, is so far as I know quite new.[29] And many may be inclined to reject that move, distancing Plato from his speaker, out of hand. However I shall close this chapter by pointing to what I take to be two additional signals of Plato's intention to hold himself aloof, at least in some respects, from his creation (Timaeus and *his* creation). The first such signal comes from a curious passage on the origin of species at the end of the dialogue: birds, it seems, are descended from 'innocent but lightweight men, experts in the things above, but who were in the habit of thinking, in their simplicity, that the firmest proofs about these things were through sight' (91D6–E1). Now in one way Timaeus is no bird, because he is aware of the shortcomings of visual and other perceptual evidence.[30] At the same time there is a sense of his beginning to sprout feathers instead of hair just at that point when he derives 'generated' from 'came into being', apparently on the basis that what we see and touch all comes to be and passes away (28A–C); and when he proposes that, when it comes to the history of the universe, and the ultimate causes of things, the best we can do is to rely on analogies with ordinary sensible experience. Just as Timaeus' account starts with a caution about its status, or the status of 'many' of its elements, so Plato closes it with another such caution – and one, I propose, that to some degree, and despite his evidently thorough philosophical grounding, also applies to Timaeus himself.

The second signal that we are meant to harbour doubts about Timaeus' status in Plato's eyes comes from what I take to be somewhat mixed mes-

---

[28] In this way, Timaeus' account does after all become a kind of *muthos*; and it might even be that 29D3 itself, which first introduces the idea of the *eikōs muthos*, in the context of the theme of 'gods and the coming into being of the whole', will contain a smidgeon of the idea of 'likely *myth*'. However the main work is in any case done by 'likely', *eikōs*, not by the term *muthos*.

[29] For a first and very rough sketch of the basic explanation of the phrase 'likely story' I have now offered, see Rowe 2003b (which the account in the present chapter now mostly replaces). I note that on my account those interpreters – beginning with Aristotle – who claimed that Plato seriously believed in a creation will be failing to take sufficiently into account the author's relationship to his characters.

[30] To that extent he will certainly be the 'true astronomer' of *Republic* VII, 530A (who will talk about 'the craftsman of the heavens': see n. 19 above).

sages, at the beginning of the dialogue, about his qualifications. True, Socrates does say of him that 'in my opinion he has reached the pinnacle (*akron*) of philosophy as a whole [all of philosophy: *philosophia hapasa*]' (20A4–5), which might be thought to be all the recommendation he could possibly need.[31] But there is more to what Socrates says about Timaeus than meets the eye, both here and in other parts of the passage: 'philosophy as a whole' is hardly the most obvious way of referring to *dialectic*; and other parts of Socrates' recommendation, too, make it look more like a general character-reference, of the sort that would appeal to politicians and statesmen of the sort that the other speakers, Critias and Hermocrates, and indeed Timaeus himself, clearly are. Timaeus is from a splendidly governed city; he's wealthy and from a good family; he's held the highest office in his city; 'and again in my opinion he has reached the pinnacle of philosophy as a whole'. In the event, he does seem to know a great deal about the outcomes of Platonic and Socratic philosophizing; but then, of course, he was part of the conversation 'yesterday', which both was and wasn't the conversation of the *Republic*. And that connection cuts both ways, because the account of the conversation that Socrates provides for the benefit of his interlocutors makes little or nothing of the idea, so central to the *Republic*, of philosophical rule. One explanation for that, I suggest, is that none of Socrates' interlocutors could even remotely claim to be philosopher-rulers, Callipolis-style; 'yesterday's' conversation would then have had partly to be, by implication, a critique of their own political conduct – but for the purposes of the *Timaeus* and *Critias*[32] they are represented as authorities in their fields.[33] Or rather, at least in Timaeus' case, an authority *up to a point*.[34]

---

[31] Cf. *akroi eis philosophian* at *Republic* VI, 499C7.

[32] And of the third member of what was evidently intended to be a trilogy, *Hermocrates*, which remained unwritten.

[33] For a more detailed discussion of the issues, see Rowe 2004a, which is in dialogue with Schofield 1999: 31–50, Schofield 1997 (1999), and Kamtekar 1997 (1999).

[34] Timaeus' main field is identified by Critias at 27A3–5 ('the biggest expert in astronomy among us, and the one who has made it most his business to know about the nature of the universe').

CHAPTER II

*Plato on the art of writing and speaking (*logoi*): the* Phaedrus

The *Phaedrus* is – like so many other dialogues of Plato's – one of a kind. It appears to reach its climax with one of the most memorable pieces of Platonic writing (the great myth of the chariot of the soul), only to go on to treat it as a starting-point for a dry discussion of what Socrates calls the 'art[1] of words (*logoi*)'.[2] What emerges at the end of this discussion, between Socrates and Phaedrus, an amateur enthusiast for rhetoric, is a critique[3] of writing as a medium of communication, and a strong statement of preference for the spoken word, in the particular form of dialectic between master dialectician and student. It is the critique of writing, together with the description of a new, philosophical rhetoric that frames it, that will be the main subject of the present short (and last) chapter.

The basic lines of a coherent interpretation of the *Phaedrus* were laid down by W. H. Thompson in the introduction to his edition of the dialogue, published in 1868.[4] The dialogue starts, after some preliminaries, with Phaedrus reading an exhibition speech by – the person we know as – the great Attic orator Lysias on the theme 'a boy should grant (sc. sexual) favours to the man who is not in love him rather than one who is'. Socrates then offers a short, rival speech on the same subject, but then pretends to repent of his implied attack on the god Eros, and gives a second, much longer speech, now in praise of Love; this is the part that includes the comparison of the soul to a charioteer (reason) and his two horses, one white (corresponding to the 'spirited' part in the *Republic*) and one black (the appetitive part). Thompson proposed, and he is surely right, that the

---

[1] Or 'expertise', or 'science': that familiar term *technē* again.   [2] I.e. of speaking and writing.

[3] By Socrates, of course. It is not clear whether, by the end of the conversation, Phaedrus has lost any of his addiction to the products of contemporary rhetoric (mostly written as well as performed: see below); at most, he agrees to think about it. Paradoxically, in a dialogue that will talk about the need to match speech to audience, Plato seems to have given Socrates an interlocutor with little talent for the Socratic sort of talk.

[4] See Rowe 1986, of which the present chapter is the briefest of summaries; some small modifications are there made to Thompson's treatment. See also Rowe 1988.

eventual function of this second speech in the economy of the dialogue is to provide a sample of Plato's own writing/Socratic speaking,[5] representing the 'art of words' as it can and should be applied; in the second part of the dialogue Socrates then shows the superiority of this kind of *logos* to the products of 'the art of speaking', i.e. rhetoric, as it is currently practised, before finally comparing it, to its disadvantage (for all its brilliance), with the process of living dialogue. One of the key moments in the *Phaedrus*, for Thompson's interpretation, is when Socrates claims of the sensible and knowledgeable writer[6] that he will not be in earnest about writing, 'with words that are incapable of speaking in their own support, and incapable of adequately teaching what is true' (the two main deficiencies Socrates has identified in writing as a medium), but will write, when he writes, 'for the sake of amusement': 'A very fine form of amusement it is you're talking of, Socrates . . .' responds Phaedrus: 'that of the man who is able to amuse himself with words, *telling stories about justice and the other subjects you speak of*' (277D2, E1–3). Thompson takes this as a reference to Socrates' second speech:

It [the speech] relates to Justice: for that virtue, according to the Platonic Socrates, consists in the due subordination of the lower appetites to Reason, aided, not thwarted, by the impulsive or irascible principle; and this subordination is figured by the charioteer holding well in hand the restive steed, while he gives the rein to his nobler and upward-striving yoke-fellow.[7] It may also justly be said to embrace the other customary topics of Socratic discourse [i.e. the fine and the good];[8] for we recognise [in the speech], under but thin disguises, all the peculiarities of the Platonic psychology: the immortality, antecedent and prospective, of the soul, its self-moving or self-determining properties . . . its heavenly extraction, its incarceration in the flesh, and the conditions of its subsequent emancipation; finally, that singular tenet of [recollection] which, in the *Phaedo* and elsewhere, is insisted on as one of the main props of the doctrine of immortality; and that not less characteristic doctrine of ideas or archetypal forms . . . It is an instance of that species of rhetoric which alone seemed to Plato desirable or salutary . . . It is intended to prove, by a living example, that the art which, as normally practised, was a tool in the hands of the designing and ambitious, is capable of being turned

---

[5] From within the context of the dialogue, of course, the speech is given orally rather than written. Until the end, when dialectic is singled out as the ideal medium, speaking and writing tend to be treated together, both insofar as Socratic speaking is also Platonic writing, and insofar as rhetoric, whether current or ideal, is implicitly treated as involving both the written and the spoken word. Thus Phaedrus has a written copy of Lysias' speech hidden under his cloak when he encounters Socrates, but he actually comes fresh from a *performance* of the speech by Lysias; and ultimately orators are, for the purposes of the dialogue, indistinguishable from (mere) speech-writers.

[6] The one who has 'pieces of knowledge' (*epistēmai*) about what is just, fine and good, 276C3–4.

[7] This is a somewhat optimistic description of the white horse as Socrates describes him; but no matter.

[8] See n. 6 above.

by the philosopher to the better purpose of clothing in an attractive dress the results
of his more abstruse speculations . . .⁹

Thus Socrates' great second speech collects together – and, I add, devel-
ops in its own distinctive way – a range of typical Platonic themes; when
Socrates comments on the speech in the later part of the dialogue, then,
Plato is commenting on his own writing. And the nature of these comments
amounts to a kind of rationale for his writing practice, one that serves to
confirm two central points which the previous chapters of this book have
attempted to establish, and to illustrate: first, that he was a writer who composed with one eye on his prospective readers; second, that he composed in
order to persuade them as much as in order to make them think.¹⁰ (And as
always in this book, 'them' as applied to Plato's readers will include us.) If
rhetoric is 'the art of using language so as to persuade or influence others',¹¹
Plato has a fair claim to be the inventor, as well as the finest proponent, of
philosophical rhetoric. This is the justification for the principle from which
this book began: that we shall not be in a position to understand what Plato
wants to say until, among other things, we have understood the degree to
which the *way* he says what he actually says may have been determined
by his perception of the needs of his audience, and of the distance that
separates them from him.

The most important passages are the following (Socrates is speaking):

Since the power of speech is in fact a leading of the soul [sc. towards the truth],
the man who means to be an expert in rhetoric must know how many forms¹²
soul has. Thus their number is so and so, and they are of such and such kinds,
which is why some people are like this, and others like that;¹³ and these having
been distinguished in this way, then again there are so many forms of speeches,
each one of such and such a kind. People of one kind are easily persuaded for one
sort of reason by one kind of speech to hold one kind of opinion, while people of
another kind are for some other sorts of reasons difficult to persuade.

---

⁹ Thompson 1868: xvii–xviii.

¹⁰ The second point is confirmed by the inclusion, in the ambit of the discussion, of Socrates' second
speech, if and insofar as that stands for Plato's own writing.

¹¹ *OED*.

¹² That is, *eidē*: the question is the one that we were left with in *Republic* X, 612A4, whether the soul
is something *polueides* or *monoeides*, and then again at the beginning of the *Phaedrus* (230A; see
chapters 2 and 3 above). Here in the later part of the *Phaedrus* Socrates has already suggested that
any rhetorician – 'both Thrasymachus and anyone else', *Phaedrus* 271A4 – who writes a manual on
the subject of rhetoric must enable us 'to see whether soul is something one and uniform in nature
or complex (*polueides*)' (271A6–7; see also 270D1–2, where Socrates says that anyone looking into
anything must ask whether it is 'simple' (*haploun*) or *polueides*).

¹³ People will be 'like this, or like that', I take it, because the different 'kinds' or 'parts' of their souls
are disposed differently; everyone will have the same parts, at least potentially (for this 'potentially',
see chapter 5, pp. 169–72 above). See further below.

Having then grasped these things satisfactorily, after that the student must observe them as they are in real life, and actually being put into practice, and be able to follow them with keen perception . . . But when he both has sufficient ability to say what sort of man is persuaded by what sorts of things, and is capable of telling himself when he observes him that *this* is the man, *this* the nature of person that was discussed before, now actually present in front of him, to whom he must now apply *these* kinds of speech in *this* way in order to persuade him of *this* kind of thing; when he now has all of this, and has also grasped the occasions for speaking and for holding back, and again for speaking concisely and piteously and in an exaggerated fashion, and for all the forms of speeches he may learn, recognising the right and the wrong time for these, *then* his grasp of the science will be well and complete finished, but not before that; but in whichever of these things someone is lacking when he speaks or teaches or writes, and says that he speaks scientifically, the person who disbelieves him is in the stronger position, (271C10–272B2)

and

Until a person knows the truth about each of the things about which he speaks or writes, and becomes capable of defining the whole by itself, and having defined it, knows how to cut it up again according to its forms until it can no longer be cut;[14] and until he has reached an understanding of the nature of soul along the same lines, discovering the form of speech which fits each nature, and so arranges and orders what he says, offering a complex (*poikilos*) soul complex speeches containing all the modes, and simple (*haplous*) speeches to a simple soul: not until then will he be capable of pursuing the making of speeches as a whole in a scientific way, to the degree that its nature allows, whether for the purposes of teaching or for those of persuading either, as the whole of our previous argument has indicated. (277B5–C6)

Socrates does not tell us what 'complex' speeches are, apart from their 'containing all the modes', but 'simple' ones will presumably be those that are offered to individuals whose souls are 'simple' because reason is in perfect and complete control; 'complex', or 'variegated', 'many-coloured' souls will be those in whom either 'spirit' or appetite dominates. (Thus, for example, the 'democratic' type of individual in the *Republic*[15] will be 'complex'

---

[14] This is the method of 'collection and division'. See 266B3–C1: 'Now I am myself, Phaedrus, a lover of these divisions and collections, so that I may be able both to speak and to think [in a roundabout way he has managed a rudimentary application of the method himself, to love (*erōs*)]; and if I find anyone else that I think has the natural capacity to look to one and to many, I pursue him "in his footsteps, behind him, as if he were a god". And the name I give those who can do this – whether it's the right one or not, god knows, but at any rate up till now I have called them "experts in dialectic".'

[15] So called because he gives equal status to all his desires, making no distinction between them (VIII, 561C–D).

because of his behaviour, but that will be explained by the domination in him of the 'complex' beast of appetite.)[16] It will hardly be a wild guess, by this stage in my argument, that the category 'complex' *logoi* will include any that in one way or another set out to address perspectives other than Socrates' (Plato's) own. By that reckoning most of the dialogues will be 'complex', and only a few – mostly ones not considered in any detail in this book[17] – will be 'simple': *Parmenides, Theaetetus, Sophist, Politicus.*

If indeed Plato intends Socrates' criticisms of writing to apply to his own output,[18] then he might appear to be proposing a disturbing devaluation of his own *oeuvre*. After all, he evidently devoted a considerable proportion of his time and energy to writing; how *could* he agree, as he surveys his own work, that

the person who thinks that there is necessarily much that is merely for amusement in a written speech on any subject, and that none has ever yet been written, whether in verse or in prose, which is worth much serious attention, or indeed spoken, in the way that rhapsodes speak theirs, to produce conviction without questioning or teaching, but that the best of them have really been a way of reminding people who know; who thinks that clearness and completeness and seriousness exist only in those things that are taught about what is just and beautiful and good, and are said for the purpose of someone's learning from them, and genuinely written in the soul; who thinks that discourses of that kind should be said to be as it were his legitimate sons, first of all the one within him, if it is found there, and in second place any offspring and brothers of this one that have sprung up simultaneously, in the way they should, in other souls, other men; and who says goodbye to the other kind – *this*, surely, Phaedrus, will be the sort of person that you and I would pray that we both might come to be? (Socrates at *Phaedrus* 277E5–278B4)

In truth, however, this is no less than we should expect from someone who, like Plato, and his Socrates, believes that the philosophical road, for human beings, is in principle never-ending. (We know that it has an end; it is just that we shall never get there. Life is too short, human reason too weak, its resources too small.) What Plato has Socrates say about writing would apply equally to anything *said*, too – indeed, even to any particular outcome of the dialectical process. The unending nature of that process,

---

[16] Democratic man as *poikilos*, 561E4; *poikilos* of the monster of appetite, 588C7.

[17] Hardly an accident, given that one of the chief themes of the book is about how Plato relates to his audiences (in which context straight discussions between two philosophers will be the least interesting).

[18] Mackenzie 1982 produces a subtle argument to suggest that the dialogues are capable of escaping Socrates' strictures on writing; for a response to Mackenzie see Rowe 1986: 114–15.

as Plato (Socrates) understands it, is nowhere better expressed than in the
Phaedrus:

PHAEDRUS: 'It's a quite beautiful form of amusement you're talking of, Socrates,
in contrast with a worthless one: if someone is able to amuse himself with
words, telling stories about justice and the other subjects you speak of.'

SOCRATES: 'Yes, Phaedrus, just so. But I think it is far finer if one is in earnest
about those subjects: when one makes use of the science of dialectic, and
taking a fitting soul plants and sows in it words accompanied by knowledge,
which are sufficient to help themselves and the one who planted them, and
are not without fruit but contain a seed, from which others grow in other
soils, capable of rendering that seed for ever immortal, and making the one
who has it as happy as it is possible for a man to be.' (276E1–277A4)

This is the picture of the master dialectician, with his pupil. The reference
to 'words accompanied by knowledge' are likely at first sight to suggest
that it is only the pupil who still has work to do. But the reference to
'knowledge' here needs to be read in context: Socrates has just talked about
the ideal 'farmer', the sower of 'seeds', as having only 'pieces of knowledge'
about the just, fine and good.[19] And in case there should be any doubt
on the matter, Socrates goes on to reaffirm – perfectly in the manner of
the *Apology* – that *wisdom*, full knowledge, belongs only to gods.[20] If any
writer – whether Lysias, or Homer, or Solon, or whoever – ever composed
what he composed

(SOCRATES) 'knowing how the truth is, able to help his composition when he is
challenged on its subjects, and with the capacity, speaking in his own person,
to show that what he has written is of little worth, then such a man ought
not to derive his title from these, and be called after them, but rather from
those things in which he is seriously engaged.'

PHAEDRUS: 'What are the titles you assign him, then?'

SOCRATES: '*To call him wise seems to me to be too much, and to be fitting only in the
case of a god*; to call him either a philosopher or something like that would
both fit him more and be in better taste.' (278C4–D6)

And then, in case we should suppose that Plato himself is the kind of ideal
writer who writes 'knowing how the truth is', he has Socrates add

---

[19] I.e. in the passage referred to in n. 6 above.

[20] It is important to bear in mind that the main contrast in the whole of the last part of the *Phaedrus*
is between the expert and the non-expert *in writing* and *in speaking*, and especially between those –
like current orators – who say that an expert in this field 'need have nothing to do with the truth
about just and good things' (272D4–5), and those – philosophers – like Socrates (if there is anyone
like him) who speak only because they care about the truth.

On the other hand, the man who doesn't possess things of more value than the things he composed or wrote, turning them upside down over a long period of time, sticking them together and taking them apart – him, I think, you'll rightly call a poet or author of speeches or writer of laws? (278D8–E2)

There is an ancient tradition about Plato's meticulousness as a writer.[21] Granted, the tradition may even have originated from this very context in the *Phaedrus*; but it is one of the few aspects of what little has been handed down about Plato that must certainly be true – and if he is here describing himself, with an appropriate degree of playfulness ('my compositions, poor things, are all I have to offer'), that would be entirely in keeping with his Socratic *persona*.

---

[21] See Hackforth 1952: 165 n. 2; and perhaps *Republic* VI, 501B9–C1, where the founders of the best city – which on one level include Socrates and the other interlocutors, on yet another Plato himself – are envisaged as looking to their model as they put together the laws like painters, 'rubbing out one thing, painting another back in'. If this is a description of repeated attempts to get things right, as I am inclined to think, then it could well be another indirect self-reference (and at a pinch might even be what is being picked up in the *Phaedrus* passage).

Epilogue: What is Platonism?

One of the main claims that I have attempted to justify in the preceding chapters is that there will usually be a range of aspects, in any given dialogue, that derive simply from the process of embedding content within a persuasive form, without themselves constituting part of that content; what might be called – by analogy with Timaeus' discourse – the by-products of a literary necessity. Only when we have identified these factors, so I have argued, will we be in a position to separate out what it is that Plato wants to say.

'What Plato wants to say': this is the 'Platonism' of the title of this short Epilogue – not the Platonism of the various kinds of 'Platonists' who followed and interpreted him, each in their own special way. I am not here concerned with them; my interest is solely in the dialogues themselves, starting from them, and not from others' interpretations. (The case of Aristotle's treatment of Plato is in any case a salutary warning of the dangers of that. Despite some recent claims to the contrary, merely being close in time to Plato gives an interpreter few advantages.) If the dialogues sometimes point beyond themselves, as they do, for example, on the subject of the good, in the present context – and probably in others – I am content to note the fact and move on, back to the solider, because more accessible, ground of the written texts.[1] My question is simply about what *these* can tell us about Plato's thinking.

My answer to that question has emerged in a piecemeal way over the preceding chapters. I now mean to try to bring some of the pieces together, by providing the briefest of sketches – and it will be no more – of what I take, on the basis of the parts of the corpus I have considered, to be the main trends of Plato's thinking: 'Platonism', then, as viewed from the

---

[1] If anyone should claim that the written texts cannot properly be understood without reference to the unwritten, I can only respond that in that case I shall happily make do with what will always in any case be a partial understanding.

perspective of a fair sample of the corpus, read as a corpus of writings that are at once philosophical and literary, philosophical and *rhetorical*.

Plato's view of things, I propose, is at once optimistic and pessimistic. It is optimistic firstly insofar as Plato maintains a fundamental belief in our power, as human beings, to control our own destiny, that is, to determine whether things will turn out well or badly for us: 'even the person who comes up last [in the lottery for the choice of lives], if he has chosen with intelligence, has a life available to him that should content him, and not a bad one, if he lives with due attention', as the Exegete (*prophētēs*) says to the gathered souls of the dead in the myth in *Republic* x (619B3–5). But Plato's view of humanity is also pessimistic, insofar as he has no faith in our capacity to 'live with due attention' (*suntonōs*). Lurking inside us, and waiting to grow and develop, should we be careless, and begin to give it encouragement, is an 'innate desire' or 'appetite' (*sumphutos epithumia*),[2] which will ruin our lives. Still, ruin is not inevitable; we can prevent it ourselves, if we are sufficiently endowed with reason, and if not, then one may dream of constructing a society that will impose rationality on the generality of humankind from outside.

Plato's view of the world at large, by contrast, is quite unaffected by pessimism: the cosmos is shot through, 'bound together', by goodness; that is, by the principle of the good. Only by grasping that principle, and the way in which it operates in nature, shall we understand the universe in which we live. And it is that same principle, the good, that we also need to grasp if we are to live a fully intelligent and satisfactory life, instead of a 'bad' one (to quote the Exegete). Since we all *want* to live a good and happy life, we all also want to live an intelligent life – that being the only way to avoid living a bad one. Unfortunately most of us fail to recognize that as what we want, because we have already failed to 'pay attention' as we needed to, and have installed things like power or money, or 'pleasure', as our ends in life. But that in itself only serves to underline the fundamental goodness of the world, insofar as we suffer misery in proportion to the poorness of our choices. Things are, despite appearances, as they should be; in fact just as they would be if they had been put together by a divine craftsman working from the best of paradigms.

Underlying all of this is a thoroughly objectivist position: the good is something that can, at least up to a point, be grasped by the intellect, but

---

[2] The phrase comes from the Great Myth of the *Politicus* (272E6), in which the pattern of behaviour of the cosmos is portrayed in human terms. See also *Phaedrus* 246A6–7, which compares the soul to the 'combined (actually 'grown [or *born*] together', *sumphutos*) power of a winged pair of horses and charioteer'.

does not depend on the intellect – even a divine intellect – for its existence. The good is the good in itself, or the *real nature* of goodness; what good *is*. And just as we need to grasp the good in order to understand the world and ourselves (and everything else), so we need to grasp the *real natures* of beauty, justice, humanity, knowledge, statesmanship . . . if we are to know what we are talking about when we talk about such things. It is no use looking at actual examples of beauty, or justice, or whatever, because these will give us a hopelessly inadequate idea of what these things actually are – indeed, in some cases, as with 'statesmanship', possibly no idea of the real thing whatsoever;[3] still, for the most part they will give us *some* idea of the real thing, whatever it may be, and enough to allow us to carry on living and communicating. But something better is available to us, through the medium of philosophy, and of dialectic. It is open to us to recognize that there are things beyond particulars: things in themselves ('forms'),[4] in which particulars 'share', which make particulars what they are, and which can be investigated and grasped, insofar as they can be grasped, by dialectical reason. And these things in themselves are not only distinct from the corresponding particulars; they turn out to encapsulate a higher specification – as it were – altogether, so that if we imagined a perfectly beautiful being, for example, or a perfectly knowledgeable and wise one (a god will serve as an example covering both cases), he or she would exemplify a beauty, knowledge and wisdom quite beyond our merely human reach. Similarly in the case of justice and the other excellences, and of humanity itself, which would differ from divinity by virtue of a lesser, time-limited, rationality, and by the requirement and consequences of embodiment. It is in this association of what things *are* with what – from our perspective from below, as it were – they *would ideally be*, along with a commitment to the power of human reason (and an awareness of its limits), that the heart of Platonism is located.

So: these things, 'things in themselves', 'real natures', 'forms', are not – mere – universals, even if they behave in some respects like universals; if they are 'present in' particulars, by virtue of the 'sharing' relationship, what is actually 'in' the particulars is no more than a shadow or 'image', 'copy', of the real thing. Nevertheless, the 'things in themselves' are accessible, by

---

[3] See the *Politicus*, e.g., at 291C (the field has been entirely taken over by imposters).

[4] It is Plato's interpreters who have turned 'forms' ('ideas'), *eidē* or *ideai*, into a technical term. Plato has no technical terms, unless in the shape of a collection of terms – and even then he is quite capable of talking about the things the terms refer to without using the terms themselves. *Variation* is one of the signature features of Platonic style (even when he is referring from one written text of his own to another).

philosophical means, from where we are now;[5] and access to them will in turn enable us to gain a better understanding *of* the here and now.[6] In fact, such access will revolutionize our lives; things will never look the same again. Even if we can only approximate to the best imaginable in thought, a society or an individual that achieved the best approximation possible would be quite different from any society, and any individual – except, perhaps, Socrates himself, despite his protestations – known to us. But we all agree – Socrates' interlocutors always agree, without a moment's hesitation – that we want what is really good. Well, proposes Plato, the choice is yours; the kind of life you live is in your hands.[7]

And this, I take it, is quite the kind of thing that – his – Socrates is proposing, in the *Apology*, under the heading of 'soul-care', and 'city-care'; as the kind of life he proposes is quite the kind of life that he exemplifies, whether in the 'Socratic' dialogues, the *Republic*, or any other dialogue. The 'Platonism' I have in mind is not restricted to any 'middle' Plato, but – in the broad terms in which I have sketched it – is there, in principle, throughout. I end with a quotation from Paul Shorey:

My thesis is simply that Plato on the whole belongs rather to the type of thinkers whose philosophy is fixed in early maturity[8] (Schopenhauer, Herbert Spencer), rather than to the class of those who receive a new revelation every decade (Schelling). (Shorey 1903: 88)

What the real Socrates in fact contributed to the thought of Plato's 'early maturity' we cannot know for sure. But Plato seems to have been happy to attribute everything – the whole of what I am calling 'Platonism' – to him; and that, I suggest, is neither an empty compliment nor a convenient fiction.

---

[5] That is, there is little or nothing *other-worldly* about the Plato whose outlines I am sketching, despite his apparent adherence to the idea of the soul's immortality: that in a way commits him to the existence of another world, but if so, that other world hardly seems to be treated as more than a waiting-room for souls awaiting reincarnation.

[6] And, up to a point, of the physical world itself: see chapter 11 above.

[7] What I have said about Platonic metaphysics above will doubtless appear somewhat thin, superficial, and lacking in bite. However, as I have indicated, my aim here is the strictly limited one of indicating the general direction of flow of Plato's thinking, as this has emerged in the course of my argument in the book as a whole. The most illuminating treatment of metaphysics in Plato I have found, after Penner 1987, is Silverman 2002.

[8] Shorey in fact takes a much less positive view of the so-called 'Socratic' dialogues than I have argued for; his Platonic Socrates can be, and not merely play, the sophist and eristic as well as the philosopher. I maintain not only that there are, so far, no clearly established examples of this, but that it would be so plainly contrary to Plato's project that – given the degree of his control as author – we should not expect to find any. On *apparent* sophistry, see e.g., Appendix to chapter 5 above, and Penner and Rowe 2005 (Shorey finds the *Lysis* especially suspect).

Bibliography

Adam, James, 1963 (1902). *The Republic of Plato*, 2 vols. (second edition). Cambridge.

Annas, Julia, 1985. 'Self-knowledge in early Plato', in Dominic J. O'Meara (ed.), *Platonic Investigations* (Studies in Philosophy and the History of Philosophy, vol. XIII), Washington, DC: 111–38.

Blondell, Ruby, 2002. *The Play of Character in Plato's Dialogues*. Cambridge.

Brickhouse, Thomas C. and Smith, Nicholas D., 2002. 'Incurable souls in Socratic psychology', *Ancient Philosophy* 22: 1–16.

Burnyeat, Myles, 1990. *The Theaetetus of Plato*. Indianapolis.

1992 (1977). 'Socratic midwifery, Platonic inspiration', in Hugh H. Benson (ed.), *Essays on the Philosophy of Socrates*, New York: 53–65 (reprinted from *Bulletin of the Institute of Classical Studies* 24 [1977]:7–16).

2003. 'Socrates, money, and the grammar of *gignesthai*', *The Journal of Hellenic Studies* 123: 1–25.

2005a. 'On the source of Burnet's construal of *Apology* 30B2–4: a correction', in *The Journal of Hellenic Studies*, 125: 139–42.

2005b. '*Eikōs Muthos*', *Rhizai. A Journal for Ancient Philosophy and Science* II.2: 143–65.

Cooper, John M., 1982. 'The *Gorgias* and Irwin's Socrates', *Review of Metaphysics* 35: 577–87.

(ed.), 1997. *Plato, Complete Works*. Indianapolis (= 'the Hackett translation' [by various authors]).

1999. 'Socrates and Plato in Plato's *Gorgias*', in John M. Cooper (ed.), *Reason and Emotion: Essays on Ancient Moral Psychology and Ethical Theory*, Princeton: 29–75.

Cross, R. C. and Woozley, A. D., 1966. *Plato's Republic: A Philosophical Commentary*. London.

Davidson, Donald, 1993. 'Plato's philosopher', in Terry Irwin and Martha C. Nussbaum (eds.), *Virtue, Love and Form: Essays in Memory of Gregory Vlastos*, *Apeiron* 26.3/4: 179–94.

2001 (1983). 'A coherence theory of truth and knowledge' (as reprinted, with 'Afterthoughts'), in Donald Davidson, *Subjective, Intersubjective, Objective*, Oxford: 137–57.

Diès, A., 1913. 'La transposition platonicienne', in F. Aveling et al. (eds.), *Annales de l'Institut Supérieur de Philosophie* (Université de Louvain), Tome II: 265–308.

Dodds, E. R., 1959. *Plato: Gorgias. A Revised Text with Introduction and Commentary*. Oxford.

Ebert, Theodor, 2004. *Platon, Phaidon*. Göttingen.

Frede, Michael, 1992. 'Plato's arguments and the dialogue form', in J. C. Klagge and N. D. Smith (eds.), *Methods of Interpreting Plato and his Dialogues* (*Oxford Studies in Ancient Philosophy* suppl. vol.): 201–19.

2000. 'The literary form of the *Sophist*', in Christopher Gill and Mary Margaret McCabe (eds.), *Form and Argument in Late Plato*, Oxford: 135–51.

Gerson, Lloyd P., 2003. *Knowing Persons: A Study in Plato*. Oxford (but see my review in *Ancient Philosophy* for 2005).

Gonzalez, Francisco, 1998. *Dialectic and Dialogue: Plato's Practice of Philosophical Inquiry*. Evanston, IL.

Grote, George, 1865. *Plato and the Other Companions of Sokrates*, 3 vols. London.

Hackforth, R., 1952. *Plato's Phaedrus*. Cambridge.

Irwin, Terence, 1979. *Plato: Gorgias* (Clarendon Plato series). Oxford.

1995. *Plato's Ethics*. Oxford.

Johansen, T. K., 2004. *Plato's Natural Philosophy: A Study of the Timaeus-Critias*. Cambridge.

Kahn, Charles H., 1983. 'Drama and dialectic in Plato's *Gorgias*', *Oxford Studies in Ancient Philosophy* 1: 75–122.

1996. *Plato and the Socratic Dialogue: the Philosophical use of a Literary Form*. Cambridge.

2002. 'On Platonic chronology', in Julia Annas and Christopher Rowe (eds.), *New Perspectives on Plato, Modern and Ancient*, Cambridge, MA/Washington, DC: 93–127.

Kamtekar, Rachana, 1997 (1999). 'Philosophical rule from the *Republic* to the *Laws*: commentary on Schofield', in *Proceedings of the Boston Area Colloquium in Ancient Philosophy* 13: 241–52.

Kraut, Richard, 1992. 'Introduction to the study of Plato', in R. Kraut (ed.), *The Cambridge Companion to the Study of Plato*, Cambridge: 1–50.

2003. 'Justice in Plato and Aristotle: withdrawal versus engagement', in Robert Heinaman (ed.), *Plato and Aristotle's Ethics*, Aldershot: 153–67.

Laks, André, 1990. 'Legislation and demiurgy: on the relationship between Plato's *Republic* and *Laws*', in *Classical Antiquity* 9: 209–29.

Mackenzie, Mary Margaret, 1982. 'Paradox in Plato's *Phaedrus*', in *Proceedings of the Cambridge Philological Society* n.s. 28: 64–76.

Moreau, Joseph, 1953. 'Platon et la connaissance de l'âme', in *Revue des Études Anciennes* 55: 249–57.

Morgan, Kathryn, 2000. *Myth and Philosophy from the Presocratics to Plato*. Cambridge.

Morrow, Glenn R., 1993. *Plato's Cretan City: A Historical Interpretation of the Laws*. Princeton.

Penner, Terry, 1987. *The Ascent from Nominalism*. Dordrecht.

1991. 'Desire and power in Socrates: the argument of *Gorgias* 466A–468E that orators and tyrants have no power in the city', *Apeiron* 24: 147–202.

Penner, Terry and Rowe, Christopher, 2005. *Plato's Lysis* (Cambridge Studies in the Dialogues of Plato). Cambridge.

Press, Gerald (ed.), 2000. *Who Speaks for Plato? Studies in Platonic Anonymity.* Lanham, MD.

Renaud, François, 1999. *Die Resokratisierung Platons. Die platonische Hermeneutik Hans-Georg Gadamers.* Sankt Augustin.

Rowe, C[hristopher] J., 1986. 'The argument and structure of Plato's *Phaedrus*', in *Proceedings of the Cambridge Philological Society* n.s. 32: 106–25.

1988. *Plato*, Phaedrus (second, corrected edition). Warminster.

1993. *Plato*, Phaedo. Cambridge.

1999. 'La forme dramatique et la structure du *Philèbe*', in M. Dixsaut (ed.), *La fêlure du plaisir. Études sur le* Philèbe *de Platon, 1: Commentaires*, Paris: 9–25.

2002a. 'Reply to Penner', in Julia Annas and Christopher Rowe (eds.), *New Perspectives on Plato, Modern and Ancient*, Cambridge, MA/Washington, DC: 213–25.

2002b. 'Handling a philosophical text', in Roy K. Gibson and Christina Shuttleworth Kraus (eds.), *The Classical Commentary: Histories, Practices, Theory*, Leiden: 295–318.

2002c. 'Socrates and Plato on virtue and the good: an analytical approach', in G. Reale and S. Scolnicov (eds.), *New Images of Plato*, Sankt Augustin: 253–64.

2003a. 'Reply to Richard Kraut', in Robert Heinaman (ed.), *Plato and Aristotle's Ethics*, Aldershot: 168–76.

2003b. 'The status of the "myth" in Plato's *Timaeus*', in Carlo Natali and Stefano Maso (eds.), *Plato Physicus. Cosmologia e antropologia nel Timeo*, Amsterdam: 21–31.

2004a. 'The case of the missing philosophers in Plato's *Timaeus-Critias*', in *Würzburger Jahrbücher für die Altertumswissenschaft*, Neue Folge, Band 28b: 57–70.

2004b (1995). *Plato:* Statesman (second, corrected edition). Oxford/Warminster.

2005a. 'Hommes et monstres: Platon et Socrate parlent de la nature humaine', in John Dillon and Monique Dixsaut (eds.), *Agonistes: Essays in Honour of Denis O'Brien*, Aldershot: 139–55.

2005b. 'What difference do Forms make for Platonic epistemology?', in Christopher Gill (ed.), *Virtue, Norms, and Objectivity*, Oxford: 215–32.

2006a. 'The literary and philosophical style of the *Republic*', in Gerasimos X. Santas (ed.), *The Blackwell Guide to Plato's* Republic, Oxford: 7–24.

2006b. 'The *Symposium* as a Socratic dialogue', in James H. Lesher, Debra Nails, and Frisbee Sheffield (eds.), *Plato's* Symposium: *Issues in Interpretation and Reception.* Cambridge, MA: 9–22.

2007a. 'Plato and the Persian wars', in Emma Bridges, Edith Hall and P. J. Rhodes (eds.), *Cultural Responses to the Persian Wars.* Oxford: 85–104.

2007b. 'The moral psychology of the *Gorgias*', in Michael Erler and Luc Brisson (eds.), *Proceedings of the Seventh Symposium Platonicum*. Sankt Augustin: 90–101.

2007c. 'The place of the *Republic* in Plato's political thought', in G. R. F. Ferrari (ed.), *The Cambridge Companion to Plato's* Republic, Cambridge: 27–54.

Rutherford, R. B., 1995. *The Art of Plato: Ten Essays in Platonic Interpretation.* London.

Santas, Gerasimos X., 1979. *Socrates: Philosophy in Plato's Early Dialogues.* London.

Schofield, Malcolm, 1997. *Saving the City.* London.

1997 (1999). 'The disappearing philosopher-king', in *Proceedings of the Boston Area Colloquium in Ancient Philosophy* 13: 213–41.

2006. *Plato* (Founders of Modern Political and Social Thought). Oxford.

Scott, Dominic, 1995. *Recollection and Experience: Plato's Theory of Learning and its Successors.* Cambridge,

Sedley, David, 1990. 'Teleology and myth in the *Phaedo*', *Proceedings of the Boston Area Colloquium in Ancient Philosophy* 5: 359–83.

1995. 'The dramatis personae of Plato's *Phaedo*', in Timothy Smiley (ed.), *Philosophical Dialogues: Plato, Hume, Wittgenstein* (*Proceedings of the British Academy* 85), Oxford: 3–26.

2003. *Plato's* Cratylus (Cambridge Studies in the Dialogues of Plato). Cambridge.

2004. *The Midwife of Platonism: Text and Subtext in Plato's* Theaetetus. Oxford.

Forthcoming. 'Myth, politics and punishment in Plato's *Gorgias*', in Catalin Partenie (ed.), *Plato's Myths.* Cambridge.

Shorey, Paul, 1903. *The Unity of Plato's Thought.* Chicago.

Silverman, Allan, 2002. *The Dialectic of Excellence: A Study of Plato's Metaphysics.* Princeton.

Slings, S. R. †, 2003. *Platonis Rempublicam recognovit, etc. S. R. S.* (Oxford Classical Texts). Oxford.

2005. *Critical Notes on Plato's* Politeia. Leiden.

Stokes, Michael C., 1997. *Plato: Apology.* Warminster.

De Strycker, E. and Slings, S. R., 1994. *Plato's* Apology of Socrates. Edited and completed from the papers of the late E. de Strycker (S. J.), Leiden.

Szlezák, Thomas A., 1985. *Platon und die Schriftlichkeit der Philosophie. Interpretationen zu den frühen und mittleren Dialogen.* Berlin.

2004. *Das Bild des Dialektikers in Platons Späten Dialogen. Platon und die Schriftlichkeit der Philosophie, Teil II.* Berlin.

Tarrant, Harold, 2002. 'Elenchos and exetasis. Capturing the purpose of Socratic interrogation', in Gary A. Scott (ed.), *Does Socrates Have a Method? Rethinking the Elenchus in Plato's Dialogues and Beyond*, Philadelphia: 61–7.

Taylor, A. E., 1928. *A Commentary on Plato's* Timaeus. Oxford.

Taylor, C. C. W., 2000. *A Very Short Introduction to Socrates.* Oxford.

Thesleff, Holger, 1982. *Studies in Plato's Chronology* (Commentationes Humanarum Litterarum 70). Helsinki.

Thompson, W. H., 1868. *The Phaedrus of Plato, with English notes and dissertations.* London.

Tigerstedt, E. N., 1977. *Interpreting Plato* (Stockholm Studies in History of Literature, 17). Uppsala.

Vlastos, Gregory, 1971. 'The paradox of Socrates', in G. Vlastos, *The Philosophy of Socrates: A Collection of Critical Essays*, New York: 1–21.

   1991. *Socrates: Ironist and Moral Philosopher.* Cambridge.

   1994. *Socratic Studies* (ed. M. Burnyeat). Cambridge.

Wardy, Robert, 1996. *The Birth of Rhetoric.* London.

White, Nicholas, 2002. *Individual and Conflict in Greek Ethics.* Oxford.

Index